The Book of Lists

The Book of Lists

REVISED AND UPDATED AND EVEN MORE CANADIAN

IRA BASEN
JANE FARROW
AMY WALLACE
DAVID WALLECHINSKY

 ALFRED A. KNOPF CANADA

Library and Archives Canada Cataloguing in Publication

Book of lists (2017)
    The book of lists : revised and updated and even more Canadian / edited by Ira Basen,
Jane Farrow, Amy Wallace and David Wallechinsky. — The Canada 150 edition.

Issued in print and electronic formats.
ISBN 978-0-7352-7306-1
eBook ISBN 978-0-7352-7307-8

    1. Canada—Miscellanea. 2. Curiosities and wonders—Canada.
I. Basen, Ira, editor II. Farrow, Jane (Jane Katherine), editor III. Title.

FC60.B68 2017   971.002   C2017-902279-2

Text design by Jennifer Griffiths

Cover design by Colin Jaworski
Cover image © Dorling Kindersley / Getty Images

Interior images: (cupid) © Victorian Traditions, (curling) © Corepics VOF, (paintbrushes)
© Karramba Production, (concert) © dwphotos, (Canadian coins) © Vladimir Sazonov, (retro TVs)
© Maxx-Studio, (crowd illustration) © HelgaLin, all Shutterstock.com; (la Justice) Anonymous,
French, 18th Century, Gift of the Estate of James Hazen Hyde; (beaver, moose, and polar bear)
lithographs by Lindner, Eddy & Claus, 1890, The Jefferson R. Burdock Collection; (beaver detail)
from "Flags of All Nations" lithograph issued by Allen & Ginter, 1890, The Jefferson R. Burdock
Collection, all The Metropolitan Museum of Art; (man in sling) cigarette card by W.D. & H.O.
Wills, 1913, The Wellcome Collection; (landscape) etching, "Gebouw aan een rivier" by Willem van
Nieulandt; (skeleton) etching, "Skelet met pijl en boog" by Hendrick Hondius; (owl) engraving,
"Uil met brill en boeken" by Cornelis Bloemaert (II); (map) "Kaart van de landen rond de poolcirkel
met de drie reizen van de Nederlanders, 1598" by Arnaud A.J. Pistoor; (giant with men in basket)
etching, "Spotprent op de Landzaten" 1795, Anonymous, all Rijksmuseum, Amsterdam

Printed and bound in the United States of America

10 9 8 7 6 5 4 3 2 1

CONTENTS

Introduction and Acknowledgements

It was hard not to feel intimidated about being asked back in 2005 to join forces with the Wallace and Wallechinsky list machine. The first *Book of Lists*, published in 1977 by David, Amy and their father, Irving, was brilliant. It, and subsequent versions, sold millions, and spawned countless imitators. David and Amy then spent several decades filing away obscure pieces of information to be included in future books of lists. And there we were, two CBC radio producers, whose brains were geared more towards finding interesting people to talk to on the radio than trying to find a Canadian who had died laughing.

Sometimes we got lucky. We hadn't really expected to be able to add Canadian content to a list of "famous events that happened in the bathtub," until we stumbled across the fact that former prime minister R.B. Bennett had died in his. It also turns out that you can actually learn a few things about the differences between Canada and the United States by working on a book of lists. We realized that our showbiz celebrity culture is not nearly as developed as theirs; our stars aren't larger than life. We could find no examples of a public kiss that equalled the buzz created by Britney and Madonna at MTV's Video Music Awards in 2003, so we started looking in different places. Our mobsters don't have nicknames as colourful as their American counterparts, but our hockey players do. We couldn't find an instance of Canadians rioting after a trial verdict, but we had no trouble finding fans going wild after rock concerts. And while the American version of the book had a list of "15 Actors Who Became Politicians," we flipped it around to suit our needs: "14 Canadian Sports Heroes Who Became Politicians." And it seemed to work. Our Canadian edition of *The Book of Lists* was a big bestseller.

So here we are 12 years later, and our publishers have asked us to update the book and add more Canadian content in honour of Canada's 150th birthday.

Most of the lists that we've kept from the 2005 book have new content added, although in some cases, like "16 Cases of People Killed by God," we decided to leave things as they were. There are lots of all-Canadian lists that weren't there before ("9 Things You Probably Didn't Know About 'O Canada'"), and dozens of new, personalized lists from people who bring their unique perspective to a particular topic.

But the question remains: Why write a book of lists in 2017? Back in 2005, social media was in its infancy, the Web was still in search of a viable business model, and if you wanted to get some information in the form of a list, you had to pick up a book like ours.

Today that's all changed. Lists are everywhere on the Web: 5 reasons you should do this, 10 things you didn't know about that. Lists are at the core of some of the Internet's most successful sites, BuzzFeed being the most obvious example. Today, there's not a news or information site anywhere that hasn't figured out that lists drive traffic, traffic attracts advertisers, and advertisers pay the bills.

The reason for the popularity of online listing is not hard to figure out. Stripped down to its bare essentials, a list is an information delivery system with a very tight focus. You know what you're going to get, and you know it will be presented to you in an easily digestible package. And in a world where it seems everyone is suffering from attention deficit disorder, and no one has time to absorb all the information we have at our fingertips, lists are a quick and easy way to get just enough information to make you feel like you're not missing out, without suffering from information overload.

That presented a challenge for us in compiling lists for this edition of the book. Lists are no longer the novelty they were in 1977, or even 2005. So what sets our lists apart? The answer is "story." We tried, wherever possible, to develop a narrative arc around our lists. We don't do ranked lists. None of them are the best or the worst of anything. These are not just bits of information to share around the water cooler, but facts that, when presented together, create a story.

For example, there's a list by media lawyer Daniel Henry about 10 important cases in Canadian media law relating to freedom of expression. Each of those 10 entries is interesting on its own, but taken together, they tell the story of a long and largely successful struggle that has played out in Canadian courts that has resulted in Canadian citizens and journalists enjoying rights and freedoms not found in many other countries. On the darker side, a list of 4 ships that brought migrants to Canada is the story of how our mistreatment of refugees sometimes had tragic consequences, a story that risks getting lost in the hoopla over our 150th birthday. So, think of this as a trove of surprising, enlightening and sometimes very odd stories, told in list form.

We had a lot of fun writing and revising this edition, and of course, couldn't have done it without the help of our friends, families and the enthusiastic staff at Penguin Random House Canada. Number one on that list would be our wise, patient and eagle-eyed editor Amanda Lewis who first proposed this new edition—many thanks for your endless insights, encouragement and improvements. We'd also like to acknowledge the contributions of Michael Schellenberg, the 2005 edition editor, whose talents and spirit still infuse this book. We're grateful to the entire PRHC team who know it takes a village of uniquely gifted and dedicated people to get a manuscript edited, designed, printed, distributed and marketed—many thanks to Knopf Random Canada publisher Anne Collins, Knopf Canada publishing director Lynn Henry, supervising editor Amanda Betts, senior managing editor Deirdre Molina, sales director Matthew Sibiga, marketing manager Jessica Scott, senior production coordinator Brittany Larkin, designers Colin Jaworski and Jennifer Griffiths and publicist Kaitlin Smith.

We'd also like to thank our resident "experts" who responded to the call to take us deep inside their areas of specialization to deliver some truly wonderful lists. While we may have come up with our own list of favourite cookbooks, for instance, we think you'll agree that it means a whole lot more coming from a pro like Naomi Duguid. We are also indebted to the Banff Centre for Arts and Creativity, in particular director of literary arts Devyani Saltzman and her team in the registrar's office, who made sure our self-directed writing residency was as magical as it was productive.

And finally, book writing is a labour of love fuelled by the generosity and support of the home team. Jane Farrow would like to thank Annabel Vaughan for her countless kind gestures and for being such a brilliant and loving co-adventurer. Ira would like to thank the people on his most important list: Lynn, without whose love and support nothing would be possible, and his four young grown-ups, Joanna, Andrea, Rochelle and Nathaniel, who have all evolved into astute list makers, solicitors and critics. The next generation?

And to you, clever reader, thank you for picking us up. We hope you enjoy reading this new edition and pass it along. If you happen to come across something we missed, a noteworthy Canadian, a fascinating fact about beavers, or another cat who travelled hundreds of miles to come home, get in touch.

—Ira and Jane

People

AGES OF 23 PEOPLE HAD THEY LIVED TO 2017

1. Jerry Garcia (1942–95), musician: 75
2. John Denver (1943–97), musician: 74
3. George Harrison (1943–2001), musician: 74
4. Freddie Mercury (1946–91), musician: 71
5. John Belushi (1949–82), comedian: 68
6. John Candy (1950–94), actor: 67
7. Gilda Radner (1946–89), comic: 71
8. Phil Hartman (1948–98), comic: 69
9. Andy Kaufman (1949–84), comic: 68
10. Joey Ramone (1951–2001), musician: 66
11. Sid Vicious (1957–79), musician: 60
12. Terry Fox (1958–81), runner: 59
13. Michael Jackson (1958–2009), musician: 59
14. John F. Kennedy Jr. (1960–99), publisher: 57
15. Dorothy Stratten (1960–80), model: 57
16. Diana, Princess of Wales (1961–97), royalty: 56
17. Chris Farley (1964–97), comic: 53
18. Owen Hart (1965–99), wrestler: 52
19. Kurt Cobain (1967–94), musician: 50
20. River Phoenix (1970–93), actor: 47
21. Tupac Shakur (1971–96), rapper: 46
22. Notorious B.I.G. (1972–97), rapper: 45
23. Michel Trudeau (1975–98), hiker/skier: 42

8 PEOPLE WHO CAME SECOND IN HISTORY

1. The Second Pope

After St. Peter, a shadowy figure known as St. Linus the Martyr reigned as the second pope from AD 67 to 79. He was probably a Jew, and was most certainly born in Tuscany, Italy.

2. The Second Cromwell to be Lord Protector of England

On September 3, 1658, Oliver Cromwell, the Lord Protector of England, died, nominating as his successor his eldest surviving son, Richard. Not the man his father was, Richard survived as ruler of the country for less than a year and was dismissed by Parliament in May 1659. Twelve months later, the monarchy was restored in the shape of Charles II, and Richard Cromwell fled to the Continent. Allowed to return to England in 1680, he became a farmer in Hertfordshire and died in 1712 at the age of 85.

3. The Second Woman to Take Her Seat in the Canadian House of Commons

In 1935 Martha Louise Black became the second woman to be elected to the House of Commons when she won the Yukon riding for the Conservatives despite a Liberal sweep in the rest of the country. Born in Chicago in 1866, she arrived in the Yukon with her father during the height of the gold rush in 1899. In 1904 she married George Black, a local Dawson City lawyer. In 1912 George was appointed Commissioner of the Yukon, and in 1921 he was elected to Parliament. He held the seat until 1935, when he was forced to step aside due to ill health. Martha ran in his place and won the seat, becoming one of only two women in the House (Agnes Macphail was the other). But Martha Black always believed her husband was better suited to political life than she was, and she gladly stepped aside in the 1940 election to allow George to regain the seat.

4. The Second Führer of the Third Reich

If the Third Reich had survived the thousand years its founder predicted it would, there would have been very many Reichsführers. In fact, there were two. After Hitler's suicide in his Berlin bunker on April 30, 1945, the dubious honour of being the second führer of Nazi Germany was bestowed on Admiral Karl Dönitz. Eight days later the new führer agreed to terms of unconditional surrender to the Allied forces. Tried by the International Military Tribunal at Nuremberg, he was sentenced to 10 years' imprisonment, which he served in Spandau Prison on the western fringes of Berlin. Dönitz died in 1980.

5. The Second Man to Run a Mile in Less Than Four Minutes

Just 46 days after Roger Bannister ran the first sub-four-minute mile, Australian athlete John Landy became the second man in history to break the four-minute barrier. Running in a race in Finland, Landy beat Bannister's record-breaking time by nearly two seconds. The stage was set for an epic confrontation between the two men, which took place in the so-called Miracle Mile at the Empire and Commonwealth Games in Vancouver on August 7, 1954. Landy led from the start but, in the home stretch, looking over his left shoulder to see where his rival was, he was overtaken by Bannister on his right. Landy tried to respond but was beaten to the tape. In later life, Landy was elected governor of the Australian state of Victoria.

6. The Second Person to Swim across Lake Ontario

When Marilyn Bell became the first person to swim across Lake Ontario on September 9, 1954, she attracted headlines all around the world. Many people were stunned that a 16-year-old schoolgirl was the first to meet one of swimming's greatest challenges. When 36-year-old John Jaremey became the second person to cross the lake two summers later, he didn't get nearly as much recognition, even though 21 men had already failed in their attempts to make the swim. A Toronto steamfitter, Jaremey left Niagara-on-the-Lake at 5:47 a.m. on July 22, 1956, and when he arrived at the Eastern Gap lighthouse at 3:02 the following morning, he was greeted by 12,000 cheering spectators.

7. The Second Member of Parliament to Come Out as Gay

There were six openly gay or lesbian MPs in the House of Commons in 2017, but it's been a long road to acceptance for members of the LGBTQ community in Canadian politics. It took NDP MP Svend Robinson nine years after he was elected in 1979 to come out. Robinson will always be remembered as the first gay MP to do so. The distinction of being the second MP to declare his homosexuality belongs to Bloc Québécois MP Réal Ménard, who was elected in 1993 and came out two years later in response to Liberal MP Roseanne Skoke's attempt to exclude gays and lesbians from a proposed hate crimes bill.

8. The Second Woman Appointed to the Canadian Senate

It's easy to mock the Canadian Senate and the people appointed to it, but winning the right to sit as a senator was an important goal for Canadian women in the 1920s, and their victory was hard won. In 1927, a group of five women activists, now known as the Famous Five, launched a legal challenge to clear the way for women to be appointed to the Upper House. But the Supreme Court of Canada ruled in 1928 that women were not "persons" as defined by the British North America Act and were therefore not eligible to sit in the Senate. The ruling in the so-called Persons Case was appealed to the British Privy Council, which reversed the decision in October 1929. Four months later, Liberal Prime Minister William Lyon Mackenzie King appointed the first woman senator, Cairine Wilson. In 1935, Conservative Prime Minister R.B. Bennett appointed the second woman, Iva Campbell Fallis. Fallis, a Conservative Party activist from

Peterborough, Ontario, never forgot the Supreme Court's ruling in the Persons Case, and never forgave. As a senator, she voted against a bill that would make the Supreme Court the final court of appeal in Canadian law. "I could never trust the Supreme Court after it decided that women aren't persons," she declared. Fallis remained a senator until her death in 1956.

14 MEN WHO CRIED IN PUBLIC

1. Todd Bertuzzi, hockey player

On March 8, 2004, Todd Bertuzzi of the Vancouver Canucks delivered a vicious sucker punch to Steve Moore of the Colorado Avalanche in an NHL game in Vancouver. Moore suffered a concussion and broke several bones in his neck. Two days later, Bertuzzi appeared in front of the media and sobbed uncontrollably as he offered his "apology" to Steve Moore. "I just want to apologize for what happened out there," said Bertuzzi, wiping his eyes with a napkin. "I had no intention of hurting you." Many observers viewed Bertuzzi's tearful performance with a dash of cynicism, noting that feeling sorry for "what happened out there" is not quite the same thing as taking personal responsibility for seriously injuring a fellow hockey player.

2. John Boehner, Speaker of the House

As Speaker of the House between 2011 and 2015, John Boehner, the pumpkin-hued Republican from Ohio, was third in line to the presidency. Though he never made it to the Oval Office, he was unquestionably the nation's Blubberer-in-Chief. To paraphrase Winston Churchill, never were so many tears shed for so little reason. Boehner cried during a tribute to golfer Arnold Palmer, while listening to Irish music on St. Patrick's Day, when he sang "America the Beautiful," and as he confessed in an interview on *60 Minutes*, he could not visit a school or even see little kids in a playground without crying. Even on election night in 2010, when the Republicans regained control of the House, propelling Boehner into the Speaker's chair, he could not turn off the waterworks. "I am ready to lead," he sobbed. "Dry up," thought millions of Americans.

3. Jesus Christ, religious leader

After Lazarus died, Jesus led his disciples to visit Lazarus's sisters, Mary and Martha. When the friends of Lazarus agreed to show Jesus the cave where Lazarus's body was laid, Jesus wept.

4. Bill Clinton, American president

On the morning of his inauguration, President Clinton and his family attended services at Washington's Metropolitan African Methodist Episcopal Church. As the choir sang hymns, tears rolled down Clinton's cheeks. Clinton teared up frequently as his years in office continued. Once, when caught on camera laughing and joking at a funeral, Clinton suddenly realized he was being filmed. Having learned "the Nixon lesson," he instantly grew serious, and tears came to his eyes. Right-wing TV host Rush Limbaugh played the tape in slow motion repeatedly, sending his studio audience into fits of mirth. Tom Lutz, the author of *Crying: The Natural & Cultural History of Tears*, observed that crying for male politicians was "a 1990s version of kissing babies."

5. David, warrior king

When David and his troops returned to the city of Ziklag after being sent home by the princes of the Philistines, they discovered that the Amalekites had invaded the city and taken captive all of the women and children, including David's two wives. David and his followers immediately "lifted up their voices and wept until they had no more power to weep."

6. John Diefenbaker, Canadian prime minister

Diefenbaker shed a few tears when the Canadian flag was first hoisted on February 15, 1965. A fierce defender of the Red Ensign, he vigorously opposed the new maple leaf design chosen by Prime Minister Lester B. Pearson. Commenting on the flag ceremony a few days later, he said, "As leader of Her Majesty's Loyal Opposition, and as an officer of Parliament, I was present at the raising of that flag. It was my duty to be there because I believe in Parliament. I confess, too, that I had a heavy heart. I was not aware that tears fell from my eyes until I saw the picture. But I cannot change my convictions."

7. Gord Downie, musician

The wonder is not that Gord Downie cried in public in 2016; it's that he held off for as long as he did. In May, the long-time leader of the Tragically Hip announced on the band's website that he was suffering from inoperable brain cancer, but that the band would go ahead with a planned cross-country summer tour. The "Man Machine Poem" tour was an instant sell-out and culminated in an emotional three-hour final concert on August 20 in the band's hometown of Kingston, Ontario, that was watched and heard by an estimated 11 million people on the CBC. Still, Downie was able to hold it all together, even as thousands of his fans broke down in tears. That all changed in December, when the singer appeared on stage at a meeting of the Assembly of First Nations in Gatineau, Quebec. In recognition of his work calling attention to the tragedy of residential schools, Downie was presented with an eagle feather, wrapped in a star blanket, and honoured with a Lakota spirit name: Wicapi Omani, or Man Who Walks among the Stars. It was at this point that the dam burst. Through his tears, Downie declared, "We must walk down a path of reconciliation from now on. Together and forever. This is the first day of forever. The greatest day of my life. The greatest day of all our lives."

8. Wayne Gretzky, hockey player

Hockey's Great One routinely choked up—while winning games, getting awards, addressing the media, retiring and once when talking about his wife's acting career. But his most memorable tears streamed down his face at the press conference announcing his trade from Edmonton to Los Angeles in 1988. Edmonton owner Peter Pocklington accused him of crying "crocodile tears," and fans responded by burning Pocklington in effigy outside the arena.

9. Michael Jordan, basketball player

Michael Jordan cried openly when, while playing with the Chicago Bulls, he won his first NBA title in 1991, and this drew no comment from the press. Then, when he won his fourth title in 1996, he wept once more, falling onto the floor in a fetal position and sobbing when the game ended. This time, TV announcers explained that Jordan's father had been murdered a year and a half before; the game was played on Father's Day, and Jordan had made an incredible comeback after retiring for two years.

10. Laurier LaPierre, broadcaster

The most talked-about tear ever shed on Canadian television fell from the eye of Laurier LaPierre, the mercurial co-host of CBC's controversial current affairs program *This Hour Has Seven Days*, in the spring of 1966. It happened while LaPierre was watching a taped interview with the mother of Steven Truscott. At the age of 14, Truscott had been convicted and sentenced to hang for the murder of a 12-year-old girl, a conviction that was later overturned. When the interview ended, LaPierre slowly rubbed a tear from his eye and proceeded to link the Truscott case to the debate over capital punishment that was about to begin in Parliament. CBC management was outraged and publicly condemned LaPierre's "unprofessional" conduct. In a statement he later came to regret, CBC president Alphonse Ouimet questioned whether the tear was real. The following year, LaPierre was fired from the program. The CBC cited the incident as proof that LaPierre was unable to control his emotions or his bias on air.

11. Richard Nixon, American president

During a 1977 television interview, Nixon told David Frost, "I never cry—except in public." Nixon's most famous public weep occurred in 1952 after he made his notorious "Checkers speech" and Dwight Eisenhower decided to allow him to remain on the Republican ticket as the vice-presidential candidate. Watching this performance, Nixon's college drama coach, Albert Upton, who had taught the future politician how to cry, remarked, "Here goes my actor."

12. Barack Obama, president of the United States

It's safe to say that no president in American history has cried in public as much as Barack Obama. There were at least a dozen sightings during his presidency, most famously when speaking following the massacre of 20 children and six adults at Sandy Hook Elementary School in 2012. In fact, nothing was more likely to drive Obama to tears than speaking about gun violence, and his inability to get any gun control measures passed by Congress. In 2015, he cried while listening to Aretha Franklin's extraordinary performance of "(You Make Me Feel Like a) Natural Woman" at the Kennedy Center. Whether he cried in November 2016 upon learning that Donald Trump would succeed him in the White House is anyone's guess.

13. Norman Schwarzkopf, American military leader

Towards the end of the 1991 Persian Gulf War, General Schwarzkopf was interviewed on television by Barbara Walters. His eyes welled up as he answered personal questions. Walters said, "Generals don't cry." Schwarzkopf replied, "Grant, after Shiloh, went back and cried. Sherman went back and cried . . . and these are tough old guys . . . Lincoln cried." He added that he held back his tears in front of his troops during the war for the purpose of morale; although he could cry in front of them during a Christmas Eve service, where he was embodying the role of father figure, rather than commanding officer.

14. Justin Trudeau, prime minister of Canada

As a self-confessed feminist and all round New Age-y kind of guy, it's probably not surprising that Justin Trudeau would be more likely to cry in public than some of his predecessors, including his father. The first public sighting of Trudeau in tears actually happened while he was campaigning for the Liberal leadership in 2013. In Belleville, Ontario, the future prime minister was presented with a picture of himself as a toddler being carried under his father's arm. Trudeau told the crowd he struggles to resist crying when people around the country tell him "great stories about my father and about my mother," but on that day he could not hold back. In his first few months as prime minister, the younger Trudeau also cried at a ceremony officially acknowledging the abuse suffered by Indigenous Canadians in residential schools, and after touring the Auschwitz death camp with a survivor.

CHARLOTTE GRAY'S 10 WOMEN WHO LIVEN UP CANADIAN HISTORY

Charlotte Gray is the author of 10 bestsellers of Canadian history and biography, the most recent of which is The Promise of Canada: 150 Years—People and Ideas That Have Shaped Our Country. *A frequent guest on television and radio, she championed Sir John A. Macdonald in CBC Television's* Who Is the Greatest Canadian? *and Jane Urquhart in CBC Radio's* Canada Reads. *Gray is an adjunct research fellow at Carleton University and a member of the Order of Canada.*

1. Ste. Marie de l'Incarnation (1599-1672)

A curious mix of mystical spirit and solid good sense, this Ursuline nun arrived in Quebec from France when she was 40, and immediately became a powerful administrator in the struggling colony. Defying the weather, the winters, Iroquois raids and ill will from some fellow settlers, she established schools for girls (both French and Indigenous), learned the Montagnais, Algonquin, Huron and Iroquois languages, and compiled dictionaries and catechisms in each. In vivid letters (about 13,000 during her lifetime) and memoirs, she recorded the early years of New France. A 2008 documentary of her life story is entitled *Folle de Dieu* (*Madwoman of God*).

2. Julie de Saint-Laurent (1760-1830)

The daughter of a French engineer, Saint-Laurent was the devoted mistress of Prince Edward, Duke of Kent and fourth son of George III, for 28 years. Ten of those years were spent in Canada, where they lived first in Quebec City and then in Halifax. Saint-Laurent charmed her contemporaries with her beauty, wit and dignity; the lieutenant governor of Nova Scotia remarked on her "intrepid fortitude . . . and refined manners." In the New World, she was treated with the same respect paid to the prince, but when they returned to the Old World she was socially ostracized. Forced by debts and dynastic pressures, Edward married a German princess in 1818 and became the father of the future Queen Victoria. Saint-Laurent retreated to Paris and privacy.

3. Mary Ann Shadd Cary (1823-93)

Born into an African-American family in Delaware that was active in the Underground Railway, Shadd immigrated to Canada in 1850 and founded an anti-slavery newspaper and a racially integrated school in Chatham, Ontario. An energetic campaigner against slavery and those who exploited freed slaves, she taught a whole generation of new Canadians that "Self-reliance is the Fine Road to Independence." She later returned to the United States and, at age 60, became the first black woman lawyer there, saying, "It is better to wear out than to rust out."

4. E. Pauline Johnson, Tekahionwake (1861-1913)

The fiery daughter of a Mohawk poet and English gentlewoman, Johnson was Canada's first performance artist as well as a gifted poet. In wealthy cities, muddy farm settlements and grubby railway towns, she would first recite blood-thirsty ballads about Indian battles while clad in fringed buckskin, then she would change into an elegant satin evening gown and murmur romantic love poetry and lyrical verses about nature. Her best-known poem, "The Song My Paddle Sings," celebrates our national love affair with the canoe, and helped make her Canada's first coast-to-coast celebrity.

5. Nellie McClung (1873-1951)

"Never apologize, never explain, just get the job done" was one of McClung's favourite axioms as she fought to secure political rights for women. Born in Ontario and raised on a farm in Manitoba, she was a passionate and witty social activist. In Winnipeg in 1914, she gave a brilliant performance of a stuffy male premier (based on Premier Sir Rodmond Roblin) in a "Mock Parliament," in which women legislators debated whether to give men the vote. Two years later, Manitoba became the first province to grant women the vote; within a few years women could vote in all federal and provincial elections, except in Quebec. McClung also wrote bestselling novels (in her day, her sales matched those of Lucy Maud Montgomery), and was one of the Famous Five who secured the right for women to sit in the Canadian Senate.

6. Charlotte Whitton (1896-1975)

A tough-minded academic who championed children's welfare, Whitton became Canada's first woman mayor when she was elected in Ottawa in 1951. During 10 stormy years in office, she worked hard to prove one of her favourite dictums: "Whatever women do, they must do twice as well as men to be thought half so good . . . luckily, it's not difficult." The *Reader's Digest* called her "hell on wheels." She didn't care: "Call me anything you like," she said, "but don't call me a lady."

7. Paraskeva Clark (1898-1986)

By the time Russian-born Clark arrived in Canada in 1931, she had already studied painting in St. Petersburg and Paris and had a strong commitment to both her own art and to socialism. Outspoken and unconventional, she had little patience for the Canadian love affair with landscape painting, preferring portraiture and socially relevant canvases. Inspired by Dr. Norman Bethune (with whom she had a brief affair), she was politically active in the cause of artists' rights and on behalf of starving Russians during the Second World War. Her self-portrait, *Myself* (1933)—jaunty hat, rose-pink lips and sensuous black velvet jacket—in the National Gallery of Canada glows with her strength and self-possession.

8. Viola MacMillan (1903-93)

This was a woman who wasn't afraid of getting her hands dirty. The 13th child of a poor farmer, Viola started her career as a typist, but her life changed when she married mining prospector George MacMillan. "We never allow women underground. It's bad luck," a mine manager told her, but in Cobalt, Ontario, she went down a silver mine anyway and was hooked. Soon she was a major rock star—prospecting full-time, finding gold, putting together deals, establishing the Prospectors & Developers Association of Canada, becoming the first woman inducted into the Canadian Mining Hall of Fame. Her life had highs (the

MacMillans became very wealthy) and lows (she spent some months in jail for manipulating gold stocks, but later received a full pardon). Today, we can share her enthusiasm for Canada's rocks in the Viola MacMillan Mineral Gallery in Ottawa's Canadian Museum of Nature.

9. Lili St. Cyr (1918–99)

Born Marie Van Schaak in Minneapolis, Minnesota, Lili was neither a franco-phone nor a Canadian. But in 1944 she changed her name, crossed the border and scandalized and seduced Montreal with a burlesque act in which she emerged from an onstage bubble bath. Quebec's Catholic clergy condemned her act, declaring that whenever she dances "the theatre is made to stink with the foul odor of sexual frenzy." She was eventually charged with obscenity, but her acquittal confirmed that, while Toronto was all about money, Montreal knew how to have fun. Marilyn Monroe is said to have modelled herself on the infamous Lili.

10. Judy LaMarsh (1924–80)

One of the first women cabinet ministers in Canada, LaMarsh established the fundamentals of medicare and the Royal Commission on the Status of Women in Canada; introduced groundbreaking legislation, including the Canada Pension Plan; and presided over the 1967 Centennial celebrations—all in the five-year span between 1963 and 1968. LaMarsh's locker-room language and outrageous hats infuriated her colleagues, who were unaccustomed to mouthy women who elbowed their way onto the front bench.

11 MEETINGS BETWEEN FAMOUS PEOPLE AND PEOPLE NOT YET FAMOUS

1. New York City, 1789. George Washington is introduced to Washington Irving

As the president browsed in a Broadway shop, a servant of the Irving family spotted him from the street and hustled inside with six-year-old Washington Irving in tow. Informed that the lad had been named after him, the chief executive stroked the head that later would conjure up Rip Van Winkle and wished the boy well. *Note:* This pat on the head has been passed on through generations of Americans to the present-day recipient. An older Washington Irving bestowed it upon his publisher, George Putnam, who in turn gave it to young Allan Nevins, the future Pulitzer Prize–winning historian.

2. London, England, 1836. Elizabeth Barrett Browning attends a dinner for William Wordsworth

Elizabeth Barrett, not yet either married to Robert Browning or very well known, was a great admirer of Wordsworth. John Kenyon, a friend of the Barrett family, arranged for Elizabeth to attend a dinner in the poet's honour. Although she was nervous (she said that she trembled "in my soul and my body") about being seated next to Wordsworth, he was kind and even recited one of Dante's sonnets for her entertainment. Eight years later, Barrett paid tribute to Wordsworth by mentioning him in "Lady Geraldine's Courtship."

3. Leghorn, Italy, 1897. Enrico Caruso sings for Giacomo Puccini

Near the beginning of his career, Caruso was hired by Arturo Lisciarelli to star as Rodolfo in a production of Puccini's *La Bohème*. Lisciarelli took advantage of Caruso's eagerness to sing the part by booking him for a mere 15 lire per performance, but added, rather vaguely, that the fee would be increased to 1,000 lire if Puccini liked him. When Caruso found out that Puccini lived nearby, he made a 40-kilometre trip to see the composer at his villa. After Caruso sang several measures, Puccini exclaimed, "Who sent you? God?" Despite the composer's praises, Lisciarelli held Caruso to the original terms of his contract.

4. Saskatoon, 1910. John Diefenbaker sells a newspaper to Wilfrid Laurier

Laurier was in Saskatoon to lay the cornerstone of a building at the University of Saskatchewan. As he left the train station, he was approached by a 15-year-old newsboy named John Diefenbaker. The prime minister paid Diefenbaker for a paper, inquired as to the state of the newspaper business and offered his hope that the young boy would one day grow up to be a great man. In his speech later that day, Laurier spoke about his meeting with the newsboy, who apparently ended the conversation by saying, "I can't waste any more time on you, Prime Minister. I must get about my work."

5. New York City, 1910. Sarah Bernhardt meets Lillian Gish in the wings

Before going west to become a star in D.W. Griffith's epic films, Miss Gish landed a dancing role in Sarah Bernhardt's show. As they waited together in the wings for the opening curtain, the Divine Sarah stroked the young girl's delicate curls admiringly and uttered something to her in French, a language Miss Gish had never before heard.

6. New York City, c. 1945. Nancy Reagan dates Clark Gable

Gable dated the future First Lady—then known as Nancy Davis and an aspiring actress—on three occasions during a visit to New York. Although gossip columnists speculated about a possible marriage, the relationship never was particularly romantic. Gable simply enjoyed seeing the town with Nancy and making her laugh, while she hero-worshipped Gable and wondered how long it would last. Once, when they attended a party, she was convinced that Gable would leave her the moment a more glamorous woman appeared. When he stayed, it gave her self-confidence a great boost.

7. Gainesville, Florida, 1962. Tom Petty meets Elvis Presley

When future rock star Petty was 11 years old, Elvis arrived in his hometown to shoot scenes for the movie *Follow That Dream*. Since his uncle was involved with making the film, Petty was able to visit the set and meet the king of rock and roll. Petty remembered, "He didn't have much to say to us, but for a kid at an impressionable age, he was an incredible sight." Straight away, Petty traded his slingshot for a friend's collection of Elvis records.

8. Washington, D.C., 1963. Bill Clinton shakes hands with John F. Kennedy

In the summer of 1963, Clinton was named one of the delegates to Boys Nation, an American Legion program in which a select group of high-school juniors travelled to Washington to watch national politics in action. The highlight of the trip was the delegates' visit to the White House, where a gangly, crew-cut Clinton briefly shook hands with President Kennedy. The moment was recorded for posterity (and future Clinton campaigns) in a photo and on film. When Clinton returned home to Arkansas, he was set on a political career. His mother, Virginia Kelley, remembered, "I'd never seen him so excited about something. When he came back from Washington, holding this picture of himself with Jack Kennedy, and the expression on his face—I just knew that politics was the answer for him."

9. Cheltenham, England, Literary Festival, 1963. John Fowles meets Iris Murdoch

When bestselling author John Fowles was on the verge of success, but not yet famous, he was a panellist at the Cheltenham Festival. He was prepared to attack the famous authoress Iris Murdoch, but instead found her "a gentle creature with a good mind." Mrs. Fowles felt Murdoch ignored them. Years later, when Fowles's fame was enormous, Murdoch invited the Fowleses to lunch. He recorded the following exchange in his diary:

I.M.: Are you religious?

J.F.: Not at all . . .

I.M.: Nor am I.

J.F.: In the normal sense of the word.

I.M.: Ah. (long Pinter-like silence, contemplation of the lawn outside.) I expect you have a nice intellectual circle at Lyme Regis? [The popular seaside resort area where Fowles lived.]

J.F.: Are you mad?

10. Ottawa, 1969. Allan Rock takes John Lennon on a Mystery Tour of Ottawa

Lennon arrived in the nation's capital by train from Montreal, where he was bedded down with Yoko Ono as part of their Year of Peace tour. They had come because future Liberal cabinet minister Allan Rock, then the 21-year-old president of the University of Ottawa's Student Union, had promised them a meeting with Prime Minister Trudeau. After speaking to some students at the university about peace, Lennon, Ono and Rock piled into Rock's Volkswagen fastback for a tour of the city. They drove up to the front door of 24 Sussex Drive and knocked on the door. Alas, the prime minister wasn't home. Lennon scribbled a note for Trudeau and left it with the housekeeper. Six months later, Lennon was back in Ottawa, and this time he was able to get his visit with the prime minister (see chapter 3).

11. Ottawa, April 1972. Richard Nixon predicts Justin Trudeau will be PM one day

The American president didn't actually meet the future prime minister, who was only four months old at the time, but he still saw big things in the toddler's future. It happened during a black-tie state dinner for Richard Nixon and his wife, Pat, hosted by Prime Minister Pierre Trudeau and his wife, Margaret, at Ottawa's National Arts Centre. In the champagne toast following the dinner, the president raised his glass and declared, "Tonight, we'll dispense with formalities. I'd like to toast the future prime minister of Canada—to Justin Pierre Trudeau." To which the prime minister responded by saying that should his son become prime minister one day, "I hope he has the grace and skill of the president," marking perhaps the first and only time that the words *grace* and *Richard Nixon* were used in the same sentence.

IF 36 FAMOUS MEN WERE KNOWN BY THEIR MOTHERS' MAIDEN NAMES

In our society, a married woman loses part of her identity through taking her husband's family name. Should her children happen to become famous, her husband's family is immortalized, while her own family is consigned to oblivion. (Picasso is one of the few famous men who chose to use his mother's name, partly because it was less common than Ruiz, his father's name.) It seems fitting to turn the spotlight, for once, on the maternal branch responsible for contributing half the genetic endowment of the world's immortals and mortals.

1. William Arden (Shakespeare)
2. George Ball (Washington)
3. John Bannerman (Diefenbaker)
4. Jean Boisvert (Chrétien)
5. Joey DeVannah (Smallwood)
6. Frank Garaventa (Sinatra)
7. Osama Ghanem (bin Laden)
8. Dan Gougeon (Aykroyd)
9. Ernest Hall (Hemingway)
10. Abraham Hanks (Lincoln)
11. Peter Harris-Jones (Mansbridge)
12. Martin Hayter (Short)
13. Charlie Hill (Chaplin)
14. Wayne Hockin (Gretzky)
15. Arnold Jedrny (Schwarzenegger)
16. Winston Jerome (Churchill)
17. Stephen Johnston (Harper)
18. Ludwig Keverich (van Beethoven)
19. Leonard Klonitsky-Kline (Cohen)
20. Albert Koch (Einstein)
21. Johann Sebastian Lämmerhirt (Bach)
22. Justin Mallette (Bieber)
23. Sigmund Nathanson (Freud)

24. Brian O'Shea (Mulroney)
25. Wolfgang Amadeus Pertl (Mozart)
26. Karl Pressburg (Marx)
27. Tiger Punsawad (Woods)
28. Napoleon Ramolino (Bonaparte)
29. Conrad Riley (Black)
30. Mordecai Rosenberg (Richler)
31. Michael Santaga (Bublé)
32. Michael Scruse (Jackson)
33. Mick Scutts (Jagger)
34. John A. Shaw (Macdonald)
35. Justin Sinclair (Trudeau)
36. Alexander Graham Symonds (Bell)

15 FAMOUS PEOPLE WHO WERE EXPELLED FROM SCHOOL

1. Lily Allen (1985-), singer

You know things aren't going well when your school resumé includes 13 entries. That's how many English schools the young Lily Allen attended, including one that boasted Prince Charles among its alumni. But Lily was a wild child and was expelled several times. In a 2007 interview with *Rolling Stone*, Allen was asked about one particular expulsion. "I was doing things that I shouldn't have been doing with boys at that young age," she replied, "smoking cigarettes and drinking." "What were you doing with boys?" the interviewer inquired. "I was giving blow jobs," the singer replied. Next school.

2. Conrad Black (1944-), media mogul and author

Conrad Black hated going to Upper Canada College, the elite private boys' school in Toronto. In 1959 he and two other students stole answers to an exam and sold them to their classmates. The trio made almost $5,000, but the scheme unravelled when one of their "customers" got caught walking into the exam with his prepared answers. The boy fessed up to authorities and, in Black's words, "sang like a canary flying backwards at three in the morning." Black was promptly expelled from UCC and next attended Trinity College School in Port Hope. He despised this school too, and, as Peter C. Newman reports in his biography of Black, *The Establishment Man*, after a short time TCS "strongly suggested that Conrad would be happier elsewhere."

3. Humphrey Bogart (1899–1957), actor

The son of a successful physician with inherited wealth, young Bogart was sent to Phillips Academy of Andover, Massachusetts, and after a year was thrown out for "irreverence" and "uncontrollable high spirits." Since attending Yale was suddenly out of the question, Bogie joined the U.S. Navy.

4. Tina Brown (1953–), magazine editor

Former editor-in-chief of *Vanity Fair* and *The New Yorker*, Brown was expelled from three boarding schools by the time she was 16. "I got other girls to run away," she recalled, "and I organized protests because we weren't allowed to change our underpants." At one school, the headmistress found her diary, "and opened it where I had described her bosom as an unidentified flying object."

5. Jean Chrétien (1934–), Canadian prime minister

While attending boarding school in Trois-Rivières in the spring of 1952, the future prime minister Jean Chrétien got caught trying to sneak back into the school after a night of carousing with his classmates and was expelled. Rather than face his strict father with the news of his expulsion, he arranged to lay low at a friend's place in Montreal and wait out the rest of the spring term. He returned to Shawinigan when "school" let out, his father still unaware of his expulsion. As the summer progressed, Chrétien made inquiries about going to another college in Prince Edward Island, but that summer he fell in love with his future wife, Aline, and lost interest in moving hundreds of miles away. As Chrétien faced the dilemma of coming clean with his father or leaving Quebec, his brother Maurice saved the day by pleading with the Trois-Rivières school to take Jean back, which they did.

6. Jackie Collins (1941–2015), novelist

At 16, Collins was expelled from Francis Holland School in England for (among other crimes) truancy, smoking behind a tree during lacrosse, selling readings from her diary of naughty limericks and waving at the neighbourhood flasher. Said Collins, "I was a *bad* girl." She later sent her own daughters to the same school.

7. Salvador Dalí (1904–89), artist

In 1926 Spanish ultra-modernist painter Salvador Dalí was expelled from the Escuela Nacional de Bellas Artes de San Fernando in Madrid when he refused to allow his professors to critique his paintings.

8. 50 Cent (1975-), rapper

50 Cent (Curtis Jackson) started selling crack cocaine when he was 12 years old. He was expelled from Andrew Jackson High School in Queens, New York, in grade 10 after he was caught by the school's metal detector bringing a gun to school, and being in possession of a large cache of drug money. He earned his high-school equivalency diploma while in jail for selling drugs to an undercover policeman.

9. Gustave Flaubert (1821-80), author

The 18-year-old Flaubert was first in his philosophy class at the College Royal. Nevertheless, he led a revolt against a substitute teacher, and when the noisy students were ordered to copy 1,000 lines of poetry as punishment, Flaubert organized a petition in protest. The headmaster was unmoved, and Flaubert and two other boys were expelled.

10. William Randolph Hearst (1863-1951), plutocrat

In 1885 American newspaper publisher William Randolph Hearst was expelled from Harvard, halfway through his junior year. He had given each of his professors a chamber pot adorned with the professor's name and picture.

11. Benito Mussolini (1883-1945), dictator

At the age of nine, Mussolini was sent 32 kilometres from home to a boarding school in Faenza, Italy, run by Salesian priests. The recalcitrant youth was nearly expelled for throwing an inkpot at a teacher who had struck him with a ruler. Finally he went too far—he stabbed a fellow student in the buttocks with a knife. The future dictator was permanently dismissed.

12. Richard Pryor (1940-2005), comedian

Pryor was expelled from a Catholic grammar school in Peoria, Illinois, when the nuns discovered that his grandmother ran a string of brothels. At 16, he was expelled from Central High School for punching a science teacher named Mr. Think.

13. Keanu Reeves (1964-), actor

Keanu Reeves was no one's idea of a model high-school student. He attended four different Toronto schools in a five-year period. The one school where the aspiring actor should have felt most at home, the famed Etobicoke School of the Arts, was the only one he was formally expelled from. Here's how he later described his experience at ESA.

"The teachers there, were like, 'HEY! Reevesy! Stop slacking, you slacker!' and I was like, 'Yeah, then make me, dude,' and then they were like, 'I will if you don't watch your attitude, young man,' and then I was like, 'Yeah, well, I won't if you don't watch *your* attitude . . . wait, what did I just say?' Anyways, I guess I was just a little too rambunctious and shot my mouth off once too often. I was not generally the most well-oiled machine in the school. That time they caught me smoking pot in the school bathroom didn't help either."

14. Leon Trotsky (1879-1940), political leader

At approximately the age of 10, Russian Communist leader Leon Trotsky was expelled from secondary school in Odessa after he incited his classmates to howl at their teacher. Trotsky, however, was the school's best pupil and was readmitted the following year.

15. Owen Wilson (1968-), actor

Owen Wilson was never a great student, which is perhaps why as a 10th grader at St. Mark's prep school in Dallas, he felt the need to steal his geometry teacher's textbook and copy out the answers to an exam. After he was caught, Wilson was expelled. He finished his year at a neighbouring high school and then agreed to go to the New Mexico Military Institute in Roswell at the behest of his parents, where, he claims, "I learned to follow the rules, even the ones I thought were stupid."

9 FAKE "DE"S

1. Honoré de Balzac (1799-1850)

The great French novelist was the son of a civil servant named Balzac. He added the aristocratic "de" to his name and passed it on to his son.

2. Pierre-Augustin Caron de Beaumarchais (1732-1799)

The author of *The Barber of Seville*, the most popular comedy of the 18th century, Caron was the son of a watchmaker. He married a widow and took over her husband's position at court, as well as his property. One of those properties was in Beaumarchais, which name he then appended to his own.

3. Amor De Cosmos (1825-1897)

Born William Alexander Smith, Amor De Cosmos was one of the founding fathers of British Columbia. A reformer and liberal at heart, he was elected several times in and around Vancouver and Victoria and served simultaneously as the premier of British Columbia and a federal Member of Parliament from 1872 to 1874. In 1854 he changed his name to something that he felt was more memorable than Bill Smith. *Amor de cosmos* means "lover of the universe." His name was a factor in one electoral defeat when he was forced to run as "William Alexander Smith commonly known as Amor De Cosmos." When one voter could not say the full name at the polling station, his vote was disqualified, and De Cosmos's opponent George Gordon won by a single vote.

4. Fabre d'Églantine (1750-1794)

Born Philippe Fabre, he was a popular playwright and politician who is credited with creating the names of the months and days that were used in the French Revolutionary calendar. Accused of "moderacy," he was guillotined on April 5, 1794.

5. Daniel Defoe (1660-1731)

Born Daniel Foe, he had already adopted his "de" before he wrote his famous novels *Robinson Crusoe* and *Moll Flanders*.

6. Mazo de la Roche (1879-1961)

The popular author of 16 books in the Whiteoaks of Jalna series was born Mazo Roche in Newmarket, Ontario, in 1879, the daughter of William Roche and Alberta Lundy. Why she decided to add "de la" to her name is not exactly clear, but in both her fiction and real life, Mazo de la Roche liked to live in a world of illusion. Part of that illusion appears to be that her family was descended from French aristocracy.

7. Portia de Rossi (1973-)

The Australian actress, model and spouse of Ellen DeGeneres (a genuine "de") was born Amanda Lee Rogers, but changed her name to Portia de Rossi at age 15. She says it was "the most daring thing" she had done in her life up to that point.

8. André de Toth (1913-2002)

Born Andreas Toth in Hungary, he transformed into a "de," moved to Hollywood and became a successful director of violent Westerns and action dramas. He also directed the 3-D classic *House of Wax* (1953).

9. Dame Ninette de Valois (1898-2001)

Born Edris Stannus and married to Arthur Connell, she was known as a dancer, a choreographer and the founder of what became the Royal Ballet, as well as the Royal Ballet School. She died on March 8, 2001, at the age of 102.

6 PEOPLE WHOSE NAMES WERE CHANGED BY ACCIDENT

1. Irving Berlin (1888-1989), songwriter

He was born Israel Baline, but the sheet music for his first composition, "Marie from Sunny Italy," credited the song to "I. Berlin." Baline preferred the mistake over his actual name.

2. William Faulkner (1897-1962), novelist

After William Falkner's first published work, a poem titled "L'Après-midi d'un Faune" (1924), appeared, he discovered that a *u* had been inserted into his last name. He decided to live with the new spelling rather than go through the hassle of correcting the error.

3. Ulysses S. Grant (1822-85), general and U.S. president

The future Civil War general was born Hiram Ulysses Grant. The prospect of entering the U.S. Military Academy with the initials H.U.G. embarrassed him, so the new cadet reversed the order of his names and started signing himself U.H. Grant. He soon learned that Thomas L. Hamer, who had sponsored his appointment to West Point, had mistakenly enrolled him as Ulysses Simpson Grant, "Simpson" being the maiden name of Grant's mother. Grant, finding nothing objectionable in the initials U.S.G., adopted the new name.

4. Buddy Holly (1936-59), singer and songwriter

When Charles "Buddy" Holley signed his first contract with Decca Records, his last name was misspelled as "Holly." Reasoning that others in the recording industry would make the same error, Buddy kept the new spelling.

5. Dionne Warwick (1940–), singer

When her first record, "Don't Make Me Over," was released in 1962, a printing error made Dionne Warrick over into Dionne Warwick.

6. Oprah Winfrey (1954–), television personality

Her parents intended to name her "Orpah" after Ruth's sister-in-law in the Old Testament. However, the name was misspelled "Oprah" on her birth certificate. Winfrey has used it ever since.

6 PEOPLE WHO DEFECTED TO CANADA

1. Igor Gouzenko, September 1945

Igor Gouzenko was a lowly cipher clerk at the Soviet embassy in Ottawa, but he played a very large role in ramping up Cold War tensions in the 1950s and '60s. Gouzenko came to Ottawa in 1943. His job, ciphering incoming and outgoing messages for the Soviet foreign intelligence agency, gave him a window into Soviet espionage activities around the world, including Canada. In September 1945, disillusioned with conditions in his homeland, and unhappy about learning that he was about to be sent back to the Soviet Union, Gouzenko walked out of the embassy with a briefcase full of documents that revealed the extent to which Soviet operatives had infiltrated Western governments by recruiting spies in those countries. Gouzenko's evidence eventually led to 39 Canadians being arrested, with 18 convicted on a variety of charges. According to the *New York Times*, Gouzenko's actions "awakened the people of North America to the magnitude and the danger of Soviet espionage." Gouzenko lived the rest of his life in a suburb of Toronto under the name George Brown. He died of a heart attack in 1982.

2. Mikhail Baryshnikov, June 1974

Mikhail Baryshnikov was considered one of the great young dancers in the world in 1974, a rising star in the great Kirov Ballet in Leningrad, a worthy successor to fellow countrymen Nijinsky and Nureyev. But the dancers who accompanied him to Toronto that spring were mostly second-string members of the legendary Bolshoi Ballet. The main troupe was performing in London. Not surprisingly, opening night, June 24, at the O'Keefe Centre (now the Sony Centre) was a disaster. Audience members walked out, and critics pounced on everyone except Baryshnikov. The young dancer was not happy. He was already feeling that his creativity was being stifled by the conservatism of Soviet dance officials. He wanted an opportunity to try more experimental works, and that wasn't going to happen in the Soviet Union. Using *Globe and Mail* dance critic John Fraser as an intermediary, Baryshnikov hooked up with some American friends to arrange his defection. Following the final Toronto show on June 29, the dancer ran from the theatre into a waiting car and was whisked off to a farmhouse north of Toronto. In August he performed his first post-defection ballet with the National Ballet of Canada, but his dream was always to dance in New York, and that's where he has lived and starred ever since.

3. Sergei Nemtsanov, July 1976

Sergei Nemtsanov was just 17 years old in 1976 when he won a spot on the Soviet diving team to compete in the Olympics in Montreal. Sergei finished 9th in the Men's 10 Metre Platform competition, but he had already made up his mind that he would not be returning to the Soviet Union after the Games. Defecting would not be easy. Soviet diving authorities were concerned that some athletes might defect when in Canada, so they ordered their divers to return to their rooms as soon as their competitions were over, and they planned to fly them home before the Games ended. But they did allow the team to attend a going-away luncheon with divers from other countries. It was at that luncheon that Nemtsanov, with the help of a Canadian diver, made a break for it. He slipped into an office that Canadian authorities had set up for just this purpose, and declared he wanted to defect to Canada. The Soviets did not respond well. They claimed that "unidentified terrorists" had brainwashed and kidnapped the young diver and threatened to cut off all sports ties between the two countries, including hockey. And then things got weird. It turned out that young Sergei was romantically involved with an American diver named Carol Lindner, whose father was a wealthy newspaper and supermarket-chain owner in Cincinnati. At her father's urging, Carol wrote Sergei urging him not to defect. After 19 nerve-racking days spent at a home on Lake Muskoka north of Toronto, Sergei, concerned about his family's safety, decided to head back to the Soviet Union. He competed for the Soviet Union again in the 1980 Moscow Olympics, and then finally immigrated to the United States after the fall of the Soviet Union.

4, 5, 6. Peter, Marian and Anton Stastny, 1979-80

They were three prolific goal-scoring brothers trapped in an oppressive Communist country, and they were desperate to escape. Peter, Marian and

Anton Stastny were not only the best players in their native Czechoslovakia, they were good enough to be among the best players in the NHL. But they'd only have a chance to prove that if they defected. Czech authorities in 1979 weren't in the habit of letting their top players just walk away to grab the riches that awaited them in the West. The opportunity for Peter and Anton came at the World Championship tournament in Innsbruck, Austria, in the spring of 1979. The brothers contacted officials from the Quebec Nordiques, who owned their NHL rights, and a plan was hatched. After the final game Anton, Peter and Peter's wife would walk past the team bus into a waiting car that would whisk them off to Vienna, and then to Canada. Marian decided to stay with his family in Czechoslovakia. But Czech authorities made his life difficult, closely monitoring his movements. The following year, the Nordiques managed to get him out as well. The three Stastny brothers were able to play together on a line in the NHL, just as they had always dreamed, and they helped turn the Nordiques from perennial also-rans into Stanley Cup contenders. The team made the playoffs for seven consecutive years after they joined.

The Screen

6 ALGORITHMS THAT CHANGED THE WORLD

An algorithm is defined most simply as a set of steps to accomplish a task. Your favourite apple pie recipe is an algorithm. Follow the steps and you'll bake a pie. But algorithms are most commonly thought of as mathematical models, not menus. One of the first algorithms was created by Euclid, the father of modern geometry, back in 300 BCE. It was used to reduce fractions to their simplest forms. Today, most people think of algorithms in a computer context. Computer algorithms are steps that a computer program takes to accomplish a task. For example, a search algorithm allows your computer to do searches. And since computers run pretty much everything these days, algorithms have taken on almost mythical status. Some have achieved enormous power over our lives. Here are six that helped change the world.

1. Dijkstra's

Let's start with an algorithm from the earliest days of the computer age that continues to have great relevance. It was developed in 1956 by Edsger W. Dijkstra, a 29-year-old Dutch computer scientist who was one of the pioneers in the field. It addressed what is known in mathematics as the "shortest path problem." Simply put, this algorithm was designed to find the shortest path between two nodes on a graph. It most commonly does this by establishing a single "source" node, and then finding the shortest path between that node and all the other ones on the graph. What does this mean to you? If you think of your house as the "source" node, and you want the shortest route to Grandma's house, Google Maps or a similar program will plot your route using a variation of Dijkstra's algorithm.

2. Archie

There was an Internet years before there was a World Wide Web, but it wasn't a very friendly place. There were files stored all over the vast cyber network, but without hyperlinks, it was hard to share them, and without a search engine, it was hard to find them.

It's almost impossible to imagine the online world without the ability to search. Search algorithms revolutionized the way we retrieve information, and the first one was developed by a McGill University graduate student named Alan Emtage. In 1989, two years before the birth of the Web, he developed an algorithm to search and index public Internet-based archives. He called it

Archie (*archive* without the *v*). It was an instant hit among students and other early adopters of the net, but Emtage neglected to tell the people running the university's computer science program what he was up to. By 1992, Archie's server was using about half the available bandwidth in eastern Canada. A few thousand devoted users were asking about 50,000 queries a day.

In a pre-Web world, Archie was an effective, if cumbersome way of finding documents on the Internet. If you typed in the name of the file you were looking for, it could look around the net and find it, though when things got busy on weekday afternoons, it could take Archie several hours to respond to your query. Still, it is widely regarded as the first search engine.

3. Google Search

By 1997, the top commercial search engines of the day (AltaVista, Lycos, Yahoo!) were crawling about 100 million documents on the Web, but the results they were yielding were often not very useful. When two Stanford graduate students named Sergey Brin and Larry Page entered "Bill Clinton" in one of those search engines, the first result that came up was a Bill Clinton "joke of the day" site— not very helpful for serious scholars like them.

In 1998, Brin and Page published a paper called "The Anatomy of a Large-Scale Hypertextual Web Search Engine," which introduced the world to an algorithm that would answer users' search queries with high-quality relevant results. Their key insight was borrowed from the world of academics. The highest quality academic papers are generally those that are cited most often. Page and Brin saw links as the online equivalent of footnotes. Their algorithm, which they called PageRank, would focus not on how popular a site was, but on how many people were linking back to it, and who those people were. If respected scholars linked to a site, the algorithm would give that more weight than if the links came from undergraduates, and would rank it more highly.

By focusing on links rather than the number of hits, Brin and Page shifted search results away from keyword quantity to page quality. They called their new search engine Google. Their algorithm is perhaps the most valuable, and most closely guarded, piece of intellectual property in the world. There are now hundreds of variables that determine where a site will be ranked on the Google search page. For businesses, the difference between being ranked number one and number 10 could be the difference between commercial success and failure.

4. Facebook Newsfeed

With about 1.7 billion active users, Facebook has become the colossus of the Web, and the heart of the giant is the newsfeed—that constantly updating list of stories that appears in the middle of your Facebook homepage. For most Facebook users, it is now their primary source of news. "What we're trying to do," company founder Mark Zuckerberg has declared, "is give everyone in the world the best personalized newspaper we can."

About 70% of stories in the newsfeed are posted by friends. The rest come mostly from traditional publishers like newspapers. The average user could get about 1,500 posts a day—way more than most people can or will read. So Facebook has developed a series of highly complex algorithms to present users with the 300 or so stories they think they're most likely to want to see.

The algorithms look at about 100,000 variables. They include things like who the post is coming from, whether the user has expressed interest in the topic, comments they've made, and posts they've shared. Surveys show most Facebook users don't even know their posts are being curated this way. They think the stories they are getting from their favourite news source on their feed are the same stories everyone else is getting. But they're not.

Human editors used to make decisions about what constituted news and what didn't, and they could be held accountable for their decisions. Increasingly, that job has been taken over by algorithms. Facebook has become the world's largest and most powerful publisher, but its algorithms are so opaque that no one, not readers nor traditional newspaper publishers, can really be sure why a story makes it into the newsfeed or doesn't.

5. Netflix Recommendation

Let's face it, recommendations systems like those featured on sites such as Netflix are kind of creepy. And the better they are at knowing exactly what movie we might like to watch, the creepier they are. But people love them because they help cut through the clutter of the 13,000 possible movie choices Netflix offers. Netflix gathers a huge amount of data about us every time we choose a movie, and then runs that data through a series of highly sophisticated ranking algorithms that can then recommend future movie choices with alarming/astonishing accuracy.

One of the most important algorithms is the Personalized Video Ranker (PVR), which, among other things, personalizes your selection according to the genre of movies it has determined you like and places them prominently on your screen. The Trending Ranker will make sure romantic comedies are featured around Valentine's Day. The Continue Watching Ranker tries to predict whether you might be going back to a movie you started but didn't finish. The Video-Video Similarity algorithm is not personalized to the individual user but lumps all Second World War movies together, for example.

So far, there's no word on a "time to go to the bathroom" algorithm, but don't bet against it.

6. Artificial Intelligence

As impressive as search and recommendation algorithms are, they have one major limitation. They can make inferences based on the data that is fed into them, but they can't do anything beyond that data; in other words, they can't think for themselves. But that's changing. Welcome to the world of artificial intelligence. It's a complicated world, but perhaps the best way of thinking about AI is machine learning: machines that can actually get smarter over time, not because more data is being fed into them, but because they can take data they already have and build the same kinds of neural networks as our brains to process that information and adapt to changing circumstances.

Take self-driving cars, for example. There is no way computers can be programmed to know all the decisions that have to be made while driving a stretch of Highway 401 in rush hour. But the car's onboard computer can be programmed, using AI algorithms, to know what things are right and wrong or safe and unsafe to do, and then make those decisions on its own.

The problem, of course, is that once we start building machines with minds of their own, they could become smarter than we are and we might lose control of them. Think Frankenstein's monster, an early form of AI, or the HAL computer in the movie 2001: *A Space Odyssey*. We've always tended to build technology first and worry about the implications later. The potential of artificial intelligence is so great that we might not have the luxury of doing that this time around.

CHUCK LAZER'S 13 CANADIAN TV SHOWS THAT MATTERED

Every list like this is subjective. Mine is no different. It's based on my taste, my childhood and my 30 years of experience in Canadian TV. I favour shows that played a role in building an industry, developing talent and attracting an audience. Canadians still make TV that competes with the best in the world without having to import the talent. The list is in alphabetical order. Oh, and why 13? We had to stop somewhere.

Chuck Lazer has written or produced two dozen series and hundreds of episodes in 30 years of working in Canadian TV. His credits include Nothing Too Good for a Cowboy, The Odyssey, Goosebumps *and* Max Glick.

1. Beachcombers (1972-90, CBC)

The CBC rejected the original *Beachcombers* pilot, but decided to pick up the series anyway. That turned out to be an excellent decision—*The Beachcombers* (later just *Beachcombers*) ran for 19 seasons. Set on the Sunshine Coast of B.C., the series followed the adventures of beachcomber Nick Adonidas, his partner Jesse, his competitor Relic and RCMP Constable Constable. Probably half of Canada's West Coast film and TV industry worked on some of the show's 387 episodes, including Hart Hanson, who went on to create his own long-running series, *Bones*.

2. Country Hoedown (1956-65, CBC)

A country music series that for 10 years gave a home and a break to many singers and musicians, including Tommy Hunter, whose own show went on to replace *Country Hoedown* when it was cancelled; Gordie Tapp, who found further success on *Hee Haw*; and Gordon Lightfoot, who started as a member of the show's dance troupe.

3. Degrassi (1982-2012, various networks)

A show that many of us grew up with. In 2012, 30 years after its first episode, *Degrassi* surpassed *Beachcombers'* 387 episodes to become Canada's longest-running scripted TV show. The franchise began as *The Kids of Degrassi Street* in 1979, about a group of teenagers living in the heart of Toronto. Because the show featured actors who were roughly the same age as the characters they played, we got to—had to—follow these kids as they grew up. *The Kids of Degrassi Street* became *Degrassi Junior High*, then *Degrassi High*, then *Degrassi: The Next Generation*. Their challenges evolved from bad-luck chain letters to drugs, teen pregnancy and then to families and kids of their own.

4. The Friendly Giant (1958-85, CBC)

"Look up. Look w-a-a-y up." That was the invitation that everyday brought children into Friendly's castle to visit him and his two friends, Rusty the rooster and

Jerome the giraffe. Was there ever a more welcoming space for young children to visit? The show was simple, sweet and gentle. A chat followed by a story and sometimes music. Day after day the format was the same, and this, along with the soothing nature of the performances, gave viewers a comforting place to spend 15 minutes.

5. Front Page Challenge (1957–95, CBC)

Such a simple concept. Four regular panellists try to guess the recent or historical news story with which this week's guest is associated. Boy, were they good! The series ran for almost 40 years, and helped make panellists Pierre Berton, Betty Kennedy, Toby Robins and Gordon Sinclair into national celebrities. The show rarely shied away from controversy, and guests included Pierre Trudeau, Indira Gandhi, Timothy Leary, Golda Meir and, in the middle of the Cold War, Soviet defector Igor Gouzenko. On a game show!

6. Hockey Night in Canada (1952–2014, CBC; 2014–, Rogers)

After 21 years on radio, *Hockey Night in Canada* moved to television in 1952. Since then, it has remained the bedrock of the Canadian broadcasting schedule. Before the franchise became the multi-network octopus it is now, *Hockey Night in Canada* was a single hockey game broadcast across all of English Canada on the CBC—usually the Maple Leafs game from Toronto. And this game was must-watch TV. It was programming that united the country and made national stars out of sportscasters and commentators.

7. The Littlest Hobo (1963–65, 1979–85, CTV)

Some have called it the "Canadian *Lassie*." In a half-hour series, the dog is usually the heart of the family. The twist here is that the dog has no home. Hobo is a drifter who moves from town to town, helping people he meets and always (except for one or two episodes) leaving at the end, much like the Lone Ranger. It's what we call a "travelling angel" series. Imagine what Ingmar Bergman would have done with a series about a dog . . .

8. Orphan Black (2013–, Space)

As the Pythons said, "Now for something completely different." Maybe this is insider baseball, but there are some people in the Canadian TV business who fear that they can't compete in the global marketplace without American stars. And they want the Canadian government to subsidize hiring these American actors. I don't know many "creatives"—writers, directors and performers—who believe that. *Orphan Black* gives the lie to their argument. The acclaimed series has won multiple international and Canadian awards, and its star, Tatiana Maslany, has won two Emmy Awards for best performance by an actress in a series. Without a requirement, or at least a strong financial incentive, to cast a Canadian in that role, Ms. Maslany would have been lucky to get a chance to read for the part she so clearly owns. Canadian television and the world would have been poorer for it.

9. Road to Avonlea (1990-96, CBC)

Ninety-one episodes of quality family Sunday-night TV. Initially based on several books by Lucy Maud Montgomery, the series expanded from there. Broadcast on CBC and on Disney in the United States (as *Avonlea*), the series won four Emmy Awards, four CableACE Awards, 18 Gemini Awards and was chosen by the public as the most popular program in Canada in 1990, 1991 and 1992. The cast, as well as the writers and directors, are a who's who of Canadian TV then and now.

10. SCTV (1976-84, various networks)

John Candy. Eugene Levy. Catherine O'Hara. Martin Short. Andrea Martin. Rick Moranis. Dave Thomas. Joe Flaherty. And many more. All in one series. All in Canada. Funny.

11. Speakers' Corner (1990-2008, Citytv)

Anyone with a loonie could record themselves in a video booth outside Citytv's buildings across the country. On any topic. There were rants, performances, political comments, even casting auditions. Before they were famous, the Barenaked Ladies recorded themselves to promote an upcoming gig happening just down the street. The recordings were culled, edited into thematic episodes and aired on Citytv. After *Speakers' Corner*, *YouTube* couldn't be far behind.

12. This Hour Has Seven Days (1964-66, CBC)

Canadian TV's first short-lived entry into muckraking investigative journalism. Its technique was often controversial and confrontational. The newsmagazine pioneered the use of the "ambush interview," where politicians were greeted by journalists at their homes or on their way to work and asked difficult questions. Less than two years into its run, the series was cancelled by the CBC, which claimed the show violated journalistic ethics. The cancellation sparked countrywide demonstrations, telephone campaigns and newspaper editorials pushing back against political interference in the news. The CBC upheld the cancellation and the firing of creator Patrick Watson and host Laurier LaPierre. But the ambush interview lives on today in a more comedic form in *This Hour Has 22 Minutes*.

13. The Wayne & Shuster Show (1955–85, CBC)

One of Canada's all-time funniest comedy teams, Johnny Wayne and Frank Shuster first came to the CBC on radio in the '40s, then moved to TV in the '50s. They achieved great success in the United States, appearing 67 times on *The Ed Sullivan Show*—more than any other guests. But they chose to live in Canada, even though they were less well received by the CBC. Two of their most popular bits were "Shakespearean Baseball," a baseball game played out in Shakespearean rhyming verse, and "Rinse the Blood Off My Toga," retelling the murder of Julius Caesar as a hard-boiled police procedural. Caesar's widow laments to the investigating officer, "I told him, Julie, don't go!"

17 ACTORS AND ACTRESSES WHO TURNED DOWN GREAT ROLES

1. Marlon Brando

Turned down the role of Frankie, the musician-junkie, in *The Man with the Golden Arm* (1955). Frank Sinatra got the part and re-established his career with an electrifying performance.

2. Montgomery Clift

Expressed enthusiasm for the role of the young writer in *Sunset Boulevard* (1950) but later turned it down, claiming that his audience would not accept his playing love scenes with a woman who was 35 years older. William Holden starred with Gloria Swanson in the widely acclaimed film.

3. Bette Davis

Turned down the role of Scarlett O'Hara in *Gone with the Wind* (1939). The role went to Vivien Leigh. Davis thought that her co-star was going to be Errol Flynn, with whom she refused to work.

4. W.C. Fields

Could have played the title role in *The Wizard of Oz* (1939). The part was written for Fields, who would have played the Wizard as a cynical con man. But he turned down the part, purportedly because he wanted $100,000 and MGM only offered him $75,000. However, a letter signed by Fields's agent asserts that Fields rejected the offer in order to devote all his time to writing *You Can't Cheat an Honest Man*. Frank Morgan ended up playing the Wizard.

5. Jane Fonda

Turned down *Bonnie and Clyde* (1967). The role of Bonnie Parker went to Faye Dunaway. Fonda, living in France at the time, did not want to move to the United States for the role.

6. Cary Grant

Producers Albert Broccoli and Harry Saltzman, who had bought the film rights to Ian Fleming's James Bond novels, originally approached Cary Grant about playing 007. Grant declined because he did not want to become involved in a film series. Instead, Sean Connery was cast as Bond, starting with *Dr. No* (1962). Fleming's comment on this casting choice: "He's not exactly what I had in mind."

7-8. Gene Hackman and Michelle Pfeiffer

Orion Pictures acquired the film rights to *The Silence of the Lambs* in 1988 because Gene Hackman had expressed an interest in directing and writing the screenplay for it. He would also star as serial killer Hannibal Lecter. By mid-1989, Hackman had dropped out of the project. Jonathan Demme took over as director and offered the female lead of FBI agent-in-training Clarice Starling to Michelle Pfeiffer, with whom he had worked in *Married to the Mob* (1988). Pfeiffer felt the film was too dark and decided not to be in it. When *The Silence of the Lambs* was made in 1990, the lead roles were played by Anthony Hopkins and Jodie Foster. Both won Academy Awards for their performances.

9. Hedy Lamarr

Turned down the role of Ilsa in *Casablanca* (1942). Ingrid Bergman took over and, with Humphrey Bogart, made film history. Lamarr had not wanted to work with an unfinished script.

10. Burt Lancaster

Turned down the lead in *Ben-Hur* (1959). The role of Judah Ben-Hur went to Charlton Heston, who won an Academy Award and added another hit to his career of spectacular blockbusters.

11-12. Ewan McGregor and Will Smith

Both of these stars turned down the role of Neo, which eventually went to Keanu Reeves, in the blockbuster science fiction epic *The Matrix*. McGregor starred as the young Obi-Wan Kenobi in *Star Wars: The Phantom Menace* instead, while Smith—who went on to star in the film version of Isaac Asimov's *I, Robot*—admitted, "I watched Keanu's performance—and very rarely do I say this—but I would have messed it up. I would have absolutely messed up *The Matrix*. At that point I wasn't smart enough as an actor to let the movie be."

13. Sarah Polley

The Canadian actress, scrrenwriter and director got her start playing Sara Stanley in the much-loved Canadian TV series *Road to Avonlea* and then found big-screen success in *The Sweet Hereafter* (1997), directed by Atom Egoyan. She was offered and almost accepted the female lead in Cameron Crowe's film *Almost Famous* (2000). The part of Penny Lane, a lovelorn groupie, eventually went to Kate Hudson, and quickly established her as a bankable Hollywood star. Polley went on to direct *Away from Her*, *Take This Waltz* and *Stories We Tell*, which won numerous international and Canadian awards.

14. Robert Redford

Turned down the role of Ben Braddock in *The Graduate* (1967). The role made an instant star of Dustin Hoffman. Redford thought he could not project the right amount of naiveté.

15. Christopher Plummer

The great Canadian actor loved *The Lord of the Rings* books, but when director Peter Jackson offered Plummer the prized role of Gandalf in his Lord of the Rings trilogy, Plummer turned it down. The prospect of spending several years shooting in New Zealand was too great a commitment. "I thought, There are other countries I'd like to visit before I croak," the actor later told Conan O'Brien. Plummer was full of praise for the performance of Sir Ian McKellen, the actor who wound up playing the wizard to great acclaim, but also indicated he might have some regrets about his decision. "I hate the son of a bitch," he said of McKellen.

16. Sean Connery

Gandalf again. Before offering the part to Plummer, director Peter Jackson first approached Sean Connery. Jackson was so keen on having Connery play the wizard that he made him an offer he thought the great Scottish actor could not refuse: $6 million per picture, plus 15% of box office. But Connery turned it down. "I never understood it," Connery later said about the part. "I read the book, I read the script, I saw the movie, I still don't understand it." Perhaps Connery should have tried harder. The trilogy earned nearly $3 billion at the box office. It's estimated that Connery's take could have been in the range of $400 million. But The Lord of the Rings series wasn't the only blockbuster that Connery has turned down in his long career. He also passed on Dumbledore in the Harry Potter series, and Morpheus in *The Matrix*, claiming, once again, that he "didn't get it."

17. James Caan

Caan has had a very successful Hollywood career, including an Oscar-nominated turn as Sonny Corleone in *The Godfather*. But Caan's radar has not always been finely tuned. He turned down the role of Popeye Doyle in *The French Connection* (1971), as did Steve McQueen, because he didn't think Doyle was "likeable enough." Gene Hackman got the part and won an Oscar. Caan also turned down the lead role in *One Flew Over the Cuckoo's Nest* (1975). It went to Jack Nicholson, who won an Academy Award. And he turned down the starring role in *Kramer vs. Kramer* (1979), a part that won an Oscar for Dustin Hoffman. "I looked at it," he recalled, "and I said, 'this is middle-class, bourgeois horsecrap! This is crap!'"

10 FILM SCENES LEFT ON THE CUTTING-ROOM FLOOR

There are lots of reasons why some scenes don't make it into a final cut: length restrictions, censorship, artistic differences between producers, writers and directors about plots and characters. For decades these sequences were seen by nobody other than studio execs and directors, but nowadays, we have "director's cuts," with longer, languorous edits replete with new scenes, alternative endings and subplots. This list pulls back the curtains on some of the more significant deletions that filled gaps in plot, character development and motivation.

Sometimes we catch these narrative jump cuts, but mostly we just sink into the joyful disbelief the silver screen demands.

1. The Wizard of Oz (1939)

The Wizard of Oz originally contained an elaborate production number called "The Jitter Bug," which cost $80,000 and took five weeks to shoot. In the scene, Dorothy, the Scarecrow, the Cowardly Lion and the Tin Woodsman are on their way to the witch's castle when they are attacked by "jitter bugs"—furry pink and blue mosquito-like "rascals" that give one "the jitters" as they buzz about in the air. When, after its first preview, the movie was judged too long, MGM officials decided to sacrifice the jitter bug scene. They reasoned that it added little to the plot and, because a dance by the same name had just become popular, they feared it might date the picture. (Another number was also cut for previews because some felt it slowed the pacing, but it was eventually restored. Its title was . . . "Over the Rainbow.")

2. Sunset Boulevard (1950)

Billy Wilder's film classic about an aging Hollywood film queen and a down-on-his-luck screenwriter originally incorporated a framing sequence that opened and closed the story at the Los Angeles County Morgue. In a scene described by Wilder as one of the best he'd ever shot, the body of Joe Gillis (William Holden) is rolled into the morgue to join three dozen other corpses, some of whom—in voice-over—tell Gillis how they died. Eventually Gillis tells his story, which takes us to a flashback of his affair with Norma Desmond (Gloria Swanson). The movie was previewed with this opening in Illinois and Long Island. Because both audiences inappropriately found the morgue scene hilarious, the film's release was delayed six months so that a new beginning could be shot in which police find Gillis's corpse floating in Norma's pool while Gillis's voice narrates the events leading to his death.

3. Spartacus (1960)

Of the 167 days it took Stanley Kubrick to shoot *Spartacus*, six weeks were spent directing an elaborate battle sequence in which 8,500 extras dramatized the clash between Roman troops and Spartacus's slave army. Several scenes in the battle drew the ire of the Legion of Decency and were therefore cut. These included shots of men being dismembered. (Dwarfs with false torsos and an armless man with a phony "break-away" limb were used to give authenticity.) Seven years later, when the Oscar-winning film was reissued, an additional 22 minutes were chopped out, including a scene in which Varinia (Jean Simmons) watches Spartacus (Kirk Douglas) writhe in agony on a cross. Her line "Oh, please die, my darling" was excised, and the scene was cut to make it appear that Spartacus was already dead. These cuts were restored to the film in the early '90s.

4. Splendor in the Grass (1961)

As filmed, *Splendor in the Grass* included a sequence in which Wilma Dean Loomis (Natalie Wood) takes a bath while arguing with her mother (Audrey Christie). The bickering finally becomes so intense that Wilma jumps out of the tub and runs nude down a hallway to her bedroom, where the camera cuts to a close-up of her bare legs kicking hysterically on the mattress. Both the Hollywood censors and the Catholic Legion of Decency objected to the hallway display. Consequently, director Elia Kazan dropped the piece, leaving an abrupt jump from tub to bed.

5. Dr. No (1962)

The first of the James Bond films ended with Honey Ryder (Ursula Andress) being attacked by crabs when Bond (Sean Connery) rescues her. The crabs moved too slowly to look truly menacing, so the ending was reshot without them.

6. Ferris Bueller's Day Off (1986)

John Hughes's classic teen comedy features Matthew Broderick as a high-school slacker who fakes being sick to drive around in his dad's Ferrari, see the sights of Chicago and eat "pancreas" at a fancy French bistro. Filmed before teens had debit or credit cards, the movie never reveals where Ferris gets the cash to finance this epic sick day; the scene of him cashing in one of his dad's bonds was removed. Director John Hughes felt this plot detail made Ferris slightly delinquent instead of an adorable rogue.

7. Jerry Maguire (1996)

Jerry Maguire originally included a fictional Reebok advertisement starring Rod Tidwell (Cuba Gooding Jr.), which was cut from the film by director Cameron Crowe. However, when the movie was broadcast on the Showtime cable network, the commercial was restored, playing under the closing credits. Reportedly, the scene was put back in because of a lawsuit filed by Reebok against Columbia Pictures over the terms of product placement in the film.

8. Titanic (1997)

The film ends with Rose (Gloria Stuart) going to the deck of the research ship investigating the *Titanic* wreck, leaning over the railing and dropping a necklace with the valuable Heart of the Ocean diamond into the ocean. As originally filmed, the crew members of the research ship see Rose, mistakenly believe that she is planning to jump overboard, and try to talk her out of committing suicide. When they realize what she is actually doing, they try to persuade her to preserve the necklace. Director James Cameron decided that he wanted the scene to focus on Rose, so he reshot it with her alone.

9. Harry Potter (2001-11)

Suffice to say, when you film an eight-part series a few bits and bobs are going to get cut. One deleted scene from *Deathly Hallows: Part 1* features Harry and his cousin Dudley saying goodbye with a touch of bromance. Dudley reassures Harry he's "not a waste of space." Harry responds, "See ya, Big D," opening the door for some intriguing fan fiction.

10. Suicide Squad (2016)

A full cast of DC Comics anti-heroes are recruited to a punishing strike force tasked with the responsibility of saving the world. Lead actor Jared Leto plays the psycho-killer Joker but was cut from so many scenes that critics dubbed his role a glorified walk-on. Early on he drives the action, torturing, blackmailing and blasting his way to the secret nanobomb facility. But then the Joker disappears in a blaze of exploding helicopter, only to inexplicably re-emerge in the final scenes unscathed. When asked where all his scenes went, Leto couldn't conceal his ire. "I have no idea. He probably went and had a drink or something. Stretched. Once you get blown up in a helicopter your muscles get a little tight."

ASTRA TAYLOR'S 6 REASONS WE SHOULD BE AFRAID OF THE WEB

Astra Taylor was born in Winnipeg and raised in the United States. She is a documentary filmmaker, writer, activist and musician. Her book The People's Platform: Taking Back Power and Culture in the Digital Age (2014) *was described by cultural theorist Douglas Rushkoff as "perhaps the most important book about the digital age so far this century."*

1. Silicon Valley

Silicon Valley is both a geographic location and an ideology. Way back in 1995, Richard Barbrook and Andy Cameron dubbed it "the California Ideology"—"a mix of cybernetics, free market economics, and counter-culture libertarianism." This ideology is embedded in most of the online platforms and services we use daily, regardless of where we live. After all, Google dominates search not just in California, or even in the United States, but globally. Every time we use Google (or Facebook, Netflix, Twitter, PayPal, Yelp and so on), profits flow back to one region and empower a specific class of people (tech workers, corporate executives, venture capitalists and shareholders) while their ideology infuses every corner of the world. Money and wealth concentrate while a technocratic, neoliberal credo spreads.

2. Peter Thiel

If the above doesn't worry you, then consider Peter Thiel, one of Silicon Valley's most successful billionaire entrepreneurs and an enthusiastic supporter of and official advisor to President Donald Trump. Thiel made his fortune from PayPal and sits on the board of Facebook. A diehard libertarian, he believes "freedom and democracy are no longer compatible" (and, to be clear, he'd prefer freedom, which for him means free markets). "Since 1920, the vast increase in welfare beneficiaries and the extension of the franchise to women—two constituencies that are notoriously tough for libertarians—have rendered the notion of 'capitalist democracy' into an oxymoron," Thiel explained in 2009. Like most libertarians, Thiel despises welfare but doesn't actually object to a strong state or raking in government cash. Thiel's data-mining company Palantir does brisk business spying on citizens for governments across Europe and also the United Kingdom, United States, Australia, New Zealand and Canada.

3. Surveillance

Which brings us to surveillance. Do you like your every digital click, search query, message and move being monitored and logged, parsed and analyzed? If the answer is *no*, be concerned. When we think of surveillance we often think of big government, something out of George Orwell's *1984*. But Peter Thiel's Palantir is proof that reality is more complicated. In keeping with the California Ideology, the state has privatized and outsourced many of its core features, including keeping tabs on citizens. Big government and big business have merged. But it's important to note that most companies involved in surveillance are less obviously menacing than Palantir, with its contracts with military, national security and intelligence communities.

4. Advertising

The dominant business model online is advertising—that is why so many of the services we use, from search to social media, are "free." Instead of paying with money, we pay with our personal data. We implicitly and often explicitly grant websites and apps permission to track us on and offline. In return, unscrupulous data brokers create remarkably comprehensive digital profiles of us and "personalize" our digital experiences and individually target ads, often discriminating against vulnerable populations and perpetuating inequity in the process. The fundamental commercial nature of the Web is a huge factor in the rise of online surveillance, and something that can only be resolved through the cultivation of public, non-commercial alternatives.

5. Inequality

While the Web's early champions were convinced that networked technologies would create a "more level playing field" and empower the little guy, things haven't quite turned out that way. As we've already seen, the Internet's global reach means that companies based in California can extract profits from users around the world. What's more, due to something called "network effects" there's a tendency towards centralization and even monopoly online. The reason Facebook is so useful, after all, is the fact that so many people from so many places are on it—and that's why rival social media platforms have a problem attracting an audience and getting a foothold. In countless instances, the Web amplifies the gulf between winners and losers, with scarce resources—namely, attention and money—gravitating to those at the top instead of down to those who need them the most.

6. The Future

Unless we drastically change course politically, networked technologies, from data tracking to artificial intelligence, are only going to intensify the economic and social pressures that are already tearing societies apart. More and more of our devices will go online (the so-called Internet of Things), which means we'll be leaking data for advertisers and governments to scoop up not just from our computers and phones, but our cars and coffeemakers as well. Our digital profiles will become more nuanced: we'll never see ads for politicians we don't already agree with, which means polarization will increase; we'll only be targeted for news we like, even if it's fake; we'll be channelled into purchasing decisions and even education and career opportunities based on our gender, race and class, deepening cultural divides. Meanwhile, advances in machine learning and automation will enable employers to fire more of their employees and squeeze wages, resulting in further financial insecurity and social animosity. Or maybe not, since the future is not written and (as yet) impossible to predict. In theory, people could use the Web to come together and demand that technology be put to positive use, connecting and enriching all of us instead of benefiting a lucky few.

13 MOVIE STARS (+1 NEWS ANCHOR) AND HOW THEY WERE DISCOVERED

1. Pamela Anderson
Comox, British Columbia, native Pamela Anderson was spotted at a B.C. Lions football game in Vancouver in 1989. A cameraman roaming the stands for crowd shots locked onto the 22-year-old blonde beauty in a tight Labatt's Blue T-shirt, causing the crowd to cheer. Labatt's quickly signed her up as their "Blue Girl," and Pamela was soon adorning the walls of bars across Canada. Within the year she was on the cover of *Playboy*, and two years later she got the starring role in the TV series *Baywatch*.

2. Ellen Burstyn
She was cast in her first major role in *Tropic of Cancer* (1969) on the basis of a political speech that director Joseph Strick heard her delivering.

3. Gary Cooper
Working as a stunt man, he was noticed by director Henry King on the set of *The Winning of Barbara Worth* at Samuel Goldwyn Studio in 1926.

4. Errol Flynn
He was discovered by Cinesound Studios casting director John Warwick in Sydney, Australia, in 1932. Warwick found some amateur footage of Flynn taken in 1930 by Dr. Herman F. Erben, a filmmaker and tropical-disease specialist who had chartered navigator Flynn's schooner for a tour of New Guinea headhunter territory.

5. Ryan Gosling

By the time he was 11 years old, Ryan Gosling knew he wanted to be in show-biz. He was living in Cornwall, Ontario, singing at weddings, performing in his uncle's Elvis Presley tribute act, and entering talent shows with his older sister, Mandi. In January 1993, 12-year-old Gosling attended an open audition in Montreal for the TV show *The Mickey Mouse Club*. He beat out 17,000 other aspiring Mouseketeers. Gosling signed a two-year contract and moved to Orlando, where he joined Justin Timberlake, Christina Aguilera and Britney Spears in the ensemble cast. "I think they needed a Canadian," he later told the New York *Daily News*.

6. Rock Hudson

Hudson, whose original name was Roy Fitzgerald, was working as a truck driver for the Budget Pack Company in 1954 when another driver offered to arrange a meeting between Fitzgerald and agent Henry Willson. In spite of Fitzgerald's professed lack of faith in his acting abilities, Willson took the aspiring actor under his wing, changed his name to Rock Hudson and launched his career.

7. Janet Leigh

She was a psychology student when MGM star Norma Shearer happened to see a photo of her at a ski lodge in northern California where her parents were employed. Shearer took it to the studio, with the result that Leigh was given a role in *The Romance of Rosy Ridge* (1947).

8. Gina Lollobrigida

An art student in Rome, she was stopped on the street by director Mario Costa. She let loose a torrent of abuse about men who accost defenceless girls, and only when she paused for breath was he able to explain that he wanted to screen-test her for *Elisir d'Amore* (1946). She won the part.

9. Carole Lombard

She met director Allan Dwan in Los Angeles in the spring of 1921. Dwan watched 12-year-old Carole—then tomboy Jane Alice Peters—playing baseball outside the home of his friends Al and Rita Kaufman.

10. Ryan O'Neal

He was befriended by actor Richard Egan in 1962 at the gymnasium where both Egan and O'Neal worked out. "It was just a matter of Ryan himself being so impressive," said Egan.

11. Telly Savalas

He was teaching adult-education classes in Garden City, New Jersey, when an agent asked him if he knew an actor who could speak with a European accent. He tried out himself and landed a part in *Armstrong Circle Theater* on television.

12. Charlize Theron

The South African–born actress studied dance and modelled in Milan and New York before heading to Los Angeles to pursue her dream of acting. After several difficult months in L.A., Theron's discovery came in a Hollywood Boulevard bank. When a teller refused to cash an out-of-town cheque for her, she threw an enormous tantrum that caught the attention of veteran talent manager John Crosby, who happened to be standing nearby. Crosby handed her his business card as she was being thrown out of the bank, and she signed with him.

13. John Wayne

He was spotted by director Raoul Walsh at Hollywood's Fox lot in 1928. Walsh was on his way to the administration building when he noticed Wayne—then Marion Morrison, a studio prop man—loading furniture from a warehouse onto a truck.

+1. Peter Mansbridge

"Transair flight 106 for Thompson, The Pas and Winnipeg, now ready for boarding at gate one." It's hard to believe that a simple flight announcement, delivered at an airport in Churchill, Manitoba, would be the launching pad for one of the most successful careers in Canadian broadcasting. But that is exactly what happened in the case of CBC anchor Peter Mansbridge. He was a 20-year-old baggage handler in September 1968, when a busy ticket agent asked him to make the now-famous flight announcement. The manager of the CBC station in Churchill was at the airport that day. He knew a radio voice when he heard one. He approached Mansbridge and asked if he would be interested in working the night shift at the station. Mansbridge said yes, and so began a career that has lasted nearly 50 years.

17 CANADIAN MUSICIANS AND THE MOVIES THEY'VE BEEN IN

1. Bryan Adams

Adams played a gas station attendant in *Pink Cadillac* (1989), which starred Clint Eastwood and Bernadette Peters.

2. Paul Anka

Anka's most memorable film role probably came when he played himself in the groundbreaking 1962 National Film Board documentary *Lonely Boy*. He starred in his first movie in 1959 at the age of 18, when he played Jimmy Parlow in the film *Girls Town*. He followed that up with *The Private Lives of Adam and Eve* (1960), *Look in any Window* (1961), and the D-Day epic *The Longest Day* (1962). He made three forgettable films in the 1990s: *Captain Ron* (1992), *Ordinary Magic* (1993) and *Mad Dog Time* (1996). In 2001, he played a pit boss in the film *3000 Miles to Graceland*, which was set in Las Vegas during an Elvis convention, and starred Kurt Russell and Kevin Costner.

3. Leonard Cohen

Cohen played himself in the wonderful 1965 National Film Board documentary *Ladies and Gentlemen . . . Mr. Leonard Cohen*, directed by Donald Brittain and Don Owen. Two years later, he played a singer in *The Ernie Game*, which was written and directed by Owen and starred Jackie Burroughs.

4. Jim Cuddy

Cuddy and the other members of Blue Rodeo played themselves in the 1990 hit *Postcards from the Edge*, which was directed by Mike Nichols, written by Carrie Fisher, and starred Meryl Streep and Shirley MacLaine.

5. Burton Cummings

Cummings played Rick in the 1982 flick *Melanie*. The movie, which starred Glynnis O'Connor and Paul Sorvino, was the story of a young woman's battle to regain custody of her son.

6. Gord Downie

Downie and the rest of the Tragically Hip were the Team Kingston curling team in Paul Gross's comedy *Men With Brooms* (2002). In 2006, Downie played "Cop 1" in *Trailer Park Boys: The Movie*, and followed that up with an appearance as a biker in the road movie *One Week* (2008), starring fellow Canadian Joshua Jackson.

7. Drake

Drake (real name Aubrey Drake Graham) was an actor before he was a singer. From 2001 to 2009 he played Jimmy Brooks in the hit TV series *Degrassi: The Next Generation*, filmed in Toronto. In 2013, he played a soul brother in the not-very-successful sequel *Anchorman II: The Legend Continues*. But he's got acting chops and movie star looks, so expect his film credits to grow over the next few years.

8. Ronnie Hawkins

Canada's favourite hillbilly has appeared in several notable movies. He played Wolcott in the colossally unsuccessful *Heaven's Gate* (1980). He also played a bar singer in *Meatballs III* (1987), and he was Desi in *Boozecan* (1994). Perhaps his most unusual role was as Bob Dylan in *Renaldo and Clara* (1978), a movie that Dylan wrote and directed. He most recently played a gas station attendant in the Red Green movie *Duct Tape Forever* (2002).

9. Chantal Kreviazuk

The Winnipeg-born singer-songwriter made her big-screen debut playing Mary in the 2001 Canadian flick *Century Hotel*. She also appears in two movies scheduled to be released in 2017, *Welcome to Nowhere* and *Kiss and Cry*.

10. k.d. lang

Lang's first screen role was as Kotzebue in *Salmonberries* (1991). She followed that with *Teresa's Tattoo* (1994), and then in 1999 she played Hilary in the thriller *Eye of the Beholder* alongside fellow Canadians Jason Priestley and Geneviève Bujold. Don't blink and you can also catch her in Brian De Palma's crime drama *The Black Dahlia* (2006), starring Scarlett Johansson and Josh Harnett. Lang played a lesbian bar singer (not much of a stretch), but she did not get a credit.

11. Avril Lavigne

She's best known as a singer, and more recently as a designer and model, but Avril Lavigne does have a couple of big-screen roles on her resumé. In 2006, she played a high-school student intent on stopping cows from being shipped to the slaughterhouse in Richard Linklater's adaptation of the book *Fast Food*

Nation. The following year she had a single scene in a movie called *The Flock*, alongside Richard Gere and Claire Danes. Despite the star power in the cast, the movie never opened in the United States.

12. Gordon Lightfoot

Lightfoot played U.S. Marshal Morrie Nathan in the seldom-seen 1982 drama *Harry Tracy, Desperado*. The movie starred Bruce Dern and fellow Canuck Helen Shaver.

13. Alanis Morissette

The Ottawa singer has appeared in two movies, *Dogma* (1999) and *Jay and Silent Bob Strike Back* (2001). Both were written and directed by Kevin Smith, and Alanis plays the role of God. She has also played some more down-to-earth roles on the small screen, including a regular gig as Dr. Audra Kitson in the TV series *Weeds* (2009–10).

14. Robbie Robertson

Robertson played himself and also produced *The Last Waltz* (1978), perhaps the best concert movie ever made. He followed that up with roles in two less impressive films. He was Patch in *Carny* (1980), a movie he also produced, and he was Roger in *The Crossing Guard* (1995), which was written and directed by Sean Penn.

15. Shania Twain

Shania played herself in the 2004 David O. Russell film, *I Heart Huckabees*.

16. Martha and Rufus Wainwright

The musical progeny of Kate McGarrigle and Loudon Wainwright III appeared as lounge singers at the Cocoanut Grove in Martin Scorsese's Howard Hughes biopic *The Aviator* (2004). In 2005, Rufus played Jeremy in *Heights*, a romantic drama set in New York City.

17. Neil Young

Young's first acting role came in a 1982 film called *Neil Young: Human Highway*, where, in spite of the movie's title, he played a character called Lionel Switch and not himself. He followed that up in 1987 when he played a truck driver in the romance *Made in Heaven*. He was Westy in *'68* (1988) and Rick in *Love at*

Large (1990). He returned to the big screen in 2003 with *Greendale*, a musical look at the lives and struggles of people in a small fictional town, which he wrote and directed. Young made a cameo appearance as his alter ego, Bernard Shakey, playing the role of Wayne Newton.

JESSE WENTE'S 8 FILMS YOU SHOULD WATCH TO PREPARE FOR THE END OF THE WORLD

One of the ideas that has stuck with me for a long time is the notion that Indigenous people on Turtle Island (a.k.a. North America) exist in a post-apocalyptic world. We have seen our environment destroyed, our way of life extinguished, and now we live among the walking dead. I've decided I have always loved zombie movies because, for us, they verge on documentaries. Timing has rarely felt as perfect to examine and revisit the stories of the end. With Mother Nature under constant siege, a Trump presidency set on rolling back progress, and mistrust of modern media at an all-time high, it's no wonder my generation feels a sense of unease. In these moments it's helpful to return to art for connection, community and even instruction. So with that in mind, I offer you a list of films to prepare you for the apocalypse.

Jesse Wente, an Anishinaabe/Canadian, is the director of film programmes at the Toronto International Film Festival. He can be heard regularly on CBC Radio's Metro Morning *and* Unreserved.

1. Dawn of the Dead (1978, USA)
DIRECTOR: George A. Romero
STARRING: David Emge, Ken Foree

A group of survivors escape to a shopping mall overrun by the walking dead intent on reliving their consumer-based existence. The zombie movie that eats other zombie movies also contains some valuable post-apocalypse survival tips, including: malls are valuable sites for materials and supplies; and, when around helicopters, duck.

2. Before Tomorrow (2008, Canada/Nunavut)
DIRECTORS: Marie-Hélène Cousineau, Madeline Ivalu
STARRING: Madeline Ivalu, Paul-Dylan Ivalu

An Inuk grandmother and her grandson set out on their annual trip to dry the community catch, but when no one comes for their usual pick-up, they begin to suspect something sinister. A stunningly beautiful film about an Inuit community's encounters with Europeans. A movie about the Inuk apocalypse that suggests love and family will help you survive the end.

3. Miracle Mile (1988, USA)

DIRECTOR: Steve De Jarnatt
STARRING: Anthony Edwards, Mare Winningham

A couple attempts to escape the nuclear apocalypse and preserve their love, something that is virtually impossible in Los Angeles—Armageddon or no Armageddon. Key survival tip: don't be in Los Angeles when Armageddon comes.

4. The Quiet Earth (1985, New Zealand)

DIRECTOR: Geoff Murphy
STARRING: Bruno Lawrence

Imagine waking up to find that you're the only person left on Earth. Cool! Then you realize maybe you're not so alone after all. Not cool. Key survival tip: bring a book.

5. On the Beach (1959, USA)

DIRECTOR: Stanley Kramer
STARRING: Gregory Peck, Ava Gardner, Fred Astaire

Atomic destruction wipes out most of the world, including the United States, so a submarine commander seeks refuge in Australia, knowing that they must return, but not knowing to what. Key survival tip: submarines are an effective mode of post-doom transportation, but they don't leave a lot of space for dancing, even if you're Fred Astaire.

6. Last Night (1998, Canada)

DIRECTOR: Don McKellar
STARRING: Don McKellar, Sandra Oh, David Cronenberg, Sarah Polley

A sardonic and distinctly Canadian apocalypse brings together six Toronto residents seeking their own version of the last night on earth, with the end scheduled for 12-midnight, sharp. Thought-provoking and increasingly funny, the film also features a who's who of Canadian filmmakers in acting roles—spot producer Daniel Iron and directors Bruce McDonald and François Girard, perfectly cast as street toughs. Key survival tip: enjoy yourself; it's the end anyway!

7. Dr. Strangelove or: How I Learned to Stop Worrying and Love the Bomb (1964, USA)
DIRECTOR: Stanley Kubrick
STARRING: Peter Sellers, Sterling Hayden, George C. Scott

A satire turned potential documentary about an insane general, an unhinged military advisor/former or present Nazi, and a dimwitted president who cause global calamity through what presents as an increasingly realistic chain of events. Russia is involved. Perhaps the greatest film satire ever made, by one of cinema's greatest masters, Stanley Kubrick. Key survival tip: beware of inept presidents and Nazis.

8. This Is the End (2013, USA)
DIRECTORS: Seth Rogen and Evan Goldberg
STARRING: Jay Baruchel, Seth Rogen, James Franco

As foretold in the ancient prophecy, the end of the world occurs during a party at James Franco's house. Key survival tip: don't go to James Franco's house.

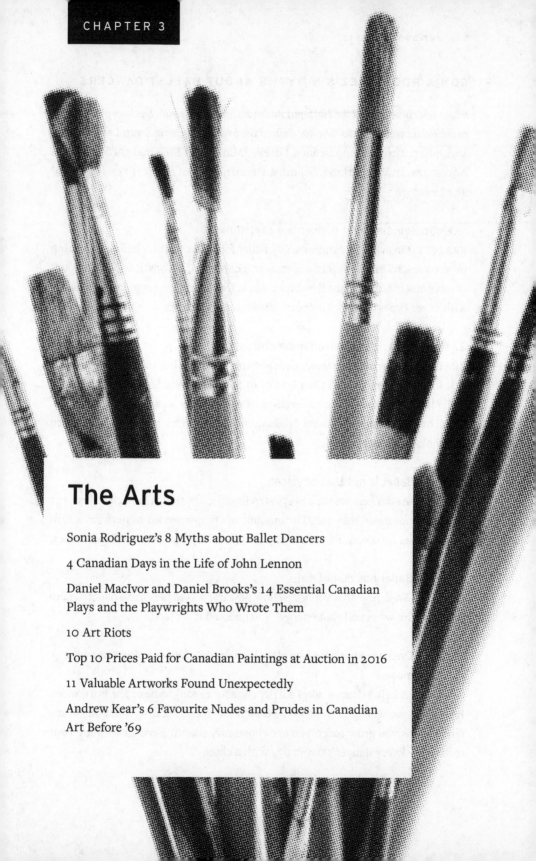

CHAPTER 3

The Arts

SONIA RODRIGUEZ'S 8 MYTHS ABOUT BALLET DANCERS

Sonia Rodriguez joined the National Ballet of Canada in 1990. She was promoted to principal dancer in 2000. She has danced the principal roles in Swan Lake, Romeo and Juliet, The Sleeping Beauty, Giselle, Manon, La Fille mal gardée, Alice's Adventures in Wonderland, Nijinsky, Hamlet, Song of the Earth *and* Opus 19/ The Dreamer.

1. Myth: Being a ballet dancer is a part-time job

REALITY: On average, dancers study ballet for about 12 years before becoming professionals. Once they join a company, a dancer's day consists of seven hours of class and rehearsal time five days a week. Dancers often supplement that day with other types of workout or strengthening programs.

2. Myth: Ballerinas are fragile creatures

REALITY: Ballerinas are fluid, delicate and graceful, but in order to embody that ideal, they must push their bodies to their limit. Studies have proven that while having a more acute experience of the sensory aspects of pain, professional ballet dancers and sports professionals have a much higher pain tolerance threshold than most people.

3. Myth: Ballet is not that physical

REALITY: As dancers we are always striving to make things look effortless, but that does not mean they are. The amount of energy needed to perform a full-length ballet is comparable to playing two football games, or running 18 miles.

4. Myth: Ballerinas do not eat

REALITY: Well, now that you know how physical it is to perform a ballet, where do you think we get all that energy? You guessed it . . . food.

5. Myth: Once you become a professional ballet dancer you do not take class anymore

REALITY: A ballet dancer takes a daily class for as long as he or she is a dancer. It is where you work and improve your technique, and because your body keeps changing as you grow older, you are constantly adapting and developing your technique. Every dancer's day starts with a class.

6. Myth: Ballerinas use one or two pairs of point shoes per year

REALITY: Most professional ballet dancers will go through two to three pairs of point shoes a week. During a performance, a lead ballerina will go through one to three pairs per show.

7. Myth: Point shoes are made of wood

REALITY: Point shoes are made of layers of fabric and glue. They do not have a sole like street shoes, but they do have a shank made of strong leather that adds support while on point. Each dancer must sew her own ribbons and elastics; some even darn the toe. This whole process can take up to 45 minutes.

8. Myth: Ballet dancers retire by age 30

REALITY: While the length of a dancer's career depends very much on the individual's body and passion, more and more dancers are lengthening their time on stage. A better understanding and awareness of the needs of our bodies, and better care to prevent and avoid injuries, have allowed dancers to keep dancing well into their 40s.

4 CANADIAN DAYS IN THE LIFE OF JOHN LENNON

1. May 30, 1969—John and Yoko record "Give Peace a Chance" in a Montreal hotel room

The famous recording session took place at about 11 p.m. in Lennon's room at the Queen Elizabeth Hotel. It was produced by a young Montreal producer and jazz musician named André Perry, who had been hired by Lennon's record company, EMI. Conditions were hardly ideal for recording. The room was small and filled with people, the ceilings were low and the acoustics were terrible. Perry had a four-track Ampex tape machine with four microphones—one for Lennon and his guitar, one for Tommy Smothers and two for everyone else in the room. The group, which included Timothy Leary, Toronto rabbi Abraham Feinberg, musician Petula Clark and members of the Canadian Radha Krishna Temple, did one quick sound check and then recorded the song in a single take. After everyone left, at about 2 a.m., Perry also recorded John and Yoko singing the flip side of the record, "Remember Love."

2. September 13, 1969–Lennon performs solo for the first time at a Toronto concert

The Toronto Rock 'n' Roll Revival was possibly the greatest concert ever held in Canada, featuring such stars as Chuck Berry, Little Richard, Alice Cooper, the Doors, Jerry Lee Lewis and a new musical ensemble called John Lennon and the Plastic Ono Band. The organizers had wanted the full complement of Beatles, but the concert was put together so hastily that it was not possible to get them all together. So John brought Yoko Ono and some friends, including Eric Clapton, over with him from London to perform without the Beatles for the first time. John looked almost messianic onstage, wearing a white robe and a heavy beard. Yoko hid behind a giant pillow and shrieked for most of the concert. But the gig appears to have helped Lennon make an important decision. When he got back to London, he informed Paul, George and Ringo that he was no longer interested in being a Beatle.

3. December 22, 1969–Lennon gives secret testimony to the Le Dain Commission

Three days before Christmas 1969, John Lennon and Yoko Ono met secretly with two members of the Le Dain Commission, which had been established by the Trudeau government to investigate Canada's marijuana laws. The session was held in secret because the commission suspected that the RCMP was harassing and sometimes even arresting people who appeared in front of them in public sessions. They were concerned that the same fate might befall the famous Beatle. In his testimony, Lennon urged that marijuana be legalized, and that its sale be controlled by the government to keep money out of the hands of the pushers. He also condemned the use of hard drugs, including LSD, which, he said, had "burned my head off." He strongly supported the commission's efforts to reform the country's marijuana laws. "We honestly think a place like Canada looks like the only hope," Lennon told the commissioners. "Canada is America without being American, without that . . . 'We-are-the-mighty-whatever scene.' Canada's image is just about getting groovy, you know."

4. December 23, 1969–Lennon talks peace with Prime Minister Pierre Trudeau

This was a meeting between a politician who often behaved like a rock star and a rock star who, by 1969, was behaving much like a politician. The location was the Prime Minister's Office. The discussion was scheduled to last just 15 minutes, and was to be followed by a 15-minute photo op, but it ended up lasting much longer. Most of the conversation dealt with the world situation and Lennon's campaign for peace. Both men agreed that a climate of mutual trust had to be created in which disarmament and peaceful diplomatic relations could begin. When it was over, Lennon said, "If all politicians were like Mr. Trudeau, there would be peace." Trudeau replied, "I must say that 'Give Peace a Chance' has always seemed to me to be sensible advice."

DANIEL MACIVOR AND DANIEL BROOKS'S 14 ESSENTIAL CANADIAN PLAYS AND THE PLAYWRIGHTS WHO WROTE THEM

When we were asked to submit a list of essential Canadian plays and playwrights, we were honoured but we also knew we were in trouble. How on earth could we come up with a finite list with so many indispensable, dazzling works to pick from? So we focused on the word *essential*: plays that had influenced us; had impacted other writers, actors and directors; had brought attention to Canadian theatre from outside Canada; and, in some cases, plays that broke new ground. Also, we only considered plays at least 10 years old (it requires some marinating to become essential). Finally, we wouldn't include anyone from our immediate circle, just to be fair. It was not easy distilling it down to 14, but the list had to end somewhere or else it's not a list so much as a book . . . hey, there's an idea!

Daniel Brooks and Daniel MacIvor are two of Canada's leading actors, playwrights and directors. Their work has been performed by theatre companies across the country. They have collaborated on several productions, including Here Lies Henry *(1995),* Monster *(1998),* Cul-de-sac *(2002),* House *(2010) and* Who Killed Spalding Gray? *(2014).*

1. Fortune and Men's Eyes by John Herbert (1964)

An extraordinary play, and subsequent movie, exploring homosexuality and violence in a men's prison. While serving six months for possession of marijuana, Smitty becomes the sexual subordinate of Rocky, who occupies the top of the prison food chain. The play draws on Herbert's own experience doing time following his conviction for dressing in drag in 1947 under the "same-sex sexual activity laws" that were only repealed in 1969. Although Herbert's work is now the most published play in Canada, back in 1967 no one here would touch this modern masterpiece with a 10-foot pole. New York's Actors Studio didn't pass up the opportunity, however, and promptly workshopped it with Dustin Hoffman and Jon Voight starring as Rocky and Smitty, the same illustrious acting duo who went on to light up the screen in *Midnight Cowboy*. Herbert lived in Toronto and wrote several more plays, but this one was the game-changer, lifting the lid on a previously unspeakable topic and the harshness of prison life.

2. Les Belle-Soeurs by Michel Tremblay (1968)

This was the play that marked a changing of the guard in Quebec theatre, and maybe even Quebec society. In the play's language, and in his choice of subject matter and characters, Tremblay brought the Quiet Revolution to the stage. He approached the subject of class in an honourable way. His characters were working-class people, they were intelligent, and he deeply respected them.

3. Creeps by David Freeman (1971)

"Groundbreaking" barely covers it. *Creeps* was the first play to ever feature stories about people with disabilities and the dysfunction bred of the silence and denial they frequently face. The original production was part of Toronto's Tarragon Theatre's first season and included incandescent performances by John Candy and Frank Moore. Freeman demonstrated how the personal could be converted into artful, incisive social commentary that touched us all.

4. Ten Lost Years by George Luscombe (1974)

Ten Lost Years began life as a book, an oral history of the Great Depression as told by its survivors to author Barry Broadfoot. It was published in 1973, and the next year, Luscombe, along with writer Jack Winter and musician Cedric Smith, brought the book to the stage of Luscombe's groundbreaking Toronto Workshop Productions. Onstage, *Ten Lost Years* was a complex collage of storytelling and music, and the words spoken by the 10 actors came directly from the pages of the book. Luscombe was a pioneer of this kind of documentary drama that told stories about the Canadian working class. Critic Jack Kapica wrote in the *Montreal Gazette* that *Ten Lost Years* "packs an emotional wallop long unmatched in the annals of Canadian theatre." Over a two-year period, more than 66,000 Canadians saw the play in the course of 42 weeks of touring in all 10 provinces.

5. Mercer family play cycle by David French (1972-88)

A transplanted Newfoundlander, French never strayed far from the rich vein of family lore and tradition he mined to create these classics, including *Leaving*

Home and *Of the Fields, Lately.* David French created the Canadian equivalents of Tennessee Williams's characters with their haunting, visceral, essential take on leaving home, politics, love and the eternal drama of families.

6. Maggie and Pierre by Linda Griffiths and Paul Thompson (1980)

There was so much to admire in this two-act monologue about the tortured relationship between Canada's brainy but aloof prime minister and his young flower child wife. Linda played all three roles, two of which were men. It was exciting to see Linda's voice emerge, and exciting to see the gender bending. It took courage for a woman to take on a man's role, especially a man everyone in the audience already knew. Perhaps most amazing of all, the play actually managed to make Canadian politics sexy.

7. The Crackwalker by Judith Thompson (1980)

The Crackwalker hit the scene like a bolt of lightning, jolting people alive with its bracing, brutal yet fragile characters and situations inspired by Thompson's own experiences as a social worker in Kingston, Ontario. Better viewed as a period piece than a timeless work, *The Crackwalker* crossed boundaries, offending and challenging many. Most importantly, Thompson broke new ground by insisting that while the play was rough and raw, it communicated critical truths about human failings and small Canadian towns.

8. Dragon Trilogy by Robert Lepage (1985)

This is the play that brought Robert Lepage to the attention of the world. It was incredibly ambitious: nearly six hours long, in four parts, and spanning 80 years, it traces the interwoven lives of two girls from Quebec City, a Chinese immigrant laundryman, and an Englishman who arrives in Quebec to open a shoe store. It asked a lot of audiences, but it was worth it.

9. Ilsa, Queen of the Nazi Love Camp by Blake Brooker (One Yellow Rabbit) (1987)

Where to start with these canny Calgary disruptors, One Yellow Rabbit? Satirical, hilarious, original, adventurous—a play that takes you on a musical journey of B-movies, European cabaret traditions, the history of fascism, and Canada's own Holocaust denier Jim Keegstra. Every bit original and inspiring, this play raised the bar for us all. Thank you, One Yellow Rabbit.

10. Toronto, Mississippi by Joan MacLeod (1987)

Like Judith Thompson before her, MacLeod used her own experiences as a social worker to shape her writing in *Toronto, Mississippi*, a play exploring the realities of mental disability, family dynamics and the creative capacity of an Elvis impersonator. MacLeod, however, invokes a tender, more lyrical voice to expose the complexities of people's lives and the determination to transform them in the face of adversity. With 11 plays and numerous awards to her credit, MacLeod has created a small universe of wonderful, fascinating characters with whom you can empathize, people you'd feel lucky to share a dinner table with.

11. 7 Stories by Morris Panych (1989)

The play opens with a man in a suit standing on the seventh-storey ledge of a building, about to jump. Suddenly a window flies open, and a sucession of inhabitants prattle on about the ups and downs of their own day, seemingly oblivious of the life and death scenario playing out before them. Provocative, cynical, whimsical, absurdist, Morris Panych has defined contemporary Canadian theatre in tone and form. He's written 30 plays, directed 90 more, and lived or had work produced in virtually every province—a true Canadian all-star.

12. Dry Lips Oughta Move to Kapuskasing by Tomson Highway (1989)

Irreverent and totally refreshing, *Dry Lips* was a much needed change-up in Canadian theatre storytelling. It told a tragicomic story of men on the Rez protesting an all-girl hockey team, drawing criticism and controversy for its portrayal of Native men's attitudes towards women. Highway's choice to use humour as his weapon to talk about enduring universal struggles and inequity was brave and inspiring. The play catapulted Highway into Canadian theatre history, becoming the first play written by a Canadian to get a commercial production at Toronto's esteemed Royal Alexandra Theatre.

13. Da Kink in My Hair by Trey Anthony (2001)

Eight black women drop their guard and dish at a Caribbean hair salon in Toronto. Trey Anthony's brilliant mashup of singing, drumming and dancing hit all the right notes. The heartfelt, funny and relatable triumphs and trials of these women's lives, captured perfectly in Anthony's dialogue, fed an audience hungry for something they weren't getting anywhere else.

14. East of Berlin by Hannah Moscovitch (2007)

Moscovitch's first full-length play marked the arrival of a fierce new playwright possessed of a unique, humorous and brave intellect. *East of Berlin* showcases her talent for plunging into complex yet familiar topics, like generational trauma and the Holocaust, and coming out the other side with refreshing, nuanced revelations about suffering and redemption. Critics have breathlessly declared her "irritatingly young," and she is! But oh, just think what lies ahead.

10 ART RIOTS

1. The appearance of William Macready at the Astor Place Opera House (New York, May 10, 1849)

William Macready, a close friend of Charles Dickens, was the most famous English actor of his day and, when he travelled to the United States to perform, he fully expected to receive the kind of acclaim he was used to in London. Instead, he found himself at the centre of a fierce controversy involving a rival actor, the American Edwin Forrest. Patriotic Americans championed Forrest over Macready, whom they saw as an arrogant, patronizing foreigner. On May 10, 1849, thousands of Forrest supporters gathered outside the Astor Place Opera House, where Macready was due to perform. Stones were hurled at the building and the police attempting to protect it. As the violence grew worse, the militia was summoned and eventually opened fire on the crowd. Twenty-three people were killed and hundreds injured.

2. Premiere performance of the Marquise de Morny's pantomime Rêve d'Égypte (Moulin Rouge, Paris, January 3, 1907)

Set in the pharaohs' Egypt, this pantomime featured the controversial French writer and music-hall actress Colette and her friend and *inamorata*, the Marquise de Morny. The women portrayed reunited lovers, with the marquise playing the male role. Colette had said, "I become my parts," and it was so on that night, for when the lovers embraced in a long kiss, Colette, almost nude, displayed uninhibited passion. The marquise's husband, his friends and the audience were outraged. When the curtain came down, the audience was in an ugly mood, and its outrage boiled over into a riotous affair, with people throwing objects at the performers and beating each other with their umbrellas.

3. Premiere performance of Arnold Schönberg's Pierrot Lunaire (Berlin, 1912)

In 1912 Schönberg had yet to develop his 12-tone system, but his composing had already evolved towards music severe in style, terse in form and atonal, with melodies that were sombre and unadorned. *Pierrot Lunaire* was such a work, and it provoked hostility, riots and scandal. Blows were traded amid hysteria and laughter. One critic wrote: "If this is music, then I pray my Creator not let me hear it again." Even years later, repercussions were still felt, as a man from the premiere audience brought assault charges against another man. In court, a physician testified that the music had been so jarring as to awaken peculiar neuroses.

4. The Armory Show (International Exhibition of Modern Art) (The Armory of the 69th Cavalry Regiment, New York, February–March 1913)

In 1913 Americans viewed a major exhibit of European and American art, and most were not impressed. The 1,600 predominantly modern works assembled at the armory included the art of Picasso, Matisse and Duchamp. Modern American art was represented by the works of such artists as John Sloan, John Marin and Maurice Prendergast. But most Americans were not ready for the brave new visual worlds. Demonstrations unprecedented in the United States marred the show. Howls of laughter and derision were common, and a frenzied mob threatened to destroy canvases, particularly the Cubist paintings and Duchamp's *Nude Descending a Staircase*. Nevertheless, the exhibition was a great success, stirring up curiosity and gaining a few supporters.

5. Premiere performance of Igor Stravinsky's Rite of Spring and the accompanying ballet by Vaslav Nijinsky (Théâtre des Champs Élysées, Paris, May 29, 1913)

The music performed that night was so revolutionary in concept that many in the audience perceived it as musical anarchy. Also, Nijinsky's dancing was too sensual for the moral and aesthetic palates of many of the ballet lovers. Together, the music and dance shocked the audience. Whistling and catcalls rocked the theatre, and sympathetic patrons tried, without success, to silence the upheaval. Fistfights cropped up in the aisles, and gendarmes arrived to expel the worst of the offenders, but pandemonium soon broke out anew and continued until the end of the performance. Years later, the composer-conductor Pierre Boulez referred to *Rite* as "the cornerstone of modern music."

6. Dada performance (Salle Gaveau, Paris, May 26, 1920)

Well known for provoking their audiences to riotous protest, the Dadaists (who opposed bourgeois values) went all out at this performance—one that many claim was the climax of the Paris Dada anti-art movement. The performers appeared onstage to present their poems, manifestos and sketches in outrageous attire. André Breton had a revolver tied to each temple, Paul Éluard was dressed as a ballerina, and the others wore tubes or funnels on their heads. These outfits, together with the content of the programme, which attacked art, philosophy, ethics and just about everything the bourgeoisie held sacred, pushed the audience beyond its endurance. Tomatoes, eggs and beefsteaks were thrown at the performers amid a tremendous uproar. Naturally, the Dadaists considered the evening a great success.

7. Initial screenings of Luis Buñuel and Salvador Dalí's L'Âge d'Or (Paris, December 1930)

A film that bombards the viewer with violent and erotic surrealistic imagery, L'Âge d'Or is concerned with the malice and hypocrisy of man. It vigorously scorns the conventions and institutions of bourgeois society. As expected, bourgeois society was not delighted with the film. One newspaper called it "obscene, repellent and paltry," and another commented that "country, family and religion are dragged through the mud." An article in an extreme rightist paper incited reactionary young Frenchmen, and they launched an attack on the theatre that did not stop for six days. By that time, 120,000 francs' worth of damage had been done. Due to the violent controversy, the film was not shown again publicly for more than 35 years.

8. Unveiling of mural by Diego Rivera (Hotel del Prado, Mexico City, June 1948)

Diego Rivera's mural Dream of a Sunday Afternoon in Alameda Park, commissioned for the dining room of the new Hotel del Prado in 1948, showed Mexican historian Ignacio Ramírez holding an open book. The words Dios no existe ("God does not exist") were clearly printed on one page. Consequently, Archbishop L.M. Martinez refused to bless the government-owned structure, and a mob of youths stormed into the dining room and scraped away the words with a knife. When Rivera restored the words with a fountain pen, local students threatened to obliterate them as often as Rivera replaced them. The hotel had the mural covered, and while its fate remained in limbo, Rivera was denied entrance to a movie house and his home was vandalized. Eventually, a priest who preferred to remain anonymous quietly blessed the hotel.

9. Concert by Paul Robeson (Peekskill, New York, September 4, 1949)

When the Cold War intensified, Robeson came under increasing fire for his leftist political views. A benefit concert for the Civil Rights Congress by Robeson and other liberal singers in Peekskill, New York, scheduled for August 27, 1949, had to be cancelled when a mob of anti-Communists reinforced by the Ku Klux Klan smashed chairs and beat concertgoers. Robeson returned on September 4 to sing for a crowd of 10,000 in a field outside Peekskill. Supporters formed a human shield around Robeson as he performed songs including "Go Down, Moses" and "Ol' Man River." At the end of the show, concertgoers found themselves having to run a gauntlet of stone-throwers lining the exit. Singer Pete Seeger used the stones thrown at his car to build a chimney for his house. Hundreds were injured trying to leave the show. A year later, Robeson was blacklisted after he refused to sign an affidavit disclaiming his membership in the Communist Party.

10. Publication of Salman Rushdie's novel The Satanic Verses (Bombay, February 24, 1989)

It's a pretty safe bet that none of the thousands of people who demonstrated against *The Satanic Verses* on that February day in Bombay had ever read the book—its publication was banned in India. But that didn't stop Indian Muslims from joining Muslims around the world to denounce it as blasphemous because of its depiction of the prophet Muhammad. Days before the demonstration in Bombay, the Iranian government had issued a *fatwa* against Rushdie, offering a bounty to anyone who would kill him. Police in Bombay were expecting a difficult day: they had detained 500 people before the protest even started, but they were largely unprepared when the demonstration turned into a riot. The crowd burned cars, buses and motorcycles, and even torched a small police station. At one point, according to police, people in the crowd opened fire on police officers, and the police fired back. When it finally ended three hours later, 12 people were dead, at least 40 were injured and 800 had been arrested.

TOP 10 PRICES PAID FOR CANADIAN PAINTINGS AT AUCTION IN 2016

All prices are "hammer prices" and do not include the buyer's premium, which the auction house charges to the buyer to cover administrative expenses. The $9,500,000 paid for Lawren Harris's *Mountain Forms* is the most ever paid for a Canadian painting. Of the top 100 paintings sold in Canada in 2016, 54 were by Harris and Jean-Paul Riopelle.

1. Lawren Harris, *Mountain Forms* (c. 1926) $9,500,000
2. Paul Kane, *Scene in the Northwest* (c. 1845–46) $4,600,000
3. Lawren Harris, *Mountain and Glacier* (1930) $3,900,000
4. Jeff Wall, *Dead Troops Talk* (1992) $3,199,000
5. Lawren Harris, *Winter Landscape* (1916–17) $3,100,000
6. Lawren Harris, *The Old Stump, Lake Superior* (1926) $3,000,000
7. Emily Carr, *The Crazy Stair* (c. 1928–30) $2,900,000
8. Jean-Paul Riopelle, *La Forêt* (1953) $2,515,918
9. Lawren Harris, *Pine Tree and Red House, Winter* (1924) $2,500,000
10. Lawren Harris, *Houses, St. Patrick Street* (1922) $2,400,000

Source: Canadian Art Sales Index 2016.

11 VALUABLE ARTWORKS FOUND UNEXPECTEDLY

1. In a Farmer's Field

In 1820 a Greek peasant named Yorgos was digging in his field on the island of Milos when he unearthed several carved blocks of stone. He burrowed deeper and found four statues—three figures of Hermes and one of Aphrodite, the goddess of love. Three weeks later, the Choiseul archaeological expedition arrived by ship, purchased the Aphrodite and took it to France. Louis XVIII gave it the name Venus de Milo and presented it to the Louvre in Paris, where it became one of the most famous works of art in the world.

2. Beneath a Street

On February 21, 1978, electrical workers were putting down lines on a busy street corner in Mexico City when they discovered a 20-ton stone bas-relief of the Aztec night goddess, Coyolxauhqui. It is believed to have been sculpted in the early 15th century and buried prior to the destruction of the Aztec civilization by the Spanish conquistadors in 1521. The stone was moved approximately 200 metres from the site to the Museum of the Great Temple.

3. In a Hole in the Ground

In 1978 more than 500 movies dating from 1903 to 1929 were dug out of a hole in the ground in Dawson City, Yukon. Under normal circumstances, the 35-mm nitrate films would have been destroyed, but the permafrost had preserved them perfectly.

4. Under a Bed

On May 11, 2001, the *Globe and Mail* reported that a 1603 portrait of Shakespeare as a young man had turned up in the suburban Ottawa home of Lloyd Sullivan, a retired engineer. A portrait of a young man in a woven doublet with a subversive smile and twinkly eyes, it was signed by John Sanders and done in oils on an oak panel. This caused a sensation in art circles. If authentic, the Sanders portrait would be the only known painting of Shakespeare made during his lifetime. Scientists duly set about investigating the painting and have concluded it was made with wood, paint and paper dating from the early 17th century. Other experts have confirmed the historical accuracy of the subject's hairstyle, the fabric pattern and silk thread in the Elizabethan collar, and the style of brush strokes. Finally, the Sanders family have demonstrated a clear genealogical connection going back centuries to the Worcester area, a few miles from the Bard's hometown of Stratford-upon-Avon. According to the Sanders family, their ancestor painted the portrait and it's been handed down through the generations, survived flood and fire, been stored in closets and under beds, and occasionally exhibited as a portrait of Shakespeare, including at the Montreal Eaton's Art Gallery in the early 1960s. Since the Sanders portrait was hailed as the "*Mona Lisa* of the Elizabethan Age" in 2011 by scientists, curators and conservators, the controversy has subsided and it has been shown at major art galleries around the world.

5. On a Wall

A middle-aged couple in a suburb of Milwaukee, Wisconsin, asked an art prospector to appraise a painting in their home. While he was there, he examined another painting that the couple had thought was a reproduction of a work by Vincent van Gogh. It turned out to be an 1886 original. On March 10, 1991, the painting *Still Life with Flowers* sold at auction for $1,400,000.

6. In a Trunk in an Attic

In 1961 Barbara Testa, a Hollywood librarian, inherited six steamer trunks that had belonged to her grandfather James Fraser Gluck, a Buffalo, New York, lawyer who died in 1895. Over the next three decades she gradually sifted through the contents of the trunks, until one day in the autumn of 1990 she came upon 665 pages that turned out to be the original handwritten manuscript of the first half of Mark Twain's *Huckleberry Finn*. The two halves of the great American novel were finally reunited at the Buffalo & Erie County Public Library.

7. At a Flea Market

A Philadelphia financial analyst was browsing at a flea market in Adamstown, Pennsylvania, when a wooden picture frame attracted his attention. He paid $4 for it. Back at his home, he removed the old torn painting in the frame and found a folded document between the canvas and the wood backing. It turned out to be a 1776 copy of the Declaration of Independence—one of 24 known to remain. On June 13, 1991, Sotheby's auction house in New York sold the copy for $2,420,000.

8. Masquerading as a Bicycle Rack

For years, employees of the God's House Tower Archaeology Museum in Southampton, England, propped their bikes against a 69-centimetre black rock in the basement. In 2000 two Egyptologists investigating the museum's holdings identified the bike rack as a seventh-century BCE Egyptian statue portraying King Taharqa, a Kushite monarch from the region that is modern Sudan. Karen Wordley, the Southampton city council's curator of archaeological collections, said it was a "mystery" how the sculpture ended up in the museum basement.

9-11. On Kijiji, in a Field and in a Dumpster

The high value and volume of sculptures, lithographs and paintings made by Jean-Paul Riopelle mark him as a popular target for art thieves. His works are widely collected and displayed in private homes, corporate offices or public spaces where security doesn't always match the value of the work. Between 1989 and 2015 there were 19 robberies reported to the police; some of the artworks turned up in strange places, much the worse for wear. In 1999 a sculpture was tossed into a dumpster and broken when the thief panicked and ran. In 2010 the police were tipped off about a few dozen Riopelle lithographs for sale on Kijiji. In 2011, two bronze statues worth over $1 million and weighing a combined

450 kilograms were stolen then dumped in a field by three men seeking to sell them as scrap metal. According to Quebec police, artworks are used to settle debts amongst criminals—Riopelle sculptures and paintings have been uncovered in raids at biker gang and Mafia homes and warehouses.

ANDREW KEAR'S 6 FAVOURITE NUDES AND PRUDES IN CANADIAN ART BEFORE '69

The idea that artists are generally a sexually liberated bunch is an enduring myth. The idea that Canada was a particularly strident backwater of conservative mores and repression prior to the 1960s, an image captured perfectly in the sobriquet "Toronto the Good," is equally enduring. Then what sort of unconventionalities and controversies might we expect from the Canadian art world over the half-century leading up to the sexual revolution? The answer: a complex and dissonant weave of politeness, perversity, prudery and pride. There is something about looking back to distant moments of surprising unconventionality, eroticism and censorship that I relish; with Canadian art, controversy (like revenge) is a dish best served cold.

Andrew Kear is curator of historical Canadian art at the Winnipeg Art Gallery.

1. The Girls

Around 1913, American-born sculptors Frances Loring and Florence Wyle began living and working together in Toronto. Their shared residence/studio—an abandoned church—was a social hub, a place around which, according to A.Y. Jackson, "the art of Canada . . . revolved." "The Girls," as they were known to their friends, bucked gender stereotypes with aplomb. And they bucked artistic trends. While their male buds in the Group of Seven were busy painting every damned rock and tree in the country, Loring and Wyle chiselled actual stone and wood, and helped design significant public memorials including the Queen Elizabeth Way Monument at Gzowski Park (Toronto). In 1914 the pair created bronze busts of each other that, today, are displayed at the Loring-Wyle Parkette in Toronto's Moore Park neighbourhood.

2. Real Barenaked Ladies

Except for the pubic hair there wasn't anything particularly novel about the painting. Nudes had been exhibited in Canada well before 1927, albeit mostly in art museums, shielded from wide public consumption. These nudes had always been smooth and fictional, though: classical goddesses, harlots from the Bible. The pubic hair in John W. Russell's *A Modern Fantasy* (private collection) cued the viewer to a distinct quantum of sordidness, namely that the painting was of *someone* in particular, a naked contemporary. Moral authorities voiced their outrage, predictably, and attendance figures to the exhibition's lively unorthodox venue, Toronto's CNE, predictably soared.

3. The Wife-Swapping Celibate

Besides his reputation as a wealthy mystic and vocal member of the Group of Seven, Lawren Harris is known for the indiscretion of leaving his first wife, Beatrice (Phillips), for Bess (Larkin), herself inconveniently wedded to Harris's childhood friend, fellow mystic and Group champion F.B. Housser. Harris and Bess fled Toronto's moral disapprobation for warmer climes, first the United States then Vancouver, in 1940, where, as you might expect, they were a hit. Harris maintained that his thing with Bess was about "real spiritual oneness," and thus entirely bereft of sexual intimacy—"There's to be none of that," he insisted to fellow artist and tennis partner Peter Haworth.

4. War and Communal Bathing

The wartime body—the mutilated male corpse in particular—is a reminder of both the hell of war and the banality of evil. With the Canadian-initiated development of the first official war art program in the early 20th century, artists suddenly gained broader and more intimate access to depicting this potent signifier. Although corpses didn't stop piling up on battlefields, as C.W. Jefferys's 1919 *Polish Army Bathing at Niagara Camp* and George Pepper's 1944 *Mobile Bath* (both at the Canadian War Museum) show, Canadian artists also began shining a new light on another sort of military body. Of course, what makes images such as these so powerful is not only their brazen sexual undercurrent, but the utter incongruity of the scenario they represent—namely, the bathing of bodies used for slaughter.

5. The Morality Squad Goes to the Gallery

Eros '65 opened at the only Toronto commercial gallery owned by a woman. The Dorothy Cameron Gallery exhibition displayed works of erotic art by 22 professional artists, including Joyce Wieland and Greg Curnoe. Although peevish Puritanism, the city's lingering default setting on matters of art and culture, was retreating by 1965, the police morality squad swooped in all the same. The lesbian eroticism of Robert Markle's imagery, found in pieces like *Lovers I* (National Gallery of Canada) and *Lovers II* (Art Gallery of Ontario), was particularly popular among the cops and prosecution when the trial convened in a basement courtroom that was traditionally used to arraign prostitutes. Cameron became the first Canadian gallerist charged and convicted under Section 150 of the Criminal Code with exposing the public to obscenity.

6. Venus in the Sweat Lodge

By the late 1960s, Odawa-Potawatomi-English artist Daphne Odjig enjoyed a growing reputation. In 1968 she was approached by Herbert Schwarz, a medical doctor with eclectic fascinations, to illustrate 15 "erotic Indian legends," later published as *Tales from the Smokehouse*. Odjig accepted and, in her words, set out to "please the buyer." Her churning, languorous paintings—many of which were later acquired by the National Gallery of Canada—capture the sweaty and bizarre salaciousness of the *Smokehouse* stories, which percolate with lively interjections of flying genitalia, bestiality and characters named "One Eye" and "Big One." The setting of one lubricious exploit is Montreal during Expo '67. Another, in which an Indigenous convert requests a missionary "to torture me with that thorn of yours," inexplicably approximates a story from *The Decameron* by Boccaccio.

CHAPTER 4

Music

LYNN COADY'S 8 CANADIAN '80S POP ACTS WHO WERE MORE '80S THAN THE '80S

The great thing about Canadian pop music in the 1980s is that it was never, no matter how hard it tried, in the mainstream. It couldn't be. Just by nature of being Canadian, our music was an outlier and our bands were weirdos. They made videos with shoddy backdrops and rickety-looking sets that didn't possess the slick production values of, say, Michael Jackson's "Beat It" or Duran Duran's "Rio." But considering we now look back at all that blow-dried '80s slickness with a touch of scorn (it was the culture in which the gold-escalator-riding new president of the United States was forged, after all), our homegrown pop music videos seem, in retrospect, all the cooler. Canadian acts were operating on a shoestring and getting their music out there nonetheless. They did what they had to do. They gathered unto themselves the biggest, cheapest cans of aerosol hairspray that Shoppers Drug Mart had available, kitted themselves out in the most colourful, geometric-patterned outfits from Le Château, resolutely applied their own damn eyeliner and away they went—into music history.

Lynn Coady is the Scotiabank Giller Prize–winning author of six works of fiction including the short-story collection Hellgoing *and a novel called* The Antagonist. *She lives in Toronto where she works as a TV writer.*

1. Jane Siberry

I remember coming home from school to watch *Video Hits* and discovering, sandwiched between the bland mall-concert stylings of Tiffany and the BritPop dirty-girl gyrations of Samantha Fox, the video for Siberry's "Mimi on the Beach." And just staring at it. Thinking: Wha? Siberry sported a rooster-esque haircut (the hair on the top of her otherwise shaved head having been crimped with a crimping iron) adorned with a "headband" that I'm pretty sure was actually just a piece of drug-store ribbon discarded after someone's birthday party. And she was dressed in an outfit somewhere between a Floridian retiree's poolside attire and a child's favourite pair of PJs. She was perhaps the coolest Canadian woman I'd ever seen on TV. The lyrics went like this: "Mimi on the beach, Mimi on the beach, Mimi on the beach." It was about a girl at sea, floating on a pink surfboard, and that was basically it. Somehow it was the most wistful thing I'd ever heard.

2. Lisa Dalbello

Holy crap, let's talk about Dalbello's video for "Gonna Get Close to You." The crazy thing about the gilded, commercial, hair-sprayed, conservative '80s was that every once in a while a crack would appear in the cultural brick wall you, as a young person, faced every day—a wall of bland sexual orthodoxy and rigorously policed heteronormativity. Annie Lennox was one of those cracks and so was Boy George. But the video for "Gonna Get Close to You" represented a damn chasm. Dalbello is crouched in her apartment, caressing her overturned grand piano, peering through her blinds at the man in an apartment across the way. And the man is in a dress—a *dress*! And Dalbello, defiantly unpretty in buttoned-up, head-to-toe black, is so aroused she becomes all tied up in her telephone cord (that's right, kids—phones were tethered to the wall in those days). And now the dress-wearing man is putting on lipstick—and pearls and heels! Dalbello, still watching him, writhes with passion against her phone-cord restraints! But oh my god, now he's in her apartment! And she's in her bathtub! I was a 14-year-old Catholic girl from Cape Breton Island and so titillated and confused! And then he pulls on her feet, and she sinks under the water, and I am worried about what's going to happen to her impeccably teased hair! This video changed me.

3. Carole Pope

Yet another damn chasm in the wall of heteronomativity that '80s teens with differing interests and inclinations were forced to bash their heads against. All you need to know about Carole Pope is that she sang the lyrics "I want her so much I feel sick" in reference to a fellow teenage girl, in a song that included a lot more physical details along these lines but lower down. And this song was played on the radio. In the '80s. Because it was that good. She sneered and smirked as she sang. This was in the age when women in pop were mostly a version of Jody Watley or Debbie Gibson or Bananarama. Her hair and eyeliner were equally amazing.

4. Lawrence Gowan

Gowan's hair was also excellent, mainly because it added height. He was a small fellow, but a piano genius with a voice that could cave in a building. His most noteworthy video, for "A Criminal Mind," was quintessentially '80s-Canadian in its hamminess and—let's face it—how cheap it looked. Yet it was also fantastic— a soaring, overwrought melodrama that made the song iconic and unforgettable.

5. The Payolas

These guys were more '80s than the '80s for two basic reasons: One, the lead singer had a British accent, which lent the band loads of cachet with Canadian audiences brought up watching *The Tommy Hunter Show* while waiting for the latest hot David Foster/Anne Murray collab to drop, therefore starved for a whiff of the exotic; and two, the video for the single "Eyes of a Stranger." The eyes of said stranger, as depicted in the video, are outlined by a blood-tingling amount of eyeliner even for an '80s video. It's unbelievable the girl can actually raise her face to the camera. But it was also a great song. The Payolas were good. I'd still happily listen to their LP *Hammer on a Drum* any day, which includes an amazing duet with Carole Pope, by the way.

6. Strange Advance

Synthesizers and serious looks! Jackets with zippers that zip lengthwise across the chest instead of up and down! Popped collars and finally—as was *de rigueur* back then—a vague sense of the songs having all been written in a fallout shelter while waiting out the nuclear winter.

7. Gino Vannelli

It wouldn't be a fair representation of '80s culture without reference to a guy who sang a song about how gross it is when women over 30 get dressed up and go out in public where people have to look at them ("Black Cars"). So here's to Gino Vannelli. Not only was he more '80s than the '80s, but he was also a '70s phenomenon, and in the '70s, he actually managed to be more '70s than the '70s. He sported a large, fluffy afro, wore silk shirts unbuttoned to mid hairy chest, and (I'm guessing, here, I can't be bothered to research this) medallions. In the '80s, however, Vannelli seamlessly slicked himself up in obligatory Patrick Bateman fashion, although he retained his penchant for keeping his top two buttons undone.

8. Platinum Blonde

In the decade-long struggle of Canadian pop music to be mainstream despite its innate (and innately delightful, I'd argue) weirdness and outsider status, Platinum Blonde is the blazingly mainstream exception that proves the oddball rule. In an era when hair was everything, Platinum Blonde's hair was . . . well, the name says it all. Every single head in the all-male ensemble sported a perfect, tousled, gloriously sun-kissed mane. These guys had everything—the clothes, the eyeliner, the funky, big-shouldered, '80s-obligatory blazers. The occasional earring dangling in a saucily androgynous way from a single ear. The synth-heavy hits, the soulless-glam videos, and, once again, the songs that nodded in a blasé, *ah well, at least I look good* kind of way at our inevitable nuclear destruction.

14 HITS WRITTEN (AT LEAST IN PART) BY CHANTAL KREVIAZUK

Winnipeg-born Chantal Kreviazuk released her first album in Canada in 1996, establishing herself as one of this country's finest pop vocalists. But it has been her songwriting that has really catapulted her to international fame (and probably fortune). Take a look at the A-list talent she has written for! It often takes a village to write a pop song, which is why Chantal usually shares writing credits with other producers and artists (including her husband, Raine Maida of Our Lady Peace), but there's no doubt that lots of today's top hitmakers have her number on their phones.

1. Avril Lavigne, "He Wasn't" (2001)
2. Gwen Stefani, "Rich Girl" (2004)
3. Kelly Clarkson, "Walk Away" (2004)
4. Mandy Moore, "Gardenia" (2007)
5. David Cook, "Permanent" (2008)
6. Carrie Underwood, "Unapologize" (2009)
7. Joe Cocker, "So" (2010)
8. Drake, "Over My Dead Body" (2011)
9. Pitbull, "Feel This Moment" (2012)
10. Josh Groban, "Brave" (2012)
11. Shakira, "You Don't Care about Me" (2014)
12. Jennifer Lopez, "Emotions" (2014)
13. Lea Michele, "Burn with You" (2014)
14. Britney Spears, "If I'm Dancing" (2016)

5 HITS MADE WITHOUT THE ARTISTS BEING IN THE SAME ROOM

by Renato Pagnani

In the 20th century, songwriters in search of a hit headed to the places where songwriters and musicians gathered to collaborate in person, like New York's Tin Pan Alley and the Brill Building, or Motown's Hitsville. But in the early years of the 21st century, you didn't have to leave your bedroom if you wanted to co-write a song, have it professionally mixed and mastered, or even launch an entire career. While songwriters, producers and engineers still tend to congregate in the same place to produce magic, modern technologies have helped to decentralize and democratize music-making. These five pieces of music prove that imagination—not access to expensive studios, fancy equipment or even proximity—is now the only limiting factor when it comes to crafting a classic.

Renato Pagnani has written about music for publications including Pitchfork, SPIN, Rolling Stone *and* Maclean's.

1. Drake, "One Dance"

The contributions from Nigeria-based Wizkid and Britain's Kyla to this transnational collaboration, Drake's first #1 as a lead artist in the United States, were all submitted via email. Once the Canadian superstar's team received the various parts, they were fit together like puzzle pieces by Paul "Nineteen85" Jefferies and Noah "40" Shebib, assembled with the kind of precision that belied the fact the three artists were never once together in the studio. The effervescent summer jam of 2016 topped charts in 15 countries and is the most-played song ever on Spotify with over a billion streams and counting.

2. Chief Keef, "Citgo"

Eighteen-year-old Polish aviation student Radoslaw Sobieraj went from zero to hero overnight with an instrumental riff he worked out in his bedroom and posted on YouTube. He awoke to see that his latest creation had amassed 30,000 views overnight, plus a note from the manager of Chicago rapper Chief Keef. The man himself had typed in "Chief Keef type beat," exactly what Radoslaw had titled his jam, and up popped a shimmering synthesizer mix that then caught fire on the Internet overnight. Chief Keef snagged it as a bed track for

"Citgo," the breakout hit on his major label debut, *Finally Rich*. Interviewed by *SPIN* in 2013, Radoslaw said it was still his dream to leave Gliwice, a small city in Upper Silesia, to meet Chief Keef and his crew in person in Chicago, "and spark some loud with them."

3. Mac Dre, "Back N Da Hood"

Phoning it in never had so much street cred. While serving four years in federal prison for conspiracy to commit robbery, legendary Bay Area rapper Mac Dre rapped the vocals for his five-song *Back N Da Hood* EP over the phone from inside the Fresno County Jail and United States Penitentiary Lompoc. Dre's vocals were later placed over the EP's funk-indebted beats by his producer and collaborator Khayree. Instead of detracting from his cautionary street tales, the grainy low fidelity of his phone-recorded vocals infuses lines like "Another sleepless night in Fresno Jail / I got a federal hold and I can't even bail" with a chilling intensity, adding another layer of realism to the music of an artist who helped define an entire region's sound before his untimely death in a 2004 drive-by shooting—a case that remains unsolved to this day.

4. Young Thug, JEFFERY

Even as recently as a decade ago, an album would need to be finalized weeks in advance of its release date so it could be sent to the manufacturing plant to be pressed and then shipped to stores in time. But with modern technologies and digital releases, there's a lot more leeway— even if sometimes it drives those involved in the process a little crazy. Case in point: at 3 a.m. the night before Young Thug's 2016 tour de force *JEFFERY* was set for release, audio engineer Alex Tumay received a text message with three pages' worth of changes that Young Thug wanted made to the album's mix. Without access to a studio, and equipped only with a set of headphones and his laptop, Tumay needed another reference point, so he got creative. He ordered an Uber, positioned himself in the rear middle seat, plugged into the vehicle's sound system via the aux cord, and asked his driver to turn up the volume as loud as it could go. With the help of the car's acoustics, Tumay would have the reference point he needed to work his magic. At first, the driver said no his request, but Tumay pressed. "You can drive around and run the tab up. Just go wherever, I don't care where you drop me off." And that's what happened: Tumay tweaked the mix of the album while his driver was miserable, but making a lot of cash. "I had him drive me to the 300 offices, so I could play it for Lyor Cohen," the 300 Entertainment label exec. Looking back at the experience, Tumay laughs. "I probably got a one-star rating from the driver."

5. Solange, "Cranes in the Sky"

Some songs take time before they take shape. A long time. Solange Knowles took eight years to finally do justice to the instrumental created for her in 2008 by musical polyglot Raphael Saadiq. Riffing out a song about a sadness she couldn't shake, and the heaviness she felt about neighbourhood gentrification and "construction cranes blocking the view," she returned to the drums, bass and strings bedtracks and knew she'd finally nailed it. But when she asked Saadiq if he had the stems for the music—the individual recordings of each instrument they'd need to mix it—he couldn't find them. So Solange built "Cranes in the Sky" over top of the original demo, combining an unfinished—and untouched—demo with polished additions written years later. The result, the critically acclaimed single on her 2016 album *A Seat at the Table*, debuted at #1 on Billboard.

8 RARE ABILITIES OF GLENN GOULD

1. As an infant, Glenn rarely cried, but by the age of three months he had begun to hum, loudly and persistently. His mother would hold him on her knee in front of the piano keys, and unlike most children, who would thump or pound the notes, Glenn would strike one key at a time, letting the note decay into silence before playing another.

2. Glenn loved to sing, and by the time he was three it was clear that he had perfect pitch. He could detect subtle differences between flats and sharps, and when asked to sing any specific note—a C-sharp, for example—was able to hit the note perfectly every time.

3. Glenn could read music before he could read words, and could play piano pieces from memory that he had heard just once.

4. When learning new piano pieces, Glenn would take the sheet music into his room and study it quietly, then play a concerto, for instance, completely from memory. This exceptionally rare musical ability is akin to being able to read a manual on how to drive, then get in a car and drive on busy streets or highways.

5. At 14, Glenn had an epiphany about his ability to hear music on different levels. While he was practising a fugue by Mozart, someone switched on a vacuum cleaner near the piano, thus drowning out the noise of the piano notes being struck. Instead of being distracted, Glenn found the mechanical wall of sound quite pleasing because it allowed him to hear the music "in his head" louder than the music being made on the piano. By heightening his physical and inner experience of the music, he was able to distinguish between the "perfect" music he heard in his mind and the sometimes less than perfect music he was producing on the instrument. Armed with this crucial distinction, he became an unstinting perfectionist in all of his performances and recordings. At times, he created this shroud of mechanical noise while he practised by loudly playing TV Westerns or Beatles records simultaneously.

6. At 22, Glenn first performed his unique interpretation of Bach's *Goldberg Variations* in public on October 16, 1954, in Toronto. He was drawn to their complex contrapuntal phrasing and mathematical precision and worked on the compositions painstakingly for months in the quiet of his family's Lake Simcoe cottage. Glenn's distinctive mannerisms and fidgeting were already very much in evidence. He swayed, hummed, sang along and conducted with one hand while playing with the other. Unfortunately, only a dozen or so people attended the concert because it was the same night that Hurricane Hazel was flooding streets, toppling buildings and wreaking havoc on the city. Within a year, he recorded his career-defining performance of the *Goldberg Variations* in New York for Columbia Masterworks. It was an instant success and, since then, has never been out of print.

7. At the age of 35, Glenn created a new art form: contrapuntal radio. Asked by CBC Radio to come up with an original production that celebrated Canada's centennial year, 1967, he set out to explore his fascination with solitude and the effect of the northern geography, climate and isolation on Canadian identity. The resulting documentary, *The Idea of North*, layered human voices on top of each other in a manner reminiscent of contrapuntal music composition to create a dense, impressionistic, non-linear narrative. Provocative and original, this work and other contrapuntal essays and documentaries cemented his reputation as a radio genius.

8. Glenn's hearing was so refined that he was able to hear things on audio tape that most people around him couldn't. He could tell exactly what tape deck was used to record a specific performance by almost imperceptible changes in the quality of the sound and tape hiss.

9 THINGS YOU PROBABLY DIDN'T KNOW ABOUT "O CANADA"

1. It was commissioned by Quebec's Saint-Jean-Baptiste Society

Today, the Saint-Jean-Baptiste Society is one of the most nationalistic of all Quebec political organizations. It's hard to imagine the society's members even singing "O Canada," let alone writing it. But in fact, the song that eventually became Canada's national anthem was commissioned by the society for an immense Congrès catholique canadien-français scheduled for June 1880 that brought tens of thousands of French Canadians from Canada and the United States to Quebec City. The song was supposed to be the crowning moment of an open-air concert on the afternoon of June 24 (Saint-Jean-Baptiste Day) on the Plains of Abraham with 40,000 people in attendance. But because of a mix-up, it wasn't performed until the evening, at the Quebec Skating Rink.

2. "O Canada" was written explicitly to be a French-Canadian national hymn

There were no English words to the original "O Canada." The French words, still sung today, were written by Quebec judge Adolphe-Basile Routhier and are steeped in religion as well as nationalism, which helps explain the connection to the Saint-Jean-Baptiste Society: "Because you know how to carry the sword, you know how to carry the cross . . ." The last verse, which even most French Canadians don't know, ends "And repeat, with our fathers, the victorious cry / For Christ and King!"

3. The composer of "O Canada," Calixa Lavallée, performed as a blackface minstrel in the United States for more than 10 years

Lavallée was born near Montreal in 1842. He was a talented musician, something of a child prodigy, who left home to join Duprez and Green's New Orleans and Metropolitan Burlesque Opera Troupe and Brass Band when he was 16. He was a musician and then bandleader with Duprez and other minstrel troupes between 1859 and 1873.

4. Lavallée joined the Union Army in the U.S. Civil War

Lavallée was a bandsman in the 4th Rhode Island Regiment in Providence from 1861 to 1862. During battle, bandsmen were given medical duties, removing wounded soldiers and attending to surgeons in makeshift hospitals behind the lines. In September 1862, Lavallée was wounded at the battle of Antietam, still the bloodiest single day in the history of American warfare—Union and Confederate losses combined totalled almost 22,720 dead, wounded or missing. Although technically a draw, the standoff at Antietam was claimed as a victory by Abraham Lincoln, and an excuse to issue the Emancipation Proclamation, decisively changing the course of the Civil War.

5. Lavallée left Quebec within weeks of writing "O Canada," never to return

After the war, and after quitting his minstrel show, Lavallée returned to Montreal where some patrons raised enough money to send him to France to study, which he did from 1872 to 1875. On his return, he became Quebec's leading classical musician (he suppressed his minstrel past) and was the obvious choice to be asked to write "O Canada." It was to be his last Canadian commission. Lavallée wanted the Quebec government to set up a National Conservatory of Music. Discouraged by their refusal, and deeply in debt, he moved to Boston in November 1880, where he became a major figure in American music history. In 1884, he gave the first recital of all-American composers in that country's history. He died in Boston in 1891.

6. "O Canada" was not a big success in Quebec after its first performance, and wasn't performed in English Canada until 1907

Toronto's Mendelssohn Choir first performed "O Canada" in 1907 using an English translation of the original French words. Performances in Pittsburgh and in Carnegie Hall followed. The *Globe and Mail* called it "a popular hit."

7. There have been hundreds of versions of possible English lyrics to "O Canada"

After the first English performances of "O Canada," it was clear that a mere translation of the French words wouldn't do. *Collier's* magazine sponsored a contest for new lyrics, which attracted 350 entries. The contest was won by Mrs. Mercy E. Powell McCulloch. "O Canada, in praise of thee we sing / From echoing hills, our anthems proudly ring." You don't want to know about the losing entries. But the "official" English words were based on a version first written by a Quebec judge named Robert Stanley Weir (yes, that makes two judges involved in the writing of "O Canada"). Weir wrote his version to mark the 300th anniversary of the founding of Quebec City. He is the person who first wrote "O Canada, our home and native land / True patriot love . . ."

8. Weir's original version included the words "thou dost in us command"

Although "O Canada" became our official national anthem in 1980, we're still arguing about the English words. MP Maurice Baril's successful bill in 2016 changed the words "in all thy sons command" to "in all of us command." What opponents of the bill did not realize is that those were close to Weir's original words—"O Canada, our home and native land / True patriot love, thou dost in us command." The words were changed to "in all thy sons command" in 1914, around the time of the First World War.

9. The tune to "O Canada" may well have been "borrowed" (i.e., stolen) from Mozart

The openings to "O Canada" and "March of the Priests" from Act 2 of Mozart's opera *The Magic Flute* are virtually identical, note for note.

Thanks to Robert Harris for this list.

12 CANADIAN BANDS AND WHERE THEY GOT THEIR NAME

1. Arcade Fire

Possibly Canada's premier band of the early 21st century, the name of Montreal's Arcade Fire came from a pretty dark place. In a 2004 interview with the blog *Gothamist*, lead singer Win Butler explained that "the first kid who beat me up when I was 12 was a high school kid who always used to talk about how the old arcade burned down and all these kids died." Appropriately, perhaps, the band's first album, released in 2004, was called *Funeral*.

2. Barenaked Ladies

A provocative but slightly puerile name the band came up with while bored and hanging out at a Dylan concert. The name has grabbed people's attention, as it was intended to do, including Toronto mayor June Rowlands, who banned the group from playing at City Hall in 1992 because the name objectified women.

3. Blue Rodeo

One of Canada's most beloved bands, Blue Rodeo was christened late in 1984, just before the band made its debut performance in Toronto in February 1985. The band's co-founders, Jim Cuddy and Greg Keelor, had been in New York City experimenting with various sounds. They were attracted to the N.Y. performance art scene, and wanted a name that combined that with country music. "The core of the band [is] this notion of rock discovering country and adding improvisation," Cuddy has said, "and we wanted to have a psychedelic cowboy name."

4. Broken Social Scene

The great Toronto indie musical collective got its name in a most random way. Kevin Drew, one of the band's founders, was on tour playing keyboards in a friend's band in the late 1990s. "I had this really elaborate set-up with lots of different keyboards," Drew told Spin.com. "I was a keyboard freak back then. When the tour was over, I came back to Toronto and played a Sunday night show under the name John Tesh Jr. and the Broken Social Scene." The John Tesh Jr. part was in honour of the acclaimed American keyboard player of the same name. The Broken Social Scene part "just sort of popped into my head, I think. But [future BSS bandmate] Brendan [Canning] said that the Broken Social Scene was a great name for a band and that's what we went with."

5. The Guess Who

Randy Bachman and Burton Cummings first made music together under this name in 1966. The name was intended to make people wonder who the hot new British supergroup was.

6. Men Without Hats

Ivan and Stefan Doroschuk of Montreal, the brothers behind the monster '80s hit "Safety Dance," say the name of the band was meant to suggest that they were non-conformists.

7. Metric

The indie rock band Metric began life as a duo called Mainstream, formed by Emily Haines and James Shaw in 1998. After releasing their first record, *Mainstream*, they changed the name to Metric, after a sound that Shaw programmed on his keyboard. "When we saw that word on the keyboard's LED screen it looked so electro," Haines later recalled in an interview. "It had a no-bullshit vibe. It was a little cold and standoffish and we're down with that. It works for us."

8. Nickelback

The story goes that the bass player Mike Kroeger used to work at Starbucks, where he uttered the phrase "here's your nickel back" all day long.

9. Rough Trade

The creative duo of Kevan Staples and Carole Pope first began singing folk songs in Toronto's Yorkville, under the moniker the Bullwhip Brothers. In 1974 they took the name Rough Trade, a gay slang term for a male sexual partner sporting a tough, working-class physicality. Men referred to as "trade" did not usually self-identify as "gay" and were usually compensated for their companionship with cash or gifts.

10. Rush

The band was having trouble coming up with a name, and in the final rush to get one John Rutsey's older brother yelled, "Why don't you call your band Rush?"

11. Sloan

Sloan took the nickname of a bass-playing friend, Jason Larsen, as their band name. His one-time boss had a French accent and referred to Jason as the "slow one," which sounded more like "sloan" when he said it, hence the nickname.

12. The Weeknd

The Weeknd, whose real name is Abel Tesfaye, hated his name growing up. He wasn't a big fan of the two Scarborough, Ontario, high schools he attended either, and so he dropped out when he was 17. He convinced one of his future bandmates to do the same. "We grabbed our mattresses from our parents," he told MTV in 2013, "threw it in our friend's shitty van and left one weekend and never came back home." In honour of his great escape, when Tesfaye started making music, he did it under the name The Weekend, but there was already a Canadian band with that name, so to avoid copyright issues, he dropped the *e* and became The Weeknd.

12 HARD-ROCKIN' WOMEN WHO MAKE CANDY PALMATER PROUD TO BANG HER HEAD

Candy Palmater is a comedian and recovered lawyer whose national television show, The Candy Show, *showcased Canadian music for five seasons on the Aboriginal People's Television Network. She can frequently be heard guest-hosting CBC Radio shows.*

1. Joan Jett
To say that the opening licks of "I Love Rock 'n' Roll" blew my 14-year-old mind is an understatement. Until then I had no idea women could shred and "not give a damn about their bad reputation" like this. I couldn't figure out if I wanted to be her or be with her. She embodied all that I dreamed of when I was a girl and she remains the queen of it all for me. May it pleasure the gods, I will get to interview her someday.

2. Holly Woods
Growing up in northern New Brunswick, access to concerts was pretty scarce. So when my friend's older brother drove us to Moncton to see the band Toronto in 1982, fronted by lead vocalist Holly Woods, I was blown away. She howled, "Your daddy don't know / What your mama's gonna do tonight" and proceeded to get in a fight with the guitarist on stage, which I thought was the coolest thing I had ever seen two women do to that point.

3. Carole Pope
I had a friend in high school that I was obsessed with. I couldn't quite understand those feelings until "High School Confidential" defined them for me. For breaking ground decades before it was "cool" to be gay, for singing her ass off with Rough Trade and for still being one kickass woman, Carole Pope has earned a righteous spot on this list.

4. Darby Mills
When asked, "What would you be if you could be anything in the world?" my answer is always, "I would be a rock star." And if suddenly I could sing, Darby Mills from the Headpins is the singer I would be. Her vocal power and rock grittiness sustained me through high school!

5. Lee Aaron

I was a metalhead who came of age in the era of New Wave and bands like Wham!, so you can imagine my excitement when Lee Aaron showed up on MuchMusic wielding a Viking sword and belting "Metal Queen." A few years later she also turned the sexist video tables on the dudes by putting a bunch of beefcake in her video for "Whatcha Do to My Body."

6. Wendy O. Williams

What's not to love about wild Wendy (may she rest in peace) and her Plasmatics, punk trailblazers who worked chainsaws and sledgehammers into their live show while Wendy sported electrical tape on her nipples. The moment that solidified her spot on this list for me was when she appeared on the Tom Snyder talk show and blew up a car. For the entire five years of my national TV show, every episode I would think, How can we compare to Wendy blowing up a car?!

7. Lita Ford

Lita was only 16 years old when she played lead guitar in the Runaways alongside Joan Jett. Four years later, she went solo and since then has never stopped strapping on her signature axe, the B.C. Rich Warlock, and thrilling audiences and guitar aficionados the world over. Both her prowess as a guitar player and her dating record impressed me. She counts among her exes Tony Iommi, Nikki Sixx and Chris Holmes. She is also on my list of dream interviews . . . here's hoping.

8. Doro Pesch

This amazing Snakebite and Warlock lead singer from Germany has been "raising her fist in the air" for 30 years. Still touring and still dressed in black leather, head to toe, she makes me excited to turn 50. My fave Doro moment was in the documentary *Heavy Metal* when she said, "They want me to be sexy without my leather, without power, this I could not do." She is five feet, three inches of pure, hard-driving metal.

9. Bif Naked

This Canadian rock goddess represents much more than just a rock legend on this list. She had arm tattoos before any other women in media had them, she beat cancer, she advocates for animals and she wrote an amazing book. And I still listen to "I Love Myself Today" before I hit the stage. I was 35 or so before

I got to see her live and I know I was the oldest person in the audience, but it didn't matter to me one bit. Bif rocks my gypsy soul!

10. Angela Gossow

Having come of age in the era of melodic metal, it took me a while to get into speed metal and the "cookie monster" vocals that often accompany it. The first time I heard Arch Enemy with Angela's growling vocals, I was intrigued, then I saw video of her in action and fell in love. She exudes raw power and domination on stage . . . she obvs didn't get the memo that we are supposed to be "sugar and spice and everything nice." I would love to inhabit her body on stage for just one night!

11. Lzzy Hale

When a woman is singing a song like "I Miss the Misery," it gives you a sense that someone else is channelling your feeling and your anger through her voice. I already loved Lzzy, then she went on tour with another member of this list, Lita Ford. I knew no list of mine would be complete without her.

12. Cristina Scabbia

This Italian is as fierce as she is beautiful. When Lacuna Coil first came to my attention with their dual vocalists and I heard Cristina's voice for the first time, I became an instant fan. In seeing how much success she has had, one can't help but think of those early days and Joan Jett having to put out her own record and how far we have come in terms of hard-rockin' women and those of us who love them.

ANNA MCGARRIGLE'S MENTIONS OF CLIMATE AND WEATHER CONDITIONS IN 10 MCGARRIGLE SONGS

Anna McGarrigle was one half of the acclaimed, award-winning folk music duo Kate and Anna McGarrigle. She continues to write music and perform in family concerts.

1. Now the sea evaporates to make the clouds for the rain and snow
    Leaving her chemical compounds in the absence of H_2O
    ("NaCl, a.k.a. Sodium Chloride Song," by Kate McGarrigle)

2. Ah we come a long way since we last shook hands
    Still got a long way to go

Couldn't see the flowers when we last shook hands
Couldn't see the flowers on account of the snow
("Come a Long Way," by Kate McGarrigle)

3. Winter's comin' on now
   I put the clocks back by an hour
   I changed the double-windows
   And cut the last of summer's flowers
   ("I'm Losing You," by Kate McGarrigle)

4. And when we get tired we'll stop to rest
   And if you still want to talk you can bare your breast
   If it's winter and cold we'll take a rooming-house room
   And if it's summer and warm we'll sleep under the moon
   ("The Walking Song," by Kate McGarrigle)

5. And the summer sun shone down on us,
   And it was fun to feel and it was fun to fall into a sloppy teenage scene.
   All those happy hours, turned green buds into flowers
   This crazy summer is past now, sunrise to sunset is fading fast now.
   ("Saratoga Summer Song," by Kate McGarrigle)

6. Monday morning, I boarded that train,
   Leaving London in the pouring rain
   ("Tell My Sister," by Kate McGarrigle)

7. There's a freezing-rain warning, gale-force winds forecast
   I need shelter until the morning or until this weather is passed
   There's a low cloud in your garden that the sun can't burn off today
   ("Hang Out Your Heart," by Anna McGarrigle)

7. In middle-fall when northern winds blow the clouds every which way
   and the temperature is variable in the course of a shortened day,
   the ghost of summer lingers on in the dying rays of the sun
   And winter waits to heap its snow upon us by the ton
   ("Bundle of Sorrow, Bundle of Joy," by Anna McGarrigle)

8. *J'me regarde pas dans les vitrines quand il fait 30 en d'sous de zéro*
   J'ai pas d'motel aux Laurentides, quand il fait frette j'fais pas du ski
   ("*Complainte pour Ste-Catherine*," by Philippe Tatartcheff and Anna
   McGarrigle)

9. The pumps is all froze,
   The horse is feet up
   The grader has levelled the mailbox away.
   Winter is turning your blue eyes to grey
   ("Forever and the Same, a.k.a. The Pump Song," by Philippe Tatartcheff
   and Anna McGarrigle)

10. The season is aging,
    Look out your window
    Our love is fading, we may part tomorrow
    ("The Season Is Aging," by Philippe Tatartcheff and Anna McGarrigle)

JOHNNY CASH'S 10 GREATEST COUNTRY SONGS OF ALL TIME

Johnny Cash, widely considered to be the greatest country music singer and composer in history, died in September 2003 at the age of 71. Known as "The Man in Black" (he always wore black), Cash recorded more than 1,500 songs. Cash contributed this list to The Book of Lists *in 1977.*

1. "I Walk the Line," Johnny Cash
2. "I Can't Stop Loving You," Don Gibson
3. "Wildwood Flower," Carter Family
4. "Folsom Prison Blues," Johnny Cash
5. "Candy Kisses," George Morgan
6. "I'm Movin' On," Hank Snow
7. "Walking the Floor over You," Ernest Tubb
8. "He'll Have to Go," Joe Allison and Audrey Allison
9. "Great Speckled Bird," Carter Family
10. "Cold, Cold Heart," Hank Williams

6 CANADIAN CONCERTS WHERE THE FANS WENT WILD

1. The Festival Express, Toronto, 1970

The Festival Express was Canada's answer to the epic concerts that brought together the twin tribes of rockers and hippies for a peace-loving music extravaganza. Montreal, Toronto, Winnipeg and Calgary had signed on for the tour, which travelled by private train between gigs and featured such rock royalty as the Band, Janis Joplin, Buddy Guy, Traffic, the Grateful Dead, and Canadian acts Ian and Sylvia and Robert Charlebois. The tour hit a snag early on, when the first gig in Montreal was cancelled by Mayor Jean Drapeau, who feared mayhem in light of the much-publicized hedonism and occasional violence associated with other festivals, including Woodstock and Altamont. So the Festival Express rolled on down to Toronto to kick things off on June 27. Waiting for them there was a large contingent of the May 4th Movement (M4M), anti-Vietnam protestors whose name commemorates the Kent State killings of four students by Ohio Guardsmen. They dubbed the event the RRRRip-Off Express, claiming that live music should be free, even though the two-day music fest was only charging $14 for a pass. Two thousand protestors stormed the gates, 350 of whom gained entry. Outside, the rest of the M4M mob sparred with 160 policemen, throwing garbage cans, bottles and rocks. Ten officers and 20 youths were injured, and 29 arrests were made. The situation was defused when the Grateful Dead agreed to play a free concert in nearby Coronation Park for the gatecrashers. When Janis Joplin took the stage later that night, she said, "Man, I never expected this of Toronto. You're really looking beautiful, man." The Festival Express continued, although M4M demonstrations were also held in Winnipeg and Calgary. The hippie paradise of a week-long trans-Canadian party and jam session on the train has achieved legendary status in the annals of rock and roll history.

2. The Clash, Vancouver, 1978

The Clash played Vancouver for the first time in 1978 at the Commodore Ballroom. The place was packed with punks revved up at the prospect of slam-dancing on the sprung dance floor. A local act, the Dishrags, got things going with a punishing, sneer-filled set, then Bo Diddley took the stage with his odd rectangular-shaped guitar and let rip with his epic riff "Hey, Bo Diddley." The punks were polite for a few songs, but clearly failed to grasp why Clash lead singer Joe Strummer would invite this old guy along for the tour. The beer and joints were starting to kick in, along with the catcalls, so Bo cut his set short. When the Clash took the stage, pandemonium hit. The punks paid tribute to their heroes by slamming into each other, jumping onstage, throwing drinks and beer bottles at the band, and spitting at them. The Clash withstood the controlled riot for four songs, ducking and dodging the fusillade, then Strummer interrupted the music to mock them: "If anybody had any balls they'd be throwing wine bottles!" At the end of the shortened set, Strummer, clearly peeved at the lack of respect shown one of the greats of rock and roll, pulled Bo Diddley out onstage for the encore to jam with them on "I Fought the Law."

3. Teenage Head, Toronto, August 20, 1981

It was a hot August night at Toronto's lakeshore amusement park. Youth had come from far and wide to attend the free concert by one of Canada's hottest punk acts. But before the gig had even started, police had closed the front gate, saying the venue was full to capacity. A crowd gathered at the gate, quickly noting that there were only a handful of police officers facing several hundred excited fans. A few rowdy ringleaders climbed the fence and beckoned the crowd to follow and storm the turnstiles. They were beaten back by the cops once, but they persisted by forcing open the gate. The crowd surged forward as the cops tried in vain to stop them. By the time reinforcements arrived, a full-scale riot was in progress. Lake Shore Boulevard was closed down as police in cruisers and boats, on horseback and in riot gear swung their batons while being pelted by garbage, bottles and rocks. Largely oblivious to the goings-on, Teenage Head continued to rock out as the melee continued for three hours. Dozens of fans and cops were injured, and 24 people were eventually arrested. The riot was front-page news in 90-odd North American newspapers, and Ontario Place pulled the plug on free rock concerts forever.

4. The Jackson Victory Tour, Montreal, 1984

The Jackson Victory Tour of 1984 was hyped as the biggest music event of the century. It was the first time all six brothers had played together since the '60s, and in the intervening years Michael had hit the big time with mega-million-selling albums *Off the Wall* and *Thriller*. The entire tour sold out before the Jacksons hit the road, including several dates in Vancouver, Montreal and Toronto. The first show in Montreal, on September 17, went off without a hitch, but the next night the mood changed. Word had spread that the show was bloated and overpriced, the tour merchandise was tacky and ridiculously expensive, and, as usual, the sound quality at the Big O was horrible. The capacity crowd grew restless as the show was delayed two hours while security patted down concertgoers for weapons or alcohol. When a local radio jock announced that scalpers were selling off their unsold tickets for $5 each, Montrealers rushed down to the stadium for a last-minute bargain. Venue staff made a foolish decision to close the doors, thus preventing all ticket holders from coming into the stadium, even those who had paid full price. An unruly mob formed outside the gates, bent on getting even with the greedy promoters and rock stars. First they swarmed the T-shirt vendor booths and threw all of their inventory into the crowd. Next they took up the metal stanchions and used them as battering rams to break into the stadium. When the glass doors shattered, they ran in and got lost in the crowd. Security finally did the right thing and radioed for the show to start, in order to quell the looming melee that could spill out into the audience of 58,000. With a huge explosion of pyrotechnics, the Jacksons took the stage and broke into the tune "Wanna Be Startin' Something."

5. Guns N' Roses, Montreal, 1992

Guns N' Roses concerts in Canada have been the occasion for two separate riots. The first unfolded in Montreal's Olympic Stadium on August 8, 1992. Front man Axl Rose, famous for his tantrums on and off the stage, incited a riot when he complained about the sound system, and seemed to imply he had a sore throat before walking offstage 50 minutes into the show. This came after Axl had made the audience of 57,000 wait for two hours before taking the stage. Fans were enraged, and began removing the bolts from their stadium seats and throwing them on the stage. Elsewhere they looted concession stands, set fires, smashed windows and damaged 30 police cruisers. Of the 300-odd police officers who tangled with the mob, eight were slightly injured, along with three concertgoers. Damages ran into the hundreds of thousands of dollars, and 12 people were arrested.

6. Guns N' Roses, Vancouver, 2002

The second Guns N' Roses riot was in Vancouver on November 7, 2002. The band was ready to kick off the North American leg of its Chinese Democracy Tour, but front man Axl was AWOL. He called 10 minutes before showtime to say that his plane couldn't get off the ground in Los Angeles due to inclement weather. When the cancellation was announced to the 8,000 fans, they rampaged through the streets of Vancouver. Their fury may have been fuelled in part by the memory of another Guns N' Roses last-minute cancellation in Vancouver, in 1992. Dozens of glass doors and windows were smashed, fireworks were set off, and rocks, beer bottles and cement bricks were thrown at the 120 police officers called out to quell the riot, who used pepper spray, attack dogs and batons to disperse the mob. Damages were estimated at over $350,000 and 12 people were arrested. Some fans were angry and proclaimed they would never listen to Guns N' Roses again, while others felt it fit in with the band's badass attitude. One fan who was arrested declared that "the riot kicked ass. It's like I told the cops—now that's how you start a motherfuckin' world tour!"

15 SONGS SUNG BY WILF CARTER

Wilf Carter (1904–96) was a pioneer in Canadian country music. Born in Nova Scotia, Carter moved to Alberta at age 19 and found work as a cowboy. To supplement his income, he accompanied tour groups through the Rockies, singing and playing his guitar. It was in the Rockies that he developed his signature yodel. He became a recording star in Canada and the United States, where he was known as Montana Slim. He recorded over 40 albums and wrote hundreds of songs in a career that spanned more than 50 years. Many of Wilf Carter's songs had rather intriguing titles. Here's a sample of some of the more unusual ones.

1. "There's a Love Knot in My Lariat"
2. "The Little Red Patch on the Seat of My Trousers"
3. "Everybody's Been Some Mother's Darling"
4. "By the Grave of Nobody's Darling"
5. "I Bought a Rock for My Rocky Mountain Girl"
6. "Don't Be Mean, I Wasn't Mean to You"
7. "My Old Lasso Is Headed Straight for You"
8. "There's a Padlock on Your Heart"
9. "Sick, Sober, and Sorry"
10. "When the Ice Worms Nest Again"
11. "I'm Gonna Tear Down the Mailbox"
12. "My Wife Is on a Diet"
13. "What Cigarette Is Best"
14. "I Wish There Were Only Three Days in the Year"
15. "No! No! Don't Ring Those Bells"

ROBERT HARRIS'S 10 LITTLE-KNOWN CANADIANS WHO CHANGED THE COURSE OF MUSIC HISTORY

Robert Harris is a long-time CBC Radio broadcaster and Globe and Mail *music critic. He is the author of* What to Listen for in Mozart *(1993) and* What to Listen for in Beethoven *(1997).*

1. Emma Albani (1847-1930)

Emma Lajeunesse was born in Chambly, Quebec, and went on to become one of the most famous opera stars in the world in the late 19th and early 20th centuries. Her musical talents were apparent at a young age, but she was unable to finance her studies in the artistically and economically impoverished Quebec of the 1850s. She eventually made her way to Italy (where a coach suggested she change her name to Albani), and from there conquered first Italy, then London, then New York. She sang a vast number of roles at Covent Garden and the Met, from *Lohengrin* to *La Traviata* to *Les Huguenots*, and was unquestionably the most famous Canadian musician in the world for many decades, even if no one knew she was Canadian.

2. Pierre Cossette (1923-2009)

Pierre Cosette was born in Valleyfield, Quebec, and became one of Hollywood's most famous press agents and managers. Dean Martin and Andy Williams were among his clients. He also started Dunhill Records, which launched the career of the Mamas and the Papas. In 1971, Cossette approached ABC with a suggestion that they televise the Grammys, the music industry's annual awards show. ABC turned him down, unless, they said, he could get someone like Andy Williams to host. Cossette did, and the rest is history. The Grammys is now the second-most important awards show in the American entertainment business, bested only by the Academy Awards. Cossette was the executive producer of every Grammys broadcast from 1971 to his death in 2009. His son now co-produces the show.

3. Nathaniel Dett (1882-1943)

Robert Nathaniel Dett was born in Drummondville, Ontario, now part of Niagara Falls. One of the first black composers to earn a significant international reputation, Dett was a pioneer in combining the world of the African-American spiritual with romantic, European musical traditions. Dett first matriculated to Oberlin College in Pennsylvania, and later studied at Harvard.

He was one of the first black composers to be permitted to join ASCAP—the American Society of Composers, Authors and Publishers. His work was played in Carnegie Hall by major symphony orchestras, at a time when racial prejudice was rampant in the United States. Dett travelled to Europe both to study and to work and was travelling with the USO Chorus when he died in 1943. He is buried in Niagara Falls, where the British Methodist Episcopal Church, where he served as organist, was renamed for him and designated a National Historic Site in 2001. The Canadian group the Nathaniel Dett Chorale is named for him.

4. Gil Evans (1912-88)

Of the few people in the world who have heard of Gil Evans, fewer still realize he was born in Toronto. Evans eventually became one of the most influential jazz arrangers who ever lived. Starting work with the Claude Thornhill Orchestra in the '40s, Evans teamed up with Miles Davis in the late '50s to create some of the most influential jazz albums ever recorded—*Miles Ahead*, *Porgy and Bess* and *Sketches of Spain*. Evans's use of traditional symphonic instruments in his jazz arrangements and his modernist approach to jazz influenced countless other arrangers and created a whole new school of jazz, summarized by the title of his first album with Miles Davis, *The Birth of the Cool*. Evans continued working for decades after his collaborations with Davis, and was planning an album with Jimi Hendrix when the guitarist died in 1971. He was active well into the '80s, writing the score for Martin Scorsese's *The Color of Money* in 1986. Evans died in Mexico in 1988.

5. Bob Ezrin (1949-)

Born in Toronto, Bob Ezrin became one of the most important rock producers of all time. Starting with Alice Cooper, Ezrin eventually produced albums by a who's who of rock legends, including Kiss, Pink Floyd, Lou Reed, Deep Purple— almost all of the hard rock classic bands of the mid-'70s and beyond. Ezrin co-produced Pink Floyd's *The Wall* and produced Lou Reed's *Berlin*, both among the 50 most important pop albums ever made. Ezrin is still active, having branched out into film and concert production and music education.

6. Bob Farnon (1917-2005)

Originally one of the members of the Happy Gang, Bob Farnon was a trumpeter and arranger who worked for the Canadian Army Show, and then led the Canadian band of the Allied Expeditionary Force in the Second World War

(Glenn Miller led the American version). Farnon stayed in England after the war and launched one of the most successful musical careers in modern history, as a bandleader, arranger, recording artist, composer and conductor. A musical god in Great Britain, and one of its most famous musicians, Farnon was also considered the best pop arranger in history. Everyone from André Previn to Quincy Jones to John Williams has acknowledged their debt to Farnon, who was the only arranger outside of the United States to work on an album with Frank Sinatra. For years librarians at the CBC Music Library in Toronto reported visits from arrangers from all over the world anxious to study scores that Bob Farnon wrote for the CBC Light Orchestra in the early '40s, to pick up tricks from the master.

7. Edward Johnson (1878-1959)

To the extent that anyone in Canada has ever heard of the operatic tenor Edward Johnson, it's probably because the University of Toronto named their Faculty of Music building after him. But Johnson was a towering figure in the world of opera in the mid 20th century. Born in Guelph, Johnson spent five years at La Scala in Milan, where he was known as Edoardo di Giovanni. He moved to New York where he debuted many famous roles, but most importantly, in 1935 he became general manager of the Metropolitan Opera, a position he held for 15 years. During his tenure, Jussi Björling, Robert Merrill, Jan Peerce, Risë Stevens and Eleanor Steber all made their Met debuts. In 1950, he relinquished the job to his protégé, Rudolf Bing, and returned to Guelph, where he died in 1959.

8. Hugh Le Caine (1914-77)

Hugh Le Caine might be the textbook example of the tragedy of being ahead of one's time. Le Caine, born in Port Arthur, Ontario, was a scientist and physicist who worked on the development of radar during the Second World War, and then on nuclear physics. But his passion was music, and the intersection of technology and music. In the end, Le Caine invented 22 new musical instruments, including the Electronic Sackbut in the 1940s, now acknowledged as the world's first synthesizer, 20 years before Bob Moog invented his. He also invented what he called the Special Purpose Tape Recorder, now understood to be the first multi-track tape recorder ever created. Le Caine was also a composer—his *Dripsody* from 1952, based on the electronic manipulations of the sound of a drip of water, was one of the earliest examples of *musique concrète*, music based on recordings of natural sounds. Le Caine was supported throughout his life by Canada's

National Research Council, but his work was almost completely unknown, even within Canada. Only after his tragic death in a motorcycle accident in 1977 was Le Caine's work fully discovered and honoured.

9. Ruth Lowe (1914-81)

Ruth Lowe was a pianist and songwriter from Toronto who wrote some of the most famous songs in American pop music history. Ruth was working in the Song Shop in Toronto when Ina Ray Hutton's famous all-woman orchestra came to town, desperate to find an emergency replacement pianist. Lowe auditioned, and stayed with the band for two years (Hutton's orchestra was the model for the all-girl band in Billy Wilder's *Some Like It Hot*). Lowe married Harold Cohen in 1938, but he died during an operation only a year later. Returning to Toronto, Lowe wrote a song about her grief called "I'll Never Smile Again." Tommy Dorsey heard the song on the CBC while touring with his band in Toronto, and eventually recorded it in 1940, with his new boy singer, Frank Sinatra. "I'll Never Smile Again" became one of the most iconic songs of the Second World War period, and one of the most popular pop tunes of all time. Sinatra's version is in the Library of Congress Registry of American Recordings. Lowe also wrote the lyrics to Sinatra's long-time closing music, "Put Your Dreams Away," which was the last piece of music played at his funeral. In 1982, a year after her death, Lowe was inducted into the American Music Hall of Fame with an honorary Grammy award.

10. The Otnorots (1940s and '50s)

The Otnorots (that's *Toronto* spelled backwards, by the way) was the original name of a group of four guys from St. Michael's Choir School in Toronto in the late 1940s, who went on to form two of the most important groups of pre–rock and roll pop music: the Four Lads and the Crew Cuts. The Four Lads came first. Two of the "Lads" (Connie Codarini and Bernie Toorish) were original members of the Otnorots. In 1950, they started performing at local clubs, got noticed by some scouts and moved to New York, where they recorded smash hits like "Moments to Remember," "Istanbul (Not Constantinople)," and "Standin' on the Corner." The other two Otnorots (Rudi Maugeri and John Perkins) formed the Crew Cuts in 1952 and had success with songs like "Sh-Boom" and "Earth Angel." Together, the Four Lads and the Crew Cuts influenced everyone from the Everly Brothers to the Beach Boys to the Beatles.

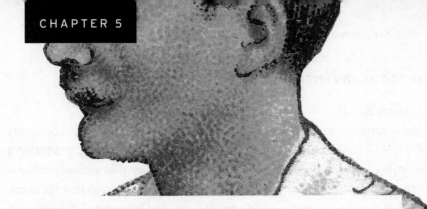

Food and Health

11 FOODS INVENTED IN CANADA

1. Maple Syrup

Maple syrup predates Canada by a few millennia, as Indigeneous people were the first to enjoy sweet water drawn from maple trees in spring, and boiled it down in clay cooking pots. The arrival of copper and iron pots allowed producers to evaporate it more efficiently, with a 40:1 ratio of sap to syrup now the norm. Canada supplies 85% of the world's maple syrup, and at roughly $1,800 a barrel, thieves routinely conspire to steal thousands of gallons of the gold nectar from secured warehouses. The biggest heist involved nearly 3,000 tonnes of syrup worth almost $19 million in 2012.

2. Butter Tarts

These lard-laced bombs of pastry, eggs, brown sugar and butter first appeared in the 1600s, a maple-syrup-infused local variation on Quebec's *tarte au sucre*, Scottish treacle pie and American pecan pie. They've been in heavy rotation ever since, a perennial bestseller at bake sales and the highlight of many a care package. Debate rages over whether an authentic butter tart contains raisins or pecans, and whether the insides should be runny or firm.

3. McIntosh Apples

McIntosh apples were discovered and first grown by United Empire Loyalist John McIntosh in 1811. While clearing land on his farm near Ottawa, he found a small stand of 20 or so apple trees growing wild. He transplanted them into his own orchard, but they all died—except one, which was exceptionally sturdy and healthy. Most importantly, the apple tree produced abundant quantities of tasty bright red apples. Neighbours and fruit growers sought out this hardy new variety, the McIntosh Red, for their own orchards, and over the years hundreds of cuttings and graftings produced similarly robust apple trees ideally suited to the Canadian climate. All McIntosh apple trees descend from this one tree, which stopped producing fruit in 1908 and died in 1910.

4. Peameal Bacon

Peameal bacon has an identity crisis. The distinctive breakfast treat made of wet-cured boneless pork loin is actually encrusted in yellow cornmeal, not peameal, and in many parts of the world it's called Canadian bacon. Most of us call it back bacon and enjoy it served up in a simple white bun or toasted on English muffins with an egg. Hogtown, a.k.a. Toronto, is credited as the birthplace of back bacon in the 1860s under the direction of veteran ham and bacon provisioner William Davies.

5. Ginger Ale

John McLaughlin was a chemist and pharmacist who opened a soda-water bottling business in 1890. While experimenting with adding flavours to the bubbly water, he hit upon the additive of ginger root. The resulting drink, Pale Dry Ginger Ale, was an instant hit with thirsty Canadians and Americans. It was patented in 1907 as Canada Dry Ginger Ale.

6. Marquis Wheat

The short growing season and harsh climate of the Canadian prairies led to the development of the hardy Marquis wheat between 1902 and 1910. Sir Charles Saunders crossed Red Fife and Hard Red Calcutta wheat to create a rust-resistant variety that yielded big crops before the killing frosts of fall. By 1920 Marquis wheat accounted for 90% of all wheat grown in western Canada.

7. Pablum

A mixture of ground and precooked wheat, oatmeal and cornmeal, Pablum was invented in 1930 by three pediatricians at Toronto's Hospital for Sick Children: Alan Brown, Theodore Drake and Fred Tisdall. At the time it was created, Pablum revolutionized infant nutrition because it was affordable, nutritious and easy to prepare. As a word, *Pablum* comes from the Latin *pabulum*, meaning "foodstuff," though it has gone on to become synonymous with anything bland and mushy.

8. Poutine

Although many claim responsibility for inventing the greasy, gooey combination of squeaky cheese curds, gravy and French fries, the first poutine was made by restaurant owner Fernand Lachance in 1957 in Warwick, Quebec. He sold the regional specialty for 35 cents, mixing the curds and fries together in a paper bag, and warned diners that it would be messy but delicious. Many variations on the original recipe exist, including one deluxe version with *foie gras* served in Montreal's Au Pied de Cochon bistro.

9. Instant Mashed Potatoes

Instant mashed potatoes were invented by Edward A. Asselbergs in 1962. He came up with this novel use for Canada's staple vegetable crop while working for the Department of Agriculture. The dehydrated flakes were never a big hit with diners, but they continue to be widely used in the creation of convenience food and military rations.

10. Canola Oil

Invented in 1974 at the University of Manitoba, canola oil is pressed from the seeds of the yellow rapeseed plant. In order to appeal to consumers, that name was dropped in favour of canola, a contraction of "Canadian oil." It has become one of the most popular cooking oils in the world.

11. Yukon Gold Potato

This hybrid potato was invented by researchers at Ontario's University of Guelph in in 1980. Named after the Yukon gold rush, it has been hailed as the perfect multi-purpose potato because its smooth, yellow, waxy flesh does well when boiled, mashed or baked. The same team developed the Red Gold, a less popular hybrid, while a team of New Brunswick researchers came up with the Rochdale Gold, which hit their local grocery stores in 2002.

GRUB LIST FOR A GUIDED 10-PERSON PACK TRAIN TRIP IN THE ROCKY MOUNTAINS, 1917

Bert and Dora Riggall were renowned backcountry guides and outfitters operating out of the Waterton Lakes National Park area of southwestern Alberta from 1908 to 1946. Their trips were often massive undertakings: six to 18 people, a couple of dozen pack and saddle horses, and enough food and equipment to last for weeks. The gear (canvas tents, bedrolls, a portable cook stove and stove pipes, pots, pans, plates, cups, bowls, washbasins, buckets, ropes, saws, spades, fishing rods, a .45 Colt and shells) and the "grub" could total upwards of 2,500 pounds. What was on the menu? Drawn from the archives of the Whyte Museum of the Canadian Rockies in Banff, Alberta, here is the "grub list" for a three-week backcountry trip for 10 people in August and September of 1917, which may have been augmented with fish caught in streams and lakes.

Flour	60 lbs
Rolled oats	12 lbs
Corn meal	10 lbs
Wheatlets	6 lbs
Rice	10 lbs
Macaroni	5 lbs
Sago	2 lbs
Bacon	28 lbs
Lard	15 lbs
Butter	15 lbs
Cheese	12 lbs
Sugar	60 lbs
Custard powder	2 lbs
Jelly powders	6 lbs
Jam	6 lbs
Raisins	12 packets
Evaporated apples	8 lbs
Evaporated prunes	5 lbs
Evaporated peaches	3 lbs
Evaporated apricots	4 lbs
Dates	10 lbs
Potatoes	25 lbs
Beans	2 lbs
Soup tablets	60
Salt	12 lbs
Pepper	1 shaker
Baking powder	5 lbs
Soda	1 lb
Bovril	2 large bottles
Dried onions	1 tin
Dried milk	1 lb
Worcester sauce	1 small bottle
Lemons	1 dozen
Catsup	2 bottles
Pickles	2 bottles
Plum pudding	12 lbs
Mince-Meat	4 lbs

Tea	2 lbs
Coffee	3 lbs
Cocoa	4 lbs
Canned milk	35 cans
Canned corn	6 cans
Canned fish	10 small cans
Canned fruit	8 cans
Canned pork & beans	12 cans
Candles	10
Matches	3 boxes
Tar Soap	2 cakes

NAOMI DUGUID'S 10 FAVOURITE COOKBOOKS

The cookbooks I most treasure are horizon-expanding, giving me a feel for the depths and richness of culinary culture through stories and recipes, and with emotional or empathetic connection. Those are also the kind of books I try to write.

Naomi Duguid—traveller, writer, photographer, cook—is often described as a culinary anthropologist. She is the author of the several highly acclaimed books that explore home-cooked foods in their cultural context. Her most recent book, Taste of Persia: A Cook's Travels Through Armenia, Azerbaijan, Georgia, Iran, and Kurdistan, *was published in 2016.*

1. Food in England by Dorothy Hartley

Dorothy Hartley's *Food in England*, first published in 1954, is a treasure of traditional English foods and foodways, from how to plant an apple tree (near an outhouse) to how to make steamed puddings. She's writing about anchored regional traditions that date back into the 19th century, before English food became ruined (following the First World War). And it's these traditions, plus an infusion of ideas and creativity from the continent and from chefs, that are the backbone of today's renewed and justly celebrated English food and restaurants.

2. Book of Middle Eastern Food by Claudia Roden

Claudia Roden's *Book of Middle Eastern Food* came out in 1972. Inspired by her own Egyptian-Jewish roots, and her family's relatives and friends who lived in many places in the old Ottoman Empire, from Turkey to Iraq to Morocco, the book is a treasure of stories and gracefully written, enticing recipes. A new edition was published in 2000.

3. The Cuisines of Mexico by Diana Kennedy

Diana Kennedy is an Englishwoman who began living in Mexico in the '60s. Her books about Mexican food traditions are deeply researched and passionately appreciative. Her first book, *The Cuisines of Mexico*, has now been edited and reissued as *Essential Cuisines of Mexico*. The food geography and human geography of Mexico come into focus as she writes about the cook who taught her each recipe and the landscape that gave rise to it.

4. An Invitation to Indian Cooking by Madhur Jaffrey

Madhur Jaffrey, born in India and a long-time resident of the United States, began publishing cookbooks in the '70s. My favourite of those is her first, *An Invitation to Indian Cooking*. In it she draws on personal experience and stories from friends and family that give heart to the recipes, and anchor them.

5. Honey from a Weed by Patience Gray

Patience Gray was a journalist and food writer beginning in the '50s. Her cookbook *Honey from a Weed*, a combination food memoir, recipe book and reference published in 1986, is a classic. She takes us deep into the lore and wisdom of Mediterranean country food in Greece, Italy, Provence and Spain, primarily through lowly plants: herbs and vegetables. We learn how and when they were traditionally grown and gathered, and how they were used in simple peasant dishes, and she gives us the word for them in many languages and dialects.

6. Life and Food in Bengal by Chitrita Banerji

Another book that combines memoir, recipes and stories is Chitrita Banerji's wonderful *Life and Food in Bengal*. The stories trace the year in food, starting in Indian Bengal, where she was born and raised in a Hindu family before moving as a bride to a Muslim Bangladeshi household. The book glows with heart and tenderness, and offers wonderful recipes and insights about agricultural seasons and the cycle of the year.

7. The Classic Cuisine of the Italian Jews by Edda Servi Machlin

Edda Servi Machlin's *The Classic Cuisine of the Italian Jews* looks back at a lost era, before the Second World War, and food traditions and daily life in her family's home village of Pitigliano. At once heart-wrenching—because of the violence that underpins the loss of that life—and warming.

8. Lebanese Mountain Cookery by Mary Laird Hamady

Lebanese Mountain Cookery by Mary Laird Hamady introduces us to a large cast of characters and recipes from Lebanon. The writer married into the Hamady family, and thus has both an outsider's and an insider's eye. She introduces us to the family food culture, often with loving and entertaining stories about the culinary arguments in the family, or the special way in which a great-aunt makes a particular dish. The book offers a glimpse of largely non-urban food traditions in a part of the world that has a long history.

9. The Old World Kitchen: The Rich Tradition of European Peasant Cooking by Elisabeth Luard

Elisabeth Luard's *The Old World Kitchen: The Rich Tradition of European Peasant Cooking* was first published in England in 1984 and the United States in 1985. It is a big book, gracefully written and full of recipes from non-Slavic Europe, from Finland to Portugal. Excerpts from the writings of travellers, poets and novelists, and personal memoirs of the author's own lived experiences in Spain and elsewhere give the recipes a rich context.

10. Please to the Table by Anya von Bremzen and John Welchman

Just before the dissolution of the Soviet Union, Anya von Bremzen and John Welchman published *Please to the Table*. It's a book of recipes and stories that give a window into the culinary traditions of the many varied peoples of that huge country, from the Baltic to Central Asia. At the time it was published it was especially valuable because so little had been written in English about the food cultures there. I turn to it still.

8 TIPS FOR HEALTHY EATING IN 1942

According to the April 15, 1942, edition of *Maclean's* magazine, "if every Canadian ate these foods in these amounts every day, there would be no nutrition problem in Canada."

1. Three glasses of milk
2. Six slices of vitamin-rich bread with butter

3. One serving of meat or fish
4. One egg
5. One serving of potatoes
6. One serving of green leaf or yellow vegetables
7. One glass of tomato juice
8. One serving of vitamin-rich breakfast cereal

8 NOTABLE EVENTS THAT HAPPENED UNDER THE INFLUENCE OF ALCOHOL

1. The Hanging of Captain Kidd (1701)

Captain William Kidd was sentenced to death for murder and piracy and led to the gallows at London's Execution Dock on May 23, 1701. The execution itself was a fiasco. As a large group of spectators sang a series of ballads in honour of the pirate, a very drunk public executioner attempted to hang Kidd, who was so smashed that he could hardly stand. Then the rope broke and Kidd fell over into the mud. Though a second attempt at hanging the prisoner succeeded, the sheriff in charge was later harshly criticized in a published editorial for the bungled performance.

2. The Boston Tea Party (1773)

In Boston, Massachusetts, 50 colonials and members of the Committee of Correspondence met at the home of a printer named Benjamin Edes at about 4 p.m. on December 16, 1773. Later that evening, they intended to destroy the tea aboard three ships in Boston Harbor as a protest against the British government's taxation of the American colonies. To bolster their resolve, Edes filled a massive punch bowl with a potent rum concoction. Edes's son Peter had the job of keeping the bowl filled, which proved to be an almost impossible task because of the ardour with which the patriots drank. Shortly after 6 p.m., the men, most of whom were now in a noisy, festive mood, with a few staggering noticeably, departed and marched to Griffin's Wharf, where the tea ships were anchored. For the next three hours they sobered up, a number becoming violently ill, as they dumped heavy tea chests into the harbour—and set off the American Revolution.

3. The Charlottetown Conference (1864)

Confederation might have happened without the champagne and the wine. But the Canadian cabinet ministers who set sail from Quebec aboard the steamer

Queen Victoria on August 29, 1864, bound for Charlottetown, were not prepared to leave anything to chance. Their mission was to convince reluctant politicians from New Brunswick, Nova Scotia and Prince Edward Island to abandon their plan for Maritime union and join with them in a larger Canadian federation. In the ship's hold were many cases of champagne and wine. After two days of inconclusive meetings, the Canadians invited the Maritimers for a late Saturday lunch aboard the *Queen Victoria*. The trap was set. Historian P.B. Waite wrote that "champagne flowed like water, and union talk with it. The occasion took hold of everyone. Champagne and union!" So much progress was made that according to George Brown, by the time the lunch ended many hours later, "the union was thereupon formally completed and proclaimed!"

4. Lincoln's Assassination (1865)

On April 14, 1865, actor John Wilkes Booth began drinking at the Kirkwood House bar in Washington, D.C., at 3 in the afternoon. At 4 p.m. he arrived at Deery's Saloon and ordered a bottle of brandy. Two hours later he was drinking whisky at Taltavull's Saloon, next door to Ford's Theater. Having made the final arrangements for his impending crime, Booth returned at 9:30 p.m. to Taltavull's, where President Abraham Lincoln's valet, Charles Forbes, his coachman, Francis Burns, and his bodyguard, John Parker, an alcoholic policeman, were all drinking. At 10:15, while Parker continued to imbibe—thus leaving the president unprotected—Booth left, went next door to Ford's Theater, and shot Lincoln. Meanwhile, George Atzerodt, Booth's fellow conspirator, who was supposed to assassinate Vice President Andrew Johnson, had become so intoxicated and frightened that he abandoned the plan.

5. The Third Battle of the Aisne River (1918)

In May 1918, during the First World War, General Erich Ludendorff's German troops reached the Marne River at Chateau-Thierry, only 60 kilometres from Paris, during the Third Battle of the Aisne River. On the verge of capturing Paris, but after living without any luxuries for years, the German soldiers invaded France's Champagne province, where well-stocked wine cellars abounded. Drunkenness quickly spread through the ranks; even the German military police joined the revelries. In the village of Fismes on the morning of May 30, the bodies of soldiers who had passed out littered the streets, making it difficult for trucks to drive through the town on their way to the front lines. The intoxication and subsequent hangovers afflicting the Germans slowed their advance and halted it completely in certain sectors. This enabled the French and Americans to establish new defensive lines, counterattack, and end Ludendorff's offensive, which proved to be the Germans' last chance for victory in the war.

6. The Exxon Valdez Oil Spill (1989)

After striking a reef, the *Exxon Valdez* spilled 250,000 barrels of oil into Alaska's Prince William Sound, forming a slick that covered 4,180 square kilometres and washed onto 1,600 kilometres of coastline. At the time of the accident, Captain Joseph Hazelwood was below deck, having left at the helm Third Mate Gregory Cousins, who was not certified to pilot the tanker in Prince William Sound. After the collision, Hazelwood attempted to pilot the tanker off the reef, despite warnings that the ship might break up if he succeeded. Hazelwood also failed to sound a general alarm. In addition, Hazelwood was observed chain-smoking on the bridge until Coast Guard officers arrived and warned him that he could set the whole ship on fire. One of the Coast Guard officers who boarded the ship two and a half hours after the collision reported that Hazelwood's breath smelled of alcohol. When a blood test was administered—a full nine hours after the accident—Hazelwood's blood alcohol level was above the legal level permissible when operating a ship. Although Hazelwood admitted that he had drunk alcohol while ashore earlier that day (and witnesses spotted him drinking in two different bars), he denied being impaired at the time of the accident and insisted that the blood alcohol test was inaccurate. Indeed, although a jury convicted Hazelwood on misdemeanour negligence charges (later overturned), he was acquitted of operating a ship while under the influence of alcohol. On the other hand, an investigation by the National Transportation Safety Board concluded that Hazelwood had left the bridge because of "impairment from alcohol."

7. The Failed Soviet Coup (1991)

In a last-ditch attempt to undo the reforms of glasnost, on August 19, 1991, Communist Party hardliners attempted to overthrow Soviet premier Mikhail Gorbachev. The coup collapsed two days later in the face of resistance led by Boris Yeltsin, president of the Russian republic. The plotters' failure to act decisively against Yeltsin ensured the failure of the coup. Heavy alcohol consumption contributed to the ineptitude of the plotters. Former Soviet vice-president Gennady Yanayev, the front man for the coup, drank heavily throughout the affair and was found "in an alcoholic haze" in his office when the coup collapsed.

Another plotter, former prime minister Valentin Pavlov, began drinking the first night of the coup, by his own admission. When Pavlov tried unsuccessfully to convince the government to declare a state of emergency, he appeared sick "or more likely drunk," according to Deputy Prime Minister Vladimir Shcherbakov. The failed coup ultimately led to the complete disintegration of the Soviet Union.

8. The Death of Diana (1997)

On August 31, 1997, Diana, Princess of Wales, her boyfriend, Dodi al-Fayed, and their driver, Henri Paul, were killed in a car crash in a tunnel in Paris. Paul had been driving at more than 160 kilometres per hour when he apparently clipped another car and lost control. An investigation found that Paul's blood alcohol level was three times the legal limit. There were also traces of antidepressants in his blood. Conspiracy theorists—including Dodi's father, Mohamed al-Fayed—have disputed the blood test results. They note that two bodyguards who were with Paul shortly before the crash said that he did not appear drunk and that he acted normally.

FOOD AND DRINK CARRIED BY FERRY FROM WINDSOR TO DETROIT (MARCH 1-JULY 5, 1850)

5,159 dozen eggs
994 lbs of butter
216 kegs of lard
2,053 bushels of oats
100 lbs of bacon
51 cases of gin
4 cases of champagne
106 cases of brandy
40 gallons of vinegar
613 bushels of barley
74 bushels of peas
900 lbs of corn meal
552 lbs of pork
127 head of cabbage

Source: W.H. Smith, *Canada: Past, Present and Future, being a historical, geographical, geological and statistical account of Canada West* (Toronto: Thomas Maclear, 1851).

13 FAMOUS INSOMNIACS

1. Barbara Amiel, journalist

Amiel is a lifelong insomniac. "My earliest memory as a child of four was being sedated to sleep," she once recalled.

2. Bill Clinton, politician

Being able to get by on five hours of sleep a night may seem like an advantage for someone as busy as a president, but Clinton was later quoted as saying, "Every important mistake I've made in my life, I've made because I was too tired."

3. Judy Garland, actress and singer

As a teenager, Garland was prescribed amphetamines to control her weight. As the years went by, she took so many that she sometimes stayed up three or four days in a row. She added sleeping pills to her regimen, and her insomnia and addiction increased. She eventually died of a drug overdose.

4. Glenn Gould, musician and composer

Pianist Glenn Gould was a lifelong insomniac. He usually stayed up into the early morning hours, working or talking on the phone. He rarely slept without the help of tranquilizers. The *Goldberg Variations*, a sequence of short compositions Bach composed at the behest of Count von Keyserling as musical therapy for his abiding insomnia, became Gould's career-defining performance.

5. Arianna Huffington, publisher

The *Huffington Post* founder and jet-setter pushed herself hard to succeed, getting by with three or four hours of sleep and a steady supply of espresso. Completely exhausted, she fainted and fell one day, breaking her cheekbone. The mishap ended up being a wake-up call: she reconfigured her life and wrote a bestseller, *The Sleep Revolution*, about the value of getting a good night's sleep.

6. Wayne Johnston, writer

Johnston, an award-winning Canadian novelist, writes by night and tries to sleep during the day, getting about four hours of shut-eye daily. When he finally succumbs to fatigue, usually after 24 hours, he sleeps in a soundproofed room with a white-noise machine to mask whatever little noise makes its way in. "The sound of a cat licking its fur three floors away once kept me up all night."

7. Franz Kafka, author

Kafka, miserable with insomnia, kept a diary detailing his suffering. For October 2, 1911, he wrote, "Sleepless night. The third in a row. I fall asleep soundly, but after an hour I wake up, as though I had laid my head in the wrong hole."

8. Madonna, musician

Madonna credits her insomnia—as well as being a "control freak, anal retentive and a workaholic"—as the reason she's not married, adding, "Who could stand me!"

9. Margaret Thatcher, politician

The Iron Lady turned insomnia to her advantage by working late and sleeping an average of four hours a night. She once famously remarked, "Sleep is for wimps."

10. Groucho Marx, comic actor

Marx first began to have insomnia when the stock market crashed in 1929 and he lost $240,000 in 48 hours. When he couldn't sleep, he would call people up in the middle of the night and insult them.

11. Theodore Roosevelt, U.S. president

His insomnia cure was a shot of cognac in a glass of milk.

12. Donald Trump, U.S. president

Ever wonder why Donald Trump sends out all those break-of-dawn tweets? The answer may be that he has nothing better to do. Critics accuse the 45th president of many failings, but oversleeping is not one of his sins. When asked about his sleeping habits on the campaign trail in 2016, Trump replied, "You know, I'm not a big sleeper. I like three hours, four hours, I toss, I turn, I beep-de-beep, I want to find out what's going on."

13. Vincent van Gogh, painter

Writing to his brother, Vincent complained of his insomnia but noted the positive results he was getting from pouring "a very, very strong dose of camphor in my pillow and mattress." Camphor was a waxy, flammable solid derived from turpentine that likely contributed to the painter's illnesses and emotional distress.

12 HAIR TIPS FOR MEN FROM *NATIONAL HOME MONTHLY*, 1938

In the 1930s and '40s, *National Home Monthly* proudly billed itself as "Canada's Greatest Magazine." Its main competitor for the loyalty of Canadian women readers, *Chatelaine*, might have taken issue with that designation, but there is no doubt that the Winnipeg-based monthly presented a highly popular mix of fiction, essays, recipes, beauty secrets and other domestic tips. Most of its advice was aimed at women, but writers would occasionally offer some tips for male grooming, such as these pointers for proper male hair care, from February 1938.

Things that are BAD for your hair
1. Tight-fitting hats
2. Cold showers on the unprotected head
3. Salt water not rinsed out of the hair after a swim
4. Deep, warm bed pillows (try flat pillows or do without one)
5. An unbalanced diet, particularly one lacking in the vitamins provided by fruits, vegetables, leafy green things
6. Strain and over-exertion (take exertion in moderation; don't go in for weekend marathons. Leave business worries at the office)

Things that are GOOD for your hair
7. A weekly shampoo, thoroughly rinsed out
8. Daily brushing
9. Hair pulling (some doctors say that the fussing, combing, curling and rearranging that women constantly give their hair exercises the muscles of the scalp. They suggest tugging gently at the hair, taking small tufts and pulling, as a substitute exercise for men's hair)
10. A sound regime, good diet, rest and recreation (falling hair and early greyness are often a symptom of failing health)

11. Exercise—in moderation
12. Sunlight—in moderation

ADRIA VASIL'S 6 LITTLE-KNOWN FACTS ABOUT CANADIAN WATER SUPPLIES

Canadians can get cocky about our fresh water. Who can blame us? We've got as many as two million lakes and nearly 20% of the world's fresh water. Trouble is only 7% of that is said to be "renewable," only 1% gets replenished by rain and snowfall annually and just 2.6% of our fresh water flows to southern Canada, where most of us live. That, and we don't always treat our water all that well, so our H_2O is more stressed than most Canadians think.

Adria Vasil is an environmental journalist and the bestselling author of the Ecoholic book series on green living.

1. Canadian lakes are warming twice as fast as most lakes around the globe

When you think global-warming hot spots, you might imagine parched African sandscapes, melting glaciers, maybe a low-lying Pacific isle. Well, a study of 235 lakes on six continents representing half the world's freshwater supply found that Canada's lakes are heating up faster than most—twice the global average. Surprisingly, Lake Superior was the second-fastest warming lake, with the rest of the Great Lakes not far behind. Cottagers may be breaking out their swim trunks sooner, but researchers warn the warming waters may lead, globally, to a 20% spike in lake-choking algae blooms, as well as major ecosystem changes, eroding lake levels and a 4% increase in potent climate-cooking methane gas releases. Gulp.

2. Canada exports trillions of litres of beefy water

Pretty much everything we consume has an invisible water footprint, from your morning cup of coffee (that grande pulls about 560 litres from, say, Brazil or Kenya) to the T-shirt on your back (about 2,700 litres). While over 70% of Canada's fresh water goes into agriculture, a steak dinner is one of the heftiest ways to drain water resources in some of the most water-stressed regions of the country (namely Alberta). According to the UN, one kilo of beef sucks up about 15,000 litres of water when you factor in the H_2O that goes into grain feed. And we're shipping much of that water far from Canadian water tables. Canada exported 577,420 tonnes of beef and cattle in 2015—with 40,000 more tonnes destined for Europe if the Canada-Europe trade agreement proceeds. That's trillions of litres in virtual water exports. Talk about taking stock.

3. Over 205 billion litres of raw sewage are flushed into Canadian rivers and oceans annually

It's one of the largest sources of water pollution in Canada—and one most of us would rather not contemplate. Despite federal regulations nudging municipalities to modernize their antiquated sewer systems, record levels of raw sewage are ending up in Canadian waters. Turns out too many Canadian towns are either pumping raw sewage directly into waterways, or their aging storm sewers are still combined with sanitary sewers, allowing the dirty mix to overflow into local lakes and rivers every time a storm backs things up. Some provinces are worse than others. Nearly a quarter of Nova Scotia's wastewater went untreated in 2015. But no province flushes more untreated wastewater in waterways than British Columbia—82.3 billion litres in 2015. Victoria's secret? It dumped roughly 24.8 billion litres of raw sewage into the Pacific that same year. Thankfully, the city of Victoria has finally agreed to build a regional sewage treatment plant.

4. Boomers are, um, putting drugs in your water

No, it's not 1969. Baby boomers aren't lacing your water with those kinds of drugs. But the aging boomer population is consuming more pharmaceuticals every year, many of which are excreted with every flush. Environment Canada says over 165 pharmaceuticals and personal care products have turned up in water samples. Sewage treatment plants aren't generally designed to screen out traces of painkillers, birth control or diabetes meds, and as we learned, billions of litres of raw sewage are pumped into waterways with a cocktail of implications for aquatic life. On the bright side, sewage treatment upgrades in Kitchener, Ontario, resulted in a 70% to 100% reduction in intersex fish, according to a 2016 study out of the University of Waterloo.

5. You can buy a million litres of fresh Canadian water for the price of one

Want to become a water bottler and help quench Canada's thirst for 2.4 billion litres of the stuff a year? This country's got some great deals for you. Set up your operation in Quebec and you'll pay just $70 for a million litres of fresh, clean groundwater. Okay, so the price is going up to $503.71 per million litres in Ontario after public outrage boiled over around Nestlé Waters taking millions of litres of groundwater a day from the province for a pittance. (Rest assured, wannabe bottlers, that just means coughing up 1/40th of a penny for every 500 mL water bottle you sell.) But if you're really looking for bargain basement prices, head to B.C., where you can get pristine Canadian groundwater you can bottle and sell around the globe for the low, low price of $2.50 per million litres. That's about the price of a large water bottle at a corner store. Told you it was a steal.

6. Mixing oil and water can get ugly

You've got to hand it to Canadians: they're pretty crafty at extracting oil and gas from between a rock and a hard place. It just so happens that it requires a lot of water to draw oil from tarry sands and force open fissures in shale to extract oil and gas (à la hydraulic fracturing). Industry says it's using 1.5 barrels of Athabasca River water to process every barrel of oil but that 80% to 95% of that gets recycled. Environmental advocates say much of that water ends up in tailings ponds, where federal research has found toxic slurries leaching into groundwater (some estimates suggest a staggering 6.5 million litres a day can leach from a single pond). And with fracking? Once you force that water/ fracking chemical mix into the ground, you don't get it back. Water loss from fracking has been pegged at 17 billion litres in Alberta and seven billion litres in B.C. And if that fracked water seeps into drinking water supplies, then your well water may not only become undrinkable but also flammable. Disturbing, yes, but it does make for a great party trick.

DR. HOWARD OVENS'S 12 WAYS TO MAKE AN EMERGENCY PHYSICIAN HAPPY

Going to the emergency room can be a frustrating experience for anyone waiting for care, but it can be hard on ER physicians too. I've been an ER doc for 35 years at Toronto's Mount Sinai Hospital, a major urban and academic centre. Emergency staff often feel like we're rolling a boulder uphill, providing good care for each patient while trying to catch up with a backlog that is long and growing. Sometimes, when you encounter a new patient with a complex problem that will take a long time to sort out, you can't help but feel your heart sink a bit. Even if the patient is stable, common complaints of pain in the belly or chest have many potential causes, from trivial to life threatening. These usually take time to sort out, and meanwhile the queue is growing.

But then there are those patients who present with problems that can be diagnosed and treated in a few minutes. This not only helps our waiting times, it also makes the patient and their family very happy. They may look at you as a combination of Dr. House and Sherlock Holmes all wrapped into one, and as doctors, we experience at least a brief moment of joy. Here are a dozen of those "joyous" presentations.

Dr. Howard Ovens is an emergency physician at Mount Sinai Hospital in Toronto, and a professor in the Department of Family and Community Medicine at the University of Toronto.

1. Beet it! I
A patient is worried about "blood" in her urine, certain it's cancer. Turns out she's just been eating a lot of beets (there is red dye from the beets in the urine, but no blood).

2. Beet it! II
A patient is worried about "blood" in his bowel movements . . . he, too has been eating a lot of beets (there is red dye in the stool, but no blood).

3. Iron It Out
A patient is worried about bowel movements that are black, the colour of digested blood. But it's more likely the iron supplements she's been taking, or even Pepto-Bismol—it's true!

4. Bloodshot Eye
A patient sees red in his eye and thinks he's having a vision-threatening bleed, or worse, a form of stroke. But the bleeding is in the white (or conjunctiva) of the eye. This is almost always a popped blood vessel, and it's extremely common and benign. Bleeding might come on spontaneously, but for bonus marks, we'll ask the patient if he's been coughing or vomiting—the increased pressure in the veins of the face can be a cause of this condition. Regardless, one glance from us and we're done!

5. Toddler's Elbow

A worried parent brings in her crying toddler, who won't move his arm. *Will he ever paint or play piano?* Probably the toddler was lifted up by his wrists, leading to the common condition of "pulled elbow," a dislocation usually easily fixed—just shake hands with the child and, presto, instant cure! Give the toddler a moment to get over his surprise and hand him a lollipop or something interesting; when he reaches for it with the sore arm, you're a hero! And you can move on!

6. Seeing Shapes

A worried patient fears he is having a stroke, or a retinal tear, maybe; he had some bizarre visual distortions that are freaking him out. But strangely, all is back to normal now, except maybe for a bit of a headache. The shapes he saw? Zigzag lines or lightning bolts, in both eyes—an "optic migraine," or a common variant of migraine headache. If the patient can describe it well, there is no need for any further tests, just some careful reassurance (and maybe some pain relievers for the headache).

7. Hands from Hell

The patient is in agony; her hands are *killing* her with a burning, unremitting pain. The pain came on while cutting hot peppers and no amount of washing helps. Yet the skin looks normal . . . This is a clear case of "Hunan Hands"—skin irritation caused by capsaicin, a chemical in hot peppers. The chemical is not soluble in water, so handwashing won't help. Some oily application like antibiotic ointment or petroleum jelly and all is fine again! What a relief.

8. Be Still, My Heart

A frantic patient's heart is *racing* at up to 200 beats per minute, but he looks fine (albeit anxious). A glance at the patient and monitor tells us it is an SVT—supraventricular tachycardia, a harmless form of arrhythmia. Press in the right spot on the patient's neck or administer a very fast-acting drug (adenosine) and, bingo—cured in less than a minute. (For bonus points, call in your medical students to watch the magic!)

9. Disjointed Finger

A young athlete after contact with a ball or maybe another competitor has a finger pointing in an odd direction and his friends are grossed out. Usually, without even delaying to give a pain reliever, we just give it a pull to cure the dislocation and all is back to normal. (If the patient is lucky, maybe we'll hand him a lollipop—see #5.)

10. A Pain in the Butt

An embarrassed patient comes in with a very painful backside. Hopefully, she has a prolapsed internal hemorrhoid (yes, this is something ER doctors hope for)—a glove and some pressure, and it goes back in, with much relief all around. But even if it's a clotted external hemorrhoid, it will take only a few more minutes to freeze the area, make a small incision and pop the clot. Either way, it's a fast procedure (and the patient is very grateful).

11. Plumbing Problems

The patient with "urinary retention"—usually an older gentleman who has a large prostate and can't pass any urine—arrives in agony. But by the time the doctor gets there, the nurse has cured him with a catheter—all the doc has to do is provide the phone number for follow-up and, voilà, done!

12. Joy Is Fleeting

As I said, pains—belly, head, chest—are usually complex problems to sort out. One exception: any pain that lasts seconds, even if it comes and goes, is nothing serious. Fleeting pains are an emergency room joy!

5 DINNERS OF THE MONTH, 1962

The following is a list of dinners recommended by *Chatelaine* magazine for Wednesdays in October 1962.

1. Wednesday, October 3
   Pan-Fried Liver
   · french fried onions
   · hashed potatoes
   · Brussels sprouts
   · pecan pie

2. Wednesday, October 10
   Cold Sliced Turkey

- mixed pickles
- green salad
- rolls
- banana nutcake
- sliced peaches

3. Wednesday, October 17
   Broiled Frankfurters
   - hot potato salad
   - fried apple rings
   - tomato slices
   - chocolate pudding

4. Wednesday, October 24
   Braised Lamb Chops
   - mixed vegetables
   - chived potatoes
   - lettuce salad
   - pineapple cake

5. Wednesday, October 31
   Steamed Wieners
   - mustard sauce
   - baked beans
   - pickles
   - chef's salad
   - doughnuts
   - hot cider

10 HOUSEHOLD TIPS FROM CANADA'S FIRST DOMESTIC GODDESS, CATHARINE PARR TRAILL

Born into English gentry in 1802, Catharine Parr Traill learned the domestic trades later in life, eventually mastering them in the rough clearings of Upper Canada. In between raising children, sewing clothes and growing and making food, she found the time to write several books filled with insights and advice for pioneer families. *The Female Emigrant's Guide, and Hints on Canadian*

Housekeeping, published in 1855, was a lifeline for thousands of settler families who lacked all mod-cons and shops, even nearby neighbours or roads. Catharine Parr Traill's boundless energy and astute observations about farming, food prep, parenting and running a household make her a role model for the contemporary woman embracing the "lean in" mantra.

1. Clothing

Flannel I also recommend, as an advisable purchase. . . . Good scarlet or blue flannel shirts are worn by all the emigrants that work on land or at trades in Canada; also Scotch plaids and tweeds, strong checks for aprons, and fine white cotton stockings. It is one of the blessings of this new country, that a young person's respectability does by no means depend upon these points of style in dress; and many a pleasant little evening dance I have seen, where the young ladies wore merino frocks, cut high or low, and prunella shoes, and no disparaging remarks were made by any of the party.

2. Seed Sharing

It is always well to save your own seeds if you can. If you have more than a sufficiency for yourself do not begrudge a friend a share of your superfluous garden seeds. In a new country like Canada a kind and liberal spirit should be encouraged; in out of the way country places people are dependent upon each other for many acts of friendship.

3. House Design

Nothing contributes so much to comfort and to the outward appearance of a Canadian house as the erection of the verandah or stoup, as the Dutch settlers call it, round the building. It affords a grateful shade from the summer heat, a shelter from the cold, and is a source of cleanliness to the interior. It gives a pretty, rural look to the poorest log-house, and as it can be put up with little expense, it should never be omitted.

4. Apple Orchards

Not only are apples valuable as a most palatable and convenient article of diet, but also as one of the most wholesome. In a climate where great heat prevails during the summer months, and even later in the fall, the cooling acid of fruit becomes essentially necessary for the preservation of health. Little children can be made to sow the stones of plums, cherries and apple pips in the nursery.

5. Beer

There is nothing that the new settler complains more feelingly of than the want of good beer and ale. Nobody brews beer in their own homes in Canada. Beer can be got in all towns, it is true, but it is not, the emigrants say, like the sweet, well-flavoured home-brewed beer of the English farm-houses. As there is no prohibition in Canada against people malting their own barley, I think it would be wise for every farmer to grow a small quantity of this useful grain, and learn the practice of malting it. The bush settler has, however, little time to attend to malting and brewing. During very hot weather some cooling and strengthening beverage is much required by men who have to work out in the heat of the sun; and the want of it is often supplied by whiskey diluted with water, or by cold water, which when drunk in large quantities, is dangerous to the health, and should, if possible, be avoided.

6. Fried Venison Recipe

Cut your meat in suitable pieces: dust them with flour and season with pepper and salt; fry in boiling lard, or with some nice thin slices of ham or fat bacon. A little seasoning of onion in the gravy may be added, if not disagreeable. A little dust of flour in the pan, with a table-spoonful of boiling water, and a little tomato catsup will make the gravy.

7. Weevil Infestations in Food

There is a small dusky beetle, with two dull red or orange bars across its body, which injures meat more than the flies: it deposits its eggs in the skin and joints. These eggs turn to a hairy worm, which destroy the meat; and unless some precautions are taken, will render it unfit for use. If you find by examining the hams that the enemy has been at work, I would recommend a large boiler or kettle of water, and when it boils, immerse each ham in it for five or even ten minutes. Take them out, and when dry, rub them over with bran or saw dust, and pack them in a box of wood ashes, or of oats, as the Yorkshire farmers do: you will have no trouble with the weevil again.

8. Framed Artwork

A few prints or pictures, in frames of oak or black walnut, should not be omitted. These things are sources of pleasure to yourselves and of interest to others. They are intellectual luxuries, that even the very poorest man regards with delight, and possesses if he can, to adorn his cottage walls, however low that cottage may be.

9. A Flour Barrel Chair

A delightful easy-chair can be made out of a very rough material—a common flour barrel. *(Saw off the staves and pass interlacing ropes through auger holes to form the seat. Finish with soft hay or sheep's wool stuffed chintz.)* Two or three of such seats in a sitting-room, give it an air of great comfort at a small cost.

10. An Ice House

An ice house in so warm a climate as the summer months present, is also a great luxury. . . . A lump of ice put into the drinking water, cools it to a delightful temperature, and every one who has experienced the comfort of iced butter, and the luxury of iced creams, will agree with me it is a pity every housewife has not such a convenience at her command as an ice-house.

10 AFFLICTIONS AND THEIR PATRON SAINTS

1. Cancer

A young 14th-century Italian, Peregrine Laziosi, once demonstrated against the papacy, but was converted and became famous for his preaching and his holiness. When he developed cancer on his foot and doctors were about to amputate, he prayed all night and was miraculously cured. He became the patron saint of cancer victims.

2. Epilepsy

St. Vitus expelled an evil spirit from a Roman emperor's child, and so became the patron of people suffering from diseases typified by convulsions—epilepsy, chorea (or St. Vitus's dance) and other neurological disorders. He is also considered the patron saint of dancers, comedians and actors.

3-4. Hemorrhoids and Venereal Disease

St. Fiacre, a seventh-century holy man who set up a hospice for travellers in France, was known for miraculously healing his visitors of a variety of ills, including venereal disease and hemorrhoids. In addition, cab drivers call on him as their protector because the Hotel St-Fiacre in Paris was the first establishment to offer coaches for hire.

5. Mental Illness

The remains of St. Dymphna, a seventh-century Irish princess murdered by her father when she tried to escape his incestuous desires, are kept in a church in Geel, Belgium. Dymphna became the patron saint of the mentally ill when many insane or mentally handicapped people were cured after visiting her shrine.

6. Paralysis

St. Giles, a hermit who lived near Arles, France, in the seventh century, became the patron of the lame and the crippled. He had protected a deer that was being hunted and took an arrow that had been meant for the animal.

7. Rabies

According to legend, St. Hubert (eighth century) converted to Christianity when during a hunt he saw a stag bearing a cross in its antlers. He became the patron saint of hunters and, because of his connection with wild animals, rabies victims.

8. Skin Diseases

The patron saint of pig herders, St. Anthony was also the fourth-century Egyptian monk who established the world's first Christian monastery. Because pork fat was used to dress wounds, he became the intercessor for people with skin problems. One type of skin inflammation is known as St. Anthony's fire.

9. Throat Infections

St. Blaise (fourth century) cured a young boy who was near death from a fishbone caught in his throat. To this day, Catholics celebrate the blessing of throats. Blaise is also the patron saint of wool combers (his enemies used iron combs on his flesh) and of wild animals (he once lived in a cave among the animals).

10. Toothaches

The intercessor for those with toothaches (and the patron saint of dentists) is St. Apollonia. She lived in Alexandria, Egypt, during the third century, at a time when gangs roamed the city and tortured Christians. When artists drew Apollonia, they showed her holding either a gold tooth or a set of pincers—her teeth were pulled out by a mob when she refused to give up her Christianity.

5-YEAR SURVIVAL RATES FOR 20 TYPES OF CANCER IN 2016

		Total Survival (%)
1.	Thyroid	98
2.	Testicular	96
3.	Prostate	95
4.	Melanoma	88
5.	Breast	87
6.	Hodgkin's lymphoma	85
7.	Bladder	73
8.	Cervical	73
9.	Kidney	67
10.	Non-Hodgkin's lymphoma	66
11.	Colorectal	64
12.	Laryngeal	63
13.	Ovarian	44
14.	Myeloma	42
15.	Stomach	25
16.	Brain and spinal cord	24
17.	Lung	17
18.	Liver	19
19.	Esophegeal	14
20.	Pancreatic	7

Source: Canadian Cancer Society (2016).

5 BODY PARTS NAMED AFTER ITALIANS

1. Organ of Corti

The organ of hearing in the middle ear. Alfonso Corti (1822–78) was an Italian nobleman who studied medicine and anatomy in Vienna, writing his thesis on the cardiovascular system of reptiles. He published his findings on the inner ear in 1851, the year that he inherited estates and titles from his father and retired from scientific research.

2. Eustachian Tube

A tube leading from the middle ear to the throat. Its purpose is to equalize pressure in the ear. It is named after Bartolomeo Eustachio (*c.* 1513–74), considered one of the fathers of anatomy, who lived much of his life in Rome, working as a physician to leading churchmen, including two future saints, Charles Borromeo and Philip Neri. It has been suggested that Eustachio's discovery of the connection between the middle ear and the pharynx was known to Shakespeare and gave the playwright the means of murder (poison poured in the ear) used by Claudius to kill Hamlet's father.

3. Fallopian Tubes

The pair of tubes that conduct the egg from the ovary to the uterus in the female. They are named after Gabriel Fallopius (1523–62), who spent much of his adult life as a professor of anatomy at Pisa and Padua (early attempts to practise as a surgeon resulted in the deaths of several patients, and Fallopius decided that an academic career was a safer option). He coined the word *vagina* and also invented a kind of contraceptive sheath, which he tested out on more than 1,000 men in what was, perhaps, the first medical trial of condom efficacy.

4. Ruffini's Corpuscles

Sensory nerve-endings that respond to warmth. Named after Angelo Ruffini (1864–1929), who used gold chloride to stain microscope slides of anatomical specimens, thus revealing the tiny and sensitive corpuscles. Ruffini began his career as a country doctor but ended it as a professor at the University of Bologna. His major researches were into the embryology of birds and amphibians.

5. Sertoli Cells

Cells of the testis that serve to nourish sperm cells. Named after histologist Enrico Sertoli (1842–1910), who discovered them in 1865, when he was still a postgraduate student of physiology in Vienna. The year after his discovery, Sertoli returned to his native country to fight for Italian forces against an invading army from Austria. His later life was spent as a professor of anatomy and physiology in Milan.

CHAPTER 6

Animals

MARK LEIREN-YOUNG'S 7 CANADIAN WHALES WHO MADE HUGE WAVES

Canada's biggest celebrities don't conquer Hollywood, release bestselling albums or move into 24 Sussex Drive. They live in the oceans, where they enlighten and inspire us—most recently inspiring us to stop taking them out of their natural habitat. Here are seven whales who made huge waves.

Mark Leiren-Young is an author, journalist and playwright. His books include The Killer Whale Who Changed the World *and* Never Shoot a Stampede Queen: A Rookie Reporter in the Cariboo, *which won the Stephen Leacock Medal for Humour.*

1. Moby Doll

When the Vancouver Aquarium set out to harpoon a killer whale (as orcas were then known, and as is still the common term in science) off the coast of Saturna Island, B.C., in the summer of 1964, the plan was to use the corpse as a model for the first anatomically accurate replica of the creature. Killer whales were considered monsters, and there was a machine gun on Vancouver Island to shoot them when they came close to shore. But when Sam Burich took aim at a young whale, his harpoon missed. Instead of landing a kill shot, he'd hooked the five-year-old male, who was mistakenly identified as a potentially pregnant female. Burich removed the whale from the Salish Sea (and his family—later named J-Pod) and took him back to Vancouver. Even though the whale named Moby Doll was publicly displayed for only one day, in a local dry dock, and lived for fewer than three months in the dry dock and then in a makeshift pen constructed by the Canadian military, he introduced us to the world of killer whales and the age of captivity, which began in earnest with . . .

2. Namu

When two fishermen near Namu, British Columbia, discovered a pair of whales in their net in June 1965, they didn't do what most fishermen in B.C. had done for decades when confronted with orcas: pick up their rifles and finish off the creatures. It was less than a year after the Vancouver Aquarium had claimed Moby Doll and changed the economic equation: big cetaceans were worth big money. One whale escaped from the nets, but the other was sold for $8,000 to Ted Griffin, owner of the Seattle Marine Aquarium. Griffin dubbed his new pet "Namu," and he quickly became the aquarium's star attraction. Even though

Namu lived less than a year, he inspired a song, a dance and a movie. He also launched Griffin's career as an orca rustler—along with partner Don Goldsberry. One of their first catches was purchased by SeaWorld in Orlando and named "Shamu"—a name given to dozens of other whales over the decades, including . . .

3. Tilikum

The star of the 2013 anti-captivity documentary *Blackfish*, Tilikum was the first killer whale to truly live up to that name. The whale, originally from Iceland, was displayed in horrific circumstances at a now defunct marine exhibit in Victoria, Sealand of the Pacific. While in captivity there, Tilikum crushed a 21-year-old trainer, Keltie Byrne. In 1992, SeaWorld purchased the whale and Tilikum became the latest Shamu in their stage shows. There, Tilikum killed another trainer, Dawn Brancheau, and a visitor who had snuck into the park after hours to meet the orca. Some whale experts believed Tilikum was clinically psychotic, but that didn't stop SeaWorld from using him as the lead sperm donor for their breeding program. In all, Tilikum had 21 offspring in captivity. He died in 2016, and his story sparked the sea change in North America that led to SeaWorld committing to end its breeding program and stop showing orcas in captivity . . . eventually.

4. Skana

The first killer whale ever displayed at the Vancouver Aquarium was a K-Pod resident captured in the Salish Sea in 1967 by Griffin and Goldsberry. The aquarium wasn't planning to buy a killer whale until they had a proper tank to display one, but Griffin baited the hook by displaying the whale he'd named "Walter" at a boat show in Vancouver. Walter was an instant sensation, and aquarium director Murray Newman took the orca home after the show. There, he discovered that Walter was female. The aquarium's new star was renamed Skana, and Newman hired neuroscientist Paul Spong to study the orca's intelligence. When he was running tests on Skana, Spong realized Skana was testing him, and he became a passionate advocate for his new friend. Spong became the first truly influential opponent of captivity. He declared that Skana and her pod-mates should be known as "orcas," declaring that humans should only call them "killer whales" if we were prepared to call ourselves "killer apes." He convinced Greenpeace leader Bob Hunter to meet Skana, which led to the Vancouver anti-nuke organization changing its mission from protesting nuclear testing to saving the whales.

5. Kavna

Skana was a star—Prime Minister Pierre Trudeau even fed the orca at the height of Trudeaumania. But the Vancouver Aquarium's most famous resident would have to be the beluga known as Kavna . . . yes, *the* baby beluga. Captured near Churchill, Manitoba, Kavna was the inspiration for Canadian children's singer Raffi's bestselling recording. The song imagining the baby beluga swimming wild and free likely inspired more kids to fall in love with whales than any other whale besides Keiko—a.k.a. Willy in *Free Willy*.

6. Moby Josephine

When a finback whale was trapped in a pond near Burgeo, Newfoundland, in 1967, the locals did what people used to do with whales back then—they took out their guns and used it for target practice. Canadian journalist, author and activist Farley Mowat was outraged and turned the whale's plight into an international cause célèbre. Mowat shared the story of Moby Jo's death in *A Whale for the Killing*, an inspiration to all young animal lovers. Mowat went on to become a prominent supporter of eco-warrior Paul Watson and the organization he founded, the Sea Shepherd Conservation Society. One of the Sea Shepherd's first boats was named the *Farley Mowat*.

7. The Beatty Blue Whale

In 1987, a dead 26-metre-long female blue whale—a true leviathan—washed onto the northwestern coast of Prince Edward Island. The P.E.I. government and Canada's Museum of Nature arranged for the 80,000-kilogram creature to be buried. In 2007, the Beatty Museum sent a team to study the remains and realized there was a chance the skeleton could be recovered and preserved. The bones were cleaned and transported to Vancouver by rail where the mammoth was meticulously restored. In 2010, the whale took up residence suspended from the ceiling of the Beatty Museum at the University of British Columbia. It is the largest such display in Canada and one of only 21 such skeletons that can be seen worldwide.

THE CAT CAME BACK: 9 CATS WHO TRAVELLED LONG DISTANCES TO RETURN HOME

The phenomenon of cats travelling long distances to reunite with their owners and familiar homes is well known, but they do stretch credulity. Recent scientific inquiries and "kittycam" research have revealed that cats navigate using some of the same instincts as migratory animals like birds and insects—they use their keen olfactory senses and orient themselves to the sun and magnetic fields. The kittycams (cameras attached to a cat's collar) have also confirmed what most cat owners already know—pussy cats make the rounds, and about 10% of them have a secondary family of sorts whom they milk for food and affection, sometimes staying overnight. Verifying some of these forays has become easy thanks to the microchips implanted by veterinarians. But these long-haul journeys are of a whole other order.

1. Jessie–3,022 kilometres
In 2011, tabby Jessie was taken to a new home with her owners in Berry Springs, near Darwin, Australia. She lingered for a couple weeks, but ultimately hit the road, crossing scorching bush and desert to get back to her original home in Ungarra, 3,022 kilometres south. It took her over a year to return home, and once there she was reunited with her best buddies, two senior cats that the original owners had arranged to leave behind with the new homeowners. Jessie has been invited to stay and is happily ensconced with the new family.

2. Silky–1,783 kilometres
Shaun Philips and his father, Ken, lost Silky at Gin Gin, about 320 kilometres north of Brisbane, Australia. That was in the summer of 1977. On March 28, 1978, Silky turned up at Mr. Philips's house in a Melbourne suburb. According to his owner, "he was as thin as a wisp and stank to high heavens."

3. Howie–1,603 kilometres
In 1978 this three-year-old indoor Persian was placed temporarily at a relatives' house near the Gold Coast in Queensland while his family was vacationing. He got outside and over the course of a year walked back to his family's home in Adelaide, Australia. Said his owner, Kirsten Hicks, "although its white coat was matted and filthy and its paws were sore and bleeding, Howie was actually purring."

4. Rusty–1,529 kilometres
Rusty distinguished himself by setting an American all-time speed record for a cat return. In 1949 this ginger tom travelled from Boston, Massachusetts, to Chicago, Illinois, in 83 days. It is speculated that he hitched rides on cars, trucks and trains.

5. Ninja—1,328 kilometres

Brent Todd and his family moved from Farmington, Utah, to Mill Creek, a suburb of Seattle, Washington, in April 1996, taking with them their eight-year-old tomcat, Ninja. After a week, Ninja jumped over the fence of the new yard and disappeared. More than a year later, on May 25, 1997, Ninja turned up on the porch of the Todds' former home in Farmington, waiting to be let inside and fed. He was thin and scraggly, but his distinctive caterwaul was recognized by the Todds' former neighbours, Marilyn and John Parker. Mrs. Parker offered to send Ninja back to the Todds, but they decided to let him stay.

6. Ernie—966 kilometres

In September 1994, Ernie jumped from the truck of Chris and Jennifer Trevino while it was travelling 97 kilometres per hour down the highway 966 kilometres west of their home. A week later, Ernie showed up at the Trevino home in Victoria, Texas. When Mrs. Trevino called the cat by name, he came forward and rubbed his face against Mr. Trevino's leg.

7. Gringo—773 kilometres

The Servoz family lost their pet tom, Gringo, from their home in Lamarche-sur-Saône, France, in December 1982. The following July they learned that the cat had moved to the French Riviera. Wishing to escape the cold winter, he had made the journey south in a week and appeared at their summer home, where neighbours took care of him.

8. Muddy Water White—724 kilometres

On June 23 or 24, 1985, Muddy Water White jumped out of a van driven by his owner, Barbara Paule, in Dayton, Ohio. Almost exactly three years later, he returned to his home in Pennsylvania. "He came and just flopped down like he was home," said Mrs. Paule. She fed him for three days before realizing he was Muddy Water White, an identification that was confirmed by the local vet.

9. Holly—320 kilometres

In November 2012 Jacob and Bonnie Richter took Holly, a four-year-old stray tortoiseshell they'd adopted as a six-week-old kitten, to an R.V. rally in Daytona Beach. There, Holly bolted out the camper door and stayed away, further spooked perhaps by fireworks the next day. The Richters looked high and low, posted notices and alerted SPCA officials, to no avail. They returned to their home in

West Palm Beach and two months later, Holly showed up in a backyard about a mile from their home emaciated, bedraggled and barely able to stand. Nursed back to health by strangers, Holly was taken to a vet who scanned her and found the identifying microchip. The reunion with the Richters turned tearful when the skittish Holly instantly relaxed when Jacob hoisted her up onto her usual perch on his shoulder.

10 ANIMALS THAT HAVE EATEN HUMANS

1. Crocodiles and Alligators

Both these creatures are effective man-eaters, though the crocodile more so, accounting for approximately 2,000 deaths a year around the world. In the southern states, especially Florida, cases of golfers, joggers and swimmers getting snapped up by alligators draw major media attention, though conservation authorities say they're only responsible for 23 fatalities between 1948 and 2016. Crocodiles were responsible for the most devastating animal attack on human beings in recorded history on the night of February 19, 1945. British troops had trapped 1,000 Japanese infantrymen, many of whom were wounded, in a swampy area in the Bay of Bengal. The noise of gunfire and the smell of blood attracted hundreds of crocodiles, and by evening the British could hear terrible screams. The following morning, only 20 Japanese were found alive.

2. Komodo Dragons

The world's largest lizard, the Komodo dragon can reach 3 metres in length and weigh more than 136 kilograms. They are the top predators on the handful of Indonesian islands where they live. Their prey normally consists of deer, wild goats and pigs, but they will eat anything they can catch, including the occasional human. Komodo dragons devour their prey completely, including the bones. All that was left of a French tourist killed in 1986 was his bloodstained shoes. All that was left of a German tourist eaten in 1988 was his mangled glasses.

3. Black Bears

There are an estimated 750,000 black bears in North American. Smaller and less aggressive than grizzlies, they account for an average of one human death a year. Recent studies indicate that it is solo, hungry males who are likeliest to attack and partially ingest humans, not mothers protecting their cubs.

4. Leopards

Considered one of the most dangerous animals to hunt, the leopard is quick and stealthy and is seldom observed. In the central provinces of India, leopards have been known to invade villagers' huts to find their prey. One, known as the Panar man-eater, is reputed to have killed 400 people. It was shot in 1910 by Jim Corbett, who also killed the Champawat man-eating tigress the following year.

5. Tigers

A tigress known as the Champawat man-eater killed 438 people in the Himalayas in Nepal between 1903 and 1911. Tigers do not usually hunt humans, unless the animals are old or injured, or have become accustomed to the taste of human flesh.

6. Lions

Like tigers, lions do not usually attack humans. Man-eating lions usually hunt in prides, or groups, although occasionally single lions and pairs have become man-eaters. In October 1943, a lone lion was shot in the Kasama District of what is now Zambia after it had killed 40 people.

7. Cougars (Pumas/Mountain Lions)

Cougars have been known to catch prey seven to eight times their own size: a 45-kilogram female has been seen killing a 360-kilogram bull elk. As human populations have expanded into mountainous areas of western Canada and the United States, cougar attacks have increased, with 20 fatalities recorded between 1890 and 2011. In 1994 two female joggers in California were killed and partly consumed by female pumas.

8. Pythons

Pythons are quite capable of killing people, and several such incidents have been reported since the snakes became a trendy pet in the 1990s. However, most reports of pythons actually eating humans have proven untrue. A picture circulating on the Internet of a boy allegedly recovered from a python's digestive tract is a hoax. However, there is at least one credible report. In 1992 a group of children playing in a mango plantation near Durban, South Africa, was attacked by a 6-metre rock python, which swallowed one of them. Craig Smith, the owner of a snake park, declared, "I've dealt with a few cases like this and I always dispel them as absolute rubbish. But in my opinion this one did happen."

9. Sharks

Of the 200 to 250 species of shark, only 18 are known to be dangerous to humans. The most notable are the great white, the mako, the tiger, the white-tipped, the Ganges River and the hammerhead. The best known of all individual "rogue" shark attacks occurred on July 12, 1916. Twelve-year-old Lester Stilwell was swimming in Matawan Creek, New Jersey, 24 to 32 kilometres inland, when he was attacked by a great white shark. Both he and his would-be rescuer were killed. In 10 days, four people were killed over a 97-kilometre stretch of the New Jersey coast. Two days after the last attack, a 2.5-metre great white was netted just 6 kilometres from the mouth of the creek. According to the Florida Museum of Natural History, between 1670 and 2003 there were 833 confirmed unprovoked shark attacks in the United States, 52 of which were fatal.

10. Wolves

Wolves and their prey have been contentious subjects ever since Farley Mowat published *Never Cry Wolf* in 1963. In it, he shares his observations from years of watching wolves in the far north, stating that they are not the apex predators responsible for the decline of caribou herds but sociable hunters that, for the most part, scavenge and prey on small rodents and animals. Still, recent cases of wolves killing and partly consuming humans are on record. Twenty-two-year-old Kenton Carnegie worked in a bush camp in Points North Landing, Saskatchewan, where local wolves were observed eating garbage at the camp's dump site. When Carnegie didn't return from a hike on November 8, 2005, his co-workers went looking for him only to discover his remains, minus 30% of his torso and upper thigh. A thorough coroner's inquiry confirmed it was a wolf pack that had attacked and partially consumed his remains.

13 FASCINATING FACTS ABOUT BEAVERS

The beaver, which has come to represent Canada as the eagle does the U.S. and the lion Britain, is a flat-tailed, slow-witted, toothy rodent known to bite off its own testicles or to stand under its own falling trees. —June Callwood

Beavers have an image problem that stems largely from their instinctive drive to build dams and cause floods. They also defecate in drinking water, leading to giardia (a.k.a. beaver fever) among humans. They feed on crops such as corn and soybeans and have been known to cause considerable damage to forests. But before we write off beavers as chubby, bucktoothed pests, let's not forget their core qualities of industriousness and ingenuity—they are mother nature's chief engineers. And everyone knows they have nice fur (as proven by the fur trade). We offer this list in the hope that we can learn to accept and even honour our national animal with the praise it so richly deserves.

1. Giant beavers roamed Eurasia and North America in the Pleistocene era, rubbing shoulders with mastodons and mammoths. They were 3 metres in length, including tail—just smaller than a Mini Cooper—and weighed up to 360 kilograms.

2. The modern beaver is the second-largest rodent in the world (the capybara of South America is the first). An average adult beaver weighs 16 to 32 kilograms and measures 1.3 metres long, including a 30-centimetre tail.

3. A large adult beaver skin yielded enough fur for 18 beaver hats, popular in the 19th century. Despite this, the beaver was hunted and trapped almost to the point of extinction. They are firmly established once more, thanks to a conservation effort started by Grey Owl, the famous English immigrant who posed as a Métis in the 1930s.

4. Grey Owl claimed to have compiled a "beaver dictionary" by listening to the utterings of his two pet beavers, Rawhide and Jellyroll. He stated that he could recognize 49 words and expressions that were intelligible to all beavers, but the manuscript of this dictionary is now missing and presumed lost forever.

5. Beavers are well adapted to working underwater. A secondary, transparent eyelid allows them to see, and specialized ducts allow them to close off their ears, nostrils and lips so they can chew without drowning.

6. The two chisel-like upper front teeth of the beaver grow continuously and are sharpened by the act of gnawing on trees. They are not "buck" teeth, but point inwards to facilitate chewing wood.

7. Beavers groom themselves constantly to keep their pelt waterproofed with the oil (castoreum) they produce in two glands near the anus. Castoreum

also keeps their soft, fine under-fur from matting. Moisture never penetrates their skin, even after a long time swimming underwater.

8. There is a misconception that male beavers will bite off their own testicles if provoked, which dates back to Aesop's fables. At that time, the beaver was hunted for its castoreum, which people believed was produced in the testicles. A story popular at the time held that beavers would see a hunter coming and would bite off their testicles and toss them to the hunter to avoid being killed. If they were chased again, they would flash the hunter to show that they had already made the "ultimate sacrifice."

9. Contrary to popular legend, beavers do not know how to fell a tree so that it falls in a certain direction. Beaver remains have been found that show that the trees they were chewing fell towards them, pinching and crushing their skulls.

10. The urge to build dams stems from an instinctive aversion to the sound of running water. Beavers will try desperately to stem the flow, thereby flooding their surroundings to create a pond deep enough that the water won't freeze in winter. They eat sticks in these lean months, so they spend the entire fall submerging twigs in the pond and poking them into the muddy bottom to store them.

11. Female beavers do most of the engineering work and lodge planning, while male beavers concentrate on inspecting the structure and patching leaks.

12. Beavers are monogamous and mate for life. They raise their babies together and appear to be able to ride out the rough spots that come with lifelong commitment—occasional philandering rarely leads to a breakdown in the beaver lodge family.

13. Beavers are critical participants in creating and maintaining wetland environments and minimizing damage caused by spring floods.

10 CASES OF ANIMALS BROUGHT BEFORE THE LAW

There has been a long and shocking tradition of punishing, excommunicating and killing animals for real or supposed crimes. In medieval times, animals were even put on the rack to extort confessions of guilt. Cases have been recorded and documented involving such unlikely creatures as flies, locusts, snakes, mosquitoes, caterpillars, eels, snails, beetles, grasshoppers, dolphins and most larger mammals. In 17th-century Russia, a goat was banished to Siberia. The belief that animals are morally culpable is happily out of fashion—but not completely, for even now, these travesties and comedies occasionally occur.

1. What's a Mayor to Do?

In Ansbach, Germany, in 1685, it was reported that a vicious wolf was ravaging herds and devouring women and children. The beast was believed to be none other than the town's deceased mayor, who had turned into a werewolf. A typical politician, the wolf/mayor was hard to pin down, but was finally captured and killed. The animal's carcass was then dressed in a flesh-coloured suit, a brown wig and a long grey-white beard. Its snout was cut off and replaced with a mask of the mayor. By court order, the creature was hanged from a windmill. The weremayor's pelt was then stuffed and displayed in a town official's cabinet, to serve forever as proof of the existence of werewolves.

2. Man 0, She-ass 1

In Vanvres, France, in 1750, Jacques Ferron was caught mid-mount with a she-ass and sentenced to hang. Normally, his partner would have died as well—but members of the community took an unprecedented step. They signed a petition that stated they had known the she-ass for four years, that she had always been well behaved at home and abroad and had never caused a scandal of any kind. She was, they concluded, "in all her habits of life a most honest creature." As the result of this intervention, Ferron was hanged for sodomy and the she-ass was acquitted.

3. A Happy Tail

In 1877 in New York City, Mary Shea, a woman of Celtic origin, was bitten on the finger by Jimmy, an organ-grinder's monkey. Mary demanded retribution, but the judge said he could not commit an animal. Miffed, Mary stormed out of the courtroom, snarling, "This is a nice country for justice!" The monkey, who was dressed in a scarlet coat and velvet cap, showed his appreciation: he curled his tail around the gas fixture on the judge's desk and tried to shake hands with him. The police blotter gave this record of the event: "*Name*: Jimmy Dillio. *Occupation*: Monkey. *Disposition*: Discharged."

4. Canine Convict No. C2559

Rarely in American history has an animal served a prison term. Incredibly, it happened as recently as 1924, in Pike County, Pennsylvania. Pep, a male Labrador retriever, belonged to neighbours of Governor and Mrs. Gifford Pinchot. A friendly dog, Pep unaccountably went wild one hot summer day and killed Mrs. Pinchot's cat. An enraged Governor Pinchot presided over an immediate hearing and then a trial. Poor Pep had no legal counsel, and the evidence against him was damning. Pinchot sentenced him to life imprisonment. The no doubt bewildered beast was taken to the state penitentiary in Philadelphia. The warden, also bewildered, wondered whether he should assign the mutt an ID number like the rest of the cons. Tradition won out, and Pep became No. C2559. The story has a happy ending: Pep's fellow inmates lavished affection on him, and he was allowed to switch cellmates at will. In 1930, after six years in prison (42 dog years), Pep died of old age.

5. Monkeying Around

As recently as January 23, 1962, an animal was called into the courtroom. Makao, a young cercopithecoid monkey, escaped from his master's apartment in Paris and wandered into an empty studio nearby. He bit into a tube of lipstick, destroyed some expensive knick-knacks and "stole" a box that was later recovered—empty. The victims of Makao's pranks filed a complaint stating that the box had contained a valuable ring. The monkey's owner contended before the judge that his pet could not possibly have opened such a box. Makao was ordered to appear in court, where he deftly opened a series of boxes. His defence ruined, Makao's master was held liable for full damages.

6. The Rising Cost of Air Travel

In Tripoli in 1963, 75 carrier pigeons received the death sentence. A gang of smugglers had trained the birds to carry banknotes from Italy, Greece and Egypt into Libya. The court ordered the pigeons to be killed because "They were too well trained and dangerous to be let loose." The humans were merely fined.

7. Free Speech for Felines

Carl Miles exhibited Blackie, his "talking" cat, on street corners in Augusta, Georgia, and collected "contributions." Blackie could say two phrases: "I love you" and "I want my momma." In 1981 the city of Augusta said the enterprise required a business licence and a fee, which Miles refused to pay. He sued the city council, arguing that the fee impinged on the cat's right to free speech. The judge actually heard Blackie say "I love you" in court. However, he ruled that the case was not a free speech issue. Since Blackie was charging money for his speech, the city was entitled to their fee. Miles paid $50 for the licence and Blackie went back to work. He died in 1992 at the age of 18.

8. Death-Row Dog

The long arm of the law almost took the life of a 50-kilogram Akita named Taro, who got into trouble on Christmas Day, 1990. Owned by Lonnie and Sandy Lehrer of Haworth, New Jersey, Taro injured the Lehrers' 10-year-old niece, but how the injury occurred was in dispute. Police and doctors who inspected the injury said the dog bit the girl's lower lip. The Lehrers said the child provoked the dog and that, while protecting himself, Taro scratched her lip. Taro had never before hurt a human being, but he had been in three dogfights and had killed a dog during one of the fights. A panel of local authorities ruled that Taro fell under the state's vicious-dog law and sentenced the Akita to death. A three-year legal nightmare ensued as the Lehrers fought their way through municipal court, superior court, a state appeals court and finally the New Jersey Supreme Court.

While the legal battle raged on, Taro remained on death row at Bergen County Jail in Hackensack, where he was kept in a climate-controlled cell and was allowed two exercise walks a day. By the time his execution day neared, the dog had become an international celebrity. Animal rights activist and former actress Brigitte Bardot pleaded for clemency; a businessman from Kenya raised money to save the dog. Thousands of animal lovers wrote to the Lehrers and offered to adopt the dog. Even the dog's jailer and the assemblyman behind the vicious-dog law interceded on behalf of Taro. But when the courts failed to free the dog, the final verdict fell to Governor Christine Todd Whitman. Although the governor did not exactly pardon the Akita, she agreed to release him on three conditions: Taro would be exiled from New Jersey; Taro must have new owners; and Taro's new owners, or the Lehrers, must assume all financial liability for the dog's future actions. The Lehrers agreed, and the dog was released in February 1994, after spending three years in jail. The Lehrers subsequently found a new home for Taro in Pleasantville, New York. When all the costs of the canine death-row case were added up, the total exceeded $100,000. Taro died of natural causes in 1999.

9. Flying Squirrel in Limbo

Teacher Steve Patterson of Mississauga, Ontario, knew that it was illegal to capture and keep flying squirrels, which roam free in the forests of Canada, but also knew that it was legal to buy them for $200 in the United States, which he did. He planned to use Sabrina the Flying Squirrel for his educational work in the preservation of the species, but not long afterwards, the Canadian Food Inspection Agency told him he couldn't keep the rodent due to the risk of humans contracting monkeypox. Patterson got Sabrina tested and she came back clear, but the agency insisted that the squirrel be deported. Patterson refused and hired attorney Clayton Ruby to defend Sabrina. His local Member of Parliament, Carolyn Parrish, got on the bandwagon and with an online petition a defence fund was established. When the case went before the Federal Court of Canada in October 2004, the judge ruled that there was no serious issue, and Sabrina was granted "permanent residency status" in Canada in March 2005.

10. IKEA Monkey

Photos of a pint-sized Japanese macaque dressed in a shearling coat and diaper wandering an IKEA store in Etobicoke, Ontario, made global headlines on December 9, 2012. Left to wait in the car while his owner, Yasmin Nakhuda, nipped in to make some purchases, dapper Darwin managed to unlock the car door, exit and trace his owner's steps into the store's entryway. There he waited, pacing and agitated, for his human to return as his adorable likeness ripped up the Internet. Authorities were notified and collected seven-month-old Darwin and fined "exotic animal enthusiast" Nakhuda $240 for keeping a prohibited animal. A lengthy court trial ensued during which Nakhuda tried and failed to get Darwin back. Darwin is now living at an animal sanctuary in Ontario with other primates where he spends his days hooting, throwing food and swinging on branches au naturel. Nakhuda currently tends an unusual menagerie of creatures at her Kawartha Lakes, Ontario, home that includes miniature donkeys, alpacas groomed like poodles, tiny marmosets and a wallaroo named Wall-E.

13 UNUSUAL ANIMAL MATING HABITS

According to zoologists and smartphone-carrying tourists everywhere, the courting and sexual habits for this planet's 8.7 million species are getting pretty cray-cray. Competition is fierce, which drives creatures to be very creative in setting the mood, choosing outfits, and getting the music and food options just right. Female and male couplings still top the list of animal action, reflecting the timeless appeal of eggs and sperm. Cases of female-female, or male-male, or even female-male-female-female-male-okay-who's-counting have been observed in over 450 species of vertebrates. This list will orient you to a few ways these creatures get their freak on and occasionally even manage to raise offspring together.

1. Flatworms

These salt-water creatures are hermaphroditic and before mating, must first figure out who is pitching and who is catching. They do this by "penis-fencing," basically waving and jabbing their "swords" into and around each other, until one successfully inseminates the other. These duels can last up to an hour and result in significant tears and gouges in their flesh. The "loser" of the battle carries the eggs to term—Happy Mother's Day.

2. Bowerbirds

The ultimate interior designer, the male bowerbird constructs an elaborate and colourful home, which prospective mates visit and evaluate. Driven to outdo their rivals, males will dance to entice visitors and have bedazzled their interiors with berries, flowers, shells, coins, broken glass, beads and shiny bits of metal. Females base their decisions on rigorous home inspections and his dance moves, of course.

3. Hippopotamuses

Hippos have their own form of aromatherapy. Hippos attract mates by marking territory, urinating and defecating at the same time. Then, an enamoured hippo will twirl its tail like a propeller to spread this delicious slop in every direction. This attracts lovers, and a pair will begin foreplay, which consists of splashing around in the water before settling down to business.

4. Lynx Spiders

When a male lynx spider feels the urge, he will capture his beauty in his web and wrap her in silk. Offering her this elegant meal (the silken web) is his way of wooing. When the mood is right, the female, distracted by her feast, will allow her suitor to mount her and begin mating. Oblivious, she ignores him and enjoys her supper.

5. Penguins

Penguins prefer to be "married," but they suffer long separations due to their migratory habits. When reunited, a pair will stand breast to breast, heads thrown back, singing loudly, with outstretched flippers trembling. Two weeks after a pair is formed, their union is consummated. The male makes his intentions known by laying his head across his partner's stomach. They go on a long trek to find privacy, but the actual process of intercourse takes only three minutes. Neither penguin will mate again that year. The male Adélie penguin must select his mate from a colony of more than a million, and he indicates his choice by rolling a stone at the female's feet. If she accepts this gift, they stand belly to belly and sing a mating song. Stones are scarce at mating time because many are needed to build walls around nests. It becomes commonplace for penguins to steal them from one another. Male penguins have been observed raising a baby penguin together.

6. Hooded Seals

Males of this species can blow a large pinkish air sac out of their nostrils and bounce it around like a balloon. According to the ladies, this is hot stuff, and the larger the nasal balloon, the more successful his chances of passing on his hot genetic action.

7. Porcupines

The answer to one of our oldest jokes—"How do porcupines do it?" "Veeery carefully!—is not quite true. The truth is more bizarre than dangerous. Females are only receptive for a few hours a year. As summer approaches, young females become nervous and very excited. Next, they go off their food and stick close by the males and mope. Meanwhile, the male becomes aggressive with other males and begins a period of carefully sniffing every place the female of his choice urinates. This is a tremendous aphrodisiac. While she is sulking by his side, he begins to "sing." When he is ready to make love, the female runs away if she's not ready. If she is in the mood, they both rear up and face each other, belly to belly. Then, the male sprays his lady with a tremendous stream of urine, soaking his loved one from head to foot—the stream can shoot as far as 2 metres. If she's not ready, the female responds by: 1) objecting verbally, 2) hitting with her front paws like a boxer, 3) trying to bite, or 4) shaking off the urine. When ready, she accepts the bath. This routine can go on for weeks. Six months after the beginning of courtship, the female will accept any male she has been close to. The spines and quills of both relax and go flat, and the male enters from behind. Mating continues until the male is worn out. Every time he tries to stop, the female wants to continue. If he has given up, she chooses another partner, only now *she* acts out the male role. To "cool off," females engage in the same courtship series, step by step, in reverse order. It is advised never to stand close to a cage that contains courting porcupines.

8. Red-Sided Garter Snakes

These small snakes live in Canada and the northwestern United States. Their highly unusual mating takes place during an enormous orgy. Twenty-five thousand snakes slither together in a large den, eager to copulate. In that pile, one female may have as many as 100 males vying for her. These "nesting balls" grow as large as 60 centimetres high. Now and then, a female is crushed under the heavy mound—and the males are so randy that they continue to copulate, becoming the only necrophiliac snakes!

9. Zebra Shark

This one is not quite a mating habit so much as the inclination of one particular zebra shark, Leonie, raised and kept in captivity at an aquarium in Townsville, Australia. Leonie was paired with a male shark in 1999 with whom she mated and produced over two dozen offspring. He was then moved to another tank in 2012, and from that point on Leonie had no contact with any other males. Despite this, Leonie became pregnant and had three babies in 2016. Genetic testing revealed that these offspring had none of her old mate's genetic material, and so it was a case of the shark self-fertilizing an ovum. While this does happen on rare occasions in nature, it was all the more unusual since Leonie had already mated successfully with a male. Immaculate conception, you say? Only her trainer knows for sure.

10. Squid

Squid begin mating with a circling nuptial dance. Pairs of squid revolve around a "spawning bed" 200 metres in diameter. At daybreak they begin having sex and continue all day long—they only take a break so the female can dive down and deposit eggs. When she returns to the circle, the two go at it again. As twilight falls, the pair goes offshore to eat and rest. At the first sign of sunlight, they return to their spot and do it all over again. This routine can last up to two weeks, ensuring a healthy population of squid.

11. Uganda Kob

Exhaustion is the frequent fate of the male Uganda kob, an African antelope. Like many species of birds and mammals, the kob roams in a social group until the mating season, when the dominant male establishes a mating territory, or lek. But the females decide which territory they wish to enter and then pick the male they think most attractive. He then mates with all the females until he is too weak to continue (usually due to lack of food) and is replaced by another.

12. Geese

Two male geese may form a homosexual bond and prefer each other's company to that of any female. Sometimes, however, a female may interpose herself between them during such a courtship and be quickly fertilized. They will accept her, and weeks later the happy family of three can be seen attending to its tiny new-hatched goslings.

13. White-Fronted Parrots

These birds, native to Mexico and Central America, are believed to be the only species besides humans to kiss. Before actually mating, male and female will lock their beaks and gently flick their tongues together. If kissing is satisfying for both parties, the male boldly takes the next step, regurgitating food for his girlfriend to show his love. White-fronted parrots also share parenting, unlike many other species. When the female lays her one egg, both parents take turns incubating it. When the baby hatches, the couple feed and care for their offspring together.

11 CHILDREN WHO MAY HAVE LIVED WITH WILD ANIMALS

1-2. Romulus and Remus (8th century BCE)

Twin brothers Romulus and Remus were allegedly raised by a wolf after being abandoned in the countryside by their uncle. A number of years later they were rescued by a shepherd, and they went on to found the city of Rome in 753 BCE. Scholars long considered their childhood adventures to be mythical, but recent studies of children known to have lived with animals have demonstrated that there could well be an element of truth to the Romulus and Remus legend.

3. Lithuanian Bear-Boy (1661)

In a Lithuanian forest, a party of hunters discovered a boy living with a group of bears. The hunters captured him even though he resisted by biting and clawing them. Taken to Warsaw, Poland, and christened Joseph, the boy continued to eat raw meat and graze on grass. Although he never dropped the habit of growling like a bear, Joseph acquired a limited vocabulary and became the servant of a Polish nobleman.

4. Irish Sheep-Boy (1672)

A 16-year-old boy was found trapped in a hunter's net in the hills of southern Ireland. Since running away from his parents' home as a young child, the boy had lived with a herd of wild sheep. He was healthy and muscular even though he ate only grass and hay. After his capture he was taken to the Netherlands, where he was cared for in Amsterdam by Dr. Nicolaes Tulp. The boy never learned human speech, but continued to bleat like a sheep throughout his life.

5. Fraumark Bear-Girl (1767)

Two hunters captured a girl who attacked them after they shot her bear companion in the mountains near the village of Fraumark, Hungary. The tall, muscular 18-year-old had lived with bears since infancy. Later she was locked up in an asylum in the town of Karpfen because she refused to wear clothes or eat anything but raw meat and tree bark.

6. Wild Boy of Aveyron (1800)

A boy estimated to be 12 years old was captured by hunters when he tried to escape them by climbing up a tree. He had been spotted by residents of Aveyron, France, over the years, and to the best of anyone's knowledge, had lived alone in the forest since he was a young child. Given the name Victor, the boy was taken to live with people offering to provide for him, but he resisted being indoors and repeatedly tried to escape. He also growled and gnashed his teeth at first, but later adjusted to being with humans. He was the subject of intense curiosity by scholars and Enlightenment writers like Rousseau and Hobbes who were writing about the "naturally good or evil state of mankind." When Victor died at the age of 40, he had only managed to learn to say and write a few words, including *lait* (milk) and *oh Dieu* (oh God).

7. Dina Sanichar (1867)

A hunting party found a seven-year-old boy living with wolves in a cave in the jungles of Bulandshahr, India. Taken to the Sekandra Orphanage near Agra and given the name Dina Sanichar, the boy refused to wear clothes and sharpened his teeth by gnawing on bones. For 28 years he lived at the orphanage, but he never learned to talk. In 1895 he died of tuberculosis aggravated by the one human habit he had adopted—smoking tobacco.

8. Misha Defonseca (1945)

When she was seven years old, Misha's mother and father were seized by Nazis. She was hidden in a safe house, but, worried that she might be turned over to the Germans, she ran off and lived in the wild. For the next four years, as the Second World War raged, Defonseca wandered through Europe, covering more than 4,800 kilometres. During this time, she lived on berries, raw meat and food stolen from farmhouses. On occasion, she lived with packs of wolves. She later recalled, "In all my travels, the only time I ever slept deeply was when I was with wolves. . . . The days with my wolf family multiplied. I have no idea how many months I spent with them, but I wanted it to last forever—it was far better than returning to the world of my own kind. . . . Those were the most beautiful days I had ever experienced."

9. Saharan Gazelle-Boy (1960)

Basque poet Jean-Claude Armen discovered and observed a boy who was approximately eight years old living with a herd of gazelles in the desert regions of the Western Sahara. For two months Armen studied the boy, who he speculated was the orphaned child of some nomadic Saharan Moorish family. The boy travelled on all fours, grazed on grass, dug roots and seemed to be thoroughly accepted by the gazelles as a member of the herd. Since the boy appeared happy, Armen left him with his gazelle family. American soldiers attempted to capture the boy in 1966 and 1970, without success.

10. Marina Chapman (1964)

Colombian-born Marina Chapman has written about her extraordinary early childhood spent with a group of capuchin monkeys. Kidnapped at four for reasons unknown to her, then abandoned in the jungle, she survived for five years by learning from the small monkeys what to eat and drink, and how to avoid dangers. She was rescued by hunters and spent the next several years in a Cucuta brothel, serving a Mafia family and on the streets. Rescued from her predicament by a neighbour, Chapman was educated and adopted into a family, and in 1977 moved to Bradford, England, where she worked as a nanny. She ultimately married and had two children. In 2013 she published an autobiography, *The*

Girl With No Name, and was the subject of a National Geographic documentary, *Woman Raised by Monkeys*.

11. John Ssebunya (1991)

Ugandan villagers captured a little boy living with a pack of monkeys. One of the villagers identified the child as John Ssebunya, who had fled the village three years earlier when his father had murdered his mother and then disappeared. John was adopted by Paul and Molly Wasswa, who ran an orphanage. Several experts who studied John were convinced that John really had lived with monkeys. When left with a group of monkeys, he approached them from the side with open palms in classic simian fashion. He also had an unusual lopsided gait and pulled his lips back when he smiled. He tended to greet people with a powerful hug, the way monkeys greet each other. After some time in the orphanage, John learned to talk and to sing. In 1999 he visited Great Britain as part of the Pearl of Africa Children's Choir. That same year, he was the subject of a BBC documentary, *Living Proof*.

AVERAGE ERECT PENIS LENGTHS FOR 10 SPECIES

	Animal	*Average erect penis length*
1.	Humpback whale	3 m
2.	Elephant	1.5–1.8 m
3.	Bull	1 m
4.	Stallion	76 cm
5.	Rhinoceros	60 cm
6.	Pig	46–50 cm
7.	Man	15 cm
8.	Gorilla	5 cm
9.	Cat	2 cm
10.	Mosquito	0.25 mm

Note: The Argentine lake duck averages 40.6 centimetres from head to foot. However, its erect penis size is 43.2 centimetres.

Source: Leigh Rutledge, *The Gay Book of Lists* (Boston: Alyson Publications, 1987).

THE DAY OF EXTINCTION FOR 9 BIRDS

1. Great Auk, June 3, 1844

This large flightless bird similar to a penguin nested along both coasts of the North Atlantic. In Canada, great auks were found in Newfoundland, New Brunswick and Nova Scotia. The great auk was the first bird known as a "penguin"; when explorers from the northern hemisphere came across the similar but unrelated species in the Antarctic, they transferred the name to the new bird. The last recorded breeding place of the great auk was Eldey Island, off the coast of Iceland. At the beginning of June 1844, three men, part of an expedition funded by Icelandic bird collector Carl Siemsen, landed on the island. They found and killed two auks, among other birds gathered on the island's cliffs, and took away an egg, which was later sold to an apothecary in Reykjavik for £9. There has since been no confirmed sighting of a great auk on Eldey Island or anywhere else.

2. Labrador Duck, December 12, 1872

This small black and white duck bred in Canada's Maritime provinces and migrated as far south as Chesapeake Bay in the winter. A strong and hardy species, its decline remains a mystery but is likely due to a combination of a severe reduction in its invertebrate food supply and predation and egg-collecting by humans. The last reported Labrador duck was shot down over Long Island in 1872.

3. Guadalupe Island Caracara, December 1, 1900

A large brown hawk with a black head and grey-striped wings, the caracara was last seen alive and collected by R.H. Beck in 1900. One of the few cases in which a bird was deliberately exterminated, the caracara was poisoned and shot by goatherds, who thought it was killing the kids in their herds.

4. Passenger Pigeon, September 1, 1914

These brownish-grey pigeons were once so numerous that a passing flock could darken the sky for days. As recently as 1810, an estimated two billion pigeons were sighted in one flock. But massive hunting by settlers and a century of forest destruction eliminated the passenger pigeon and its native forest habitat. In 1869, 7.5 million pigeons were captured in a single nesting raid. In 1909 a $1,500 reward was offered for a live nesting pair, but not one could be found. Martha, the last of the passenger pigeons, died of old age in 1914 in the Cincinnati Zoo.

5. Carolina Parakeet, February 21, 1918

The striking green and yellow Carolina parakeet was once common in the forests of the eastern and southern United States, but because of the widespread crop destruction it caused, farmers hunted the bird to extinction. The last Carolina parakeet, an old male named Incas, died in the Cincinnati Zoo. The zoo's general manager believed it died of grief over the loss of Lady Jane, its mate of 30 years, the previous summer.

6. Heath Hen, March 11, 1932

A relative of the prairie chicken native to the East Coast of the United States, the heath hen was once so common around Boston that servants sometimes stipulated before accepting employment that heath hen not be served to them more than a few times a week. But the bird was hunted to extinction, and the last heath hen, alone since December 1928, passed away in Martha's Vineyard at the age of eight, after the harsh winter of 1932.

7. San Benedicto Rock Wren, August 1, 1952

Endemic to a small island off the coast of Mexico, the rock wren went extinct when a volcano threw ash and pumice across the island. The bird was terrestrial, so it was destroyed simultaneously with its habitat when the island erupted.

8. Euler's Flycatcher, September 26, 1955

Known only from two specimens and one sighting, Euler's flycatcher was an 22-centimetre olive and dusky yellow bird. The flycatcher was believed by James Bond (the authority on Caribbean birds, not Ian Fleming's 007) to have perished in Jamaica in 1955, during Hurricane Janet.

9. Dusky Seaside Sparrow, June 18, 1987

This sparrow was once common in the marshes of Merritt Island, Florida, and along the nearby St. John's River. In the 1960s, Merritt Island was flooded to deal with the mosquito problem at the Kennedy Space Center, while the marshes along the St. John's were drained for highway construction. Pesticides and pollution also contributed to the bird's demise. In 1977, the last five dusky seaside sparrows were captured. Unfortunately, they were all male, with no female to perpetuate the species. The five were relocated to Disney World's Discovery Island to live out their last days. The last one, an aged male blind in one eye, named Orange Band, died 10 years later.

RECORD LIFE SPANS OF 25 MAMMALS

	In the wild	In captivity
Bison	20	40
White-tailed deer	10	16
Caribou	15	20.2
Giraffe	25	28
Hippopotamus	50	40
Coyote	14.5	21.8
Grey wolf	16	20
Cheetah	12	17
Tiger	18	25
Lion	15	25
Leopard	12	20
Striped skunk	6	10
Racoon	16	20
Grizzly bear	25	50
Polar bear	30	38
Koala bear	17	20
Grey seal	31	43
Gorilla	50	54
Chimpanzee	60	53
Orangutan	35	50
African elephant	60	80
Spiny rat	2	4.8
Field mouse	1	4.4
Grey squirrel	12.5	23.5

Source: James R. Carey and Debra S. Judge, *Longevity Records: Lifespans of Mammals, Birds, Amphibians, Reptiles and Fish*, Odense University Press, 2000.

JANN ARDEN'S 5 MOST IMPORTANT THINGS YOU NEED TO TRAVEL WITH A 5-POUND DOG

When I was nine years old my dad moved us out to southern rural Alberta. One of the things he promised us kids *and* our mother was that we could get a dog. We picked him out of a litter of nine other puppies from a farm about 40 kilometres from us. My mother named him Aquarius. That was the beginning of my long relationship with dogs and cats and geese and rabbits and birds over these past 45 years. I've had my dear sweet Midi for the last 8 years.

Jann Arden is a Canadian singer, songwriter, broadcaster and author. She's released 12 albums, had 19 top-ten singles and won eight Juno awards including Female Artist of the Year in 1995 and 2001.

1. A fashionable dog bag that looks like a big purse so you can sneak your dog into the fanciest restaurants in any town you happen to be in. (It works every single time because I have a very well-behaved, amazing dog.)

2. A well-fitted black T-shirt that keeps your dog warm on the plane. It can get chilly for takeoffs and landings, especially in the old Beaver planes. I also have a small blanket that always comes in handy, plus a well-fitted black T-shirt for myself.

3. Never be without poo bags. I once had to use a five-dollar bill to pick up my dog's small turd, which was an expensive poo day as you can well imagine.

4. A small pet water bottle. I use one called the Water Rover. Be prepared to drink your dog's slobbering backwash when you go through security 'cause you're gonna forget to empty it every single time. Dogs always need a drink, and so will you.

5. And lastly, treats and a small can of dog food. Customs is always pretty good about letting you bring it over the border if you're up front about it. I've been tempted to eat it myself but have so far avoided that.

8 "VICE-REGAL" PETS BURIED ON THE GROUNDS OF RIDEAU HALL

1. The beloved companion of the Duchess of Connaught, 1914—dog
2. "Moses," friend and companion of Viscount Willingdon, April 29, 1930—dog
3. "Lassie," belonging to Rose, Shane and Brian Alexander (1946–52)—English sheep dog
4. "Tessa," belonging to Rose, Shane and Brian Alexander (1946–52)—English sheep dog
5. "Prince," belonging to Rose, Shane and Brian Alexander (1946–52)—English sheep dog
6. "Cachou," family of Governor General Jules Léger (1974–79)—beagle
7. "Reggie," family of Governor General Edward Schreyer (1979–84)—Irish setter
8. "Kato," family of Governor General David Johnston (2011)—Chesapeake Bay Retriever

7 LARGE ANIMALS DISCOVERED BY WESTERN SCIENCE SINCE 2000

In 1812, the "Father of Paleontology," Baron Georges Cuvier, rashly pronounced that "there is little hope of discovering a new species" of large animal and that naturalists should concentrate on extinct fauna. In 1819 the American tapir was discovered, and since then a long list of "new" animals has disproved Cuvier's dictum. Here are a few of the more recent "discoveries."

1. Three-Toed Pygmy Sloth (2001)

At 3 kilograms and about 50 centimetres long, the pygmy species is the smallest of the three-toed sloths. Discovered in 2001 on a small island off Panama, this slow-moving creature has adapted well to the mangrove swamp habitat by becoming a good swimmer. In the swamp its fur gets coated in green algae that acts as camouflage, protecting it from predators.

2. Highland Mangabey (2004)

A new species of monkey was discovered in 2004 by two separate research teams working in the remote mountains of southern Tanzania. Considered a relative of the baboon family, the highland mangabey is critically endangered, with an estimated population between 500 and 1,000. It has an unusual, gentle "honk bark," a black face and long brown fur that keeps it warm in high altitudes. Tom Butynski, one of the first scientists to spot the monkey in the wild, reported the thrill of seeing it for the first time: "Your mouth drops open and a big smile appears on your face. You say, 'Wow!'"

3. Sunda Clouded Leopard (2006)
Found on two Indonesian islands, Borneo and Sumatra, this wildcat averaging about 20 kilograms was classified as a new species in 2006. It took four more years for biologists to snap a picture of the beautiful leopard with distinctive dark-edged oval spots, stalking through the jungle underbrush. With an estimated 10,000 roaming in a quickly shrinking habitat, the Sunda clouded leopard is considered a vulnerable species.

4. Myanmar Snub-Nosed Monkey (2010)
This critically threatened species of colobine monkey found in parts of China and Myanmar has a long tail, a beard and a small stubby nose. According to local witnesses, raindrops get caught in its nasal passages, causing it to sneeze, so it sits with its head pointing downward between its knees when it rains.

5. Burrunan Dolphin (2011)
Scientists have identified a sub-species of the bottlenose dolphin found primarily in the waters near Victoria, Australia. Measuring approximately 2.5 metres in length, their combined numbers are estimated at 150. The Burrunan dolphin is the third new species of dolphin to be recognized since the late 19th century.

6. Lesula Monkey (2012)
This magnificent species of Old World monkeys was known to locals in the Lomami Basin of the Congo but only confirmed by scientists in 2012. Having distinctive human-like eyes and a naked face, a plush coat with blond and amber patches, and, on the males, bright blue buttocks and scrotum, it's surprising this eye-popping primate did not come to the attention of the outside world sooner. Adult lesula monkeys weigh between 4 and 7 kilograms and are about 50 to 60 centimetres long. Like many primates, they are threatened by loss of habitat and poaching.

7. Little Black Tapir (2013)

Small for a tapir and resembling a pig, this resident of the Amazon rainforest weighs in at an average of 110 kilograms, and measures roughly 130 centimetres long and 90 centimetres tall. The little black tapir may have avoided detection for so long because, like its relatives, it is good at avoiding contact with humans and generally leads a solitary life, sleeping and wallowing in mud by day and foraging for fruit, berries and tender foliage by night.

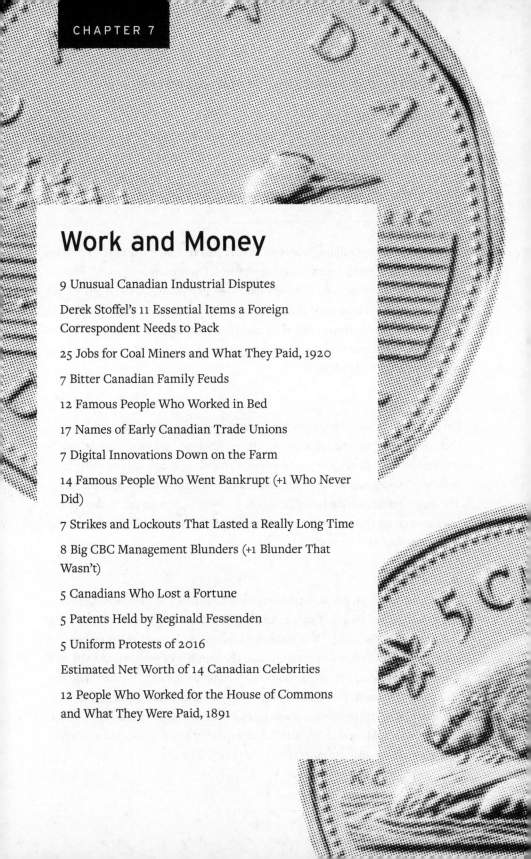

CHAPTER 7

Work and Money

9 Unusual Canadian Industrial Disputes

Derek Stoffel's 11 Essential Items a Foreign Correspondent Needs to Pack

25 Jobs for Coal Miners and What They Paid, 1920

7 Bitter Canadian Family Feuds

12 Famous People Who Worked in Bed

17 Names of Early Canadian Trade Unions

7 Digital Innovations Down on the Farm

14 Famous People Who Went Bankrupt (+1 Who Never Did)

7 Strikes and Lockouts That Lasted a Really Long Time

8 Big CBC Management Blunders (+1 Blunder That Wasn't)

5 Canadians Who Lost a Fortune

5 Patents Held by Reginald Fessenden

5 Uniform Protests of 2016

Estimated Net Worth of 14 Canadian Celebrities

12 People Who Worked for the House of Commons and What They Were Paid, 1891

9 UNUSUAL CANADIAN INDUSTRIAL DISPUTES

1. A Very Thin Blue Line

In Quebec City, on June 25, 1921, 200 policemen and firemen went on strike, demanding a 25% increase in their wages. The city promptly put out a call for unemployed men who wanted to become policemen and firemen. Four days after walking off the job, the strikers were back at work.

2. Silent Nights

Before there were "talkies," theatre owners had to hire musicians to provide the musical accompaniment for silent pictures. On September 5, 1921, a couple dozen musicians went on strike against three movie houses in Calgary. They were protesting the owners' plans to reduce their wages. A mediator from the Department of Labour was called in, and after four days, he arrived at a settlement. The musicians would continue to get the same daily rate, but a half hour was added to their workday.

3. Time This . . .

On April 3, 1930, 50 brass workers, metal polishers and buffers in London, Ontario, walked off the job after spotting "efficiency experts" carrying stopwatches in their plant. They were worried that their boss's idea of being more "efficient" was going to mean they would be forced to work harder and faster. The employer immediately began to hire workers to replace the strikers, causing the men on the picket line to reconsider their position. On April 22, they began heading back to work.

4. Reel Trouble

On August 26, 1931, 80 projectionists were locked out of 19 movie theatres in Montreal, part of a wave of strikes and lockouts involving projectionists across the country in the 1930s. The issue in Montreal, as in most other places, was the attempt by theatre owners to reduce the number of projectionists by half. The old rules called for two projectionists to be on duty at all times. The theatre owners thought they could get by with just one. Some of the strikes were successful, and the projectionists were able to delay the inevitable. But that was not the case in Montreal. Theatre owners quickly hired replacement workers, and the striking projectionists never got their jobs back.

5. Bowling Strikes

In March 1932 six pin boys went on strike against the Bowlerdrome in Prince Albert, Saskatchewan. They were angry that they had been asked to shovel the snow in front of the building without getting paid. The boys were fired the next day. It was the first of nine strikes waged by pin boys in Canada in the 1930s.

6. Playing Around

In July 1937, 500 caddies at the Royal York Golf Club in Toronto went on strike, demanding a raise from 60 cents a round to 75 cents. The strike lasted 11 days, making it the longest of the 19 caddy strikes that hit Canadian golf courses between 1932 and 1939. The Toronto caddies were unsuccessful in getting a pay raise, but they were granted the privilege of playing one free round of golf every week.

7. Butt Seriously...

Twenty-nine construction workers building a road near Coboconk, Ontario, walked off the job on August 16, 1937, as a protest against a "no smoking" order. They returned victorious later that day.

8. Some Like It Hot

Forty furnace-factory workers walked off the job in Ingersoll, Ontario, on October 10, 1951, to protest a lack of heat in the furnace department. They returned the next day.

9. Safety First

Two hundred copper miners in Levack, Ontario, walked out on April 10, 1956, in a protest against wearing safety glasses. They were back two days later, wearing their glasses.

DEREK STOFFEL'S 11 ESSENTIAL ITEMS A FOREIGN CORRESPONDENT NEEDS TO PACK

Derek Stoffel is the CBC Middle East Bureau Chief.

1. Incoming

Flak jacket and Kevlar helmet. You don't leave home without it.

2. Staying in Touch
BGAN satellite phone. You need to get your story in, and the 4G doesn't always work when bullets are flying over your head.

3. Getting There
Maps. I mean the kind printed out on paper. Google Maps doesn't work in war zones, and making the wrong turn can get you seriously messed up.

4. Java
Sachets of Starbucks instant coffee. If you haven't developed a taste for Arabic coffee, you need to bring your own.

5. Chilling
An iPad loaded with some favourite TV shows. After 18 hours covering conflict, you need to unwind. An episode of *30 Rock* or *Seinfeld* helps.

6. First Aid
MedKit (or medical kit); 911 doesn't work in the Middle East and there likely isn't a hospital around the corner.

7. A Shot (the Good Kind)
Small bottle of Scotch. War is hell. You need to take the edge off a bit.

8. $$$$
Cash. Several thousand crisp American dollars. Credit cards don't work when you need to pay a local driver or convince a rebel fighter you need to get past his checkpoint.

9. Heating Up
Sriracha hot sauce. A few small bottles are always tucked away in the depths of my suitcase. Middle Eastern food isn't spicy, so you need a do-it-yourself solution.

10. Looking Good
Medium-blue button-up shirt. Wrinkled somewhat, with sleeves perfectly rolled-up to complete the Dashing ForCorr Look™.

11. Where in the World?

Tracker/Emergency Signal App. Lets your editors know where you are, and can be used to send a distress call when you're being carted off to a dank Turkish jail, as I was in 2013.

25 JOBS FOR COAL MINERS AND WHAT THEY PAID, 1920

In October 1920 the Western Canada Coal Operators' Association signed an agreement with District No. 18 of the United Mine Workers of America. Among other things, the pact outlined what jobs were available for coal miners and what their daily rate of pay would be. The agreement provides an interesting window into life in a Canadian coal mine in the 1920s. Here's a sample, taken from that year's *Labour Gazette*, published by the Canadian Department of Labour.

	Job	Daily Wage
1.	Tail rope engineers	$7.88
2.	Tipple engineer	$7.61
3.	Incline engineers	$7.61
4.	Endless rope engineers	$7.50
5.	Bottom man	$7.08
6.	Tipple dumper (man)	$7.08
7.	Breaker picker boss	$7.08
8.	Fan fireman	$6.85
9.	Screen engine tender	$6.76
10.	Tipple dumpers' helper	$6.75
11.	Top cagers	$6.75
12.	Water tender	$6.71
13.	Washer or tipple oiler	$6.71
14.	Slate pickers (men)	$6.58
15.	Fan men	$6.58
16.	Dirt bank man	$6.58
17.	Rock bank man	$6.58
18.	Wiper (man)	$6.58
19.	Breaker screen (man)	$6.58
20.	Ashman	$6.58
21.	Car oilers (men)	$6.58

22. Car oilers (boys)	$4.40
23. Tipple dumper (boy)	$4.40
24. Slate pickers (boys)	$4.03
25. Tally boys	$4.03

7 BITTER CANADIAN FAMILY FEUDS

There are more than a million family-owned businesses in Canada, and one of the most difficult challenges many of them face is succession. Seventy percent of family firms don't survive into a second generation; 90% don't make it to a third. Predictably, as the stories in this list reveal, the higher the stakes, the more bitter the fight over succession becomes.

1. The Billes Family

The fight for control over the massive Canadian Tire retail empire was one of the longest and most acrimonious in Canadian business history. It was the late 1980s when the three offspring of company founder A.J. Billes began their feud. On one side were brothers Fred and David, who had always assumed that the prize would eventually be theirs. But their middle sister, Martha, had other ideas. She believed she was being excluded because of her gender, and she had no intention of being pushed around by her brothers. After an attempt to sell the company to its dealers failed in 1986, Martha sued her brothers for their shares. The brothers countersued, trying to force Martha to sell her stock to them. The stalemate lasted 10 years, during which time the two brothers saw their sister only for business reasons. The deadlock was finally broken in 1997 when David and Fred sold their shares to Martha for $45 million in cash and shares, resigned from the board and agreed that their children would never inherit the Canadian Tire mantle.

2. The Cuddy Family

Mac Cuddy spent 43 years building his company into one of the world's largest suppliers of turkeys. By the mid-1990s, Cuddy International Ltd., based in London, Ontario, was a $300 million company that controlled 45% of the Canadian processed turkey market. It should have been a nice legacy to hand off to his five sons, but instead, in the late 1990s, a pitched battle began between father and sons. The heart of the dispute was that, for Mac Cuddy, profit was thicker than blood. He was happy to welcome his sons into the business, but he was never confident that any of them had the right stuff to run the company. "You can hire better than you can sire," Mac liked to say, as he went about hiring outsiders to manage the business. His sons, however, didn't like taking orders from non–family members. Ultimately, Mac felt he had no choice but to fire two of them. A third son, Peter, who had previously held an executive position, was reassigned to the job of writing the company's corporate history. Peter responded by quitting and suing his father for misappropriating nearly $12 million of the company's money. The lawsuit was eventually dropped, and the sons went off to find other work, but the distraction caused by the bitter family feud drove the company to the brink of bankruptcy.

3. The Irving Family

Most family feuds among the ultra-rich are, not surprisingly, about money. Whether it's an inter-generational squabble or an intra-generational dispute, the fight is usually about how vast piles of money are going to be divvied up. And there's no doubt that money played a big role in the estrangement between Kenneth Irving and his father, Arthur. But there's one other factor in this case that is rare in these stories: mental illness.

The Irving fortune is estimated at about $8 billion. The family dominates the New Brunswick economy. It is the province's largest employer, owns most of its media outlets and has huge holdings in shipyards, refineries, pulp mills, railway lines and gasoline retailing. The empire was founded in the 1920s by K.C. Irving, who then turned it over to his son Arthur, who in 2000 bequeathed the most valuable part of the empire, Irving Oil, to his oldest son, Kenneth. But by 2009, the relationship between father and son had deteriorated. Arthur had decided to establish a trust, worth an estimated $1 billion, and stipulated that the proceeds of the trust be distributed equally among his five children. Kenneth apparently objected, arguing that as CEO of Irving Oil, he deserved a bigger share of the family pie. The argument over the trust was eventually fought out in a court in Bermuda between 2011 and 2012, but by that time, Kenneth had left his post at Irving Oil, never to return.

It was widely believed that Kenneth's departure was the result of disagreements with his father over the trust and other business decisions. But in a remarkable interview with the *Globe and Mail* in January 2017, Kenneth revealed that he left the family business in 2010 because he had suffered a serious mental breakdown and desperately needed treatment. He believes his father may have never understood the severity of his mental health issues.

Whatever the reason, father and son have not seen each other since 2010. It's a rift that Kenneth would clearly like to heal. "I would happily meet my dad any place, anywhere, any time, to talk about anything he wants to talk about."

4. The McCain Family

Growing up together in Florenceville, New Brunswick, Wallace and Harrison McCain were about as close as two brothers could be. They even shared the same bed. In 1957 they went into business together, and by the 1990s they were both billionaires, having created a food processing company responsible for one-third of the world's frozen french fries. That's when the issue of who would run the company after they were gone raised its ugly head. Wallace saw his son, Michael, as the natural heir apparent. Harrison did not want to turn the company over to Michael. The dispute over succession marked the end of the brothers' close relationship. Wallace left McCain Foods and bought Maple Leaf Foods for Michael to run. For years, Wallace and Harrison did not see each other socially. Harrison eventually turned control of McCain Foods over to another nephew after his own son died in a snowmobile accident. The cold war between Harrison and Wallace eventually began to thaw as Harrison's health deteriorated. Harrison died in March 2004.

5. The Oland Family

There are actually two Oland family feuds here. The first ended in money. The second ended in death.

And it was all about the beer—Moosehead beer from New Brunswick, the last nationally distributed independent Canadian beer. It was a big prize to have, and in 1981, the family patriarch, P.W. Oland, had to choose which of his two sons would run the company after he was gone: Richard (Dick) or Derek. Dick was the logical choice; he was older, after all, but P.W. felt Dick lacked the temperament and the skills for the job, and handed the company to Derek. Dick left to run a trucking company in St. John. But losing the brewery to his younger brother did not sit well, and after P.W. died in 1996, Dick, who was still a large minority shareholder, made life difficult for Derek in the courts and at the company's annual general meetings. The two brothers never fully reconciled.

Meanwhile, Dick's relationship with his only son, Dennis, was also going south. The son never felt he could win his father's approval. But Dennis had financial woes, and he was forced to borrow hundreds of thousands of dollars from his father. He was also upset about Dick's long-running, too public affair with a St. John real estate agent.

Perhaps all of these topics were on the agenda the last time father and son talked at Dick's office on the evening of July 7, 2011. All we know for sure is that at some point that evening someone bludgeoned Richard Oland to death with a blunt object, possibly a drywall hammer. The blood soaked through three layers of flooring into the office below. He was 69 years old.

Dennis was the logical suspect, but for two years police tried to build a case against him without success. His family rallied around him, including his uncle Derek. Finally, in November 2013, police laid a second-degree murder charge against Dennis. The trial began in September 2015 and captivated the nation as the secrets of the Oland family came pouring out. In December, the jury returned a guilty verdict. Dennis was sentenced to life in prison, with no possibility of parole for 10 years. But in October 2016, the New Brunswick Court of Appeal overturned the verdict, and Dennis Oland walked out of jail, awaiting the next chapter of this sordid family saga.

6. The Phelan Family

Most Canadians have never heard of Cara Operations. But they have certainly heard of Swiss Chalet, Second Cup and Harvey's. Those are just three of the more visible parts of the Cara empire, a billion-dollar restaurant and food conglomerate based in Toronto. The company was founded in the 1880s by the Phelan family, but it didn't become a major player in the food industry until it was taken over by Paul J. (P.J.) Phelan in the 1950s. Thinking about succession was never high on P.J.'s list of priorities. Most people assumed that the company would be turned over to his only son, Paul Jr. But those who thought that underestimated the ambition and the tenacity of his two daughters, Gail and Rosemary, and his granddaughter, Holiday. As P.J. became increasingly incapacitated by alcoholism and dementia in the late 1990s, the three Phelan women moved to squeeze Paul Jr. out of the company by buying up his shares and taking the company private. They finally accomplished their objective in February 2004, leaving Paul Jr. on the outside looking in, bitterly reflecting on "the controlling bullies" who had deprived him of his birthright. "You wake up and you're not you anymore," he told a magazine writer after it was all over. "You're not the person you've always been."

7. The Steinberg Family

"I've had so much fun building and running this business," Sam Steinberg once said, "that I wouldn't deprive my family of running it." It is not hard to understand why the patriarch of the grocery store empire would feel that way. Starting with nothing in 1917, by the 1970s he had built Montreal-based Steinberg's into a $4.5 billion giant with 37,000 employees. Sam was determined to keep the business in the family, but out of his four daughters and their husbands, only one was qualified to take over. Rita's husband, Leo Goldfarb, was Sam's chosen successor, although the other sisters objected. After Rita and Leo's marriage broke up, Leo left the company. Rita died of cancer a year later. That left things in the unsteady hands of daughter Mitzi and her underachieving husband, Mel Dobrin. They took over after Sam's death in 1978, but succeeded mainly in alienating employees and other family members. Before long, the bitter family feud became the company's main preoccupation. Its stock and sales nosedived. In 1989 the board finally convinced the sisters to sell their shares for the sake of the company. It was the best decision they could have made. Each of them walked away with $112 million when the company was sold to the Quebec pension fund. Within a few years, Steinberg's was bankrupt, and the pension fund was out $800 million.

12 FAMOUS PEOPLE WHO WORKED IN BED

1. King Louis XI (1423-83)

This French king was ugly, fat and sickly, but also ruthless and clever, earning the title "the universal spider." He introduced the custom of the *lit de justice* ("bed of justice"), a ceremonial appearance of the monarch, in bed, before *le parlement* with the princes of the realm on stools, the greater officials standing and the lesser ones kneeling. No one is sure exactly why he began the practice, but it caught on and lasted until the French Revolution. Fontenelle, a critic of Louis XV, was asked on the eve of the revolution, "What, sir, is a 'bed of justice'?" He replied, "It is the place where justice lies asleep."

2. Leonardo da Vinci (1452-1519)

Leonardo earned unique fame as an artist and scientist, and according to his *Notebooks*, he spent some time each night "in bed in the dark to go over again in the imagination the main outlines of the form previously studied . . . it is useful in fixing things in the memory."

3. Cardinal de Richelieu (1585-1642)

In the last year of his life, the diabolically clever and scheming cardinal took to his bed and stayed there because of his rapidly deteriorating health. This did not prevent him from working—he directed his highly efficient secret police in exposing the treasonous machinations of the youthful royal favourite Cinq-Mars. Nor did it hinder the peripatetic cardinal from travelling—his servants carried him about in his bed, and if the door of the house he wanted to stay in was too narrow, they would break open the walls.

4. Thomas Hobbes (1588-1679)

Hobbes, the great British political philosopher, was renowned for his mathematical approach to natural philosophy and found bed a comfortable and handy place to work on his formulas. He wrote the numbers on the sheets and, when he ran out of room, on his thighs. He wrote his 1661 *Dialogue on Physics, or On the Nature of Air* entirely in bed. Hobbes also sang in bed because, according to John Aubrey's *Brief Lives*, "he did believe it did his lungs good, and conduced much to prolong his life."

5. Florence Nightingale (1820-1910)

Florence Nightingale's claim to fame stems mainly from the two years she spent helping British soldiers fighting in Crimea from 1854 to 1856. Wounded soldiers were more likely to die from infections cause by unsanitary hospital conditions than from injuries suffered in battle. Nightingale helped change all that, and in so doing revolutionized the way medicine was practised on the front lines. But when she returned to Britain in 1857, her health began to deteriorate, and she spent most of the last 50 years of her life in bed, suffering from what most researchers now believe was a chronic case of brucellosis, a disease found mostly in animals, and severe depression. But despite her illnesses and isolation, she remained extraordinarily productive. She was widely recognized as an authority and advocate for health-care reform, and public sanitation. She also wrote and consulted on planning for civilian and military field hospitals.

6. Robert Louis Stevenson (1850-94)

For years Stevenson was racked by coughing spells caused by tuberculosis, and consequently he wrote most of *Kidnapped* and *A Child's Garden of Verses* in bed at his home in Bournemouth, England. Bed sometimes brought him inspiration in the form of dreams. One night his unconscious mind spun "a fine bogey tale," as he called it, based on a real-life criminal he had read about. Stevenson's dream became *Dr. Jekyll and Mr. Hyde*.

7. Marcel Proust (1871-1922)

Bundled in sweaters, a hot-water bottle at his feet, the French author worked to refine his series of novels called *À la recherche du temps perdu* ("Remembrance of Things Past") while lying virtually flat in bed in a cork-lined room. He had all the necessities within arm's reach: more than a dozen pens (if he dropped one, he refused to pick it up because of dust); all of his notes, notebooks and manuscripts; even fumigation powder, which he believed helped his asthma. In spite of all his precautions, he died of pneumonia at the age of 51.

8. Winston Churchill (1874-1965)

Churchill loved to lie abed in comfort for several hours each morning while dictating letters and going through boxes of official state papers. Although he much preferred to write his books while standing up, declining health in his later years forced him to write and correct most of *The Second World War* and *A History of the English-Speaking Peoples* in bed.

9. Mae West (1892-1980)

The legendary sex queen with the hourglass figure was famous for her double entendres. She wrote several of her own screenplays, including *Diamond Lil*, and in 1959 she published her autobiography, *Goodness Had Nothing to Do with It*. She did all her writing in bed, she reported, noting, "Everybody knows I do my best work in bed."

10. F. Scott Fitzgerald (1896-1940)

During the last two years of his life, while writing *The Last Tycoon*, Fitzgerald found that he could work longer hours by staying in bed. He'd retire to bed with a dozen Coca-Colas (which had replaced alcohol in his drinking habits) and prop himself up on pillows. Using a lapboard, he'd work for about five hours a day. A fatal heart attack prevented him from completing *The Last Tycoon*.

11. Frida Kahlo (1907-54)

Painting in bed? It's not usually recommended. Things can get pretty messy. But it's what the great Mexican artist Frida Kahlo learned to do at the beginning of her brilliant career. At age 18, Kahlo was severely injured in a near-fatal bus accident. She suffered several broken bones, and was placed in a plastic corset and confined to bed for three months. To occupy herself during her recovery, Kahlo began to paint in bed using an easel. She placed a mirror above the easel so she could paint pictures of herself. The experience was life-changing. She later said that those months in bed made her realize that what she wanted to do with the rest of her life was "painting things just as I saw them with my own eyes and nothing more."

12. Hugh Hefner (1926-)

It seems appropriate that a man who made his fortune in sex should have done so in bed. For decades, Hefner controlled the Playboy empire from a massive bed in his Chicago mansion, where he stayed awake for 60-hour stretches, fuelled by amphetamines and Pepsi.

17 NAMES OF EARLY CANADIAN TRADE UNIONS

1. Wholesale Boot and Shoemakers Union
2. Cigar Makers' International Union
3. International Union of Machinists and Blacksmiths
4. International Brotherhood of Bookbinders
5. Iron Molders' International Union
6. Coopers International Union
7. Coach Builders' Union
8. Boot and Shoe Workers International Union
9. Bindery Women's Union
10. International Printing Pressmen's Union
11. Toronto Printing Press Assistants and Feeders' Union
12. Journeymen Tailors' Union
13. Female Operatives' Union
14. Brotherhood of Telegraphers
15. Amalgamated Flint Glass Blowers' Union
16. United Hatters of North America
17. The Brotherhood of Carpenters and Joiners

7 DIGITAL INNOVATIONS DOWN ON THE FARM

by Courtney Denard

With only 1% of Canadians engaged directly in growing and raising the food we eat, farmers have to be very productive. To achieve this, farming increasingly involves high-tech inputs and applications. Here are a few innovations happening in a barn or furrow near you.

Courtney Denard is a field reporter for Ontario Farmer Publications and owner/operator of Valleykirk Farms, a family-run dairy farm in Owen Sound, Ontario. Together with her family, Courtney manages a 49-head Holstein milking herd.

1. Driverless Tractors
Autonomous and driverless tractors controlled remotely are here, but so far uptake is slow. The idea has been around since the 1940s, but issues around pricing, insurance, programming and training are giving farmers pause. Still, the potential savings in labour costs are strong incentives, and John Deere and Case IH are blazing the trail. The technology uses GPS and transponders to guide the tractor in a set route programmed into computer controls, and the vehicles are often monitored remotely by a supervisor in a central command position. Safety concerns have also been cited as a strong disincentive, with people on and off farms worried about the possibility of a hayride gone very wrong.

2. Precision Agriculture
In 1900 one farmer produced enough food for 10 people; today they're expected to feed 120 on the same footprint. Precision agriculture makes that job easier by using data collected by computers and GPS installed on their tractors. Farmers now continually harvest data about the moisture and quality of the soil, the changing impacts of drought, heat and rain, and the actual physiology of the ripening crop. These data help farmers make more precise decisions about when to water, fertilize, cultivate and harvest crops. It all adds up to money saved while trying to feed a world population that's projected to reach up to 10 billion by 2050.

3. Inland Aquaculture

Once the exclusive domain of fish farmers located on lakes and coastal waterways, aquaculture is now being practised in landlocked rural areas. The company First Ontario Shrimp, run by the Cocchio family, grows Pacific white shrimp in an enclosed, temperature-stable, saltwater tank system originally built as a hog barn. The Cocchios researched and toured similar operations in the United States before securing an aquaculture licence to import shrimp larvae on their Campbellford, Ontario, farm. The facility features a closed-loop system with zero discharge. With local restaurants and foodies clamouring for delicious, fresh shrimp, and eager to avoid unsustainable international harvesting, this is one high-tech farming trend that's likely to catch on.

4. Milking Robots

Dairy farmers use state-of-the-art mechanical milkers that are computer operated and programmed specifically for the herd. About 5% to 7% of Canadian farmers are making the shift to robotic milkers. The cows wear collars with computer chips that allow them entry into a milking stall on their own volition, day or night, where they're washed, milked and rewarded with a treat—all in about four minutes. The computer tracks how much milk each cow produces and how often they enter the stall, preventing them from being milked too often in case they're just coming through for the treat. Though the start-up costs are steep, robots are becoming more popular because they save farmers untold thousands of hours of labour.

5. Agricultural Drones

Until recently, if farmers wanted to check their crops or fields, they'd walk into their fields and have a gander. It's still something farmers do every day, but with drone technology, they can photograph and monitor large swaths of land in a small amount of time. With more accurate information and readings on moisture, pests and crop growth, farmers can produce more food per hectare. This is especially important given the skyrocketing cost of farmland. Statistics Canada data show that farmland values have increased 13,000% since 1941, taking inflation into account.

6. Smartphones

Many farmers' eyes are cast down looking not at their crops but at their smartphones, the most powerful farm management tool they have. Beyond the obvious convenience of staying connected through social media and email, there's the wildly obvious convenience of not having to run into the farmhouse to make a phone call. Smartphones have facilitated the arrival of "agvocates," savvy social media–using farmers who advocate for themselves and build bridges between the agricultural producers and consumers. Finally, the smartphone is a vital connection to other farmers and dealers with whom they can share data, stay connected and research market projections and prices. Most farming deals today are done from the cab of a tractor or the mow of a hay barn, all thanks to smartphone technology.

7. Farming Apps

Farmers are using thousands of agricultural apps to run more efficient and sustainable farms. Take Dairy Health Check, for example. This app allows dairy farmers to test their milk's bacteria level directly on-farm instead of having to send milk samples to a lab and wait days on end for the results. A laboratory slide of milk is slipped into a specialized device that attaches the iPhone camera to a precision microscope to analyze the sample. Results are transmitted back to the iPhone instantly. Benefits also include improved herd health, increased milk production and a safer food chain for all. There are also apps specifically designed for crop farmers, such as Weed ID, which helps farmers identify invasive plants that have the potential to kill an entire crop. Once a weed is properly identified, farmers can select a suitable herbicide and apply it at the appropriate rate. Doing so is not only more environmentally friendly, it's also more cost effective for the farm.

14 FAMOUS PEOPLE WHO WENT BANKRUPT (+1 WHO NEVER DID)

1. P.T. Barnum (1810-91)

Barnum, who made more than $2 million hawking freaks and wild animals, and who allegedly said, "There's a sucker born every minute," often played the fool himself by making embarrassingly bad investments. The final humiliation came in 1855, when he invested more than $500,000 in the Jerome Clock Co., only to find he'd been swindled again. The loss plunged him into bankruptcy and caused him to contemplate suicide briefly. It also provided a theme for countless moralistic newspaper editorials.

2. Kim Basinger (1953-)

Basinger was forced into bankruptcy in 1993 after losing a lawsuit and being ordered to pay $7.4 million for failing to honour a verbal contract to star in the movie *Boxing Helena*. As a result, she lost the Georgia town of Braselton, which she had purchased in 1989 for $20 million, to her partners in the deal.

3. Lorraine Bracco (1954-)

The actress racked up more than $2 million in legal bills during a six-year custody battle with actor Harvey Keitel over their daughter Stella. The debts forced her to declare bankruptcy in 1999. Despite that, 1999 ended up being a good year for Bracco—she was cast in HBO's *The Sopranos*, which she described as "a big turning point. It allowed me to put myself back on my feet."

4. Gary Coleman (1968-)

When he starred in *Diff'rent Strokes* in the 1980s, Coleman earned $64,000 a week, making him the highest-paid child star of his day. Although he found few roles after the series went off the air, he still had $7 million as of 1990. A bitter legal battle with his adoptive parents (he accused them of stealing as much as $1 million) and ongoing medical problems (he underwent two kidney transplants) drained his bank account. In 1995 he filed for bankruptcy, unable to pay $72,000 in debts. "I can spread the blame all the way around," Coleman said, "from me to my accountants to my adoptive parents, to agents to lawyers and back to me again."

5. Francis Ford Coppola (1939-)

The Oscar-winning director observed, "As they say, cash doesn't stay in my pockets very long." In 1992 he filed for bankruptcy with assets of $53 million dwarfed by liabilities of $98 million. Coppola came back financially in 1993 when he earned $10 million for directing *Bram Stoker's Dracula*.

6. Walt Disney (1901-66)

In 1921 Disney started the Laugh-O-Gram Corp. in Kansas City, Missouri, with $15,000 from investors. But he was forced to file for bankruptcy two years later when his backers pulled out because of problems with New York distributors of his animated fairy tales. Then, in July 1923, Disney left for Hollywood with all his belongings: a pair of pants, a coat, one shirt, two sets of underwear, two pairs of socks and some salvaged drawing materials.

7. 50 Cent (1975-)

You'd think a guy whose mantra is "Get Rich or Die Tryin'" would know how to take care of his money, but that's not the case with rapper Curtis James Jackson III, otherwise known as 50 Cent. In 2015, Jackson filed for bankruptcy, citing debts of $36 million, and assets of less than $20 million. Some of that debt (about $6 million) was owed to a woman who sued Jackson after he acquired a sex tape she made with her boyfriend, added his own commentary and posted it online. In July 2016, a judge approved a plan for the singer to pay back $23 million over five years. But in February 2017, another judge discharged Jackson from bankruptcy after he managed to come up with the $23 million, helped by $13.65 million he received in a settlement of a legal malpractice suit filed against other attorneys.

8. Ulysses S. Grant (1822-85)

Late in life, Grant became a partner in a banking house called Grant and Ward. In 1884 the firm went bankrupt, and the ensuing stock market crash left Grant so buried in debt that he was forced to hand over all his property, including his swords and trophies. Broke and dying of cancer, he spent his remaining days writing his memoirs to provide an income for his widow. Mark Twain published the book, and 300,000 copies were sold door to door. Twain generously offered the former president 70% of the net profits; after Grant died, his wife received $350,000 in royalties.

9. Dorothy Hamill (1956-)

After winning a gold medal at the 1976 Winter Olympics, figure skater Hamill became the first female athlete to sign a $1-million-per-year contract—with the Ice Capades. After the Ice Capades went bankrupt, Hamill bought it in 1993. She was unable to halt the skating tour's continuing slide into financial chaos. She sold the Ice Capades to televangelist Pat Robertson and filed for bankruptcy in 1996 with debts of $1.6 million.

10. M.C. Hammer (1962-)

His *Please Hammer Don't Hurt 'Em* (1990) remains the bestselling rap album of all time. M.C. Hammer earned $33 million in 1991 alone. He spent equally lavishly, buying 17 cars, a Boeing 747 and a racehorse. In 1996 M.C. Hammer filed for bankruptcy with debts of $13.7 million. He had to sell his $10 million mansion, which came with two bowling alleys and an indoor basketball court, at half its purchase price.

11. Burt Reynolds (1936-)

Reynolds was Hollywood's top star from 1978 to 1982. In 1996 he filed for bankruptcy with assets of $6.65 million and debts of $11.2 million. His creditors ranged from the IRS to the firm supplying his hairpieces. Reynolds blamed his financial troubles on an expensive divorce from actress Loni Anderson. "I'm paying the third-highest alimony and child support in the world," he told NBC's *Dateline*. "And the only two ahead of me are sheiks." In addition, the divorce hurt his reputation, costing him endorsement deals with Quaker State Oil and the Florida Citrus Commission.

12. Mark Twain (1835-1910)

Twain lost around half a million dollars on a wide range of inventions that included steam generators and marine telegraphs. But his downfall came when he decided not to invest $5,000 in Alexander Graham Bell's telephone company because he saw possibilities in the Paige typesetting machine. Ultimately, he backed its inventor with more than $250,000. The machine complicated rather than simplified the typesetting process, and in 1894 Twain's losses caused him to declare bankruptcy.

13. Mike Tyson (1966-)

The youngest heavyweight champion in boxing history, Tyson earned an estimated $300 million during his career. He spent extravagantly on mansions, cars, gifts for his entourage, even a pair of Bengal tigers. In 2003 he filed for bankruptcy with $23 million in debts, including $13.4 million to the IRS, $4 million to British tax authorities, $300,000 to a limo service and $173,000 to a Las Vegas jeweller.

14. James Abbott McNeill Whistler (1834-1903)

Whistler often had to borrow money or pawn his pictures to pay his debts. When a bill collector would come and carry off one of his chairs or beds, Whistler did not get upset; he simply drew a picture of the missing piece of furniture on the floor where it had stood. A bailiff who had taken possession of Whistler's house was once joshed into dressing up as a butler and serving tea for Whistler and his friends. But such madcap antics could not prevent the inevitable, and on May 8, 1879, Whistler went bankrupt with debts of $10,000.

+1 Who Never Did: Donald Trump (1946–)

Let's be clear. Donald Trump the person has never declared bankruptcy. As for Donald Trump's companies, well, that's a different story. Trump boasts (?) that his companies have declared Chapter 11 bankruptcy four times, but an investigation by the *Washington Post* revealed that in fact, the correct number is six times. It turns out that Trump was counting the first three cases as one. Under Chapter 11, a corporation can continue to operate while it is restructuring and reducing its debt, but the assets of the corporation's shareholders and directors are not at risk. So Donald Trump has never lost any money through bankruptcy, which is probably why he has described his use of the bankruptcy laws as "brilliant."

7 STRIKES AND LOCKOUTS THAT LASTED A REALLY LONG TIME

1. Local 145 of the Communications, Energy and Paperworkers Union vs. the Montreal Gazette

DURATION: 9 years

The newspaper employed 200 typographers in the mid-1980s, but by 1993 there were only 74 left. The company offered separation incentives to the workers. Sixty-three accepted; 11 refused and were locked out. The main issue was job protection in the face of technological change. On May 13, 2002, after being locked out for nine years, the 11 workers accepted management's offer.

2. The International Typographical Union vs. the Toronto Star, Toronto Telegram and Globe and Mail

DURATION: 8 years

This strike began in July 1964 as a relatively minor dispute over the issue of automation in the newspapers' composition rooms. There had been two years of negotiation before the strike was called, and most issues had been settled. But the union headquarters in the United States apparently wanted to make Toronto a testing ground for upcoming battles over technological change in the industry. The papers used managers and strikebreakers to continue publishing. In 1965 the workers voted to return to work, but management refused to take back 27 who had been involved in incidents on the picket line, and the other workers would not go back without them. By the time the dispute was settled in 1972, many of the striking workers had lost their life savings.

3. Local 950 of the United Steelworkers of America vs. Goldcorp Inc.

DURATION: 3 years, 10 months

The longest strike in Canadian mining history proved to be a disaster for the unionized miners. One hundred and eighty-seven workers went on strike at the company's mine in Red Lake, Ontario, on June 23, 1996, over job security and safety. But after nearly four years on the picket line, the union concluded that the company was not interested in settling the dispute at the bargaining table. The settlement that was finally reached in April 2000 offered employment for only 45 miners at a neighbouring mine, and they could no longer be represented by a union. The other workers received a generous severance package.

4. The International Typographical Union vs. the Vancouver Province

DURATION: 3 years, 6 months

Printers belonging to the International Typographical Union walked off their jobs at the Vancouver *Province* in June 1946. The action was actually part of a much larger strike against Southam papers in Hamilton, Winnipeg, Edmonton and Ottawa. In each case, the issue was the union's demand for a five-day week for all its members. The Vancouver strike was by far the most acrimonious and damaging for the company. The *Province*, the largest paper in the Southam chain, did not publish for the first six weeks of the strike. When management then tried to put out a paper using replacement printers brought in from other Southam papers, there were mass demonstrations in Vancouver's Victory Square. Trucks were overturned, papers set on fire and replacement workers roughed up. A full-scale riot broke out on July 22, and 17 people were arrested. Eventually, management was able to get a regular daily edition of the paper published, but not before thousands of readers had deserted the paper and it had fallen into second place behind its rival, the *Sun*. In 1947 a judge declared the strike illegal and ordered the union to pay the company $10,000 in damages. But the dispute dragged on until late 1949, when the two sides finally reached a settlement and the company agreed to waive the $10,000 payment.

5. Local 6917 of the United Steelworkers of America vs. S.A. Armstrong

DURATION: 2 years, 8 months

S.A. Armstrong is a major manufacturer of industrial pumps in Toronto. The strike by 76 workers began in April 1996, and the company immediately took advantage of new laws passed by Ontario's Conservative government that allowed for the use of replacement workers to keep the plant running. With little incentive to settle, the strike dragged on until 1999, when the workers eventually agreed to substantial wage cuts, as much as $3 an hour in some cases.

6. Local 9176 of the United Steelworkers of America vs. Crown Metal Packaging

DURATION: 1 year, 10 months

If you drink your beer out of a can, chances are you're familiar with the product produced by Crown Metal Packaging (formerly Continental Can). The highly profitable U.S.-based multinational, which operates 140 plants in 41 countries, makes cans for more than 120 different beers, including Molson, Labatt and Coors.

In September 2013, 120 workers at a Crown plant in north Toronto walked off the job after the company demanded pay cuts from its workers and declared that new hires would receive 42% less than current employees. The plant had recently been declared Crown's safest and most productive in North America.

The strike dragged on for 22 months, over two bitterly cold winters. In the end, the striking workers got some improved severance and pension provisions, and they were given the option of returning to work, but at substantially reduced salaries for them and all future hires.

On July 19, 2015, the strikers voted narrowly to accept the agreement. Many long-time employees were not planning to return to work, and they were afraid the company would withdraw the enhanced pension and severance terms if they rejected the deal. "We're pleased that the strike's over," commented Lawrence Hay, the Steelworkers' lead negotiator. "We're not so pleased with the terms and conditions."

7. Local 4 of the Canadian Association of Smelter and Allied Workers vs. Royal Oak Mines

DURATION: 1 year, 7 months

This strike/lockout at Royal Oak's Giant Mine in Yellowknife was one of the most bitter and violent in Canadian labour history. In May 1992, 234 gold miners voted to strike, but Royal Oak's president, Margaret Witte, chose to lock them out the day before the strike was to begin and bring in replacement workers to keep the mine operating. This set the stage for months of escalating violence and sabotage that culminated on September 18, 1992, with a bomb explosion in an underground mine shaft that killed nine of the replacement workers. A striking miner was eventually convicted of setting the bomb. In November

1993, the Canadian Labour Relations Board ruled that the company had been bargaining in bad faith and ordered the two sides to come to an agreement. The miners returned to work a month later.

8 BIG CBC MANAGEMENT BLUNDERS
(+ 1 BLUNDER THAT WASN'T)

Jane Farrow and Ira Basen had nothing to do with the compilation of this list. In all their years at the CBC, neither of them can recall a single blunder made by CBC management. Much of the information below comes from the book *The Microphone Wars: A History of Triumph and Betrayal at the CBC* by Knowlton Nash. Blame him if you must.

1. The Quebec Producers' Strike (1958)
The worst strike in CBC history, and one of the most significant strikes in the history of Quebec, began on December 29, 1958, after a producer of French children's programming refused a reassignment and began organizing his fellow producers. But CBC management did not believe producers had the right to unionize, so 74 producers hit the picket lines, backed by other Quebec unions. They were expecting a quick resolution to the dispute, but the CBC dug in its heels, at one point even sending out letters of dismissal to all the producers still on the picket line. The strike became a *cause célèbre* among Quebec artists and intellectuals. In February, a full-scale riot broke out in front of the CBC building. The strike finally ended eight weeks after it began, with the producers winning the right to bargain collectively. The whole unhappy incident seriously damaged the CBC's reputation in Quebec, fuelled French-Canadian national-ism and helped set the stage for the Quiet Revolution. It also boosted the public profile of one of the strike leaders. His name was René Lévesque.

2. Cancelling Preview Commentary (1959)
The CBC has always prided itself on its "arm's-length" relationship with the government. It is, after all, a public broadcaster, not a state broadcaster. But there have been times when CBC management has allowed the distance between it and its political masters to shrink to uncomfortable lengths. One such occasion was in June 1959, when the CBC came under attack over a radio program called *Preview Commentary*. Prime Minister John Diefenbaker and others in the Conservative government believed that too many of the

opinions expressed on the program were critical of government policy. Word came down to acting CBC president Ernie Bushnell that "heads will roll" unless something was done about the program. All of the parties involved denied that direct political pressure had been applied by the government, but the president was clearly spooked. Without consulting the programmers involved, Bushnell abruptly cancelled the program. When the CBC board endorsed the decision, several senior managers and dozens of producers resigned in protest. As the outrage spread across the country, the board reversed its position and ordered the program back on the air.

3. The Seven Days Firings (1966)

This Hour Has Seven Days had been a thorn in CBC management's side since its debut on October 4, 1964. It was irreverent, unconventional, sometimes taste-less, highly opinionated and hugely popular with everyone except politicians in Ottawa. They were not fond of the show's withering "hot seat" interviews. The show's unpopularity in Ottawa caused CBC management many sleepless nights. Finally, in April 1966, Bud Walker, who ran the English TV network, met with one of the show's hosts, Patrick Watson, and fired him and his co-host, Laurier LaPierre. The decision touched off an unprecedented wave of outrage from viewers and from inside the CBC. A subsequent report by a parliamen-tary committee was highly critical of CBC management's conduct in the firing of the two hosts. By July 1966 Bud Walker was gone, but so too were Watson, LaPierre, their producer Douglas Leiterman and their program.

4. Cancelling Don Messer (1969)

CBC management is forever looking for ways to attract a "younger audience," and almost every time it tries, it winds up getting itself into a whole bunch of trouble. One of the most dramatic examples occurred in 1969 with the decision to cancel the popular musical program *Don Messer's Jubilee* after more than 30 years on CBC radio and television. "I am bloody well going to kill the geriatric fid-dlers," boasted program director Doug Nixon, who then proceeded to notify the much-beloved Messer of his program's cancellation by sending him a telegram. And even though the popularity of *Don Messer's Jubilee* was not what it used to be, the decision, and the crude way in which it was undertaken, sparked howls of anger from loyal viewers. Demonstrations were held in front of Parliament Hill and at CBC offices in Ottawa and Toronto. MPs rallied to Messer's defence, but to no avail. Don Messer's days at the CBC had come to an end.

5. Prime Time News (1992)

For more than a decade, the combination of *The National* and *The Journal* had been a popular destination for Canadian TV viewers between 10 and 11 p.m. But by 1990 a new management team had taken over, led by a new president, Gérard Veilleux, and it was looking to "reposition" the TV network. Veilleux, his powerful communications chief, Robert Pattillo, and Ivan Fecan, the head of English TV, had concluded that "from a marketing point of view, *The National* and *The Journal* just don't make sense." So in 1992 they made two fateful decisions. They cancelled *The Journal* and merged the unhappy staff of that current affairs program with the people who had been producing the news. Then they changed the name of the show to *Prime Time News* and moved it to 9 p.m. The result was a ratings disaster. Seventeen percent fewer people watched *Prime Time News* than had watched its predecessor. By 1994 *The National* was back, and so too was its 10 p.m. start time.

6. The Valour and the Horror (1992)

The Valour and the Horror was a series of three documentaries produced by two of Canada's leading filmmakers, Terence and Brian McKenna, and broadcast on the CBC in January 1992. The documentaries took a revisionist look at the record of Canada's military leadership during the Second World War, and found it wanting. It was predictable that Canadian war veterans were going to be unhappy with the series. The only question was, once the inevitable political firestorm began, would CBC management stand behind the films it had partially paid for and agreed to broadcast? The answer, for the most part, was *no*. In November 1992 the McKennas suffered a setback when the CBC ombudsman ruled that the series was "flawed" and didn't measure up to CBC standards. President Gérard Veilleux responded by apologizing and promising that the corporation's "scrutiny of programming of this kind will be improved substantially." To many CBC journalists and members of the public, Veilleux's comments smacked of management interference in CBC journalism. The *Globe and Mail* attacked the "servile timidity of the CBC." Ultimately, the series went on to win several awards, and historians generally supported the filmmakers' interpretation of events. But the controversy dealt a serious blow to Veilleux's credibility and that of other senior managers.

7. Cancelling Regional TV News (2000)

In 2000, after years of devastating budget cuts that saw hundreds of millions of dollars lopped off the corporation's budget, CBC management decided to cancel all regional TV supper-hour newscasts and replace them with a single national supper-hour news program. Many of these newscasts were not highly rated, which may have led some managers to believe that their presence would not be greatly missed. Wrong! Two thousand people protested outside the CBC building in Charlottetown, P.E.I. Their anger was echoed by MPs of all parties who rose up to condemn the decision. In the face of mounting opposition, CBC management backtracked—but only a little. In May 2000, it announced that 14 half-hour regional news shows would be added to the national broadcast, but the new hybrid program failed to attract much of an audience. Nationally, the CBC lost 200,000 viewers in that time period. In some parts of the country, ratings have dropped by more than 50%.

8. The Jian Ghomeshi Sex Scandal (2014)

Where to begin? Maybe they never should have hired him in the first place. There were enough stories circulating of Ghomeshi inappropriately hitting on women during his university and rock star days that red flags might have gone up way back then. But he was good at what he did, and when CBC management went looking for a show and a host that could reach a younger, hipper audience, it created Q and installed the former musician and TV personality as its host. But there was more to the job than just being behind the mic. Ghomeshi was to be the new face of CBC: younger, social media–savvy, non-white. Between April 2007, when the show debuted, and Ghomeshi's firing in the fall of 2014, he was everywhere, on and off the air. Ghomeshi was on a fast track to the stars, and CBC management was only too happy to help him get there.

Which is perhaps why managers ignored for too long reports coming out of the program unit about the host's bullying and abusive behaviour, and inappropriate behaviour towards women all over town. To its credit, when presented with video evidence of Ghomeshi's violent sexual practices, CBC management fired him immediately. But it then dropped the ball again. A botched investigation into what happened cost two senior managers their jobs, and damaged the reputation of others.

Jian Ghomeshi wasn't the first "difficult" CBC host to get a free pass from management; he was just the worst. CBC management has pledged there will now be zero tolerance for host misbehaviour, but no chase producer who has ever been yelled at by their host believes that's likely to happen.

+ 1 Blunder That Wasn't: Hockey Night in Canada

Sometimes a decision that looks like a blunder might not actually be one. Sometimes, not having much money to throw around can be an advantage. In November 2013, the National Hockey League announced it was ending its association with the CBC and entering a new partnership with rival Rogers Communications, selling the English-language broadcast rights to all NHL games for the next 12 years for the staggering price of $5.23 billion. The NHL's partnership with the CBC went back more than 60 years, and the public broadcaster made an aggressive offer to continue broadcasting hockey, but in a time of budget cutbacks and shrinking ad revenues, there was no way the CBC could match Rogers' bid.

When the deal was announced, many critics faulted CBC management for letting its signature broadcast slip through its fingers, but from the perspective of 2017, the CBC's decision not to break the bank to keep *Hockey Night in Canada* is looking pretty smart. Rogers has struggled with declining ratings and weaker than expected ad revenues. Many observers now believe it probably overpaid for the NHL rights, and will have a hard time making a profit over the length of the contract.

It was the second time in five years that CBC management had dodged a bullet when it came to *Hockey Night in Canada*. In 2008, the CBC lost the rights to the iconic *Hockey Night in Canada* theme when it was outbid for the rights to the song by rival CTV, owner of TSN. It was reported that CTV may have paid as much as $3 million for the right to use the theme on its hockey broadcasts in perpetuity. The public broadcaster had negotiated for months with the song's composer, but in the end, the CBC walked away, declaring that the theme was simply not worth that kind of money. The CBC was criticized for losing a song that had opened *Hockey Night in Canada* since 1968, but it turned out to be a wise decision. When Rogers won the rights to the NHL in 2013, CTV was stuck with a $3 million song, but no hockey broadcasts.

5 CANADIANS WHO LOST A FORTUNE

1. Charles Bronfman
FORTUNE LOST: $2.8 billion over 18 years

Poor Charles Bronfman. As odd as that might sound, it's hard not to feel a bit sorry for a guy who watched his starry-eyed nephew blow a sizable chunk of the family fortune chasing his showbiz fantasies. The Bronfman empire used to be based around two reliable money-spinners: booze and chemicals. But in the late 1990s, Charles's nephew and company president Edgar Jr. decided to sell off both Seagram and the family's 25% ownership of DuPont to invest in the glamorous but highly unstable world of Hollywood. He bought into movies (MCA Inc.) and music (PolyGram), and struggled to make money in both. Then, in 2000, he essentially swapped about $7 billion in Seagram's shares for a stake in the French water utility company Vivendi SA, whose president, the egomaniacal Jean-Marie Messier, had showbiz aspirations that rivalled Edgar's. But the deal went horribly wrong. Vivendi sank under a load of debt, reducing the value of the Bronfmans' stake from $6.8 billion in June 2000 to under $1 billion just two years later. As for Uncle Charles, *Canadian Business* pegged his net worth at $5.3 billion in 1999, making him the fourth-wealthiest man in Canada. By 2016 his rank had slipped to 35th, as his net worth had plummeted to a paltry $2.5 billion.

2. Robert Campeau
FORTUNE LOST: $10 billion OPM (other people's money) in four years

In the 1970s and '80s, Robert Campeau was one of Canada's most successful developers, but between 1986 and 1988 he bit off way more of the Big Apple than he could chew. He took advantage of Wall Street's love affair with junk bonds and leveraged buyouts and managed to borrow more than $10 billion to buy two major U.S. department store chains, including New York's fabled Bloomingdale's. But simply servicing the debt would have cost over $800 million a year, and by 1990 Campeau's deck of cards had collapsed, leaving 10,000 employees without jobs and about 300,000 vendors and suppliers unpaid. Campeau himself was on the hook to the Bank of Montreal for $30 million, but he never allowed that small detail to get in the way of his opulent lifestyle.

3. Jim Cohoon

FORTUNE LOST: $500,000 in 77 days

In September 1986, Jim Cohoon was a ship's hand on a freighter tied up in Thunder Bay when he discovered he had won $500,000 in the lottery. What followed was a whirlwind of reckless spending and extravagant acts of charity as Cohoon made his way back to his home in Nova Scotia. He began by giving $1,000 to a hooker in Thunder Bay. "It made her happy for one night," he remarked. Then there was the $50,000 he gave to a drifter he met outside the Salvation Army in Toronto, the $50,000 to one friend and the $100,000 to another. At that rate, it wasn't going to take long for Jim to kiss half a million dollars goodbye. Sure enough, 77 days after his spree began, Jim Cohoon was in Ginger's Tavern in Halifax with a total of $11 to his name. "I mean, it's gone and I don't have it," he remarked philosophically, adding, "I would have done it different if I hadn't been drinking so much."

4. The Eaton Brothers

FORTUNE LOST: more than $700 million in 13 years

There was no single bad decision that led to the collapse of the Eaton retail empire. Rather, it was more than a decade of mistakes by four brothers who, in the end, were not smart enough, focused enough or motivated enough to make the difficult choices that could have prevented Canada's oldest and most established department store chain from disappearing from the landscape. There is no need to hold a tag day for George, Fred, John Craig and Thor Eaton; they are still very wealthy men. But the decline in their fortune has been precipitous. Between 1992 and 1999 their net worth dropped by more than half a billion dollars. For decades, the Eatons had been listed among Canada's richest families, but by 1999 their ranking in *Canadian Business* magazine's list of wealthiest Canadians had dropped to 55th, and by 2005 they were no longer even in the top hundred.

5. Sir Henry Pellatt

FORTUNE LOST: $17 million in 13 years

At the dawn of the 20th century, Sir Henry Pellatt bestrode the Toronto business world like a colossus. His companies held monopolies on the city's electricity and public transit, and he was poised to begin developing the massive hydroelectric potential of Niagara Falls. By 1911 his fortune was estimated at $17 million, or about a quarter of a billion dollars in today's money. But by 1914

Sir Henry's world was beginning to collapse. He lost his electrical monopoly when Ontario opted for public ownership. His real estate schemes foundered when war broke out, and he sank $3.8 million into building his castle, Casa Loma, in Toronto. By 1924 he was $1.7 million in debt. He had to surrender his castle to the city when he could no longer afford to pay the taxes. By the time of his death in 1939, he had almost no money left, but thousands lined the streets to watch the funeral procession of a man who had dreamed big—and fallen spectacularly.

5 PATENTS HELD BY REGINALD FESSENDEN

Ask most Canadians to identify Reginald Fessenden (1866–1932), and you're likely to be met with blank stares. Those who do know him would probably name the Quebec-born inventor as one of the fathers of modern radio, and they would be correct. On December 24, 1906, he made wireless history by transmitting readings and music from a station in Massachusetts. But his radio achievements, as impressive as they were, barely begin to capture the creativity and prescience of a man who was probably the greatest "out of the box" thinker Canada has ever produced, although to be fair, he lived almost his entire life in the United States, where he filed for more than a hundred patents. Many of them never got to market. Many others were pilfered by other inventors, and Fessenden spent years in court seeking compensation. Here are five of his lesser-known patents that demonstrate both how eclectic and far ahead of the curve he often was.

1. U.S. Patent 1,002,141, "Determining Positions of Vessels" –August 29, 1911

"The invention herein described relates to means for locating the position of ships at sea more especially during nighttime and cloudy or foggy weather."

Navies began to incorporate submarines as part of their arsenal in the early years of the 20th century, but their usefulness was limited. They had no good way of locating ships and other dangerous obstacles in their path. The need for effective underwater sonar detection for subs and ships was brought home in tragic fashion when the *Titanic* hit an iceberg and sank in 1912. Fessenden's sonar device, built in 1914, used an electromagnetic moving-coil oscillator that emitted a low frequency, and then switched to a receiver so it could capture the echo coming off the object. It could detect an iceberg from 3 kilometres away, but because the frequency was so low, it had trouble locating precisely where it was.

2. U.S. Patent 1,576,735, "Infusor for making tea"–March 1926

"My invention relates to the making of infusions, such as tea, and has for its objects greater efficiency, convenience, reliability, uniformity, purity, economy, cleanliness and avoidance of deterioration of the infusive material and prevention of fraud."

The tea bag was already in widespread use when Fessenden came up with his idea for a tea "infusor," which he believed would overcome two of the bag's greatest deficiencies: it was unsanitary because the bag's cloth collected dirt, and it facilitated fraud because he had observed that "some restaurants served the same bag to more than one guest." Fessenden's idea was for "tea money," a perforated thin aluminum foil disc that held the tea leaves, about the size of a silver dollar. The "tea dollars" worked much the same way tea bags did—boil water and insert into cup—but because they were sealed and not made of cloth, they could not be tampered with and would presumably be more sanitary.

3. U.S. Patent 1,863,841, "Method and Apparatus for Coordinating Radio and Phonograph Reproductions"–June 21, 1932

"My invention relates to improving the efficiency of radio and wire telephone and phonograph reproduction, and more especially to co-ordinating these methods of reproduction, and still more especially to convenience in said co-operation and to the production of new effects and results thereby."

It seems hard to imagine now, but the arrival of radio in the 1920s fuelled fears that the era of recorded music would soon be over. Sound reproduction was initially much truer on radio than on phonographs. But the shift from acoustic to electric recording and reproduction gave the recording industry the ability to compete with radio, and by the late 1920s some companies were building units that housed both radios and record players, using a common speaker. Fessenden wanted to make it easier to go from listening to a phonograph to listening to the radio, and improve the sound quality of both. His patent called for wiring a speaker mechanism into the back of a piano or violin, and fastening its vibrating element to the back of the sound board, effectively using the musical instrument as a speaker.

4. U.S. Patent 1,882,183, "Means for Parking Cars"–October 11, 1932

"The present invention relates to means and methods of parking cars, particularly motor vehicles in garages, or in public or private parking spaces."

With this patent, Fessenden seems to be taking on the age-old problem of trying to park a large vehicle in a very confined space. The patent application describes a device that is similar to a turntable on wheels. It would allow cars to be parked more closely together than they could be if they needed room to back in and out and turn around on their own.

5. U.S. Patent 1,901,503, "Rotary Brush"—March 14, 1933

"My improvement relates to motor-driven brushes, more particularly adapted to be used for cleaning the teeth, and characterized in particular by being detachable and driven from a flexible shaft."

The product Fessenden was envisioning was a direct precursor to today's electric toothbrush. There would be a driveshaft with detachable brushes, but unlike today's devices, the motor would not be encased inside the shaft. Instead, there would be a small motor suspended from a swinging arm attached to the wall of the bathroom.

5 UNIFORM PROTESTS OF 2016

1. Bunnings Warehouse, New Zealand

In March 2016, workers at 29 Bunnings Warehouse stores in New Zealand took off their shop aprons and vowed not to put them back on until they had reached an agreement with the company on the issue of "rostering," a practice that would allow managers to set shifts without consulting employees. Bunnings is a giant Australian-based chain of hardware and home renovation stores. Workers were expected to wear shop aprons while on the floor, but to protest the slow pace of negotiations, they showed up for work without them. The company responded by suspending the apronless employees, a move that outraged union representatives. "To send them away on no pay for taking off an item of clothing, even though they are prepared to do all their other duties, proves the point that workers have been making all along, that this dispute is about power and control," declared union representative Maxine Gay.

2. WNBA Players, United States

In July 2016, players on three Women's National Basketball Association teams—the Indiana Fever, the New York Liberty and the Phoenix Mercury—showed up on court before their games wearing black warm-up shirts rather than shirts featuring their teams' logos. The move was made to protest recent police violence against black people in several American cities. The league responded by fining each of the teams $5,000 and each of the players $500, although it later decided not to collect the fines. "While we expect players to comply with league rules and uniform guidelines, we also understand their desire to use their platform to address important societal issues," WNBA president Lisa Borders explained.

3. NFL Players, United States

The summer of 2016 saw another uniform protest by a group of professional athletes. The National Football League's Dallas Cowboys showed up at training camp with a decal stuck to their helmets that depicted the team's logo and the words "Arm in Arm." It was a gesture of solidarity with the Dallas police force. Five Dallas police officers had been killed earlier that summer when a sniper opened fire on them following a peaceful Black Lives Matter protest. But the NFL cried foul and declared the decal to be in violation of the league's uniform policy. The players complied, but were not happy with the decision. "I understand the NFL has uniform rules and guidelines they have to follow," declared Cowboys tight end Jason Witten, "but that still doesn't mean we aren't going to support and honor our community and stand arm in arm with them now and in the future. The decal not being on the helmet is not going to stop that."

4. Chris Sale, United States

Chris Sale, the star pitcher of the Chicago White Sox, made quite a fashion statement on July 23, 2016. For that evening's game, team management had asked players to wear the uniforms worn by the White Sox during the 1976 season. Teams frequently get their players to wear these "throwback" uniforms during the season, mostly as a marketing tool to sell more jerseys. The problem was that the 1976 Sox uniforms are widely considered to be among the ugliest in baseball history. Instead of the sleek, collarless look preferred by players today, these shirts had spread collars and were so billowy that on slender players like Sale, they looked like nightshirts. When Sale discovered that he would have to wear the throwback jersey during a game for which he was scheduled to be the starting pitcher, he decided to take matters into his own hands. He went into the clubhouse while the team was taking batting practice and cut up the shirts so the players would not be able to wear them during the game. Management was not amused, and pulled Sale from the lineup.

5. Montreal Police, Canada

The dispute between the Montreal police force and the Quebec government began in July 2014, when the government tabled a proposal that would require police officers to contribute more to their pension plans. The cops took exception to the proposal, arguing that those kinds of changes needed to be settled through collective bargaining. Police are legally prohibited from striking, so they turned to other, more colourful forms of protest. Instead of wearing their regulation police trousers, officers showed up for duty wearing camo pants, leopard-print leggings, pink clown pants, and other decidedly non-official-looking trousers. The pension reform was approved by the Quebec National Assembly in December 2014, but the protest continued. In 2016, the Quebec government threatened to introduce legislation to force police to put their regulation pants back on. It never followed through, possibly because many experts believe the law would not have stood up in court. They argue that not wearing a regulation uniform is a legitimate form of protest protected by the liberty of expression and opinion provision of the Charter of Rights and Freedoms. But the government's patience eventually ran out. In May 2017, it introduced legislation to end the protest. It called for fines of between $500 and $3,000 a day for officers who weren't wearing regulation pants on duty.

ESTIMATED NET WORTH OF 14 CANADIAN CELEBRITIES

	Name	Estimated net worth	Source
1.	Kevin O'Leary	$400 million	investopedia.com
2.	Celine Dion	$380 million	forbes.com
3.	Keanu Reeves	$350 million	celebritynetworth.com
4.	Justin Bieber	$244 million	moneynation.com
5.	Wayne Gretzky	$200 million	therichest.com
6.	Kim Cattrall	$75 million	celebritynetworth.com
7.	Drake	$60 million	forbes.com
8.	Alanis Morissette	$45 million	therichest.com
9.	Gordon Lightfoot	$30 million	celebritynetworth.com
10.	Don Cherry	$12 million	therichest.com
11.	Milos Raonic	$5.8 million	moneynation.com
12.	Stephen Harper	$5 million	therichest.com
13.	Eugenie Bouchard	$3.3 million	therichest.com
14.	Justin Trudeau	$1.2 million	huffingtonpost.ca

12 PEOPLE WHO WORKED FOR THE HOUSE OF COMMONS AND WHAT THEY WERE PAID, 1891

Number		Job	Pay
1.	1	Chief messenger	$1,300/year
2.	1	Assistant to the chief messenger	$1,000/year
3.	1	Curator of reading room	$800/year.
4.	1	Doorkeeper	$500/year
5.	2	Night watchmen	$600/year (each)
6.	1	House carpenter	$700/year
7.	45	Sessional messengers:	$250/year (each)
8.	16	Pages	$1.50/day (each)
9.	4	Servants (washrooms)	$2.00/day (each)
10.	11	Permanent charwomen	.50/day (each)
11.	15	Sessional charwomen	.50/day (each)
12.	1	Gasman (during sessions)	$125/year

Source: *Canada Estimates for the Fiscal Year Ending June 30, 1891.*

CHAPTER 8

Sex, Love and Marriage

FIRST SEXUAL ENCOUNTERS OF 17 PROMINENT CANADIANS

Just about everyone can recall their first sexual experience. But even years after the event, it's a story most of us will share only with our closest confidantes. Rarely are people prepared to tell their tale to the outside world. Even rarer are those who feel compelled to include it in their memoirs or published diaries. So let's be grateful to those few brave Canadians (almost all of whom, predictably, are men) who have chosen to share their adventures with us. Without them, this rather unusual list could not exist.

1. Pierre Berton, author, journalist and broadcaster

In August 1939 Berton was a 19-year-old virgin working at a mining camp in Dawson City, Yukon. It was Discovery Day in the Yukon, a time of much drinking and debauchery. Berton was well fortified with gin when a friend suggested they visit one of the local brothels, a small log cabin rented by two enterprising women from Juneau, Alaska, in town to make some quick cash during the holiday. "I don't remember much about it because it all happened so quickly," Berton wrote in his autobiography. "One moment she was sitting on my knee, the next she was scrubbing my genitals in a china basin in the bedroom." "Not that way, sport," the woman counselled after Berton awkwardly threw himself on top of her. Two minutes later, it was all over, and Berton was back in the parlour with his buddies.

2. Earle Birney, poet

At the age of 16, Birney visited a brothel in his hometown of Banff, where he paid for the services of a young prostitute named June Nightingale. Birney later wrote, "My girl, young but motherly, seemed unaffectedly pleased to be priestess at my deflowering."

3. Toller Cranston, figure skater

In the summer of 1968, Cranston was a 19-year-old virgin, working on his skating in Lake Placid, New York. "Mrs. S." was the mother of one of his fellow skaters. She was 36, unhappily married, sexually frustrated and very interested in young Toller. He shared none of those feelings for her, but one evening Mrs. S. drove Toller home from practice and followed him into the house. "She lunged from hand to thigh to crotch within less than a minute," he wrote in his autobiography. "She undid my fly with amazing dexterity and without a moment's hesitation, performed oral sex on me." Many years later, Toller wrote that he believed the encounter with Mrs. S. had left its mark. "My first experience was in many ways destined to repeat itself for the next thirty years in a series of clinical, physical encounters with no overtones of love and romance."

4. Hume Cronyn, actor

The location was a brothel on Ste-Catherine Street in Montreal. The girl was named Michelle. It cost $3. "She lay back on the bed, held out her arms and the whole business was completed in perhaps sixty seconds," Cronyn wrote in his autobiography. He then paid another $3 and got to do it again. "It was neither a glamorous experience nor a disgusting one. It wasn't the best way, nor was it the worst. I'm not prepared either to bless or to judge it."

5. Peter Gzowski, broadcaster

Things weren't working out very well in the romance department for the teen-aged Peter Gzowski. Just as he entered high school in Galt, Ontario, and started to become interested in girls, he developed a horrible case of acne on his face and back. His nickname at Galt Collegiate was "Pus." Girls stayed well away, especially on the beach. Except for one. She was "an apple-cheeked daughter of a farm family on the edge of town," and it was there, in the barn, that she pinned Peter "to the barnyard sod and brought a hitherto unknown—well, unknown in someone else's company—feeling" to his loins.

6. Margaret Laurence, author

Margaret Wemyss had been dreaming about having sex since the age of 14, but in the highly restricted rural Manitoba world where she grew up, girls simply did not engage in sex before marriage. And so it was not until she married Jack Laurence on September 13, 1947, that the opportunity presented itself. Even though Margaret and Jack had been living in the same house, she was still a virgin on her wedding night. But that didn't seem to pose a problem. "Not only did we love one another, we wanted one another," she later recalled. "Our love and our love-making were marvellous, amazing."

7. Irving Layton, poet

Layton's deflowering was supposed to occur with a $1 black prostitute at a brothel in Harlem. He had been taken there by his brother, who felt it was time young Irving expanded his range of life experiences. But nothing happened.

"She was interested in poetry," Layton later recalled, "so I read her some. She liked it."

8. Ashley MacIsaac, fiddler

By the time he was 12 or 13 years old, MacIsaac had already figured out that "I wasn't exactly the same as all the other boys." While his friends were fantasizing about *Playboy* centrefolds, MacIsaac's fantasies included naked men. But growing up in a small, conservative and heavily Catholic town in Cape Breton, he had no way of knowing what it meant to be gay, and no opportunity to act out his fantasies. After he turned 16, MacIsaac got a car, and he would drive to Halifax to play music and cruise for sex. His first sexual experience was in the back seat of his Pontiac Parisienne. His partner was a clothing store clerk from a local mall. "It wasn't a real relationship, and it wasn't hard core, but it was my first real gay encounter, and I knew then that there was no going back."

9. William Lyon Mackenzie King, prime minister

It is probably only fitting that Mackenzie King's sex life would be as opaque as almost everything else about the man. Nowhere in his copious diaries does King ever explicitly mention sex, but some historians have seized upon a particularly intriguing entry in the summer of 1894. By then, King had developed a particular interest in Toronto's prostitutes. Like the good social reformer he was, he wanted to save them from a life of degradation. Sometimes he would even pray with them. But on one night, the 20-year-old King may have been down on his knees for reasons other than prayer. He had taken a "little stroll," when something happened that deeply disturbed him. "I wish I could overcome sin in some of its most terrible forms," the future prime minister wrote, but now he realized that he was "very weak." The following night's diary entry was even more suggestive. "I feel very sorry for something I did last night. What kind of man am I to become?" We will never know what great weakness King succumbed to that evening. There are several possibilities. But historian C.P. Stacey is convinced that he knows the answer. "It can hardly be doubted," Stacey wrote, "that these 'strolls' were visits to prostitutes."

10. Rita MacNeil, singer

In 1964, Rita MacNeil was 20 years old, living in Toronto, and just starting to perform on stage when she met her first love. He was Italian, and very handsome, but there were two points of contention between them. She wanted to become a singer, and he didn't want that; and he wanted to have sex, and she didn't. Finally, one night in a park in Toronto's east end, he threatened to leave her for good if she didn't have sex with him right there. She gave in. "I was frightened. It seemed rough and painful, and it seemed wrong. It felt dirty to me . . . there was no real pleasure in it for me," she wrote in her 1998 memoir *On a Personal Note*. "It seemed to me that everything had changed that night and I wasn't sure it was for the best."

11. Greg Malone, actor, writer, activist

Greg Malone attended a boys-only Jesuit-run high school in St. John's, in the 1960s, when studying Latin was still an important part of the curriculum. And it's probably safe to say that not many students enjoyed studying their Latin textbook as much as Greg. He liked to fantasize about being a Roman slave owner, and the main attraction in the textbook was an ink drawing of a slave wearing a short tunic that barely covered his muscular legs. Finally, Greg's fantasy reached its climax. As he wrote in his 2009 memoir *You Better Watch Out*,

> I took the slave into the shade of the villa to administer some light punishment for some imaginary infraction. The strong surge between my legs was not unfamiliar, but now it burst over me like electricity, and I felt the full force of its pleasure. The fact of the final climax was a shocking and dizzying revelation and at the sight of the virgin white semen, tears sprang without warning to my eyes, and I wept in defeat.

12. Murray McLauchlan, folk singer

McLauchlan was just beginning his career as a folk singer when he enjoyed his first sexual tryst. The girl was a classmate from his Toronto high school. The two young lovers were playing hooky from school one afternoon when they ended up in McLauchlan's bed in his parents' home. "I was a deaf-mute in a minefield, praying for guidance," he wrote in his autobiography. "She gave it to me! She taught me the dance steps slowly, carefully, one by one. She laughed good-naturedly at my clumsiness and eased me through my nervousness." When it was over, McLauchlan and friend fell asleep in his bed, which is where they were when his sister discovered them. She never told their parents about what she saw.

13. Farley Mowat, author

Mowat's sexual awakening occurred one Saturday afternoon in the cellar of his Saskatoon home. Having recently arrived with his family from Ontario, 12-year-old Farley was taken down to the cellar by an older boy he had met. Mowat later wrote that "he introduced me to bestiality, onanism and homosexuality all in one fell swoop by first masturbating his dog, then himself, and finally me."

14. Peter C. Newman, journalist and author

Newman saved his first sexual experience for his wedding night. He was 21 years old in May 1951 when he married his first wife, Pat McKee. His best man had warned him against getting married without first discovering if he and his fiancée were sexually compatible. "Why would you buy a horse you haven't even tried to ride?" he asked Newman. But Newman didn't listen. Pat and Peter spent their opening night at the Statler Hotel in Buffalo, New York. Pat retired to the bathroom and emerged moments later wearing an oversized nightgown that looked like "a Bedouin tent," her hair was in a net, and her face was slathered with Noxzema. "We somehow managed The Act," Newman recalled in his memoirs, "after which Pat rolled over and turned off the light."

15. Christopher Plummer, actor

For 17-year-old Christopher Plummer, it seemed the stars were perfectly aligned. This would be the night he would lose his virginity. First there was the girl: "the local nympho, raver, sex fiend, you name it," he wrote in his lively 2008 memoir *In Spite of Myself*. "She was tall, skinny, long of leg, not pretty, but outrageously kinky!" Then there was the setting: the back of the balcony of the local Montreal movie house. The movie was Plummer's favourite, *Laura*, starring Clifton Webb as a priggish radio host who falls in love with a beautiful young woman and ends up killing her (he thinks) rather than lose her to another man. Plummer had already seen the movie six times and prided himself on knowing all of Webb's lines.

The evening started well. In the theatre "her hands were everywhere, her tongue beating at the door of my taut terrified mouth." On the walk back to her house, she put her hands in Plummer's pants pockets and "what she didn't do with her fingers as we waddled along the streets was nobody's business." But then it all fell apart. Instead of going with the flow, Plummer summoned up a Clifton Webb line from the movie. "Young woman," he told her, "you must gain for yourself a modicum of control." The girl was not amused. "You selfish fuck," she screamed. "All you think of is yourself." She slammed the door in his face, leaving "a frustrated Clifton Webb standing all by himself, shivering in the Arctic night as dry and celibate as the ice under his feet."

16. Neil Young, musician

That old cliché that young men start playing rock and roll in order to get laid did not seem to apply to Winnipeg's Neil Young. "I don't think I got laid for fuckin' years after I got into rock and roll," he once lamented. "I think I was in Fort William when I got laid. Me and a nice little Indian and a deejay. The first time was not really that great . . . at least I didn't get any diseases. So it was good."

17. The Weeknd, singer

The Weeknd was 16 years old, still in high school in Scarborough, Ontario, and still known as Abel Tesfaye when a friend in college took him to a toga party. He met a girl, told her he was a student at York University, and the rest is a sordid bit of history. "I could have been a student at fuckin' McDonald's, she was so drunk," he told *Rolling Stone*. "I was drunk too. It was the worst experience of my life. Losing your virginity to an older woman sounds good, but it was kinda like, 'Oh shit, it's done?'"

4 CANADIAN POLITICIANS WHO RUSHED TO THE ALTAR

1. George Brown

Brown was 43 years old when he met Anne Nelson in Edinburgh in September 1862. He proposed five weeks later, and they were married on November 27.

2. Wilfrid Laurier

Wilfrid Laurier had loved Zoé Lafontaine for several years, but when she became engaged to another man, he left Montreal and moved to Athabasca to practise law. On May 12, 1868, he received a telegram requesting that he return to Montreal on "a matter of urgent importance." When he arrived the following morning, he was informed that Zoé had changed her mind about whom she wanted to marry. Wilfrid and Zoé were married at 8:00 that same evening.

3. John A. Macdonald

John A. began dating his cousin Isabella shortly after she moved to Kingston with her family in the summer of 1843. They were married on September 1, 1843.

4. William Lyon Mackenzie

The firebrand editor, reformer and first mayor of Toronto married Isabel Baxter three weeks after first meeting her.

ROMANTIC MUSINGS OF 4 CANADIAN PRIME MINISTERS

1. Sir John Thompson (prime minister, 1892-94)

"Now your ugly coward boy that nobody likes but Annie and that nobody ever did like but Annie, is far away. . . . I wish I could give you a kiss now and get a box on my ears and then a hug and a kiss and be called your darling."
—24-year-old Thompson to his future wife, Annie Affleck (December 3, 1869)

2. Sir Wilfrid Laurier (prime minister, 1896-1911)

"I love you so much. You have no idea. My love is not flashy or noisy, but it is deep. My mouth says little, but my heart feels greatly. I do not know how to define the effect you have on me. When I am close to you, I feel happy, serene, calm. . . . You have been my good angel, indeed, you have made me do all that you wanted me to do, you have led me and it goes without saying, you have always led me in the right path."
—Written to his wife, Zoé (1867)

3. William Lyon Mackenzie King (prime minister, 1921-26, 1926-30, 1935-48)

"She is, I think, the purest and sweetest soul that God ever made. She is all tenderness and love, all devotion, knows nothing of selfishness and thinks only of others. . . . The more I think and see of her the more I love her and the greater I do believe her to be. She is young too in heart and feeling as a girl of 15, in beauty she is wonderfully fair. Everyone looks with admiration on her."
—Writing about his mother, Isabel King (1900)

4. R.B. Bennett (prime minister, 1930-35)

"I shall think tonight as I journey west of a week ago and the sunlight. . . . And I will be sad and pity myself and be thankful that I know you and grateful for all you have meant to me . . . it would so please me to see your handwriting and have a few words from you. . . . I miss you beyond all words and I am lonesome beyond cure without your presence and so I go on with all my love."

—To Hazel Kemp Colville, a young, wealthy, attractive widow whom Bennett courted in 1932–33. She refused his offer of marriage, and he remained a bachelor for the rest of his life.

9 NAKED AND NOTEWORTHY WOMEN IN CANADIAN HISTORY

1. Bare-Breasted in Battle

Eric the Red's illegitimate daughter Freydis travelled from Iceland to the shores of present-day Newfoundland twice, first as a colonist and then as the leader of an expedition and fighting force. It was during her first sojourn in "Vinland," as they called it, that she engaged in battle with the Natives. For the most part the Vikings had been getting along with the Beothuks, but when relations soured, the newcomers beat a retreat—right past Freydis's house. Vulnerable and outnumbered, the very pregnant Freydis tried to ridicule and shame her Viking countrymen into standing their ground. When that failed, she picked up the sword of a fallen comrade, brandished it at the Natives, then stroked her bare breasts with the blade and charged them. According to legend, the Natives turned and ran.

2. Naked Doukhobor Demonstrations

Seven thousand Doukhobors settled in Saskatchewan in 1898–99 after they were expelled from Russia for resisting military conscription. Their religious beliefs emphasized pacifism, frugality, equality and industriousness. The communal farms they built in western Canada flourished, but within a few years they clashed with the government in their newly adopted country because they refused to assimilate and swear allegiance to the Crown. In May 1903 a small sub-sect of the Doukhobors, the Sons of Freedom, decided to demonstrate their faith by marching naked through the towns and villages of Saskatchewan. They were chased and whipped by neighbours and non-believers until the RCMP stepped in, arresting and imprisoning them for "indecent exposure." Over the next few decades, the Sons of Freedom periodically marched nude to demonstrate their zealous beliefs and also began firebombing homes and government buildings. Their actions resulted in mass trials, detainment and prison sentences that were still being handed out into the 1960s. The images of naked Doukhobors splashed across the newspapers of the day forever coloured Canadian perceptions of sect members as religious fanatics.

3. Cinema's First Nude Scene

Author, actress, director and conservationist Nell Shipman was a woman ahead of her time. Born in Vancouver in 1892, she produced, starred in and directed her own breakthrough film, *God's Country and the Woman*, at the age of 23. As in most of her films, Nell played a strong and brave woman who thrived in the cold northern climate while coexisting harmoniously with wild animals such as bears, wolves and walruses. In 1919 Nell wrote the screenplay for and starred in *Back to God's Country*, a sequel to her first big hit. Nell appeared completely nude in the film as she plunged into the icy waters of Lesser Slave Lake. *Back to God's Country* cemented Nell's free-spirited reputation and became the most successful silent film ever made in Canada. She lost a legal battle to receive royalties for the film, however, and ended up homeless in New York City.

4. The Wreck Beach Nude-In

In the 1960s and into the 1970s, Vancouver's "underground" newspaper, the *Georgia Straight*, promoted an annual "nude-in" at Wreck Beach. The sandy shores just under the cliffs of the University of British Columbia campus were a well-known haven for nudists, hippies and counterculture types who routinely frolicked naked there. The nude-in served to protest the occasional police presence and harassment Wreck Beach regulars had endured over the years. Police arrested 13 people in August 1970 including Sheila Beaupre, who was fined $50 for "committing an indecent act." She fought her case right up to the British Columbia Supreme Court and got it overturned on a technicality. The Crown then dropped the charges on everyone else who had been arrested that day. The police have never again arrested anyone on Wreck Beach for being naked in a public place.

5. Legally Topless in Ontario

Gwen Jacob was walking down a street in Guelph, Ontario, on July 19, 1991. It was humid and hot—33°C—and Jacob decided to take off her shirt to cool down, as the men she was with had done. But things heated up considerably when she was ticketed and fined $75 for indecent exposure. An Ontario court judge declared that female breasts were "sexually stimulating to men" and should therefore be covered in public. Jacob appealed the decision, and on December 10, 1996, the Ontario Court of Appeal made it legal for women to go topless in Ontario. It is still considered "indecent" to bare female breasts in public for sexual or commercial purposes.

6. Legally Topless in Canada

Because the Jacob decision was provincial in scope, like-minded women across the country have stripped off their shirts in an effort to make the Ontario law apply elsewhere. In August 1997 Regina residents Kathleen Rice, 42, and Evangeline Godron, 64, challenged the law in their province by going topless in a downtown park. They were charged with public indecency, but a year later a Saskatchewan judge affirmed their right to bare their breasts in public, effectively establishing the Ontario ruling as a legal precedent for all of Canada. Victorious defence lawyer James Rybchuk said, "Let's face it, if a woman can walk topless down the streets of Regina, Saskatchewan, she can probably walk topless down any city street in Canada."

7. Breastfeeding in Public

Lactation advocates and hungry babies everywhere rejoiced at the 1997 British Columbia Human Rights Tribunal decision that upheld Michelle Poirier's right to breastfeed in a public place. Poirier was asked to leave a staff meeting at her workplace when she began breastfeeding her baby in front of her peers. According to managers, other female staffers were made uncomfortable by the breastfeeding, which Poirier usually did over her lunch break, sitting at her desk. The tribunal decreed that it was against the law to expect Poirier to miss meetings in order to breastfeed her child.

8. Barenaked Ladies Save Gulf Island Paradise

Forty-year-old Briony Penn rode naked through the streets of downtown Vancouver on a horse to bring attention to the campaign to stop logging and development on Salt Spring Island, British Columbia. Wearing only flesh-coloured panties and a blonde wig, Penn took her chilly ride on January 22, 2001. Another 35 Salt Spring Island women posed naked for a calendar that was sold to raise funds to save the Salt Spring old-growth trees and habitat. One week after Penn's ride, the British Columbia government announced its plan to purchase the 770 hectares of land in question and turn it into a park. "It did what it was supposed to do," said Penn. "People entered into it with a spirit of fun, and it helped infect the whole island with enthusiasm."

9. Getting Naked for Affordable Education

Quebec has a long-standing commitment to accessible education with affordable tuition rates that are the envy of young people across Canada. Jean Charest's

Liberals proposed tuition hikes starting in 2011 of $325 a year over five years, for a total of a 75% increase. This sparked a student strike featuring massive street protests and civil disobedience. In response, the Liberals proposed Special Law 78 with slight increases and the requirement that protestors notify police of their protest route and tactics at least eight hours in advance. This only served to intensify protests. On June 7, 2012, thousands of students bared it all at a Formula One Canadian Grand Prix event in Montreal. Protestors chose to protest nude or semi-naked to model "transparency" in their demands, to bring increased attention to their cause and to discourage police from being aggressive with them. Police responded by dispersing crowds with their batons, pepper spray and tear gas, arresting almost 40 people. A few months later, Jean Charest lost his seat and the government in the provincial election. The newly elected Pauline Marois of the Parti Québécois quickly repealed the tuition increases.

19 MEMORABLE KISSES

1. The Kiss of Life
It was a kiss from God that infused the "spirit of life" into man, according to Genesis 2:7. God is said to have formed Adam from slime and dust and then breathed a rational soul into him. This concept of divine insufflation, which surfaces frequently in religious teachings, is often viewed through the kiss metaphor.

2. The Betrayal Kiss of Judas (c. ad 29)
As told in the New Testament, Judas Iscariot used the kiss as a tool of betrayal around AD 29, when he embraced Jesus Christ in the Garden of Gethsemane. Jewish leaders under the high priest Caiaphas had paid Judas 30 pieces of silver to identify Jesus. With a kiss, Judas singled him out. Jesus was arrested, charged with blasphemy and condemned to death.

3. The Kiss That Cost Thomas Saverland His Nose (1837)
At the dawn of the Victorian era in Great Britain, Thomas Saverland attempted to kiss Caroline Newton in a lighthearted manner. Rejecting Saverland's pass, Miss Newton not so lightheartedly bit off part of his nose. Saverland took Newton to court, but she was acquitted. "When a man kisses a woman against her will," ruled the judge, "she is fully entitled to bite his nose, if she so pleases." "And eat it up," added a barrister.

4. The First Kiss Recorded on Film (1896)

The first kiss ever to be recorded in a film occurred in Thomas Edison's Kinetoscope production *The Kiss*, between John C. Rice and May Irwin, in April 1896. Adapted from a short scene in the Broadway comedy *The Widow Jones*, *The Kiss* was filmed by William Heise and produced by marketers Raff and Gammon for nickelodeon audiences. Its running time was less than 30 seconds.

5. The Most Often Kissed Statue in History (late 1800s)

The figure of Guidarello Guidarelli, a fearless 16th-century Italian soldier, was sculpted in marble by Tullio Lombardo (*c.* 1455–1532) and displayed at the Academy of Fine Arts in Ravenna, Italy. During the late 1800s a rumour started that any woman who kissed the reclining, armour-clad statue would marry a wonderful gentleman. More than five million superstitious women have since kissed Guidarelli's cold marble lips. Consequently, the soldier's mouth has acquired a faint reddish glow.

6. The Movie with 191 Kisses (1926)

In 1926 Warner Brothers Studios cast John Barrymore in *Don Juan*. During the course of the film (2 hours, 47 minutes), the amorous adventurer bestows a total of 191 kisses on a number of beautiful señoritas—an average of one every 53 seconds.

7. The Longest Kiss on Film (1941)

The longest kiss in movie history is between Jane Wyman and Regis Toomey in the 1941 production of *You're in the Army Now*. The Lewis Seiler comedy about two vacuum-cleaner salesmen features a scene in which Toomey and Wyman hold a single kiss for 3 minutes and 5 seconds (or 4% of the film's running time).

8. The VJ-Day Kiss (1945)

When the news of Japan's surrender was announced in New York City's Times Square on August 14, 1945, *Life* photojournalist Alfred Eisenstaedt photographed a jubilant sailor clutching a nurse in a back-bending passionate kiss to vent his joy. The picture became an icon of the cathartic celebration that erupted over the end of the war. Over the years, at least three nurses and 10 sailors claimed to be the people in the photo. Since Eisenstaedt had lost his notes and negatives by the time the claimants came forward, he was never able to say definitively who was in the photo.

9. The Kiss at l'Hôtel de Ville (1950)

A 1950 photograph of a young couple kissing on the streets of Paris—"Le Baiser de l'Hotel de Ville"—found itself under an international media spotlight when, four decades after the picture was taken, the photo became a commercial success, drawing out of the woodwork dozens of people who claimed to have been the photo's unidentified kissers. The black-and-white snapshot—originally taken for *Life* magazine by Robert Doisneau as part of his series on the Parisian working class—made Doisneau wealthy when, between 1986 and 1992, it became a bestseller through poster and postcard reprints. Among those who subsequently identified themselves as the kissers were Denise and Jean-Louis Lavergne, who sued Doisneau for $100,000 after he rejected their claim. They lost their case when it was determined, in 1993, that the kissers were actually two professional models (and real-life lovers), Françoise Bornet and Jacques Carteaud.

10. The First Interracial Kiss on U.S. Television (1968)

NBC's *Star Trek* was the first program to show a white man kissing a black woman. In the episode "Plato's Children," aliens with psychic powers force Captain Kirk (William Shatner) to kiss Lieutenant Uhura (Nichelle Nichols).

11. The Majorca, Spain, Kiss-In (1969)

In 1969 an effort was made to crack down on young lovers who were smooching in public in the town of Inca on the island of Majorca. When the police chief began handing out citations that cost offenders 500 pesetas per kiss, a group of 30 couples protested by staging a kiss-in at the harbour at Cala Figuera. Following a massive roundup by police, the amorous rebels were fined 45,000 pesetas for their defiant canoodling and then released.

12. The Kiss of Humility (1975)

In an unprecedented gesture of humility, Pope Paul VI kissed the feet of Metropolitan Meliton of Chalcedon, envoy of Patriarch Demetrios I, who was head of the Eastern Orthodox Church, during a mass at the Sistine Chapel in Rome in 1975. The two men were commemorating the 10th anniversary of the lifting of excommunications that the churches of Constantinople and Rome had conferred on each other during the 11th century. Taken aback by the pontiff's dramatic action, Meliton attempted to kiss the pope's feet in return, but the pope prevented him from doing so. Meliton instead kissed his hand.

13. The "Coach's Corner" Kiss (1990-93)

The irascible and bombastic ex-player and coach Don "Hotlips" Cherry has planted a few kisses on his favourite hockey players over the years on "Coach's Corner," his regular segment of *Hockey Night in Canada*. Many recall the Doug Gilmour kiss, which happened on May 19, 1993, during the playoffs, when the Leafs and "Dougie" were playing their hearts out. But before that Cherry kissed two other much-admired players in 1990: Dale Hunter of the Washington Capitals on May 5 and legendary Boston Bruin Bobby Orr on December 15. Outspoken gay comedian and actor Scott Thompson, of *Kids in the Hall* and *Larry Sanders Show* fame, took it upon himself to reciprocate the warm feelings and nuzzled up to tough-guy Cherry when they were both guests on the *Friday Night! with Ralph Benmergui* television show on October 30, 1992.

14. The First Lesbian Kiss on U.S. Commercial Television (1991)

The first visible kiss between two women on an American network television series took place in 1991 on the show *L.A. Law*, when Michele Greene kissed Amanda Donohoe. However, it was a later kiss, on the March 1, 1994, ABC broadcast of the situation comedy *Roseanne*, that caused a sensation. In a controversial scene well publicized in the press, guest star Mariel Hemingway kisses series star Roseanne Arnold on the mouth. The kiss occurs in a "gay bar" setting, and Hemingway portrays a lesbian stripper whose kiss causes Roseanne to question her own sensibilities. The episode (whose script originally included a second kiss between two additional women) became the subject of much high-profile bickering between ABC executives and series producers Tom and Roseanne Arnold during the weeks prior to its airing. Up to the eleventh hour, the very inclusion of the kiss appeared to remain in question, prompting protests by gay rights organizations. ABC finally let the kiss happen, but added a viewer warning at the start of the episode.

15. The Sexual Harassment Kiss (1996)

Six-year-old Johnathan Prevette, a first-grader at Southwest Elementary School in Lexington, North Carolina, kissed a classmate on the cheek. A teacher saw the September 19, 1996, incident and reported it to the school principal, Lisa Horne, who punished Johnathan by keeping him from attending an ice cream party and ordering him to spend a day in a disciplinary program. But Johnathan's mother called a local radio talk show, word of the incident spread, and within six months the U.S. Department of Education had rewritten its sexual harassment guidelines to omit kisses by first-graders. For the record, Johnathan said that the girl asked him for a kiss.

16. The MTV Faux Lesbian Kiss (2003)

For the opening number of the 2003 MTV Video Music Awards, Britney Spears and Christina Aguilera sang Madonna's 1984 hit "Like a Virgin" while wearing white wedding gowns. As the music segued into Madonna's latest hit "Hollywood," Madonna stepped out of a wedding cake wearing a tuxedo. What followed was a drag show of sorts with Madonna playing the groom and Britney and Christina the virginal brides. The performance climaxed with a French kiss between Madonna and Britney and then between Madonna and Christina. The kisses overshadowed the awards themselves and were front-page news around the world.

17. The Hockey Riot Kiss (2011)

In the wake of the riot following the Vancouver Canucks' loss in the Stanley Cup final in 2011, young lovers Scott Jones and Alex Thomas locked lips in full view of the fuming mob, police and cameras. Bathed in the dramatic glow of flash bombs and tear gas, the couple looked as if they were caught in the heat of the moment; in reality, they had been pushed to the ground by police moving through the crowd. Scott told reporters the next day that Alex "was a bit hysterical afterwards, obviously, and I was just trying to calm her down."

18. The World Cup Kiss (2015)

Immediately following the U.S. women's soccer victory at the 2015 World Cup, star forward Abby Wambach rushed to the stands to kiss her wife, Sarah Huffman. The crowd roared their approval and images of the smooch flashed around the world, burnishing the game's reputation for being beautiful and now gay-friendly. The kiss was timely, too, coming one week after the U.S. Supreme Court legalized gay marriage (the two had married in Hawaii in 2013).

19. The Welcome Home Kiss (2016)

History was made when two men kissed on the gangplank of HMCS *Winnipeg* on February 24, 2016. Far from the first military personnel same-sex kiss, this was the ceremonial kiss between a sailor and a loved one when returning from a long deployment at sea. Master Seaman Francis Legare won the raffle allowing him the honour of being first off the ship to kiss his life-mate, Corey Vautour.

6 INCESTUOUS COUPLES OF THE BIBLE

1-2. Lot and His Daughters

After the destruction of Sodom and Gomorrah, the only survivors, Lot and his two virgin daughters, lived in a cave. One night the daughters plied their father with wine, and the elder daughter seduced Lot in order to "preserve the seed of [their] father." The following night they got him drunk again, and the younger daughter took her turn. Lot apparently had no memory of the events, although nine months later his daughters gave birth to two sons, Moab and Ben-ammi (Gen. 19:30–38).

3. Abraham and Sarah

Abraham and Sarah had the same father but different mothers. Sarah married her half-brother in Ur, and they remained together until she died, at the age of 127 (Gen. 20:12).

4. Nahor and Milcah

Abraham's brother, Nahor, married his niece, the daughter of his dead brother Haran and the sister of Lot (Gen. 11:27, 29).

5. Amram and Jochebed

Amram married his father's sister, and Aunt Jochebed bore him two sons, Aaron and Moses (Exod. 6:20).

6. Amnon and Tamar

Amnon raped his half-sister Tamar and was murdered in revenge two years later by Tamar's full brother Absalom (II Sam. 13:2, 14, 28–29).

8 CELEBRITY COUPLES MARRIED 3 WEEKS OR LESS

1. Rudolph Valentino (actor) and Jean Acker (actress)—6 Hours

Married November 5, 1919, Hollywood's smouldering Great Lover was locked out on his wedding night by his lovely bride. His first marriage lasted less than six hours.

2. Zsa Zsa Gabor (professional celebrity) and Felipe de Alba (socialite)– 1 Day

After surviving her one-day marriage, Gabor commented, "I'm a wonderful housekeeper. Whenever I leave a man, I keep his house."

3. Jean Arthur (actress) and Julian Anker (nice Jewish boy)–1 Day

Before she gained fame in such films as *Mr. Deeds Goes to Town*, *Mr. Smith Goes to Washington* and *Shane*, Arthur fell in love with "a nice Jewish boy" named Julian Anker because "he looked like Abraham Lincoln." They married on a whim, but both sets of parents were horrified and the couple filed for annulment the following day.

4. Britney Spears (singer) and Jason Alexander (childhood friend) –2 Days

Pop superstar Britney Spears was married for 55 hours to an old Kentwood, Louisiana, buddy. The marriage took place in Las Vegas at the Little White Wedding Chapel. The bride wore a baseball cap and torn jeans. Both were 22 years old, and claimed they were not intoxicated at the time. Said the groom, "It was just crazy, man. We said, 'Let's do something wild. Let's get married, for the hell of it.'" Spears made no comment. Calling it "a mistake," the couple had a judge annul the marriage, which took two days.

5. M.M. and J.H.–5 Days

While not celebrities of Hollywood proportions, two Toronto lesbians have the dubious distinction of being the world's first and fastest gay divorcees. The two women got married on Friday, June 18, 2004, a week after the Ontario Court of Appeal legalized gay marriage. The two women, identified only as M.M. and J.H. (the initials of their lawyers), filed for divorce five days later on Wednesday, June 23, 2004. The women had lived together for seven years, but got cold feet immediately after getting hitched. Court documents indicate that the women believed that marriage would solve problems in their relationship.

6. Gloria Swanson (actress) and Wallace Beery (actor)–3 Weeks

Married in Hollywood in March 1916, Swanson and Beery separated three weeks later. Said Beery, "She wanted the fancy life—to put on airs and all of that. Me, I like huntin' and fishin' and the simple life." Said Swanson, "I wanted to have a baby and Wally didn't want that responsibility."

7. Germaine Greer (writer/feminist) and Paul du Feu (model)—3 Weeks
The first male nude centrefold model for the London edition of *Cosmopolitan* magazine, du Feu lured Greer into marriage in May 1968. However, in Greer's words, "the marriage lasted three weeks. Three weekends, to be precise."

8. Drew Barrymore (actress) and Jeremy Thomas (Welsh barman)—3 Weeks
In 1994 the pair was married for three weeks. Barrymore later admitted that she was trying to help Thomas obtain a green card to stay in the United States.

10 FAMOUS COUPLES WHO FELL IN LOVE ON SET

1. Brad Pitt and Angelina Jolie
Hollywood's most captivating power couple met on the set of the comedy action movie *Mr. and Mrs. Smith* in 2003. They played a bored married couple surprised to discover that they have been hired by competing agencies to kill each other. At the time, Jolie was divorced from actor Billy Bob Thornton and was the single mother to a five-year-old adopted son. Pitt was married to everyone's favourite girl-next-door, Jennifer Aniston. "I think we were the last two people who were looking for a relationship," Jolie later told *Vogue* magazine, but "because of the film, we ended up being brought together to do all these crazy things . . . and we just found a lot of joy in it together and a lot of real teamwork. We just became kind of a pair." It was the third time Jolie had fallen for one of her co-stars. In 1995, she starred with British actor Jonny Lee Miller in the movie *Hackers*. They eloped the following year, but divorced in 1999. She then met Thornton on the set of *Pushing Tin,* where they played a married couple. They married in 2000, and divorced three years later. *Mr. and Mrs. Smith* finished shooting late in 2004. Pitt and Aniston announced their split in January 2005, and for the next decade Brad and Angelina ("Brangelina") were prime tabloid fodder. Their family grew to include six kids. They finally married in August 2014, but two years later announced they were splitting up and embarking on what could be one of the most expensive divorces Hollywood has seen in a while.

2. Ronald Reagan and Jane Wyman
Jane Wyman had a hard time getting going with Ronnie, as he was known on the set of *Brother Rat* (1938). Even before they were cast as lovers she had noticed him around the studio and suggested, "Let's have cocktails at my place." He innocently replied, "What for?" Wyman didn't realise how straightlaced Ronnie

was—although she was divorcing her husband, she was still officially married. When they finally began dating, they discovered they had little in common. She liked night-clubbing; he jabbered away about sports. Wyman loathed athletics, but she took up golf, tennis and ice-skating to be near Ronnie. "She's a good scout," Reagan told his mother after one date.

Reagan lived near his parents and visited them every day. Jane found his devotedness and general goodness intimidating. It wasn't until the sequel to *Brother Rat—Brother Rat and a Baby* (1940) —that they began to date seriously. While their courtship was romantic, the proposal, Wyman recalled, "was about as unromantic as anything that ever happened. We were about to be called for a take. Ronnie simply turned to me as if the idea were brand-new and had just hit him and said, 'Jane, why don't we get married?'" They were wed in 1940 and divorced in 1948.

3. Helena Bonham Carter and Kenneth Branagh

The elegant Bonham Carter, famous for, among others, her feminine period roles in E.M. Forster adaptations, met director/actor Kenneth Branagh when he directed her in *Frankenstein* (1993), a film in which they also played lovers. At the time, Branagh was married to the actress Emma Thompson; their marriage ended shortly after *Frankenstein* was released. Said Bonham Carter, "A third party doesn't break up a relationship. It just means you weren't meant to be." The British tabloids made things "very difficult for Ken and I at first." When the pair went on to co-star in *The Theory of Flight* (1998), the press let up. As for that film's love scenes, Bonham Carter remarked, "It doesn't help to be emotionally involved with the person. It's all acting. Your emotions are never present really." Said Branagh, "Nothing could be more embarrassing than somehow doing anything other than your job. . . . For this to be an excuse to play out your relationship . . . that's all bollocks!" The two were together for five years before Bonham Carter moved on to director Tim Burton, whom she met while filming *Planet of the Apes* (2001).

4. Vivien Leigh and Laurence Olivier

Cast as lovers in *Fire over England* (1937), Leigh and Olivier had little difficulty playing the parts convincingly. They were both married when they became powerfully infatuated with each other. Leigh was the opposite of Olivier's cool, calm wife, and he was a contrast to her intelligent but rather dry and unromantic husband. The affair was ill-timed: Olivier's wife was about to give birth and she guessed what was going on. At the christening party for his newborn son, Olivier stepped outside with Leigh and returned with lipstick on his cheek. On the set they were known as "the lovers." This was all too true for Olivier, who complained to another actor that he was exhausted. "It's not the stunts," he groaned. "It's Vivien. It's every day, two, three times. She's bloody wearing me out." He also felt guilty, "a really wormlike adulterer, slipping in between another man's sheets." Eventually the two passionate actors divorced their respective spouses and married in 1940. Twenty years later they divorced, and Olivier married his third wife, actress Joan Plowright.

5. Katharine Hepburn and Spencer Tracy

Having seen Tracy's work, Hepburn got him to act opposite her in MGM's *Woman of the Year* (1942), in which they would play feuding columnists who fall in love. The first time they met she said, "I'm afraid I'm a little tall for you, Mr. Tracy." Their producer, Joseph Mankiewicz, turned to Hepburn and said, "Don't worry, Kate, he'll soon cut you down to size."

After a few days of sparring on the set—at first Tracy referred to his co-star as "Shorty" or "that woman"—an attraction began to develop. Tracy was married and, although he lived apart from his wife, was a Catholic who wouldn't consider divorce. As the pair fell in love, their relationship was treated with unusual respect by the gossip columnists and was rarely referred to in print. One of the great Hollywood love affairs, the romance lasted 25 years, until Tracy's death in 1967 from a heart attack.

Explaining the phenomenal success of their screen chemistry, Hepburn said, "Certainly the ideal American man is Spencer. Sport-loving, a man's man. . . . And I think I represent a woman. I needle him, I irritate him, and I try to get around him, yet if he put a big paw out, he could squash me. I think this is the sort of romantic ideal picture of the male and female in the United States."

6. Humphrey Bogart and Lauren "Betty" Bacall

When Bacall was cast opposite Bogart in *To Have and Have Not* (1944), she was disappointed. She was 19, and it was her first movie role. She said, "I had visions of playing opposite Charles Boyer and Tyrone Power. . . . But when Hawks said it was to be Bogart, I thought, 'How awful to be in a picture with that mug, that illiterate. . . . He won't be able to think or talk about anything.'" Bacall soon learned that she was confusing Bogey with the characters he played. She was so nervous the first day of shooting that her hands were shaking; Bogart was kind and amusing and teased her through it. Soon they were falling in love. He was 25 years her senior, and unhappily married. Though the affair became serious, Bogart was reluctant to leave his wife. His friend Peter Lorre told him, "It's better to have five good years than none at all." Meanwhile, the courtship grew intensely romantic. In honour of Bacall's famous line in the movie, "If you want me, just whistle," Bogart gave Betty a small gold whistle. "Bogey," she said, "is the kind of fellow who sends you flowers." They were married in 1945—he cried profusely at the wedding—and had 12 happy years until Bogart's death from cancer in 1957.

7. Ryan Reynolds and Blake Lively

They didn't fall in love while co-starring in *The Green Lantern* (2010). At least, that's the story they like to tell. Instead, it wasn't until late 2011, a year and a half after they stopped working together on the film, that Vancouver native Ryan Reynolds and *Gossip Girl* star Blake Lively realized they were something more than friends and co-workers. The former *People* magazine Sexiest Man Alive had just ended his marriage to actress Scarlett Johansson when he went out on a date with a new woman friend. Lively and her male friend came along as well. The double date was "a most awkward date" for his friend, Reynolds later told *People*, because he and Lively "were just like fireworks." Things got serious pretty quickly after that. Reynolds and Lively were married in September 2012, and have since had two children.

8. Liz Taylor and Richard Burton

The furor that attended the Burton–Taylor affair during the making of *Cleopatra* (1962) in Rome was as bombastic as the film they were starring in. Newspapers all over the world carried photos of the courting couple. Taylor was married at the time to Eddie Fisher, her fourth husband; Burton was also married.

In her memoirs, Taylor recalled their first conversation on set. After the usual small talk, "he sort of sidled over to me and said, 'Has anybody ever told you that you're a very pretty girl?' And I said to myself, *Oy gevalt*, here's the great lover, the great wit, the great intellectual of Wales, and he comes out with a line like that." Chemistry prevailed, however, and soon there was electricity on-screen and off. There were breakups and reconciliations, stormy fights and passionate clinches, public denials and private declarations, Liz's drug overdose and Richard's brief affair with a model. "Le Scandale," as Burton called it, grew so public that Liz was denounced by the Vatican and accused of "erotic vagrancy." Liz wondered, "Could I sue the Vatican?" During one love scene, director Joseph Mankiewicz yelled, "Cut! I feel as though I'm intruding."

Burton and Taylor married for the first time in 1964, divorced, remarried, and finally re-divorced in 1976. Taylor said of *Cleopatra*, "It was like a disease. An illness one had a very difficult time recuperating from."

9. Hayden Christensen and Rachel Bilson

He was the Vancouver-born actor who, in 2000, came out of nowhere to win the coveted role of Anakin Skywalker in *Star Wars* Episodes II and III. She rose to fame playing Summer Roberts in the popular TV series *The O.C.* In 2007, Hayden Christensen and Rachel Bilson found themselves co-starring in the sci-fi adventure film *Jumper.* He played a teenager who discovered he had the power to teleport. She played the girl of his dreams in the movie, and, as it turned out, in real life as well. The couple got engaged in 2008, shortly after the movie was released, but called it off in 2010. Christensen had moved back to Canada, and Bilson continued to live in L.A. But they got back together a few months later, and in 2014, the couple announced the birth of their first child.

10. Ryan Gosling and Eva Mendes

It was not exactly a case of life imitating art. London, Ontario–born Ryan Gosling and American actress and model Eva Mendes played ex-lovers with a baby on the way in the 2011 movie *The Place Beyond the Pines.* In the movie, Mendes rejects Gosling's attempts to get involved in their child's life. Gosling turns to crime to get money to support the child, and is eventually killed by a police officer during a robbery. In real life, Gosling and Mendes became an "item" even before shooting ended in Schenectady, New York. At one point, the two stars escaped for a romantic date at Disneyland. By the time the film had its premiere at the Toronto International Film Festival in September 2012, they were officially a couple. For Gosling, this was the second time he had fallen for one of his co-stars. He met fellow Canadian Rachel McAdams in 2004 on the set of *The Notebook* and wound up dating her off and on for four years. He and Eva Mendes have never married, but are now the parents of two children.

PERCENTAGE OF SEXUALLY ACTIVE 15- TO 24-YEAR-OLDS WHO HAD MULTIPLE SEXUAL PARTNERS (2009/10)

	Percentage
Canada	32.5
Newfoundland and Labrador	31.1
Prince Edward Island	36.1
Nova Scotia	28.7
New Brunswick	33.2
Quebec	34.3
Ontario	30.4
Manitoba	32.6
Saskatchewan	32.3
Alberta	34.8
British Columbia	32.6
Yukon	54
Northwest Territories	38.6
Nunuvut	36.6

Source: *Canadian Community Health Survey 2009/10.*

CHAPTER 9

Crime and Justice

8 CANADIAN MOB HITS (+ 1 MESSAGE SENT)

Canadian mobsters may not have the colourful nicknames of their counter-parts south of the border, but they can be every bit as nasty when crossed. This list is largely based on information contained in two books: *King of the Mob: Rocco Perri and the Women Who Ran His Rackets* by James Dubro (1987) and *The Enforcer: Johnny Pops Papalia: A Life and Death in the Mafia* by Adrian Humphreys (1999).

1. Bessie Perri, Hamilton, August 30, 1930

Bessie Perri was the wife of Hamilton mobster Rocco Perri, but she was no stay-at-home pasta-cooking mob mamma. Bessi was heavily involved in the family business, which in this case mostly meant drugs and bootlegging. On the evening of August 30, 1930, Bessie and Rocco were returning home from an evening on the town. They had pulled into the garage of their 17-room Hamilton mansion. Bessie got out of the car and was heading towards the front door when she was ambushed by two hit men. She died instantly from several gunshot wounds. Ten thousand people attended her funeral. Bessie's killers were never found. Some people suspected Chicago mobsters who were upset because Bessie was refusing to pay for a drug shipment. Others thought it might be Hamilton's Papalia family, who wanted a piece of Rocco and Bessie's action. Rocco Perri disappeared on April 23, 1944. His remains were never discovered.

2. Paolo Violi, Montreal, January 22, 1978

There simply wasn't enough room in Montreal in the 1970s for both Paolo Violi and Nick Rizzuto. One of them was going to have to go. Violi, a Calabrian, became the leader of the Cotroni mob family in the early '70s, a development that did not sit well with some of the city's Sicilian mobsters, most notably Nick Rizzuto. Several peace conferences were organized by New York mob leaders throughout the 1970s, but the gap between the two sides proved too wide to bridge.

Meanwhile, the situation in Montreal continued to deteriorate. Frank Cotroni was serving time in the United States for drug running. Vic Cotroni and Paolo Violi were both sent to jail for refusing to co-operate with a Quebec inquiry into organized crime. Finally, in 1977, Nick Rizzuto and Paolo Violi had one last face-to-face meeting, but the talks failed to resolve their differences. It was just a matter of time before one of them would have to die.

On January 22, 1978, Violi was invited to a card game at his old café in the north end of Montreal. According to reports, he was given a traditional *bacio della morte*, the "kiss of death," by one of the men at the table. Then, someone pushed a shotgun behind his ear and squeezed the trigger. He was 46 years old. Three people with ties to Rizzuto were eventually convicted of the murder.

3. Paul Volpe, Toronto, November 14, 1983

Paul Volpe was a man who got too big for his own good, and he paid the price. Volpe was first introduced to crime through his family's bootlegging business in Toronto. In 1961, at the age of 34, he was initiated into the Mafia, and he rose to become one of the city's leading crime bosses. But he became restless and wanted to extend his influence. He decided Atlantic City would be fertile ground for his various illegal activities. In the 1970s he started moving his operation there. But the New Jersey city was already controlled by mobsters from Philadelphia, who felt the Canadian interloper did not pay them proper respect or provide them with adequate compensation.

What happened next is speculation, since Volpe's killers have never been caught. It is believed that the boys from Philly hired two gangsters from Hamilton who knew Volpe well enough to get close to him. They got so close that they were able to fire a few shots into the back of his head. Volpe's body was eventually discovered in the trunk of his wife's leased BMW in the parking lot at Toronto's Pearson Airport. Some Mafia observers have interpreted this as a signal from the Philadelphia mob that Volpe's fate would await others who tried to move their business out of town.

4. Domenic Racco, Milton, Ontario, December 1983

Domenic Racco was a Mafia purebred. His father, Mike, was the leader of Toronto's Calabrian mob, and Domenic was being groomed to take over the reins. But Domenic had two problems. First, he was a bit of a hothead. In the 1970s he had served time in prison for attempted murder after he shot and injured three men at a shopping plaza. Domenic thought they were being rude to him. Second, he had a major cocaine habit. Mike Racco knew his son needed someone to look after him. He asked Johnny Papalia to keep an eye on the kid, even though Johnny was not a Calabrian. Johnny had served time with Domenic and he liked him. But Domenic's coke habit had got him deeply in debt, and he was probably too proud to ask Johnny for help. In December 1983, Domenic's body was found stretched across a railroad track in Milton, Ontario, halfway between Hamilton and Toronto, a .38-calibre bullet in his head. He was 32 years old. "He was killed for no good reason," Johnny lamented. "They could have come to me [for the money]; it was really a lack of respect." Police ultimately linked the murder to Johnny's great rivals, the Musitano brothers.

5. Johnny Papalia, Hamilton, May 31, 1997

Johnny "Pops" Papalia was the long-time boss of all of southern Ontario, but by the late 1990s his iron grip was starting to weaken. Other families were chafing under Johnny's autocratic rule, and he had not put any succession plans in place. Hamilton's Musitano brothers thought they saw an opportunity to extend their power if only Johnny were out of the way. They approached a local hit man by the name of Ken Murdock, who agreed to do the hit in exchange for $2,000 and 40 grams of cocaine. On May 31, 1997, Murdock visited Johnny at the Papalia family headquarters on Railway Street in Hamilton. The two men went for a walk in the parking lot, and just as Johnny started to walk back inside, Murdock pulled out his .38-calibre revolver and shot the mob boss in the head. Johnny was 73 years old when he died. Murdock was eventually caught and convicted for the crime, but not before he fingered the Musitano brothers as the people who had ordered the hit.

6. Nicolo Rizzuto, Montreal, November 10, 2010

What goes around comes around. Live by the sword, die by the sword. Any way you care to describe it, 32 years after the killing of Paolo Violi, "justice" Mafia-style was finally meted out to Sicilian crime boss Nick Rizzuto. A sniper snuck up to Rizzuto's suburban Montreal mansion and shot him through double-paned glass with a high-powered rifle, killing him instantly. He was 86 years old, but police still considered him to be active in the family business. True, he preferred to spend his time playing with his great-grandchildren, but with his family under relentless attack from rival families (his grandson and name-sake had been gunned down earlier that same year), Rizzuto must have felt like Michael Corleone in *Godfather III*: "Just when I thought I was out they pull me back in." Police were never able to positively identify Rizzuto's assassin, but in July 2013, a Calabrian hit man named Salvatore "Sam" Calautti was shot and killed during a stag party in Toronto. It was widely seen as a settling of scores for the murder of Nick Rizzuto.

7. Salvatore Montagna, Montreal, November 24, 2011

He was known as "Sal the Ironworker" because he owned a company called Matrix Steel in the Bronx, but his real passion was lead, the kind you find in bullets. Montagna was born in Montreal in 1971, and raised in Sicily. His family moved to the Bronx when Sal was 15. It's not known when exactly he began his life of crime, but we do know that he rose through the ranks of New York's Bonanno family so quickly that by the age of 36, he had become the family's acting boss, earning the nickname "the Bambino Boss." In 2003, he was convicted of illegal gambling, and the U.S. government was able to deport him back to Canada in 2009. He settled in Montreal and proceeded to try to fill the power vacuum left by the crumbling Rizzuto empire. His efforts were not appreciated by those in the Rizzuto circle. On November 24, 2011, Montagna's waterlogged body was found on the banks of L'Assomption River in Charlemagne on Montreal's North Shore. He had been shot twice in the back of the head. Apparently, he had jumped into the river in an unsuccessful attempt to escape his assailants. Seven people eventually pleaded guilty to the murder, including Raynald Desjardins, a former Rizzuto family lieutenant.

8. Angelo Musitano, Hamilton, May 2, 2017

Angelo (Ang) Musitano thought he had put his past behind him, but like the proverbial elephant, the mob never forgets. Sure, Ang and his older brother Pasquale (Pat) had been involved in some pretty nasty business. They had been convicted for arranging the hit on Hamilton crime boss Johnny Papalia, but that was a long time ago. Ang was just 21 years old in 1997 when Papalia was gunned down. He was sentenced to ten years in prison.

Upon his release, he found it hard to stay clean. "Nobody seemed willing to take a chance on a man with a record," he wrote in an unpublished memoir. "For a time I still walked on the wrong side of life . . . And then God found me." Eventually, Ang got married, had three sons and lived quietly in a Hamilton suburb, his life revolving around his family, his work and his Church.

But there are no second acts in the organized crime business. At 4 p.m. on Tuesday, May 2, Ang was sitting in his pick-up truck in the driveway of his home when a car pulled up. A man got out of the car, walked up to Musitano, and fired multiple shots at close range. Musitano died later in hospital. He was 39 years old.

"He was a devoted father and was devoted in his faith. He was a good person," his friend Mike King told reporters. There were no arrests in the immediate aftermath of the shooting. Hamilton police expressed concern that the killing might spark a new crime war in the city.

+1 Message Sent: Max Bluestein, Toronto, March 21, 1961

Johnny Papalia didn't want to kill Maxie Bluestein. He just wanted to send him a message. Maxie controlled the Toronto gambling scene in the 1950s. According to some estimates, he took in about $13 million a year. Johnny Papalia was the boss in Hamilton, and he wanted to extend his reach into Toronto. The problem was that Max Bluestein stood in his way, and Max was not a guy who could be pushed around—not by Papalia; not by anyone. So when Johnny asked Max for a piece of the action, Max said no. Nobody said no to Johnny Pops. It was the immovable object meeting the irresistible force.

On the night of March 21, 1961, Max, Johnny and three of Johnny's goons were at the Town Tavern at Queen and Yonge. When Max got up to leave, Johnny and his friends met him near the exit and proceeded to beat him over the head with an iron bar and brass knuckles. Then, for good measure, they ground a broken bottle into his mouth. Miraculously, Max survived, and he refused to finger Johnny for the hit. So did the hundreds of people at the bar that night who witnessed the beating. Columnist Pierre Berton called it "the most remarkable case of mass blindness in scientific history." Eventually, the police were able to gather enough evidence to convict Johnny Papalia and his buddies. Johnny spent 18 months in jail for the beating, but he had succeeded in delivering his message—you don't mess with "the Enforcer."

"ROSIE" ROWBOTHAM'S 9 STEPS ALONG THE ROAD TO MARIJUANA LEGALIZATION

In 2017 Justin Trudeau's Liberal government introduced legislation to legalize the use of marijuana for recreational use under certain restrictions. Cannabis has been a prohibited substance in Canada for nearly a hundred years, and the government's decision is an important, though likely not the final step on the long road towards legalization.

Few Canadians have been more closely involved in the war against pot than Robert "Rosie" Rowbotham. In the 1960s and early '70s, Rosie was one of Canada's leading importers of marijuana and hashish. He supplied a substantial portion of the soft drugs that fuelled the infamous drug scene at Toronto's Rochdale College. But federal authorities did not appreciate Rosie's entrepreneurial spirit. He spent most of the years between 1977 and 1997 locked up in various federal institutions. After his release, Rosie spent several years working as a journalist for CBC Radio.

Here are some of his musings from the front lines of the struggle.

1. Cannabis Gets Criminalized (Thanks, Emily)

You've heard of *Reefer Madness*? Well, meet Canada's reefer madwoman.

Emily Murphy is a Canadian feminist hero. She was the first woman to serve as a police magistrate in the British Empire, and was one of the Famous Five "persons" to win the fight to have women appointed to the Senate. But she was also an ignorant racist whose ill-informed rantings about marijuana helped criminalize marijuana in 1923—even though no one was smoking pot in Canada back then, there was no evidence that it caused any harm, and there were still no federal laws regulating marijuana in the United States.

"When coming from under the influence of [marijuana]," she wrote in *The Black Candle*, an anti-pot, anti-immigrant screed published in 1922, "the victims present the most horrible condition imaginable. They are dispossessed of their natural and normal willpower, and their mentality is that of idiots. If this drug is indulged to any great extent, it ends in the untimely death of its addict."

Emily clearly knew nothing about pot. She made no distinction between it and opium. The real agenda behind her anti-drug crusade was to put an end to non-white immigration, especially black and Chinese immigration. Her great fear was that "aliens of colour" would "bring about the degeneration of the white race" through drug trafficking. She was especially concerned that white Canadian women would be unable to resist the rapacious advances of Chinese and black men.

The Black Candle was based on a series of widely read articles that Emily had written for *Maclean's* in 1920 under the name Janey Canuck. No one knows what motivated Canadian lawmakers to add marijuana to the list of prohibited substances in 1923. It was never debated in Parliament so we can't be sure why the decision was made, but it's not a big stretch to believe the reefer madwoman played an important role.

2. Pot Gets the Blues (Sprinkled with Jazz)

There may not have been any pot in Canada back when it was criminalized in the 1920s, but by the 1930s, weed had made its way north of the border. In 1934, the *Canadian Medical Association Journal* reported that 30 young people in

Windsor, Ontario, were addicted to pot that had been brought across the river from Detroit, and was being "peddled in dance halls." It was also showing up in jazz and blues clubs in Montreal and Toronto. Black musicians were bringing it up from the States for their personal use, and that caught the attention of the authorities. They didn't really care what those musicians were doing, but they weren't pleased when their white Canadian audiences started getting interested in pot. The first seizure of marijuana in Canada took place in 1937, but marijuana use, and seizures of the drug, remained pretty rare in Canada until the 1960s. Only six people were arrested for marijuana offences in B.C. between 1946 and 1961, and of all the illegal drugs seized in Canada in that period, only 2% was pot. But then came the '60s.

3. Pot Comes to Belleville (and I Was There)

It was the summer of 1965, in Belleville, Ontario, and I was about to turn 15. I smoked my first joint at a friend's house while her parents were away. We were just a small group of bored small-town white kids. I'm guessing that pot came from Mexico, into the United States, up to Yorkville in Toronto, and on to Belleville. In the early 1960s, there wasn't much pot in Belleville, but there was lots of it in Yorkville. By 1966, I was travelling to Toronto to buy pot and hash. In 1968, I got busted for the first time and spent 30 days in jail for possession of an ounce of hash with intent to traffic. Although people often associate the Yorkville scene with pot, there was far more hash and LSD there than weed.

By 1969, Yorkville was dying. Toronto officials were screaming about "the hippie disease," warning about a massive outbreak of hepatitis C. It wasn't true, of course, but as we've already seen, truth was never really important when it came to pot. There was hepatitis in Yorkville, but it was the speed freaks who were getting it. Once Yorkville was shut down, people like me needed somewhere else to buy drugs. "You should check out Rochdale," people told me.

4. The Rock

When I first started going to Rochdale College (a.k.a. "the Rock") in downtown Toronto in 1969–70, it was a pretty scary place, full of bikers and speed freaks. Not a happy home for a hippie, which is what I desperately wanted to be. In late 1969, I brought in my first ton of Lebanese hash. I was also bringing in LSD from San Francisco, and pot from Mexico. Ex–American air force pilots, who had been trained in Vietnam to fly low to avoid radar, were flying pot in from Mexico to Texas, Arizona, New Mexico and California, and it was coming north from there. The quality wasn't great but that was all that was available. You could get a better high for less money on hash than you could on the pot that we were selling. But that was about to change.

5. Pot Goes Global

By 1971–72 the market for pot exploded, and Rochdale was at the centre of it. People came from all over. We ran one of the biggest pot and hash markets in North America, and I was living my dream. It was no longer just mediocre Mexican pot that we were offering. First up was Jamaican pot, then Colombian, then Durban Poison from South Africa, then Panama Red, Maui Wowie and Kona Gold from Hawaii. And then came the elite stuff: Thai sticks and elephant sticks. We were offering the best pot menu anywhere. The Mexican stuff was still around. It was a lot cheaper—about $400 a pound compared to $900 for the good stuff—but once you had a taste of the top-of-the-line bud, it was hard to settle for less. So while hash sales remained strong, thanks to some very good stuff arriving from Lebanon and Afghanistan, you could get a really good high from this high-quality pot and demand went through the roof. People in the Canadian government were starting to notice that an entire generation of white, middle-class Canadian kids was breaking the law and many were winding up with criminal records. They thought that maybe they should do something about that.

6. The Le Dain Commission (Thanks for Nothing, Pierre)

The Canadian Government Commission of Inquiry into the Non-Medical Use of Drugs—more commonly known as the "Le Dain Commission" after its chairman, Gerald Le Dain—was set up by the government of Pierre Trudeau in 1969. About 12,000 people attended or participated in the hearings that were held across the country. When the commission issued its final report in 1972, its conclusions raised the hopes of potheads in Canada, and indeed, around the world. Le Dain confirmed what most of us already knew.

> The costs to a significant number of individuals, the majority of whom are young people, and to society generally, of a policy of prohibition of simple possession are not justified by the potential for harm of cannabis and the additional influence which such a policy is likely to have upon perception of harm, demand and availability. **We, therefore,**

recommend the repeal of the prohibition against the simple possession of cannabis [emphasis added].

Unfortunately, whatever good intentions motivated Pierre Trudeau to set up the commission in 1969 had disappeared by 1972, and the report's recommendations were largely ignored by his government, and every government since then. Over to you, Justin.

7. Bonjour, Quebec

It was the late 1980s, and for the first time, domestic pot started appearing on the Canadian scene in large quantities. The source was La Belle Province. You could find Quebec outdoor pot everywhere from the Atlantic provinces to Thunder Bay. The quality wasn't great, but there wasn't much competition.

Quebec dealers were divided along ethnic lines. You had Jews, Italians, French and Irish all competing with each other. They were buying up entire fields from cash-starved farmers, paying them about $700 to $900 a pound, and selling it for about $1,200 to $1,600, depending on the strain. That was considerably cheaper than the $2,000-plus you had to pay for imported stuff back then, but you got what you paid for.

Meanwhile, the cops were stepping up enforcement, launching huge military-style raids that netted some dealers (including me) and made for some great photo ops, but they were fighting a drug war they couldn't possibly win, and they knew it. After the Charter of Rights and Freedoms came into effect in 1982, the cops had to worry a lot more about things like unlawful search and seizure.

8. Weed Goes West (and Indoors)

In the early '90s, the centre of the Canadian pot scene began to shift from Quebec to B.C., and with it came a shift from the great outdoors to garages, apartments and warehouses. People in B.C. were growing indoor pot in soil and hydroponically, stealing electricity off the grid, running huge gas-fuelled generators, and going to elaborate lengths to avoid tipping off cops and neighbours about what they were up to.

B.C. indoor pot was more expensive than the outdoor stuff from Quebec, but the quality was off the charts. B.C. growers were getting as much as $6,000 a pound selling to Washington, Oregon and California, but the risks of getting busted cooled their enthusiasm for shipping south. So they looked east, where in Toronto, people were paying $2,000 to $3,000 for B.C. bud. Northern Lights and Skunk were two of the most popular strains back then. Everyone was asking, "Do you have B.C. pot?"

Within a few years, B.C. had pushed the Quebecers out of the picture, and most people were happy to see them go. Today, the vast majority of pot sold in Canada comes from B.C. It is that province's biggest export, although now that California, Oregon and Washington have all legalized marijuana, most of it is staying within Canada. Where there used to be a couple of hundred strains available, now there are a few thousand.

Meanwhile, the idea that pot could be used for medicinal purposes was finally being taken seriously, even among medical professionals. Recreational users welcomed this development. They saw it a potential step along the path to ending prohibition. Pot was emerging from the shadows. If growing and possessing were going to be okay for some people, how long would it be before the door was opened for everyone?

9. Medicine and More

In the early 1980s, a 25-year-old Toronto man named Terrence Parker began using marijuana to control the severe epileptic seizures that had plagued him his entire adult life. In 1987, he was charged with possession of marijuana. It was the first of many such charges against him. After one arrest in 1996, Parker's lawyer decided to argue that preventing his client from accessing marijuana violated his Charter rights, and the following year, an Ontario Court judge agreed. He ruled that "it does not accord with fundamental justice to criminalize a person suffering a serious chronic medical disability for possessing a vitally helpful substance not legally available to him in Canada." After nearly 80 years of prohibition, the wall had finally cracked.

There are now more than 70,000 Canadians licensed to use marijuana for medicinal purposes. Many of them get their pot from so-called compassion clubs, but given the outrageous prices these clubs charge, I don't think there's anything compassionate about them.

Even worse are the few dozen companies who have secured federal licences to be the exclusive suppliers of medical marijuana. They, too, are looking to cash in on the suffering of others. Among the people now trying to get into the game are two former premiers, a former Ontario health minister, and a former Toronto deputy police chief. That's right, some of the same people who wanted to throw me in prison now want to get into the pot business themselves. And those of us who actually know something about growing and selling pot can't participate because we have criminal records.

If these former lawmakers think marijuana is so great, why didn't they speak up while thousands of pot smokers were being thrown in jail under their watch? The "war on drugs" had many casualties, and I was one of them. It bothers me to see people who were on the wrong side of that war now hoping to profit from policy changes that they never supported. They are investing millions in these operations. I hope they lose everything. I think they will. (And good luck to them trying to sell pot cheaper than the local dealer.)

Almost a hundred years after it started, the criminalization of cannabis is slowly coming to an end. It's taken way too long, and way too many lives have been ruined because of a decision that never should have been made in the first place.

CANADIAN JUVENILE DELINQUENTS OF 1935

Before there were "young offenders," there were "juvenile delinquents." The Canadian Parliament passed the Juvenile Delinquents Act in 1908. It was designed to treat crimes committed by young people more as a social welfare problem than a criminal justice issue. The act declared that "the care and custody and discipline of a juvenile delinquent shall approximate as nearly as may be that which should be given by its parents, and that as far as practicable, every juvenile delinquent shall be treated, not as a criminal, but as a misdirected and misguided child."

Provinces were given the discretion to set their own definitions of what constituted a juvenile delinquent. The act stipulated that the minimum age that someone could be charged with a criminal offence was seven. Some provinces chose to impose an upper age limit of 16, while others chose 18. The Juvenile Delinquents Act was replaced by the Young Offenders Act in 1984.

In 1935, a total of 7,679 young Canadians were convicted under the Juvenile Delinquents Act (7,121 boys, 558 girls). Of these, 5,454 were considered guilty of "major delinquencies" and 2,165 of "minor delinquencies." Most minor offences were dismissed with a reprimand or a suspended sentence. Major offenders were often sent to "industrial schools."

Here's a snapshot of some of the offences that got young people into trouble in 1935.

Major Delinquencies

Offence	Number committed
Aggravated assault	72
Common assault	124
Indecent assault	30
Carnal knowledge	6
Endangering life on railway	49
Receiving stolen goods	136
Theft	3,257
Theft of money	174
Theft of bicycle	224
Willful damage to property	803
Attempt to commit suicide	2
Immorality	12
Sodomy	6

Minor Delinquencies

Offence	Number committed
Begging on street	26
Bicycle on sidewalk	13
Carrying firearms	25
Using catapult or air gun	114
Playing ball on street	35
Throwing missiles on street	31
Nude bathing	10
Disorderly conduct	149
Disturbing the peace	293
Incorrigibility	568
Smoking and buying cigarettes	14
Trespass on railway	179
Trespass	165
Truancy	380
Vagrancy	294
Wandering away from home	120
Indecent conduct	51

DANIEL HENRY'S 10 MEMORABLE MOMENTS IN FREE EXPRESSION AND THE MEDIA

There was no mention of freedom of speech or the press in the British North America Act, the British statute that created Canada in 1867. They were part of England's unwritten constitution, which Canada inherited at the time. In 1982, those freedoms were finally made explicit in Canada's Charter of Rights and Freedoms, and it suddenly became much easier for laws that limit those freedoms to be challenged, and challenged successfully. Section 2(b) of the Charter gives everyone "freedom of thought, belief, opinion and expression, including freedom of the press and other media of communication," subject to (Section 1) "such reasonable limits prescribed by law as can be demonstrably justified in a free and democratic society."

Here are some notable court successes that have made a difference in how our media communicate with us, and how we communicate with each other.

Daniel Henry practises media and entertainment law in Toronto at danieljhenry.com. He is co-founder and former president of the Canadian Media Lawyers Association (adidem.org), and former senior legal counsel at the CBC.

1. Protecting journalists' sources
Alberta (Attorney General) v. Canada (Attorney General), 1938; Globe and Mail *v. Canada (Attorney General), 2010.*

Politicians rarely like what the media say about them, and in 1937 the Social Credit government of Alberta decided to try to do something about it. The Accurate News and Information Act gave the government the right to demand and get a newspaper's sources, and force newspapers to print government replies. Newspapers failing to comply would lose the right to publish. Writers could be barred from publication. Sources could be barred from having their information published. This was all done in the interests of "accuracy." In 1938, the Supreme Court of Canada (SCC) struck the bill down, noting that free expression is built into our form of government. "It is axiomatic," wrote Chief Justice Duff, "that the practice of this right of free public discussion of public affairs, notwithstanding its incidental mischiefs, is the breath of life for parliamentary institutions." In 2010, in the *Globe and Mail* case arising out of the federal "sponsorship scandal" in Quebec, the SCC determined that, despite some reservations, a journalist-source privilege is a constitutional imperative under the Canadian and Quebec Charters. Justice LeBel wrote: "Some form of legal protection for the confidential relationship between journalists and their anonymous sources is required."

2. Television camera access to Canadian courts gets a high profile boost
Patriation Reference (1981)

Canadians have a right to see court proceedings, but few can attend. Over the years, the media have advocated for camera and microphone access to court to facilitate that public access. In 1981, the SCC permitted cameras in their court for the first time to see Chief Justice Bora Laskin read live on TV the court's judgment in the historic Patriation Reference case. It took over 10 years for the court to let cameras in again. After a few experiments in 1993, the court began recording all its cases and permitting them to be routinely broadcast. Now, legal arguments before them are available live or on demand to anyone through the court's website. There has been occasional televised coverage of trial and appellate proceedings in other Canadian courts. In the United States, many state courts have permitted television coverage of their proceedings, but the U.S. Supreme Court has yet to allow cameras in.

3. Public access to sworn police statements used in court to authorize a search (before charges are laid)
Attorney General (Nova Scotia) v. MacIntyre, 1982; Toronto Star Newspapers Ltd. v. Ontario, 2005

In this case decided just a few months before the Charter came into effect, the public's right of access to court documents was clearly declared. CBC reporter Linden MacIntyre was investigating kickbacks to the governing Liberal party in Nova Scotia from liquor sales when he heard about a related police raid. A court officer denied him access to the sworn police "Information" document, used to obtain the search warrants in court. Ultimately, the SCC confirmed he should have been given access to it because of a broad right of public access to court records. Justice Dickson wrote: "Many times it has been urged that the 'privacy' of litigants requires that the public be excluded from court proceedings. It is now well established, however, that covertness is the exception and openness the rule. Public confidence in the integrity of the court system and understanding of the administration of justice are thereby fostered." The SCC built on this principle post-Charter in the 2005 Toronto Star Newspapers case, holding that any court document filed at any stage in court proceedings, even the investigative stage, is presumptively available for public access. Justice Fish opened with this now classic statement: "In any constitutional climate, the administration of justice thrives on exposure to light—and withers under a cloud of secrecy."

4. "Scandalizing the court" declared unconstitutional
R. v Kopyto, 1987

Harry Kopyto was a Toronto lawyer who was never shy about speaking his mind. In 1986, the *Globe and Mail* quoted Kopyto expressing his dissatisfaction with a judgment his client received: "This decision is a mockery of justice," Kopyto declared. "It stinks to high hell. . . . We're wondering what is the point of appealing and continuing this charade of the courts in this country which are warped in favour of protecting the police. The courts and the RCMP are sticking so close together you'd think they were put together with Krazy Glue." Not surprisingly, he was charged and convicted of a form of contempt of court called "scandalizing the court." The following year, the Ontario Court of Appeal reversed the decision, finding that "scandalizing the court" couldn't survive the Charter's free expression guarantee. Justice Houlden wrote: "I feel confident that our judiciary and our courts are strong enough to withstand criticism after a case has been decided no matter how outrageous or scurrilous that criticism may be."

5. Striking down a broad publication ban on matrimonial court proceedings
Edmonton Journal *v. Alberta (Attorney General), 1989*

In 1935, the government of Alberta passed the Judicature Act, which stipulated that if you were getting separated, divorced or were before the courts for any other "matrimonial proceedings" in the province, the media were banned from reporting all but the most rudimentary details of the case. An ostensible purpose of the act was to prevent sensational media accounts about adulterous affairs, et cetera, but the result was that the evidence and other information that should have been made available to the public, including potential litigants who needed to understand and use the system, was hidden behind a practical wall. And details of civil cases were banned broadly before trial. In one of the first big media victories under the Charter, the SCC found these bans to be unconstitutional. Justice Cory's observation has been quoted often since: "It is difficult to imagine a guaranteed right more important to a democratic society than freedom of expression. Indeed a democracy cannot exist without that freedom to express new ideas and to put forward opinions about the functioning of public institutions. The concept of free and uninhibited speech permeates all truly democratic societies and institutions. The vital importance of the concept cannot be over-emphasized."

6. A new test for publication bans involving court proceedings
Dagenais v. Canadian Broadcasting Corp., 1994; R. v. Mentuck, 2001

The Boys of St. Vincent was a 1992 CBC TV miniseries about child abuse carried out by priests somewhere in Canada. The story was fictional but inspired by real events, including the infamous Mount Cashel case in Newfoundland, and cases in Ontario. Lawyers for the real-life priests facing trial were initially able to get an Ontario court to ban broadcast of the movie nationwide until all of their cases were over, arguing that because the series dealt with a similar subject matter, their clients' right to a fair trial would be jeopardized. The CBC objected, and in 1994, the SCC decided that the ban should never have been issued. Chief Justice Lamer wrote that the common law had to adapt to the Charter, under which free expression and fair trial rights were now equal. Under the court's new test, anyone wanting a publication ban has to prove that it is "necessary to prevent a real and substantial risk to the fairness of the trial, because reasonably available alternative measures will not prevent the risk," and the benefits of the ban outweigh its negative effects on free expression. The default position is court openness and free expression.

7. "Fair comment"—bolstering the defence for defamatory opinion
WIC Radio Ltd. v. Simpson, 2008

The "fair comment" defence in defamation law is used to defend the expression of opinion, but its name led to its being misunderstood and misapplied. Some judges thought that for comments to be defensible, the judge or jury had to decide they were "fair." This decision put that interpretation to rest. Rafe Mair was a controversial radio host who broadcast an editorial that in part compared the rhetoric of Kari Simpson, a Vancouver activist against homosexual teachers in schools, to the rhetoric of segregationist Governor George Wallace and Hitler. Simpson sued Mair and his employer, WIC Radio, for defamation. The SCC decided in favour of Mair, and clarified the "fair comment" defence: As long as the comment is identifiable by the reader or viewer as an opinion on a matter of public interest, and the opinion is based on provable facts which are set out or generally known, then the reader or viewer can figure out for themselves if the comment is "fair." If the judge or jury had to decide what was "fair," the only opinions that could be published would be those that the courts agreed with, and that would not be democratic. Justice Binnie noted: "Chilling debate on matters of legitimate public interest raises issues of inappropriate censorship and self-censorship. Public controversy can be a rough trade, and the law needs to accommodate its requirements."

8. "Responsible communication on a matter of public interest" —a new defamation defence
Grant v. Torstar Corp., 2009; Quan v. Cusson, 2009

Truth is a defence in a defamation case, but what if you can't prove in court that your message is true? These decisions by the SCC introduced a new defamation defence to Canada to deal with that: "responsible communication on a matter of public interest." This defence is not only for journalists but also for anyone who communicates on matters of public interest, like bloggers. Now, if you can prove that your message is on a matter of public interest, and that before publication you were diligent in trying to verify the truth, your defence will succeed, even if what you published turns out to be untrue. The logic is that no one should have to guarantee the truth of what they write as they write it. Sometimes truth emerges only after public debate. Chief Justice McLachlin wrote: "People in public life are entitled to expect that the media and other reporters will act responsibly in protecting them from false accusations and innuendo. They are not, however, entitled to demand perfection and the inevitable silencing of critical comment that a standard of perfection would impose." And a "matter of public interest" is not limited to discussion of government or public officials, as in some other jurisdictions. It is broad: "The public has a genuine stake in knowing about many matters, ranging from science and the arts to the environment, religion, and morality."

9. Access to video exhibits filed in court
R. v. Canadian Broadcasting Corporation, 2010

On October 15, 2007, 19-year-old Ashley Smith choked herself to death in a federal prison in front of security guards and a security camera. Smith had a long history of mental health issues and minor juvenile offences. At age 15, she'd been jailed for one month for throwing crabapples at a mailman, but never left custody. In four years, she had 17 transfers to various Canadian prisons, lived significant portions of that time in isolation, and was never properly treated for her mental illness. After Smith's death, the CBC, with the consent of her mother, fought to obtain and broadcast the video recording of her death to help the public understand what had occurred and demand answers. The recording was already an exhibit in a related court proceeding. The Ontario Court of Appeal granted the CBC's application, and made clear that there should be presumptive public access to full video exhibits filed (and relied upon) in court, not just the portions played during the public hearing. The video itself prompted significant public and legislative debate. A coroner's jury eventually made 104 recommendations for change.

10. Links and defamation—updating defamation for digital media
Crookes v. Newton, 2011

As digital media take over our lives, digital media law issues come to the fore more and more in our courts. This SCC case, involving the relationship between hyperlinks and defamatory content online, is of real practical use. The court decided that the creator of a link is not responsible for damages caused by the defamatory pages to which the link leads. Part of the reason was because the person creating the link has no control over those other pages, which can be amended without notice or consultation, and the person defamed can always sue the original publisher of those defamatory pages directly. The court wanted to facilitate free expression on the Internet, which they recognized as "one of the great innovations of the information age." Of course, the publisher of the link continues to be responsible independently for any defamatory content on his or her own page. With links everywhere in digital media, it's reassuring to know that using one won't automatically subject you to liability.

4 NOTORIOUS CANADIAN "KIDNAPPINGS"

1. John Labatt (1934)

August 14, 1934, started out like any other day for beer mogul John Labatt, but it certainly didn't end that way. Labatt was driving on a deserted country road from his summer home on Lake Huron to his office in London, Ontario, when he was pulled over by three gunmen. They ordered him to write a note to his brother, Hugh, informing him that he had been kidnapped. They then drove Labatt north towards Muskoka cottage country. The three men were American rum-runners who had fallen on hard times with the repeal of Prohibition in 1933. But they were clearly amateurs when it came to kidnapping. They took their hostage to a well-populated area of Muskoka, where their American accents and city-slicker clothes made their neighbours suspicious. Three days after seizing Labatt, the kidnappers concluded they were probably in over their heads. They drove their hostage back to Toronto and released him unharmed. But the story doesn't end there. Having only gotten a brief glimpse of his kidnappers, Labatt incorrectly identified an innocent man, David Meisner. Labatt's testimony helped convict Meisner, who spent months in jail before the real kidnappers were picked up the following summer.

2. Marilyn Lastman (1973)

Was she or wasn't she? More than 30 years after the event, that's the question many people still ask about the "kidnapping" of Marilyn Lastman. Lastman was the flashy blonde wife of flamboyant millionaire appliance salesman turned politician Mel Lastman. On January 15, 1973, the day her husband chaired his first council meeting as mayor of the Toronto borough of North York, Marilyn Lastman disappeared. She returned home in a taxi nine hours later, shaken and confused. She claimed she had been kidnapped by two men who told her they had injected her with a poison that would kill her within 48 hours. They would give her the antidote only if she paid them $800,000 the following day. They allegedly told her "there was a big revolution coming" and they needed the money. In her statement to police, Marilyn said she was able to negotiate her release by turning over two diamond rings worth $92,000, and by promising to give the kidnappers $1 million. But the kidnappers demurred. "It doesn't have to be that high," they apparently told her.

Right from the beginning, there were doubts raised about Lastman's story. The rings turned up in her drawer under her pyjamas; there was no evidence of any injection; no ransom note or other contact from the kidnappers was ever received; and no arrests were ever made. Despite the fact that Marilyn Lastman passed a lie detector test, many believe that the true story of what happened that afternoon has yet to be told.

3. Signy Eaton (1976)

June 15, 1976, could have been a very bad day for 14-year-old Signy Eaton, daughter of retail mogul John Craig Eaton. Instead, thanks to a sharp-eyed neighbour and a bungling would-be kidnapper, Eaton's unfortunate adventure lasted only a few scary moments. The intruder had broken into the family's Toronto home in the middle of the night. He seized the young girl at gunpoint, but despite several tries, he never succeeded in tying a bag over her head to conceal his identity. Eaton was struck by how slightly built the man was. Her original impulse was simply to push him over. But that proved to be unnecessary. A neighbour had spotted the intruder scurrying across the Eatons' front lawn and had called for help. When the police arrived, Eaton broke free and ran upstairs to rejoin her family. The hapless kidnapper managed to escape, but he was discovered a couple of hours later in a trench he had dug not far from the Eatons' home. He turned out to be a 47-year-old Frenchman with an extensive criminal record who had already been deported twice from Canada. He was convicted and sentenced to life in prison.

4. Dar Heatherington (2003)

On May 3, 2003, Lethbridge, Alberta, alderman Dar Heatherington disappeared in Great Falls, Montana. Three days later, she was found at the Treasure Island Hotel and Casino in Las Vegas. What happened in between depends on whom you talk to. Heatherington's story was that she had been kidnapped, taken to Las Vegas and possibly drugged and sexually assaulted. But police in Great Falls weren't buying it. They proclaimed that Heatherington's story was "not credible," and charged her with making false statements. After questioning by police, Heatherington dropped the claim that she had been kidnapped. She later recanted, arguing that police had coerced her to change her story. She continued to insist that a man she had met while riding along a bike path in Great Falls had indeed abducted her and taken her to Las Vegas, where she was forced to do things that were "very disturbing." In July 2004 Heatherington was convicted of public mischief in Calgary. Not only had her kidnapping story been proven unfounded, but so too had more than a year of complaints to police about being stalked and threatened. The court concluded that Heatherington had been writing sexually explicit letters to herself.

12 AMERICAN UNDERWORLD NICKNAMES

1. Frank "The Dasher" Abbandando

A prolific hit man for Murder, Inc.—organized crime's enforcement arm in the 1930s—and with some 50 killings to his credit, Frank Abbandando once approached a longshoreman on whom there was a "contract." Abbandando fired directly into his victim's face, only to have the weapon misfire. The chagrined executioner dashed off, circling the block so fast that he came up behind his slowly fleeing target. This time, Abbandando managed to shoot him dead, picking up his moniker in the process.

2. Israel "Ice Pick Willie" Alderman

This Minneapolis gangster liked to brag about the grotesque murder method that earned him his nickname. Israel Alderman (also known as "Little Auldie" and "Izzy Lump Lump") ran a second-storey speakeasy, where he claimed to have committed 11 murders. In each case he deftly pressed an ice pick through his victim's eardrum into the brain; his quick technique made it appear that the dead man had merely slumped in a drunken heap on the bar. "Ice Pick Willie" would laughingly chide the corpse as he dragged it to a back room, where he dumped the body down a coal chute leading to a truck in the alley below.

3. Louis "Pretty" Amberg

Louis Amberg, the underworld terror of Brooklyn from the 1920s to 1935—when he was finally rubbed out—was called "Pretty" because he may well have been the ugliest gangster who ever lived. Immortalized by Damon Runyon in several stories as the gangster who stuffed his victims into laundry bags, Amberg was approached when he was 20 by Ringling Bros. Circus, which wanted him to appear as the missing link. "Pretty" turned the job down but often bragged about the offer afterward.

4. "Scarface" Al Capone

Al Capone claimed that the huge scar on his cheek was from a First World War wound suffered while fighting with the lost battalion in France, but he was never actually in the armed service. He had been knifed while working as a bouncer in a Brooklyn saloon and brothel by a hoodlum named Frank Galluccio during a dispute over a woman. Capone once visited the editorial offices of William Randolph Hearst's *Chicago American* and convinced the paper to stop referring to him as "Scarface Al."

5. Joseph "Junior Lollipops" Carna

A long-time member of the Colombo crime family, Carna was given his nickname by his father when he was a kid. Dad owned a Brooklyn eatery called Lolly's. The younger Carna was suspected, although never convicted, of accidentally killing an ex-nun in a shootout in 1982. When he died from natural causes in 2012, the *New York Daily News* reported, "Junior Lollipops has gone to that great big candy store in the sky."

6. Anthony "Tony Bagels" Cavezza

An accused Gambino family mobster known for his affection for New York bagels, Cavezza was among the 127 suspected Mafiosi arrested in New York in January 2011, in the largest single organized crime bust in American history.

7. Vincent "Mad Dog" Coll

Vincent "Mad Dog" Coll was feared by police and rival gangsters alike in the early 1930s because of his utter disregard for human life. Once, he shot down several children at play while trying to get an underworld foe. When he was trapped in a phone booth and riddled with bullets in 1932, no one cried over his death, and police made little effort to solve the crime.

8. Charles "Pretty Boy" Floyd

Public enemy Charles Arthur Floyd hated his nickname, which was used by prostitutes of the Midwest whorehouses he patronized; in fact, he killed at least two gangsters for repeatedly calling him "Pretty Boy." When he was shot down by FBI agents in 1934, he refused to identify himself as "Pretty Boy" Floyd. With his dying breath, he snarled, "I'm Charles Arthur Floyd!"

9. Jake "Greasy Thumb" Guzik

A long-time devoted aide to Al Capone, Jake Guzik continued until his death in 1956 to be the payoff man to the politicians and police for the Chicago mob. He often complained that he handled so much money he could not get the inky grease off his thumb. This explanation of the "Greasy Thumb" sobriquet was such an embarrassment to the police that they concocted their own story, maintaining that Jake had once worked as a waiter and gained his nickname because he constantly stuck his thumb in the soup bowls.

10. "Golf Bag" Sam Hunt

Notorious Capone mob enforcer "Golf Bag" Sam Hunt was so called because he lugged automatic weapons about in his golf bag to conceal them when on murder missions.

11. Alvin "Kreepy" Karpis

Bank robber Alvin Karpis was tabbed "Kreepy" by fellow prison inmates in the 1920s because of his sallow, dour-faced looks. By the time he became public enemy No. 1 in 1935, Karpis's face had become even creepier thanks to a botched plastic surgery job that was supposed to alter his appearance.

12. Charles "Lucky" Luciano

Charles Luciano earned his "Lucky" when he was taken for a ride and came back alive, although a knife wound gave him a permanently drooping right eye. Luciano told many stories over the years about the identity of his abductors—two different criminal gangs were mentioned, as well as the police, who were trying to find out about an impending drug shipment—but the most likely version is that he was tortured and mutilated by the family of a cop whose daughter he had seduced. Luciano parlayed his misfortune into a public relations coup, since he was the one and only underworld figure lucky enough to return alive after being taken for a one-way ride.

STEPHEN REID'S 10 TOUGHEST PRISONS IN NORTH AMERICA

Stephen Reid has spent nearly two decades in more than 20 different prisons in Canada and the United States, making daring escapes at least three times. In the 1970s, Reid and two cohorts made up the "Stopwatch Gang," so named for their ability to rob banks and armoured cars in less than two minutes. In more than 100 robberies, the gang netted roughly $15 million. Reid is also an accomplished writer of fiction and non-fiction. Reid was paroled in 1987, but in 1999 he was convicted of bank robbery and attempted murder and sentenced to 18 years in jail. He is currently serving his sentence at William Head, a minimum-security prison on Vancouver Island.

1. Alcatraz (Northern California)

Any list of tough prisons has to begin with the granddaddy of them all—"the Rock." I did time with the last man to escape from Alcatraz. He made it to shore, but was so exhausted from swimming the treacherous channel that he passed out on the rocks and was reported to the local sheriff's deputies by a young boy who thought he had found a drowned body. The prison was mostly closed down by 1960, but Alcatraz remains the original supermax and a true American legend.

2. USP Marion (Illinois)

Located in the bottomlands of Illinois, in the middle of an insect sanctuary, Marion took the place of Alcatraz as America's toughest pen. The tower guards wear helmets and flak jackets and carry handheld rocket launchers to combat helicopter escapes. In the mid-'70s, a Canadian was the last to successfully escape, by devising a remote control that opened all the electronic barriers up to and including the front gate. I spent four years there in the early '80s after it became a lockdown joint, a place where we went to the showers wearing handcuffs. The mainline numbered less than 200, and I never once heard a heated argument between two prisoners—because an argument didn't have time to develop before someone was stabbed. Two guards were killed in H Unit on the same day in 1984, and one of the killers, Tommy Silverstein, lives to this day with a no-human-contact order, inside a Plexiglas cage in the basement of Leavenworth. Marion remains locked down.

3. Kingston Penitentiary (Ontario)

Built in 1835, Kingston Pen is one of the oldest penitentiaries in North America, but the bloody riot of April 1971 forever altered the course of KP. After the riot, the prison became a reception centre for the Ontario region; then, in 1978, it was transformed into a protective-custody institute. Before the riot, old Kingston at times housed up to 1,000 of the toughest cons in the country. The last escape from the old pen was in 1954, when Nick Minelli and Mickey McDonald climbed the wall behind the East Cell Block. Nick was recaptured days later in Ottawa, but Mickey McDonald's name is still on the count board in the Keeper's Hall, next to the words "At Large." Kingston Penitentiary was known for its harsh environment and strict discipline. Cramped cells, rats in the toilet, steel trays, tin cups, mailbag repair workshops, 4:30 smokeups, the silent system and the strap stayed legal and in regular use until 1970. It was a place feared and revered by crooks far and wide. I once got talking with an old swamp convict in Pensacola, Florida, and he went all wide-eyed at the mention of Kingston Penitentiary, saying to me, "You did time in that place?" The Kingston Pen was finally shut down in September 2013, and is now sometimes open for public tours.

4. The Haven (Kingston, Ontario)

Millhaven Institution opened prematurely in 1971 to accommodate the aftermath of the Kingston Pen riot. The guards formed a gauntlet all the way down T Passage, and as each busload of prisoners arrived they were beaten with oak batons all the way to their cells. No one was spared. The joint went in the crapper on opening day and stayed there. A Native prisoner from the nearby area told me that the prison was built on an Indian burial ground and was therefore cursed to forever remain a place of deep and abiding human misery. I did nine years in Millhaven, and nothing in my experience ever contradicted that theory.

5. Maricopa County Jail (Arizona)

I didn't know there were this many ugly people in Arizona. I slept on a concrete floor for 11 days in a bullpen with one open toilet for 60 people. We were given a white bread pimento sandwich and a warm Tetra Pak of milk twice a day. I wanted to hang myself, but I never saw a sheet or blanket for my whole time there.

6. Terre Haute (Indiana)

I spent a record-hot summer locked down in what is known as I-Up, a long range of cells in a tin-roofed building well segregated from the mainline. I-Up houses all the bad actors and potential escape risks in transit from all over America. Three men to a cell, walking up and down in the yard every second day for 30 minutes in a dog run with a rusted corrugated cover. Indiana in the summertime, inside an airless concrete box. It didn't surprise me that Terre Haute is where they eventually built a death house and sent Timothy McVeigh to his own hell.

7. San Quentin (California)

Never been there, but I've walked the big yard with too many who have. Quentin has to be mentioned because any joint with a death row is a tough joint, and plenty of state joints have them. But San Quentin is the West Coast Big House, and the birthplace of the dominant prison gangs that have spread into the federal system. Quentin in the '70s was famous for the phrase "DA rejects," which meant that the state attorney's office refused to prosecute cases of prisoner-on-prisoner homicides. Imagine how that policy played out in the gang-ridden, racially divided two acres of dirt and concrete that held 5,000 of the most violent men in the state of California.

8. McAlester (Oklahoma)

Corn cereal, corn mush, cornmeal, cornbread, corn on the cob, corn ad nauseam. Who knew you could make so many dishes from the golden kernel? And all shoved through our food slots by a shift of blond giants who looked like the practice squad for the University of Oklahoma Sooners football team. These Oklahoma farm boys moonlighting as prison guards made it abundantly clear they didn't like us come-from-away city types. If you didn't like corn, they didn't want to see the leftovers. I learned to speak in a drawl and never to rise above two syllables in the same word.

9. Angola (Louisiana)

The Louisiana state prison has to be named because it has a death house and an annual rodeo in which prisoners are routinely injured and killed for the pleasure of the spectators. It is where you can find the best prison magazine in the United States, where the solitary confinement huts are known as the Red Hats for the colour of their little roofs, and where the warden for some 30 years is named Burl Cain. Both he and his institution look like stereotypes from a bad prison movie.

10. Florence ADX (Colorado), Pelican Bay (California), et al.

These are the new breed of supermax prisons. Hundreds are being built by federal and state governments at breakneck speeds across the length and breadth of America. Canada has not yet been caught up in the frenzy of prison-building and privatization of the industry that is taking place south of the 49th parallel. The new supermax model is a bloodless, antiseptic and remote-monitored environment. The cells are prefab, the furnishings fixed, moulded and as cold as their designers. Many of the newer prisons are literally buried beneath the ground, saving the prisoner the imaginative leap to understanding the metaphor. A farmer standing within the vicinity of Tamms Correctional Center in Illinois (now closed) described the bone-chilling cries he heard coming across his fields on some nights. Perhaps, when a more compassionate age dawns, the new supermaxes will be kept as museums of man's inhumanity to man. Until then, the unfortunate souls who remain imprisoned inside these sterile tombs will continue to howl as they descend into their madness, void of witnesses, void of human contact.

LORRAINE JOHNSON'S 7 GARDENS BROUGHT BEFORE THE LAW

Front lawns are contested zones. Neighbours and city inspectors have a long tradition of squabbling over a manicured versus a natural look. To the dismay of the fertilizer industry and neat freaks everywhere, there seems to be a growing realization that the function and form of a front yard needn't be at odds. Who knew—the birds, shrubs, pollinators, herbs and grasses can actually coexist without the sky falling. Here are some of the rebel plants and gardeners that have blazed the trail for front yard freedom in Canada.

Lorraine Johnson is the author of numerous books on gardening and environmental issues, including The New Ontario Naturalized Garden, The Gardener's Manifesto, *and* City Farmer: Adventures in Urban Food Growing. *A perennial favourite with north-of-the-49th gardeners,* 100 Easy-to-Grow Native Plants for Canadian Gardens *was reissued by Douglas & McIntyre in 2017.*

1. Grow It, Don't Mow It

When Cathy Smallwood and her husband were looking to buy a house in St. John's, Newfoundland, in 1985, they were particularly drawn to a subdivision called Woodlands. "The building lot was set in a forest," she explains. By the time construction was complete, though, the trees had been clear-cut, so Smallwood set about to "bring the landscape back," planting spruce and fir trees and blueberry bushes for a naturalized garden. In 1992, a neighbour complained, and Smallwood received a notice ordering her to conform to neighbourhood standards within three days. Smallwood turned the complaint on its head, arguing in a presentation to the city's Planning Committee that the neighbourhood standard was in fact a forest, since that was the original landscape. The battle to defend her garden lasted for three months, with a close council vote on the matter. The deputy mayor, a gardener, cast the deciding vote in favour of Smallwood's woodland. "A lot of people felt I was challenging authority," Smallwood says now, "but I wasn't doing it for that reason. I did it to encourage biodiversity, to have a naturalized garden that attracted bees and butterflies." Or, as the sign she put on her front yard said: "Grow it, don't mow it."

2. Freedom of Plant Expression

It began with a celebration of her environmental beliefs and a desire to land-scape *with* nature instead of maintaining a lawn, with its endless regimen of watering, weeding and mowing. But celebration turned to outrage when, in 1993, Sandy Bell was slapped with a $50 fine for "excessive growth of grass and weeds" in her front-yard Toronto garden. Bell decided to fight the ticket, lost and then appealed the conviction to the Ontario Court of Justice, arguing that, under the Charter, she had a protected right to express her environmental values in her garden. The judge ruled in her favour, writing in his 1996 deci-sion that "There are now thousands of private naturalized gardens in Toronto, and I think that the inevitable consequence of routine exposure to them is that they no longer shock one's sensibilities." As a result of Bell's battle, the city was forced to include a "natural garden" exemption in its tall grass and weeds bylaw. And Bell got her $50 back.

3. Suburban Prairie Showdown

In the early 2000s, all of the drainage ditches in front of the houses on Doug Counter's quiet residential street in Etobicoke were uniformly maintained with closely clipped turf grass. But Counter decided to do something different on his little bit of city-owned boulevard: he planted a stormwater infiltration garden using native meadow species, mimicking what grows naturally in low, wet places to encourage water to seep into the ground rather than overburdening the storm sewers. The city declared his garden an illegal encroachment on the boulevard. Counter, a graphic designer by profession, found this ironic because he had designed a brochure for the city called "55 Ways to Green Etobicoke Naturally," in which homeowners were encouraged to plant wildflowers on city road allow-ances. But Counter's boulevard wasn't the only target of the city's ire. A continu-ing dispute with a neighbour, over a fence, led to complaints about Counter's front garden, too—a tallgrass prairie. When officials arrived in September 2000 to cut down his garden, a 45-minute standoff ensued: four city trucks, six city employees, two police cruisers, two policemen, and Counter's elderly father, Victor, in his socks, demanding to see a copy of the bylaw the garden contra-vened. Nobody could produce such a document, so the officials left. Counter took the city to court and, in 2003, the Ontario Court of Appeal ruled that Counter had the protected right to express his environmental beliefs on the public land of the boulevard, subject only to safety considerations. Counter's ditch garden and tallgrass prairie could stay. Further, the judge had a directive: "The City can and ought to avoid problems of this sort by developing and implementing specific guidelines to deal with the critical issue of natural gardens and their enormous environmental significance."

4. 20 Centimetres or Else

When landscape architect and certified arborist Marc Willoughby moved into his North Toronto home in 1996, one of his first acts of property maintenance was to rip out the front lawn. He planned a biodiverse garden of native species, but the sandy soil required improvement, so Marc imported topsoil and planted alfalfa—a cover crop used by gardeners and farmers to enrich the soil—along with some native trees, shrubs and perennials. Someone complained, and in 2003 Willoughby received a notice of violation from the city, ordering him to cut the garden down to 20 centimetres within 72 hours or the city would do it for him and add the cost to his tax bill. As an environmentalist lacking a lawn mower, Willoughby got down on all fours and cut the plants by hand to the requisite height in time for the inspection. Twenty years later, his yard is flourishing with many trees, tall eastern white cedars near the house, and dozens of native wildflower species. "Some people still like a manicured front yard," he acknowledged a decade after his brush with the garden police. "Mine is being maintained . . . it's just being maintained differently."

5. Criminally Tall Grasses

Deborah Dale arrived home on a summer day in 2007 and discovered that her Scarborough garden had been razed to the ground, 10 years of work and growth in her front yard and boulevard reduced to stubble. Distraught, she phoned the police, only to discover that *she* was the one considered a criminal—it was city workers who had cut down her trees, shrubs and native plants due to a neighbour's complaint about "weeds" and tall grass. Dale, a past president and longtime board member of the North American Native Plant Society, had planted her garden with more than 200 native plant species, such as culver's root and vervain, and the week before the destruction she had taught a city-funded seminar on gardening with wildflowers. Incensed, she sued the city for damages. The case was settled out of court in 2014—seven years after the precipitating cut—and the city gave Dale a written apology and rescinded the bill for cutting her garden.

6. Flower Power Fail in Cobourg

Miriam Mutton, a landscape architect who designs gardens for a living, was an elected town councillor in Cobourg, Ontario, when the municipality cut down her boulevard garden—three times in 2013—because her meadow plants were taller than 20 centimetres. Even after the boulevard rules changed to allow plants 76 centimetres tall, Mutton continued to have visits from bylaw officers. Two showed up in 2014 to order her to cut down a few tall milkweed plants, the only rogues over the height limit. "It felt like a personal and political issue," says Mutton, who is philosophical about the many ironies of her saga. She is no longer a councillor, and things seem to have turned around in her garden battle: in 2016, the town requested photographs of her boulevard garden so they could include them in their submission for a Communities in Bloom award.

7. To the Boulevards!

They live on a Mississauga street called Mineola Gardens, and they call themselves "a proud team of Mineola Gardeners." Strangers leave notes in their mailboxes thanking them for the beauty they've added to the streetscape with their boulevard gardens. But in the summer of 2015, three couples of the street received notices from the city, ordering them to cut down their "illegal encroachments" on city property and either return the boulevard to turf grass or apply for a permit to garden—at a cost of roughly $2,000. They rallied a defence team, including Liz Primeau, founding editor of *Canadian Gardening* magazine and author of the book *Front Yard Gardens*, and a number of local horticultural societies, and made deputations to council to allow for boulevard gardens. Says Primeau, "These gardeners were bold and brave, and they persevered." And they were successful, but with a catch: boulevard gardeners in Mississauga still need to apply for a $50 permit and they aren't allowed to plant vegetables.

12 UNUSUAL STOLEN OBJECTS

1. Gene Kelly's Lamppost

Bryan Goetzinger was part of the labour crew that cleared out the Metro-Goldwyn-Mayer film company vaults when MGM ceded its Culver City, California, lot to Lorimar-Telepictures, in 1986. Among the items scheduled to be dumped was the lamppost that Gene Kelly swung on in the Hollywood musical classic *Singin' in the Rain*. Goetzinger took the lamppost home and installed it in the front yard of his Hermosa Beach home. Four years later it was stolen. It was never recovered.

2. 15-ton Building
In August 1990 businessman Andy Barrett of Pembroke, New Hampshire, reported the unexpected loss of an unassembled 15-ton prefabricated structure, complete with steel girders and beams 11 metres long and 1 metre thick.

3. Vintage Airplane
Israeli air force reserve major Ishmael Yitzhaki was convicted in February 1992 of stealing a Second World War Mustang fighter plane and flying it to Sweden, where he sold it for $331,000. He had managed to remove the plane from an air force museum by saying it needed painting.

4. Buttons
Felicidad Noriega, the wife of Panamanian dictator Manuel Noriega, was arrested in a Miami-area shopping mall in March 1992. She and a companion eventually pleaded guilty to stealing $305 worth of buttons, which they had removed from clothes in a department store.

5. Fake Bison Testicles
In celebration of the 2001 World Championships in Athletics, the host city of Edmonton, Alberta, erected statues of bison, painted in colours representing the competing nations. Twenty of the statues were vandalized, with thieves removing the testicles from the bison. Although two vandals were caught red-handed in August, police considered the remaining cases unsolved. Ric Dolphin, chairman of the project that erected the statues, suggested that if the vandals were caught, "Let the punishment fit the crime."

6. Cabin
Kay Kugler and her husband, B.J. Miller, bought 16 hectares in California's El Dorado County and erected a 3-by-6-metre prefabricated cabin on the property, which they used as a vacation home. In July 2003 they arrived at their property to discover that someone had stolen the cabin, a shed, a generator, an antique bed, a well pump and a 9,842-litre water tank.

7. Wedding Dresses

Hundreds of wedding dresses worth more than $250,000 were stolen from Lisange Wedding World in Vancouver, British Columbia, on the evening of August 29, 2004. The thieves breached the security system, smashed the front door and made off with 300 new wedding gowns, 150 bridesmaids' dresses and 150 nightgowns. The store also rented gowns, but none of these were stolen. So far, none of the dresses has been recovered, nor has anyone been charged.

8. Beach Sand

So why would thieves in Jamaica target beach sand, of all things? You'd think that would be the one commodity in that island nation that would not have a lot of resale value. Well, think again. There's definitely a lot of sand, but it's not always in the right place. So if you can steal tons of sand from one beach and deliver it to another—and get away with it—you can presumably make some decent money.

And that's precisely what happened in July 2008. Hundreds of tonnes of white sand (about 500 truck loads) disappeared from a beach in the northern part of the island, the site of a proposed $8 billion resort development. The developers were understandably outraged. "It looks like a mined out quarry," fumed one as he surveyed his now sandless beach.

Suspicion immediately turned to other resort owners, who may have been looking for a sand upgrade for their own properties, or perhaps just wanted to make sure that rival resort never got built.

It appears we'll never know. A three-month police investigation that included forensic tests on beaches around the country failed to turn up any trace of the purloined sand. There were whispers of possible police collusion in the crime, but nothing was ever proven. No one has ever been charged in the case, and that northern resort never got built.

9. 10-ton Railroad Bridge and 183 Metres of Track

How do you steal a 10-ton bridge and almost 200 metres of track? If you are thieves in the eastern Czech Republic town of Slavkov, it turns out you just have to show up and ask for it. The gang arrived at the Slavkov depot in the spring of 2012 with forged paperwork, claiming that the bridge and the track had to be removed to make way for a new cycle path. Railroad employees gave them the go-ahead and stood by and watched as the thieves hauled the metal away. It was only afterward, when they checked the paperwork more closely, that they realized they had been duped. But the thieves were gone, and the metal was undoubtedly being sold for scrap on the black market.

10. 3,000 Tons of Maple Syrup

How many pancakes can you smother with 3,000 tonnes of maple syrup? If you stacked all those flapjacks on top of each other, they would probably reach to Mars and back. But it was money, not pancakes, that motivated the thieves who stole all that syrup in 2012 from a warehouse belonging to the Fédération des producteurs acéricoles du Québec (FPAQ)—the regulatory body that tightly controls and manages the syrup trade.

The FPAQ has been called the OPEC of the syrup world. Its 7,300 members produce 94% of Canadian maple syrup, and 77% of the world's supply. And that rankles syrup producers in other provinces who have trouble selling their product without the marketing muscle of the FPAQ behind them.

So a group of New Brunswick producers decided to do something about it. Over the course of a year, they were able to siphon all that syrup, worth an estimated $18.7 million, out of the barrels in the Fédération warehouse, and replace it with water. Then they took the stolen syrup back to New Brunswick, where they labelled it as official FPAQ-authorized Quebec syrup and took it to market.

It was a sweet deal while it lasted, but in July 2012, inspectors doing a routine inventory check at the warehouse discovered the water-filled barrels, and the hunt was on for the criminals and the stolen syrup. Twenty-six people were eventually arrested for their part in the heist. Only about a quarter of the syrup was ever recovered.

11. Colonoscopy Equipment

Thieves broke into a secured area of Toronto Western Hospital in February 2017 and made off with 26 fibre-optic scopes and video scanners used for medical examinations of the digestive tract. The purloined instruments, valued at $1.2 million, were packed into wheeled duffel bags by three men and rolled out of the hospital in broad daylight. Reviewing surveillance video, Detective Darren Worth speculated it might be an inside job: "It didn't look like they were randomly searching for whatever they could find. They specifically went to a specific location." Hospital staff were stunned by the heist but hope that the equipment will be put to good use in the end.

12. Brother André's Heart

You have to be a pretty heartless thief to steal a guy's heart, especially when that heart belongs to a man whose ability to heal the sick and comfort the afflicted earned him a reputation as a "miracle worker." André Bessette was born in a small town east of Montreal in 1845. He joined the Brothers of the Holy Cross when he was 25, and quickly became known around the world for his healing powers. In 1904, he began work on a small chapel on Mount Royal devoted to St. Joseph. Today, St. Joseph's Oratory is one of the largest basilicas in the world, and is a fixture of the Montreal skyline. After Brother André died in 1937, his heart was removed, placed in a jar and kept on display in a small room of the original chapel. In March 1973, thieves broke into the chapel and stole the heart. They contacted a local newspaper and demanded $50,000 for its return, insisting they would destroy the heart unless they got the money. Police thought the ransom demand might have been a hoax, and the priests refused to pay. The waiting game began. Days before Christmas 1974, the thieves blinked. Police received a tip from a lawyer who directed them to a house in southwest Montreal where they recovered the heart in a basement.

In 2010, Brother André was canonized as the first Canadian-born saint.

No one was ever charged with the heart heist, but in 2015, a Montreal criminal named Peter Fryer insisted that he and a buddy had stolen the heart on behalf of two associates who wanted to use it to negotiate a plea deal to reduce a pending sentence for robbery. Overcome with fear and guilt, they decided to return it with no conditions. That story has never been verified.

WITTICISMS OF 9 CONDEMNED CRIMINALS

1. George Appel (electrocuted in 1928)
As he was being strapped into the electric chair, Appel quipped, "Well, folks, you'll soon see a baked Appel."

2. Jesse Walter Bishop (gassed in 1979)
The last man to die in Nevada's gas chamber, Bishop's final words were, "I've always wanted to try everything once . . . Let's go!"

3. Guy Clark (hanged in 1832)
On the way to the gallows, the sheriff told Clark to pick up the pace. Clark replied, "Nothing will happen until I get there."

4. James Donald French (electrocuted in 1966)

Turning to a newsman on his way to the electric chair, French helpfully suggested, "I have a terrific headline for you in the morning: 'French Fries.'"

5. Robert Alton Harris (gassed in 1992)

The last person to die in the gas chamber at San Quentin, Harris issued a final statement through the prison warden that stated, "You can be a king or a street-sweeper, but everybody dances with the Grim Reaper." The quote was inspired by a line from the film *Bill & Ted's Bogus Journey* (1991).

6. William Palmer (hanged in 1856)

As he stepped onto the gallows, Palmer looked at the trap door and exclaimed, "Are you sure it's safe?"

7. Sir Walter Raleigh (beheaded in 1618)

Feeling the edge of the axe soon to be used on him, Raleigh said, "'Tis a sharp remedy but a sure one for all ills."

8. James W. Rodgers (shot in 1960)

Asked if he had a last request, Rodgers stated, "Why yes—a bulletproof vest."

9. Frederick Charles Wood (electrocuted in 1963)

Sitting down in the electric chair, Wood said, "Gentlemen, you are about to see the effects of electricity upon wood."

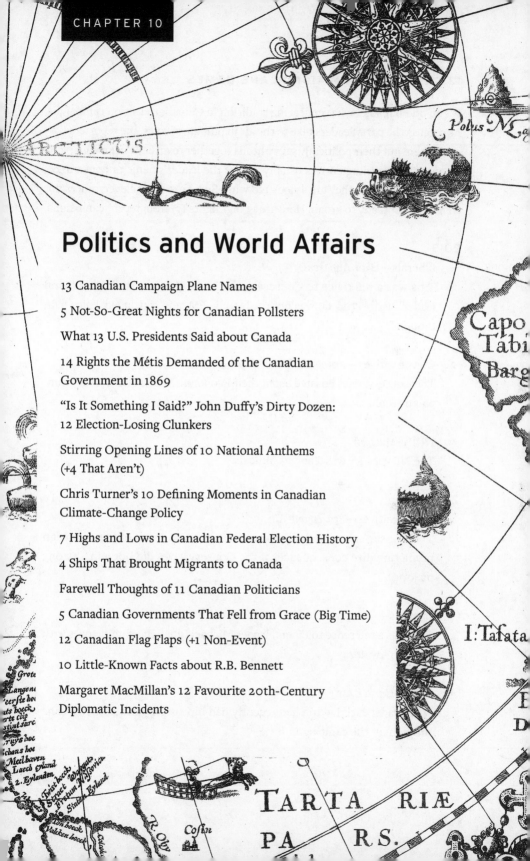

CHAPTER 10

Politics and World Affairs

13 CANADIAN CAMPAIGN PLANE NAMES

It's an odd but somewhat endearing tradition in Canadian election campaigns. As soon as the party leaders take to the air in pursuit of votes, the reporters covering them put their politically savvy heads together to give the campaign plane a name. The winning entries usually riff off the leader's name or appearance, or a campaign issue they are associated with. Some are quite clever, others not so much. Get ready to groan. Here are 13 highlights (?) from recent campaigns.

2015

1. Liberals—*H'air Apparent*
   This was a reference to Conservative TV ads that asserted that Liberal leader Justin Trudeau was not ready to be PM, and concluded, "nice hair, though."

2. Conservatives—*Economic Action Plane*
   The Conservatives boasted about their Economic Action Plan at every campaign stop.

3. NDP—*Mulc Air*
   The NDP leader was Thomas Mulcair.

2011

4. Conservatives—*Scaremong Air*
   The Conservatives under Stephen Harper spent much of the campaign predicting dire consequences if the Conservatives did not win a strong majority.

5. Liberals—*CzarForce One*
   This was a reference to Liberal leader Michael Ignatieff's family roots with Russian royalty.

6. NDP—*Hipster Air*
   NDP leader Jack Layton had recently had hip surgery and needed a cane throughout the campaign.

2008

7. Conservatives—*Sweater Vest Jet*
   Stephen Harper wore a sweater vest during a much-mocked Conservative campaign ad.

8. Liberals—*Profess Air*
   This was a reference to the professorial style of Liberal leader Stéphane Dion.

2006

9. Conservatives—*Mr. Happy's Flying Circus*
   Conservative leader Stephen Harper spent much of the campaign with a scowl on his face.

2000

10. Canadian Alliance—*Prayer Force One*
    The Alliance leader was Stockwell Day, a fundamentalist Christian.

1993

11. Progressive Conservatives—*Helicopt-Air*
    The Conservatives had signed a controversial deal to buy EH-101 helicopters that the Liberals promised to cancel.

1984

12. Progressive Conservatives—*Billion-Air*
    Conservative leader Brian Mulroney was making very expensive campaign promises.

13. Liberals—*Derri Air*
    Liberal leader John Turner was criticized for patting the posterior of party president Iona Campagnolo during a campaign appearance.

5 NOT-SO-GREAT NIGHTS FOR CANADIAN POLLSTERS

It seems as if either voters are getting more unpredictable or polling is getting harder to do right. Maybe it's a combination of both. Whatever the reason, there's no denying that 2016 was a particularly bad year for the polling industry.

In the United Kingdom, most polls before the June 23 "Brexit" vote had the Remain side winning by at least a couple of percentage points, but on voting day, the Leavers won by over a million votes. In the United States, pollsters consistently underestimated Donald Trump's support, both during the fight for the Republican nomination and in the general election against Hillary Clinton.

In Canada, pollsters have also had more than their share of embarrassing election nights in recent years. Here are some of them.

All projections are from ThreeHundredEight.com, which aggregates polling data from a variety of pollsters. Most polls have a margin of error of plus or minus two, so any time the actual vote deviates from the projected vote by more than about 2%, pollsters consider it to be a "miss."

1. Federal Election, 2011

Polls shifted wildly in this election, as the NDP came from third place to overtake the Liberals for second, thanks largely to an "orange crush" in Quebec. And while the final polls reflected this shift, pollsters failed to capture the magnitude of it. They overestimated the Liberal vote, and underappreciated the NDP surge. A projected five-point gap between the two parties turned out to be closer to 12 points.

Progressive Conservatives
> Projected vote: 36.4%
> Actual vote: 39.6%

Liberal
> Projected vote: 22.8%
> Actual vote: 18.9%

NDP
> Projected vote: 27.3%
> Actual vote: 30.6%

2. Newfoundland and Labrador Provincial Election, 2011

The polls accurately projected another big PC majority government, but missed the Liberal and the NDP vote pretty significantly. They projected a 16% gap between the two opposition parties. The actual gap turned out to be five points.

Progressive Conservatives
Projected vote: 55.2%
Actual vote: 56.1%

Liberal
Projected vote: 14.1%
Actual vote: 19.1%

NDP
Projected vote: 30.5%
Actual vote: 24.6%

3. Alberta Provincial Election, 2012

This was not a good night for pollsters. They all predicted that the Wildrose Party would form the next government of Alberta. It seemed as if the only question was whether it would be a majority or minority government. Instead, the Conservatives under Alison Redford won a comfortable majority. The polls underestimated the actual PC vote by 8%.

Progressive Conservative
Projected vote: 35.8%
Actual vote: 43.97%

Wildrose
Projected vote: 38.4%
Actual vote: 34.28%

NDP
Projected vote: 11.4%
Actual vote: 9.89%

4. British Columbia Provincial Election, 2013

B.C. pollsters were very red-faced after this one. They all seriously underestimated the Liberal vote, and wildly inflated the NDP vote. The Liberals easily won a majority government. The final projection by ThreeHundredEight.com had the NDP with a 98.3% probability of winning the popular vote. Oops!

Liberal
> Projected vote: 37.7%
> Actual vote: 44.14%

NDP
> Projected vote: 46%
> Actual vote: 39.71%

5. Alberta Provincial Election, 2015

After their epic fail in 2012, Alberta pollsters did much better in 2015. They predicted the upset victory of NDP leader Rachel Notley, but they were four points too high on her popular vote, and continued to underestimate the PC vote, even as it sank to third place, missing their total by four points.

Progressive Conservative
> Projected vote: 23.7%
> Actual vote: 27.80%

NDP
> Projected vote: 44.5%
> Actual vote: 40.57%

Wildrose
> Projected vote: 25.9%
> Actual vote: 24.23%

WHAT 13 U.S. PRESIDENTS SAID ABOUT CANADA

1. John Adams

"The Unanimous Voice of the Continent is 'Canada must be ours; Quebec must be taken.'"

—1776, while a delegate to the Continental Congress

2. Thomas Jefferson

"The acquisition of Canada this year, as far as the neighborhood of Quebec, will be a mere matter of marching, and will give us experience for the attack

of Halifax the next, and the final expulsion of England from the American continent."
—1812, letter to Colonel William Duane

3. Franklin Roosevelt
"The Dominion of Canada is part of the sisterhood of the British Empire. I give my assurance that the people of the U.S. will not stand idly by if domination of Canadian soil is threatened by any other empire. We can assure each other that this hemisphere, at least, shall remain a strong citadel wherein civilization can flourish unimpaired."
—1938, during a convocation speech at Queen's University in Kingston, Ontario

4. Harry S. Truman
"Canadian-American relations for many years did not develop spontaneously. The example of accord provided by our two countries did not come about merely through the happy circumstance of geography. It is compounded of one part proximity and nine parts good will and common sense. . . . We think of each other as friends, as peaceful and cooperative neighbours on a spacious and fruitful continent."
—1947, address to Parliament

5. Dwight Eisenhower
"Our forms of government—though both cast in the democratic pattern—are greatly different. Indeed, sometimes it appears that many of our misunderstandings spring from an imperfect knowledge on the part of both of us of the dissimilarities in our forms of government."
—1958, address to Parliament

6. John F. Kennedy
"Geography has made us neighbours. History has made us friends. Economics has made us partners. And necessity has made us allies. Those whom nature hath so joined together, let no man put asunder. What unites us is far greater than what divides us."
—1961, address to Parliament

7. Lyndon B. Johnson

"We of the United States consider ourselves blessed. We have much to give thanks for. But the gift of Providence that we really cherish is that we were given as our neighbours on this great, wonderful continent, the people and the nation of Canada."

—1967, address at Expo 67, Montreal

8. Richard Nixon

"I would say quite candidly that we have had very little success to date in our negotiations with our Canadian friends, which shows, incidentally, that sometimes you have more problems negotiating with your friends than you do with your adversaries."

—1972, press conference in Washington, D.C.

9. Ronald Reagan

"We are happy to be your neighbour. We want to remain your friend. We are determined to be your partner and we are intent on working closely with you in a spirit of cooperation."

—1981, address to Parliament

10. Bill Clinton

"In a world darkened by ethnic conflicts that tear nations apart, Canada stands as a model of how people of different cultures can live and work together in peace, prosperity, and mutual respect."

—1995, address to Parliament

11. George W. Bush

"I want to thank all the Canadians who came out today to wave to me—with all five fingers!"

—2004, during his first visit to Canada

12. Barack Obama

"Our relationship is so remarkable precisely because it seems so unremarkable—which is why Americans often are surprised when our favourite American actor or singer turns out to be Canadian! The point is we see ourselves in each other, and our lives are richer for it."

—2016, address to Parliament

13. Donald Trump

"America is deeply fortunate to have a neighbour like Canada. We share the same values, we share the love—a truly great love—of freedom. . . . American and Canadian troops have gone to battle together, fought wars together and forged the special bonds that come when two nations have shed their blood together."
—February 2017, after meeting Prime Minister Justin Trudeau in Washington

"People don't realize, Canada's been very rough on the United States. People always think of Canada as being wonderful—so do I, I love Canada—but they've outsmarted our politicians for many years."
—April 2017, speaking at the White House

14 RIGHTS THE MÉTIS DEMANDED OF THE CANADIAN GOVERNMENT IN 1869

The Canadian government purchased Rupert's Land, a vast swath of wilderness and prairie covering a third of modern-day Canada, from the Hudson's Bay Company in 1869 for $1.5 million. Unfortunately, Prime Minister John A. Macdonald chose not to consult with the inhabitants, setting into motion events that would culminate in the Red River Rebellion and the execution of elected leader Louis Riel. Their first response, however, was to form a Provisional Governing Council made up of Métis, anglophones and aboriginal representatives and draw up a list of conditions for their entry into the union of Canada. This is the complete list of the Métis Bill of Rights, written and supported unanimously by the Provisional Governing Council on December 1, 1869.

1. That the people have the right to elect their own legislature.
2. That the legislature have the power to pass all laws local to the Territory over the veto of the Executive by a two-thirds vote.
3. That no act of the Dominion Parliament (local to the Territory) be binding on the people until sanctioned by the Legislature of the Territory.
4. That all Sheriffs, Magistrates, Constables, School Commissioners, etc., be elected by the people.
5. A free Homestead and Preemption Land Law.
6. That a portion of the public lands be appropriated to the benefit of schools, the building of bridges, roads and public buildings.

7. That it be guaranteed to connect Winnipeg by rail with the nearest line of railroad, within a term of five years; the land grant to be subject to the Local Legislature.

8. That for the term of four years all military, civil and municipal expenses be paid out of the Dominion funds.

9. That the Military be composed of the inhabitants now existing in the Territory.

10. That the English and French languages be common in the legislature and courts and that all public documents and acts of the legislature be published in both languages.

11. That the Judge of the Supreme Court speak the English and French languages.

12. That treaties be concluded and ratified between the Dominion Government and the several tribes of Indians in the Territory to ensure peace on the frontier.

13. That we have a fair and full representation in the Canadian Parliament.

14. That all privileges, customs and usage existing at the time of the transfer be respected.

"IS IT SOMETHING I SAID?" JOHN DUFFY'S DIRTY DOZEN: 12 ELECTION-LOSING CLUNKERS

National elections are a conversation held at 120 decibels in an over-lit echo chamber. In an intense campaign, or in the nail-biting run-up to one, a perfectly intelligent, thoughtful politician can incinerate a lifelong dream with a single ill-judged remark. But today's gaffes are just part of a long tradition. And the decade since we last surveyed the wreckage has contributed some spectacular new fender-benders.

Liberal strategist John Duffy is the author of Fights of Our Lives: Elections, Leadership, and the Making of Canada. *This bestselling account of the country's five greatest federal elections was honoured in 2014 as one of Canada's four best political books of the quarter-century.*

1. Thomas Mulcair (2015)
". . . our first budget will be a balanced budget."

It took Canada's democratic socialists 82 years to get a serious shot at winning a federal election—and about a week to load, take aim, point the gun downward and blow their own foot off. The New Democratic Party went into the 2015 campaign as the frontrunner. The articulate, steady Québécois veteran Mulcair was poised to dispatch the tired, cranky Conservative government of Stephen Harper, and in so doing, probably extinguish the last of the third-place Liberals and their wobbly rookie leader, Pierre Trudeau's kid. Late in August, seeking to reassure voters of the NDP's fitness to govern, Mulcair promised to continue the Tories' tight-fisted austerity policies. Justin Trudeau outflanked Mulcair to the left, pledging to choose pro-growth economic policies over deficit control. At a stroke, he seized the high ground of offering "real change" to Canadians. The Liberals surged past the NDP, setting up the greatest come-from-behind win in the history of Canadian federal politics. Mulcair was asked that fateful week if he would run a deficit to fund his promises. "We are not entertaining any thought of that," he replied. Nor of winning, evidently.

2. Michael Ignatieff (2011)
"What you are saying is democracy is important in Parliament but it is also important getting out to the people."

Less a gaffe on Ignatieff's part and more the muffled cry of a man taking a well-aimed knee to the shorts. The date: April 11, four weeks to Election Day. The scene: high-stakes televised leaders' debate. The players: controlled, crafty Conservative Stephen Harper, the Bloc Québécois's wily, worldly Gilles Duceppe, New Democrat Jack Layton having the campaign of a lifetime while battling terminal cancer, and in this corner, *en direct* from London and Harvard, the sophisticated, cosmopolitan Liberal Michael Ignatieff. The action: Iggy triggers the election with an abstruse argument about the rights of Parliament and how Harper is gnawing away at our treasured democratic institutions. Harper dodges, talks economy instead of boring political-science stuff. Iggy presses the attack as the debate unfolds, raining defence-of-democratic-institutions punches at Harper. But wait! Here's Layton, pointing out that Iggy never even bothers to show up and vote in his big, sacred House of Commons. Stunned, Iggy wheels and sputters about how busy his schedule is . . . then trails off . . . then staggers through the rest of the campaign, leading "Canada's Natural Governing Party" to an unprecedented, life-threatening third-place finish. Gotta watch your back when you're in the ring, Michael.

3. Randy White, MP (2004)

"Well, the heck with the courts, eh?"

In the final see-saw days of Campaign 2004, backbench B.C. Conservative MP White declares on video that he doesn't care for gays' human rights, he doesn't think the courts should uphold them, and he will trash the Charter of Rights to thwart the courts. In so doing, White proves every single scare about Stephen Harper's Conservatives that Paul Martin's Liberals have been trying to monger. Conservatives skid in the final week; Liberals retain a reduced hold on power.

4. Stockwell Day (2000)

"No Two-Tier Health Care."

The newly minted Canadian Alliance under rookie leader Day sallies smartly in the campaign's run-up against a tired Liberal government under Jean Chrétien. Then, in week two, a CA backbencher wrong-foots himself on private health care. Against the unanimous advice of his handlers, Day decides that the TV debate will feature a stupid little hand-drawn sign that draws attention to this misstep, the CA's greatest vulnerability, when the whole country is watching. Day's "Kick Me Hard" sign entices all four other leaders to join in the fun. Chrétien romps to his third majority.

5. Kim Campbell (1993)

"An election is no time for a serious discussion of policy."

After nine years of chafing under the increasingly remote and arrogant rule of Prime Minister Brian Mulroney, Canadians welcome his successor, our first female PM, as a breath of fresh air. A wicked case of halitosis intervenes when Campbell makes it clear she has no more time for the views and impulses of Canadians than did her loathed predecessor. Stumbling from one gaffe to another, Campbell takes the PCs from 151 seats on dissolution to two on election night.

6. John Turner (1984)

"I had no option."

After years of chafing under the increasingly remote and arrogant rule of Prime Minister Trudeau, Canadians welcome John Turner as something different.

First, Turner erases his differentiation from Trudeau by appointing 13 of his predecessor' s buddies to patronage posts. Then, in the campaign' s TV debate, he lamely defends the move, arguing he "had no option." Turner transforms himself into same-old same-old—only weaker! Mulroney poleaxes Turner on TV and wins a massive majority three weeks later.

7. Joe Clark (1979)
"Short-Term Pain for Long-Term Gain."

Less a matter of wording than of the dreadful strategy behind it. With a shaky minority in a four-party Parliament, Clark and his finance minister, John Crosbie, decide to tackle the country's fiscal woes with a get-tough budget that includes a whopping 18-cents-a-gallon hike to the gas tax. They figure the Liberals, leaderless since Trudeau's exit the previous month, will fold in the budget vote. Wrong. The three opposition parties bring down the government; Trudeau rescinds his resignation; the Grits storm home to a majority; and Clark loses his leadership three years later. "Short-term pain for long-term pain" is more like it.

8. Lester Pearson (1958)
"His Excellency's advisers should . . . submit their resignation forthwith."

Having suffered a shocking upset defeat in '57 to John Diefenbaker' s Tories, the Liberals, under rookie leader Pearson, show that they have utterly failed to grasp the public's rejection of their arrogant ways while in power. On his first day in the House as leader, Pearson calls for the PC minority government to resign and let the Liberals return to power without an election. Dief goes ape: he trashes the entire smug Liberal mindset, dissolves Parliament and barnstorms the country to bag the largest majority in history.

9. William Lyon Mackenzie King (1930)
"[For] these alleged unemployment purposes, with these governments situated as they are today . . . I would not give them a five-cent piece."

A government nears the end of its mandate. A devastating global depression threatens our entire way of life. All eyes turn to Ottawa. There, Prime Minister King rises in the House to explain—he was windy even when making a gaffe—that dealing with the Great Depression was . . . a provincial responsibility! And he won't give any money to Conservative provincial governments! *Niiiiice.* Bennett' s Tories cream King's Liberals in the campaign four months later.

10. Arthur Meighen (1925)

"Before there was anything in the way of participation involving the despatch of troops, the will of the people of Canada should first be obtained."

This one's complicated. In an extremely dicey minority situation, Opposition Leader Meighen struggles to lift from his neck the albatross he had donned when he imposed conscription in Quebec. This he does by telling hard-core Anglo Conservatives in Hamilton, Ontario, that if war broke out, he'd conscript the army, send it overseas, then hold an election, and if he lost, bring the army back. This absurd position both fails to convince Quebecers and infuriates his Ontario base. Thanks to the "Heresy in Hamilton," when the vote happens 10 months later, his core stays home, he loses Ontario, and King sneaks back into power.

11. Wilfrid Laurier (1891)

"Commercial union."

Rookie Liberal Laurier is up against the old Tory pro Macdonald. Laurier chooses to invigorate his troops by boldly repackaging his party's support for free trade with the United States as "commercial union." Oooopsie. Macdonald calls an election, ignores the policy substance and goes for the Liberals on two fronts. In English Canada, he paints Grit pro-Americanism as treason to Britain. In Quebec, it's depicted as anti-Catholic heresy. Old pro: 1; Rookie: 0.

12. John A. Macdonald (1873)

"I must have another ten thousand . . . Do not fail me. Answer today."

These words were not, of course, meant for anyone to actually hear. This mid-campaign plea for political lubricant was sent in a secret telegram from PM Macdonald to Sir Hugh Allan, a Montreal businessman. In return, Allan was promised the contract to build the Canadian Pacific Railway. Macdonald got his money and actually won the election. But the telegram leaked and, two years later, Macdonald was forced to resign in disgrace.

STIRRING OPENING LINES OF 10 NATIONAL ANTHEMS
(+4 THAT AREN'T)

1. **Algeria**

   We swear by the lightning that destroys,
   By the streams of generous blood being shed
   By the bright flags that wave
   That we are in revolt . . .

2. **Burkina Faso**

   Against the humiliating bondage of a thousand years
   Rapacity came from afar to subjugate them
   For a hundred years.
   Against the cynical malice in the shape
   Of neocolonialism and its petty local servants,
   Many gave in and certain others resisted.

3. **East Timor**

   Fatherland, fatherland, East Timor our Nation
   Glory to the people and to the heroes of our liberation
   Fatherland, fatherland, East Timor our Nation
   Glory to the people and to the heroes of our liberation

4. **Georgia**

   Praise be to the heavenly Bestower of Blessings,
   Praise be to paradise on earth,
   To the radiant Georgians,
   Praise be to brotherhood and to unity,
   Praise be to liberty,
   Praise be to the everlasting, lively Georgian people!

5. **Namibia**

   Namibia land of the brave
   Freedom fight we have won
   Glory to their bravery
   Whose blood waters our freedom

6. Russia

Russia—our sacred State,
Russia—our beloved country.
A mighty will, a great glory—
Is your legacy for all time!

7. Senegal

Everyone strum your koras,
Strike the balafons,
The red lion has roared,
The tamer of the bush with one leap,
Has scattered the gloom.

8. Serbia

God of Justice, You who saved us
From disasters till this day,
Hear from now on, our voices,
And from now on, save us!
Defend with Your mighty hand,
That very future Serbia walks to.

9. Taiwan

The three principles of democracy our party does revere.

10. Uruguay

Eastern landsmen, our country or the tomb!

+ 4 That Aren't

These four countries have no official lyrics for their national anthems, stirring or otherwise.

1. Bosnia and Herzegovina
2. Kosovo
3. San Marino
4. Spain

CHRIS TURNER'S 10 DEFINING MOMENTS IN CANADIAN CLIMATE-CHANGE POLICY

In the quarter-century since climate change landed on Canada's policy radar, it has been a source of considerable action, constant controversy, occasional triumph, and middling results. In 1990, the baseline year for the Kyoto Protocol, Canadians produced 613 megatonnes of greenhouse gas emissions. That total rose steadily through the 1990s before peaking at 758 megatonnes in 2004 and then falling away to a slightly spiky plateau. In 2014, the total was 732 megatonnes. But if the results aren't breathtaking, the political machinations have never been dull. Here are the 10 defining moments in Canadian climate-change policy.

Chris Turner is the author of five books and one of Canada's leading writers and speakers on energy and sustainability. His bestsellers The Leap *and* The Geography of Hope *were both National Business Book Award finalists.* The Patch, *the definitive story of Alberta's oilsands, will be published by Simon & Schuster in 2017.*

1. Toronto Climate Conference (1988)

Canada earned a reputation for environmental leadership in the 1980s by spearheading global efforts to combat acid rain and ozone depletion. Brian Mulroney's Progressive Conservatives were remarkably bold on environmental issues, and so when climate change began to emerge as a significant problem, the federal government jumped into the lead, organizing the first major international meeting of climate scientists and policymakers ever. The event was given the wonky name "Our Changing Atmosphere: Implications for Global Security," with proceedings unfolding in Toronto over four ferociously hot days in late June 1988. Mulroney spoke at the conference, which was chaired by Stephen Lewis, Canada's United Nations ambassador at the time. The conference's closing statement is bolder than many governments would dare endorse today: "Humanity is conducting an unintended, uncontrolled, globally pervasive experiment whose ultimate consequences could be second only to a global nuclear war."

2. Rio Summit (1992)

The 1992 Earth Summit in Rio de Janeiro, Brazil, was the event that put climate change permanently on the world's political agenda. Canada played an outsized role in its organization and proceedings. The summit's secretary general was Maurice Strong, a Canadian business leader who had been active in environmental policy circles for decades. "Like it or not, from here on in, we're in this together," he said in his opening statement. "The industrialized world cannot escape its primary responsibility to lead the way in establishing this partnership and making it work." One of the most memorable speeches of the conference was delivered by Severn Suzuki, the daughter of legendary broadcaster and environmental activist David Suzuki; she was only 12 years old at the time.

3. Canadian Government Joins Kyoto Protocol (1998-2002)

In the aftermath of Rio, the UN convened a series of climate summits culminating in a 1997 accord in Kyoto that committed signatory nations to begin reducing their greenhouse gas emissions and agree to binding targets. In 1998, Prime Minister Jean Chrétien signed on to the Kyoto Accord, making Canada one of the first nations to commit to it. The Kyoto Protocol was formally ratified and went into force in 2002. Canada's initial commitment was to reduce greenhouse gas emissions to 6% below 1990 baseline levels by 2012.

4. The One-Tonne Challenge (2005)

In the wake of ratifying Kyoto, the Liberal government—now under Paul Martin—unveiled a range of initiatives aimed at jump-starting Canada's pursuit of its Kyoto Protocol targets. They were tepid and mostly voluntary, however, as exemplified by the only one most Canadians even noticed: "The One-Tonne Challenge." The "Challenge" was a $26 million publicity campaign to cajole Canadians into finding enough energy-saving tricks in their daily lives to reduce their personal carbon footprints by one tonne each. It was launched with a series of charming, energetic TV ads starring beloved CBC host Rick Mercer. Given that most Canadians were barely familiar with the concept of a carbon footprint at the time, the ad was met mostly with shrugs and question marks. Like much of Canada's climate action under Chrétien and Martin, it accomplished almost nothing and was scrapped the following year.

5. Ontario's Coal Phase-Out (2004-14)

While the feds dithered, provincial governments achieved the most dramatic results of the first wave of climate action in Canada—none more significant than Ontario's phase-out of all the coal-fired power on its electricity grid. Responding in part to climate change and even more so to the growing smog problem in the

Toronto area, Dalton McGuinty's Liberals pledged to shutter all of the province's coal plants as a 2003 election campaign promise. The pledge became a plan in 2004 and gathered steam after the Nanticoke Generating Station—the largest coal plant in North America—began decommissioning in 2010. Ontario also passed Canada's most ambitious renewable energy policy, the Green Energy Act, in 2009 to bring wind and solar power onto the grid in place of coal. The last of the province's coal plants, the Thunder Bay Generating Station, burned its last lump of lignite in April 2014.

6. British Columbia's Carbon Tax (2008)

For years, energy economists and climate-policy wonks agreed a crucial first step in fighting climate change was to put a price on carbon dioxide emissions. In 2008, British Columbia became the first jurisdiction in North America to do so. The province's carbon tax began with a $10 per tonne levy on carbon dioxide, ramping up to $30 by 2012. The revenues collected by the province are returned to B.C. residents through tax cuts in other areas, making the tax "revenue-neutral." The carbon tax reduced per capita gasoline consumption by 16 percent and became a widely admired and closely studied example for other jurisdictions around the world.

7. Federal Election (2008)

Stephen Harper's Conservatives were barely clinging to power in a minority government when they unveiled their "Turning the Corner" plan, a proposed replacement for Canada's Kyoto commitments—which Harper had opposed since the day Chrétien pledged them. The plan called for emissions cuts of 20% below 2006 levels by 2020—meaning about 3% below the 1990 baseline, less ambitious than the Kyoto target of 6%. As an election loomed, new Liberal leader Stéphane Dion built his platform on a far more ambitious climate-policy package: "the Green Shift," an array of climate initiatives with a national carbon tax and a host of accompanying tax cuts as its centrepiece. In the end, the Conservatives won a slightly larger minority and little was ever said again about "Turning the Corner."

8. Canada Withdraws from Kyoto (2011)

By the time Harper's Conservatives were handed a majority in the 2011 election, they had made it abundantly clear that they intended to abandon Canada's Kyoto commitment at the first available opportunity. Hours after returning from the

December 2011 UN climate talks in Durban, South Africa, Environment Minister Peter Kent announced the government's formal withdrawal.

9. Paris Climate Summit (2015)

After years of diminishing returns at UN climate talks—for the world in general as well as Canada—the Paris summit in December 2015 was an unexpected breakthrough. With the new government of Justin Trudeau vociferously committed to major action on climate change, the Canadian delegation played a central role in a new global climate deal that for the first time included the United States and China, the world's two largest greenhouse gas emitters.

10. National Climate Plan (2016)

In the wake of the Paris triumph, Trudeau and the heads of all 12 provinces and territories met in Vancouver in March 2016 to hammer out a national climate plan. At its centre was an obligation for each province to put a price on carbon dioxide emissions by 2018 or else pay a levy on them set by the federal government. The plan's details are still being worked out, but it already stands as the most significant coordinated climate change action in Canada's history.

7 HIGHS AND LOWS IN CANADIAN FEDERAL ELECTION HISTORY

1. Highest number of election victories: 13

Both John Diefenbaker and Herb Gray were elected to Parliament 13 times. Diefenbaker also lost twice.

2. Highest number of election defeats (without ever winning): 22

This dubious distinction belongs to John C. Turmel, who lost seven general elections and 15 by-elections running as an independent candidate between 1979 and 2000. H. Georges Grenier, of "Esprit Social," and two Communist candidates, William Kashtan and William C. Ross, hold the record for losing in nine general elections.

3. Highest voter turnout in a general election: 93.91%

The politically active voters in the Quebec riding of Îles-de-la-Madeleine set this record in the general election of 1965. They broke their own record of 93.69% set in 1949.

4. Lowest voter turnout in a general election: 23.71%

The voters of Toronto South set this record for apathy in the general election of 1921.

5. Lowest number of candidates running in a single constituency: 1

Over the years, several candidates have won federal seats by acclamation. But the last one to do it in a general election was a Liberal, Chesley William Carter, who was all alone in the Newfoundland riding of Burin–Burgeo in 1957.

6. Highest number of candidates running in a single constituency: 13

The general election of 1993 saw the city of Vancouver caught up in an electoral frenzy. Three of the city's ridings, Vancouver East, Centre and Quadra, each had 13 candidates vying for the big prize. The Liberals wound up prevailing in all three ridings. One of the defeated candidates was Prime Minister Kim Campbell, who lost her seat in Vancouver Centre.

7. Margins of victory in recent general elections:

Highest

Year	Candidate	Riding	% of votes cast
2015	Judy Foote (L)	Bonavista–Burin–Trinity	81.8
2011	Kevin Sorenson (C)	Crowfoot	83.9
2008	Kevin Sorenson (C)	Crowfoot	82.0
2006	Kevin Sorenson (C)	Crowfoot	82.5
2004	Kevin Sorenson (C)	Crowfoot	80.2
2000	Irwin Cotler (L)	Mont-Royal	81.24

Lowest

Year	Candidate	Riding	% of votes cast
2015	Brigitte Sansoucy (NDP)	Saint-Hyancithe–Bagot	28.5
2011	Hedy Fry (L)	Vancouver Centre	31.03
2008	Richard Nadeau (BQ)	Gatineau	29.1
2006	Marcel Proulx (L)	Hull-Aylmer	32.67
2004	Bradley R. Trost (C)	Saskatoon–Humbolt	26.8
2000	Larry Bagnell (L)	Yukon	32.48

4 SHIPS THAT BROUGHT MIGRANTS TO CANADA

1. SS Komagata Maru (May 1914)

The *Komagata Maru* was a Japanese freighter chartered by Gurdit Singh, a wealthy Punjabi businessman determined to test Canada's policy of excluding immigrants from South Asia. The *Komagata Maru* set sail for Canada in April 1914 with 376 passengers aboard. Almost all were men, and almost all were Sikhs. The ship dropped anchor in Vancouver on May 23, 1914, but Canadian authorities refused to allow passengers to come ashore. The standoff lasted for months and conditions aboard the ship deteriorated. Both sides agreed to take the dispute to the B.C. Court of Appeals, which ruled that the migrants had no legal right to be admitted to Canada. In July, the *Komagata Maru* left Vancouver for the long trip back to India. By the time they arrived, the First World War had begun, and the British were uncertain about the loyalty of those on board. British Indian police shot and killed 20 of the passengers shortly after they disembarked at the port of Budge Budge. Many others were arrested. In May 2016, Prime Minister Justin Trudeau offered a formal apology in the House of Commons for the treatment the passengers of the *Komagata Maru* received at the hands of Canadian authorities.

2. MS St. Louis (June 1939)

The *St. Louis* left Hamburg, Germany, on May 13, 1939, with 937 refugees aboard. Nearly all were Jewish. Most were German citizens. The Second World War had not yet begun, but conditions for Jews in Germany and other Nazi-occupied territories had already become intolerable. The ship was bound for Cuba, where, after a short stopover, most passengers hoped to move on to the United States. But when the *St. Louis* arrived in Havana on May 27, Cuban authorities refused permission to land all but a handful of passengers. The ship then set sail for the United States, but officials in Florida also had no interest in accepting the refugees. Canada was the last hope before the ship would be forced to sail back to Europe. But the Canadian government of Prime Minister Mackenzie King had no interest in accepting refugees, especially Jewish refugees. There was little sympathy for the plight of European Jews within the Canadian government or the population at large. Between 1933 and 1945, Canada admitted only 5,000 Jewish refugees, the lowest number among all developed nations. After being turned down by Canadian authorities, the *St. Louis* sailed back to Europe, landing in Antwerp on June 24. Hundreds of the passengers wound up in concentration camps, and 254 of them died there.

3. The Amelie (July 1987)

The *Amelie* was a Costa Rican–registered freighter that was seized by Canadian authorities on July 12, 1987, after dropping off 174 Sikhs (173 men and one woman) in Charlesville, a rocky outpost on the southern coast of Nova Scotia. The three crew members were arrested. The passengers claimed they were fleeing persecution in India by the majority Hindu population. But the government of Prime Minister Brian Mulroney was not impressed. There were already concerns about Sikhs in Canada, following the bombing of an Air India plane by suspected Sikh militants in Canada two years earlier. All 329 people aboard were killed. But Canadian immigration rules at the time allowed refugee claimants to live and work in Canada until their claims were settled, a process that could potentially take years. In response to the landing of the *Amelie* migrants, Prime Minister Mulroney ordered an emergency recall of Parliament and tabled Bill C-84, the Refugee Deterrents and Detention Bill. Despite the "emergency," the draconian bill was not passed for a full year, by which time most of the migrants had already begun their lives in Canada.

4. MV Sun Sea (August 2010)

The *Sun Sea* was a Thai cargo ship that was intercepted off the waters of British Columbia and escorted to CFB Esquimalt in August 2010. Aboard were 492 Sri Lankan Tamils trying to escape the bloody civil war that had ravaged their country for decades. They had been at sea for three months. The welcome by the Conservative government of Stephen Harper was less than generous. It declared the migrants to be "suspected human smugglers and terrorists" and decided that harsh treatment would serve as a deterrent to others trying to gain refugee status in Canada by "jumping the queue." Officials from the Canadian Border Services Agency immediately placed all the migrants into detention camps— men in one camp, women and children in another—where they remained for months, sometimes years, while the government fought off attempts by various refugee and human rights groups to secure their release. In the end, the government spent approximately $25 million detaining and investigating the *Sun Sea* migrants. In January 2017, the Immigration and Refugee Board announced that of the *Sun Sea* passengers who have had their refugee claims finalized, more than two-thirds, or 230 people, have been accepted. More than a hundred cases still have to be finalized.

FAREWELL THOUGHTS OF 11 CANADIAN POLITICIANS

There are two kinds of memoirs that politicians tend to write. The first is written while the politician is still in office. They've had a successful career, but maybe they're thinking of moving up the political ladder, so the attention they get from writing a book and going on tour to promote it can only help the cause. Think about Justin Trudeau's memoir, *Common Ground*, published in 2014, a year before his first election as Liberal leader.

The second kind of memoir is reserved for the retired politician, most of whom, at this point in our history, tend to be men. You know the drill: leave office; get a book deal. The memoir is a golden opportunity to settle old scores, cast a brighter sheen on unpopular policies, maybe even admit to a mistake or two. Most importantly, it's perhaps the last chance for the politician to cement his or her legacy. It's often their final word to Canadians, so the final words of that final word count for a lot, as if to say, "Here's the last thing I want you to remember about me." In that spirit, here (in alphabetical order) are the last words from the memoirs of 11 memorable Canadian politicians.

1. Kim Campbell, prime minister of Canada (June 1993–November 1993)

I will always be haunted by the question of what I could have done differently that fateful summer of 1993. Still, I regard my time in public life positively. For every example of pettiness, self-serving, or narrowness I encountered in people, there are ten examples of courage, broad-mindedness, and generosity of spirit. I am much more worldly-wise than when I started. For every devastating failure, there are real accomplishments in which I take pride. Not only do they give me some comfort, they confirm my belief that individuals can make a difference.

Kim Campbell, Time and Chance: The Political Memoirs of Canada's First Woman Prime Minister (*1997*)

2. Jean Chrétien, prime minister of Canada (1993–2003)

Sometimes Aline and I will go to a police event or state occasion if we're invited, but that happens less and less. It's healthier for us to live with the fact that when you're out, you're out. We're in the stage of our lives in which we would rather be with our children and grandchildren, enjoy a home-cooked meal with friends and relatives, savour each moment together as it passes, and prepare for our next journey, hopefully hand in hand, to a paradise as beautiful as Lac des Piles. *Vive le Canada!*

Jean Chrétien, My Years as Prime Minister (2007)

3. John Diefenbaker, prime minister of Canada (1957-63)
I feel privileged to have had the opportunity to continue serving Canada in the House of Commons. The Canadian people, without regard to political affiliation, have given me their affection. I bear no ill-feeling to those who, in the past, opposed me. But I stand today, as I have always stood, for principle:

Freedom and Equality for all Canadians, however humble in their lot in life and whatever their racial origin. One Canada, One Nation.

John G. Diefenbaker, One Canada: Memoirs of the Right Honourable John G. Diefenbaker; The Tumultuous Years, 1962–1967 (1975)

4. Preston Manning, leader of the Reform Party (1993-2000)
No doubt we will see and hear some things on the frontiers of the twenty-first century that require more than "discussion" around the campfire. In that case, it will be the duty of the scout to urge action—action to avoid the dangers and embrace the opportunities that lie ahead. Then, as always, decisions will have to be made—whether to continue huddling around the campfire of the status quo, endlessly discussing the future possibilities, or to break camp and move forward. I'm all for saddling up and moving forward! How about you?

Preston Manning, Think Big: Adventures in Life and Democracy (2002)

5. Paul Martin, prime minister of Canada (2003-6)
I cannot say for sure whether my aspirations for an African common market will come to fruition, whether the Congo rain forest can be saved to the extent it must, whether my ideas and plans for aboriginal education, mentoring and entrepreneurship will be as successful as I hope, or whether the G8 will expand in the way it should. I am going to give them all the energy I have, and I have

found some very interesting and determined travelling companions for the trip. I imagine there are going to be some surprises along the way, some disappointments and some unanticipated joys. I am looking forward to it.

Paul Martin, Hell or High Water: My Life In and Out of Politics (2008)

6. Brian Mulroney, prime minister of Canada (1984-93)

We spent two days at Harrington Lake as a family before our final departure. I had many calls—Bill Clinton called to wish me well—and my first Clerk of the Privy Council, Gordon Osbaldeston, also telephoned. In 1984, when I took office, his account of Canada's bankrupt state had appalled me. Now, as I left office, his message was much more welcome. "Your achievements such as FTA, NAFTA, GST, privatizations, deficit reduction have been heroic—that is the only appropriate word—and they shall live on long after the critics have been silenced," he said. "I'm only calling to tell you that you have done a magnificent job for Canada and we have admired you greatly." Those were just the words a retired prime minister needed to hear.

Brian Mulroney, Memoirs, 1939–1993 (2007)

7. Lester B. Pearson, prime minister of Canada (1963-68)

My last personal observation on this long road will concern the night of the press gallery dinner for me. It was a very happy occasion with a good many old friends. At the conclusion of the evening, I took a taxi home. I sank back, and began dozing and wondering about the vagaries of life, about what was going to happen now, when I suddenly realized that the driver had gone by the driveway on Sussex Drive. I banged him on the back and said: "In there, in there." The taxi driver turned around and looked at me in a friendly but pitying way: "Mr. Pearson, you don't live there any more."

Lester B. Pearson, Mike: The Memoirs of the Right Honourable Lester B. Pearson, Vol. 3 (1975)

8. Bob Rae, premier of Ontario (1990-95)

All in all, I am happy to have done what I did. I helped to take my party from protest to power. Once in power, we were able to do many good things, as well as learn much about what it is possible to do. Our courage may have been shadowed by weakness, but we were also able to carry some sweetness into the heart of the building.

Bob Rae, From Protest to Power: Personal Reflections on a Life in Politics (1996)

9. Joey Smallwood, premier of Newfoundland (1949-72)

Never say die! Never give in! Turn a deaf ear to the timid and faithless. And then at last, if the very fates do defeat us, go down, not with a whimper, but defiantly to the end. With that spirit there will be no going down. I'd like to have said of me what Kingsley Martin imagined Sir William Beverage might say: "I ruled over an empire in which the concrete never set."

Joey Smallwood, I Chose Canada: The Memoirs of the Honourable Joseph "Joey" Smallwood (1973)

10. Pierre Elliott Trudeau, prime minister of Canada (1968-79, 1980-84)

I look back on those days, and the people I met, with warm memories. And now, as long as there are fascinating new places to explore, new pathways to discover through the forests, new stars to notice in the wilderness sky, new experiences to share, and books to read, I will—God willing—remain a happy man.

Pierre Elliott Trudeau, Memoirs (1993)

11. Eugene Whelan, member of the federal Cabinet (1972-79, 1980-84)

As a boy my only ambition was to drive one of those big black steam locomotives. I just loved the sound of those old trains as they went hissing and roaring by our farm. I loved it when the engineer tooted his whistle and blew steam before the train disappeared off into the distance. Those steam engines are gone now. But I'm still around. And unlike those old-fashioned engines, you haven't necessarily heard the last from Gene Whelan. Not yet.

Eugene Whelan, Whelan: The Man in the Green Stetson (1986)

5 CANADIAN GOVERNMENTS THAT FELL FROM GRACE (BIG TIME)

1. The Conservative Government of Ontario (1934)

The 1930s were not a good time to be in government. Voters were suffering during the Great Depression, and they took out their frustrations on whoever was in office. In Ontario, the recipient of their anger was the Conservative government of Premier George Henry. The Tories had won 90 seats in the 1929 vote, but had only 17 when the election of 1934 was over.

2. The Conservative Government of Prince Edward Island (1935)

Political fortunes can shift quickly in Canada's smallest province. In the provincial election of 1931, the Conservatives won 18 of 30 seats. Four years later, the government of Premier William MacMillan met the same fate as many Depression-era governments. The Tories lost all 30 seats to the Liberals. It was the first time in the British Commonwealth that a government would face no opposition in the House.

3. The Progressive Conservative Government of New Brunswick (1987)

The New Brunswick Tories, led by Richard Hatfield, had been in power since 1970. In the 1982 election, they had won 39 of the province's 58 seats. But in 1987, they lost every single seat to Frank McKenna and the Liberals.

4. The Progressive Conservative Government of Canada (1993)

The federal Tories had 151 seats and were completing their second majority mandate when Prime Minister Kim Campbell called an election for October 25, 1993. On voting day, the Conservatives were reduced to just two seats and went from being the party with the most seats in the House to fifth place. Kim Campbell lost in her own riding and her seat in Parliament.

5. The NDP Government of British Columbia (2001)

The NDP held 39 of the province's 75 seats when the legislature was dissolved by Premier Ujjal Dosanjh. But after the votes were counted on May 16, 2001, the governing party had been reduced to just two seats, as Gordon Campbell and the Liberals swept the province. Like Kim Campbell, Dosanjh lost his own seat.

12 CANADIAN FLAG FLAPS (+ 1 NON-EVENT)

The history of flag flaps in Canada is intriguing because our national colours have not produced the type of patriotic fervour and drama that can be found in other countries. In true Canadian fashion, we have been comparatively civil in our adoption and treatment of the flag. Predictably perhaps, it isn't against the law to destroy our flag, though some firmly worded etiquette discourages committing "indignities" against it. That said, there have been some high-profile incidents involving the Maple Leaf. For the full story on our national symbol, consult Rick Archbold's excellent history *I Stand for Canada: The Story of the Maple Leaf Flag* (2002), which is our source for several of these stories.

1. Grand Designs (1964-65)

Until 1965, when the current version of the flag was adopted, the Union Jack or Red Ensign stood in as our national flag. William Lyon Mackenzie King first raised the idea of getting our own flag in 1919, but it went nowhere with Canadians. He tried again during the next world war, with the same result. But in 1964 Prime Minister Lester B. Pearson proposed a bold new flag, designed by graphic artist Alan Beddoe, which featured three red maple leaves floating on a white background, framed by two blue vertical stripes. Opposition leader John Diefenbaker led the charge to stop the design from being adopted, calling it Pearson's Pennant, and he was joined by an unusual alliance of loyalists, Quebec separatists and veterans. But popular support for the cheerful design grew, and after six months of debate and dramatics, a modified design that dropped the blue bar and featured a lone maple leaf was adopted. The red and white Canadian flag was first hoisted on February 15, 1965. According to Pearson's wife, Maryon, "The flag was the achievement he prized the most."

2. Burning Anger (1987-95)

In the years between the Meech Lake Accord in 1987 and the 1995 Quebec referendum, the Quebec fleur-de-lys and the Canadian flag became targets for Anglo/Franco anger and hostility. In Brockville, Ontario, a few men stomped, spit on and burned a Quebec flag. In retaliation, a few Canadian flags were burned in Quebec.

3. Banned in Quebec City (1990-98)

Following the failure of the Meech Lake Accord in 1990, Jean-Paul L'Allier, the mayor of Quebec City, ordered the Canadian flag removed from the roof of City Hall. It returned in 1998.

4. Costly Giveaway (1996)

In 1996 Heritage Minister Sheila Copps announced a program to give away one million Canadian flags to promote national unity. The total cost was $23 million. The program drew criticism from all sides of the political spectrum.

5. Flag-Waving in the House (1998)

On March 11, 1998, a group of Reform MPs raised a ruckus in the House of Commons by waving Canadian flags while singing "O Canada." Their hijinks were a response to comments made by Bloc Québécois MP Suzanne Tremblay, who had suggested that there were too many Canadian flags being waved at the Nagano Winter Olympics. The flag-waving disruption in the House dragged on for weeks, culminating when the Speaker, Gilbert Parent, declared that the Canadian flag was a "prop" and as such could not be brought into the House "except to quietly adorn individual desks."

6. Flaming Homophobia (1999)

In 1999 a small group of protestors from Topeka, Kansas, burned a Canadian flag in front of Ottawa's Supreme Court building after the court ruled in favour of granting spousal benefits to same-sex partners. They called it "the fag flag."

7. Patriotic Eyesore? (2001)

In 2001 Chris Hollingworth of St. Albert, Alberta, got into a dispute with the building manager of his condo over a Canadian flag in his window. Craig said he put it there after the September 11 terrorist attacks against the United States, but the building manager insisted he take it down because it was "aesthetically unpleasing."

8. The Red Rag (2001)

In 2001 Quebec premier Bernard Landry referred to the Canadian flag as "le chiffon rouge," a red rag. Ottawa voiced its displeasure, and Landry quickly back-tracked, saying he was referring only to bits of red rag used to provoke bulls.

9. Remembrance Day Flag (2004)

In November 2004 André Bellavance, a rookie Bloc Québécois MP, refused to provide a Canadian flag to veterans marking Remembrance Day in his riding. Bellavance said he was a separatist and did not feel obligated to provide the flag. Conservative leader Stephen Harper sent the veterans 10 flags from his own stash, but Prime Minister Paul Martin quickly devised a way to appear even more patriotic: he gave them the flag that flew on Parliament Hill.

10. Newfoundland Furls Its Flags (2004)

On December 23, 2004, Danny Williams, premier of Newfoundland, ordered that all Canadian flags on provincial government buildings be pulled off their official flagpoles to pressure Ottawa for a new offshore oil deal. Ottawa refused to budge, saying there would be no further talks until the flags went back up. Williams caved, but not before the debate whipped up considerable anti-Newfoundland sentiment in mainlanders.

11. G20 Protests (2010)

Vancouver demonstrators wearing face-covering bandanas declared solidarity with their Toronto black bloc counterparts by burning a flag at the corner of Clark Street and East 12th Avenue on the day of the massive arrests at G20 protests. Some participants stomped on the burning flag, and wrote chalk messages on the pavement such as "Up with trees, down with capitalism."

12. Environmental Inaction (2015)

Rick Ainsley of Caledon, Ontario, flew five Canadian flags upside down to protest the town's perceived inaction on environmental issues. Local residents objected and, with Remembrance Day fast approaching, veterans like Joe Brown were particularly vocal: "It's a disgrace. The guy should be arrested." Town councillor Joanna Downey explained that while Ainsley's act was brazenly disrespectful, it was not illegal. Ainsley was encouraged to submit his concerns in writing to the town clerk.

+1 Non-Event. No Hard Feelings (1992)

October 18, 1992. During Game 2 of baseball's World Series in Atlanta, between the Toronto Blue Jays and the Atlanta Braves, the U.S. Marines Color Guard flew the Canadian flag upside down. It could have become an international incident; instead, the mix-up became a source of amusement. Fans at the next game displayed hand-painted signs with both flags and an upside-down caption that said "no hard feelings." To make up for their mistake, the Color Guard flew to Toronto for the next game and flew the Maple Leaf right side up. Toronto ended up winning that game and the World Series.

10 LITTLE-KNOWN FACTS ABOUT R.B. BENNETT

Richard Bedford Bennett (1870–1947) was Canada's prime minister between 1930 and 1935, during the darkest days of the Great Depression. It is hard to imagine that any leader could have achieved much success navigating the ship of state through those dangerous waters, but R.B. Bennett was a singularly unlikable politician. By the time he left office, he was as unpopular as any prime minister before or since. In public, Bennett was widely viewed as uncompromising, unfeeling, imperious, arrogant and rude. The private R.B. Bennett was a kinder, gentler man than his public image would suggest, but he was still, by all accounts, a very unusual man. How unusual? Well, unlike his great political rival and fellow oddball William Lyon Mackenzie King, Bennett did not keep copious diaries, so we do not know as much about his eccentricities as we do about King's. But while R.B. Bennett may not have conducted séances with the dead, he was unquestionably a strange duck in his own unique way. Here's a glimpse inside the hidden world of R.B. Bennett.

1. He promised his mother when he was a child that he would never drink alcohol or smoke, and he never did. Later in life, he would allow sherry to be included in his consommé because he believed that the heat had burned off the alcohol.

2. He had no interest in games, sports, athletics, dancing, hobbies or amusements of any kind.

3. He never went to sleep without first reading a chapter from the Bible.

4. He never married, and as a youth showed little interest in sex. According to a document found in the archives of the Conservative Party, it appears he may have suffered from a condition called phimosis, which caused his foreskin to be wrapped so tightly around his penis that it was painful for him to have an erection. He may have had this condition treated in later life.

5. He preferred to live in expensive hotels rather than houses or apartments. After moving to Calgary in 1897, he checked into the Alberta Hotel and stayed there until 1923, when he moved into suite 759 of the Palliser Hotel. He maintained that suite until he left for England in 1939. When he entered federal politics and moved to Ottawa, he took up permanent residence at the Chateau Laurier hotel.

6. Despite his reputation for not caring about the poor, he was actually very generous and gave away lots of money to people who wrote him seeking help. He also gave each of the 178 employees of the Palliser Hotel a box of chocolates at Christmas.

7. In 1937 he fell madly in love with the widowed mother of future prime minister John Turner. He sent her a dozen roses every day and unsuccessfully tried to convince her to marry him.

8. He was very self-conscious about his clothes. He dressed like a turn-of-the-century banker, favouring a top hat, striped pants and morning coat. He purposely gained weight so as to better fill out his clothes and more closely conform to his carefully cultivated image of a stuffed shirt.

9. He was obsessed with negative press coverage and intensely disliked the ink-stained wretches of the parliamentary press gallery. In 1928, concerned about his lack of favourable coverage in Saskatchewan, he quietly arranged for the purchase of the *Regina Daily Star* to provide a pro-Conservative voice for the province. But the paper was a financial disaster, and Bennett occasionally wound up having to meet the payroll out of his own pocket.

10. He carried on a rather public flirtation with Agnes Macphail, the only female member of the House of Commons. "You have very nice ankles, Agnes," he once said *sotto voce* as she walked past him. For her part, Macphail much preferred Bennett to Mackenzie King, whom she described as a "fat man full of words." And although it is undeniably true that politics makes strange bedfellows, the ultra-conservative prime minister from the country clubs of Calgary and the CCF member from rural Ontario would have made an unlikely couple indeed.

MARGARET MACMILLAN'S 12 FAVOURITE 20TH-CENTURY DIPLOMATIC INCIDENTS

Margaret MacMillan's Paris 1919 *won the Samuel Johnson Prize, the PEN Hessell-Tiltman Prize and the 2003 Governor General's Literary Award for Non-Fiction. She is a professor at the University of Oxford, a senior fellow of Massey College in Toronto and most recently wrote* The War That Ended Peace *and* History's People.

1. Nikita Khrushchev's Shoe
At the United Nations in the fall of 1960, Krushchev heckled and jeered and leapt to his feet at every opportunity to rail against the West. When the representative from the Philippines suggested that the Soviet Union was scarcely in a position to talk about imperialism, given its own record in Eastern Europe, the shoe came off and an enraged Khrushchev banged the desk in front of him. Khrushchev, who actually turned out to be a reasonable man, looked like everyone's image of a brutish Soviet leader.

2. Mussolini's Boat
As the European statesmen gathered in Locarno in 1925 to sign a far-reaching agreement to bring peace to Europe, Mussolini astonished them all by arriving at the wheel of a fast speedboat, splashing many of the onlookers. His aim was to show the virility and modernity of the new Fascist movement and its leader. In the 1920s, though, Mussolini was still prepared to work with the European democracies. In the 1930s his grandiose ambitions to shine on the world stage and to build a second Roman Empire led him and his unfortunate country into the arms of Nazi Germany.

3. Arafat's Choice
In November 1974, over the objections of the United States, Israel and their allies, Yasser Arafat, the chairman of the Palestinian Liberation Organization, was invited to speak to the UN's General Assembly. With his head covered by his checked keffiyeh, wearing his usual dark glasses and a gun holster, he asked the world to decide whether it wanted an olive branch or a freedom fighter's gun. Arafat had wanted to bring the gun as well, but that was not allowed in the UN so he had to make do with the holster.

4. Stalin's Toast

The German-Soviet non-aggression pact of 1939 signalled the start of another European war. Its secret clauses, which only became public after the war, divided up the centre of Europe between the two totalitarian regimes. Hitler now had a free hand to turn on Poland, which Britain and France had promised to defend. After Joachim von Ribbentrop, a smooth-talking former champagne salesman turned German foreign minister, and Vyacheslav Molotov, his dour Russian counterpart, had signed the pact, Stalin held a late-night celebration dinner in the Kremlin. Ribbentrop congratulated the Soviet dictator on his 60th birthday. Stalin replied with a toast to Hitler, and spoke warmly of the friendship between the Germans and the Russians, "forged," as he put it, "in blood."

5. De Gaulle's Mischief

In 1967, the French president, Charles de Gaulle, came to Canada, ostensibly to share in the nation's centenary celebrations. As he entered the Hotel de Ville in Montreal, he told the mayor, Jean Drapeau, that he wished to address the crowd from the balcony. None of his party, including the French ambassador to Canada, knew that the old man intended to declaim the separatist slogan, "Vive le Quebec libre." The Liberal government of Lester Pearson, in an un-Canadian display of anger, declared de Gaulle's statement "unacceptable."

6. Chamberlain's Piece of Paper

In September 1938, Neville Chamberlain flew to Munich in a last-ditch effort to dissuade Hitler from invading Czechoslovakia. Britain and France, both of which still hoped that appeasing Hitler would prevent a general European war, persuaded a reluctant Czech government to hand over the Sudetenland, where the German minority lived. Hitler, who had already swallowed up Austria, now acquired a valuable strategic territory and many of Czechoslovakia's industrial plants. The British prime minister got Hitler to sign a declaration stating that both countries intended to avoid war with each other and to settle their differences peacefully. When Chamberlain landed in England, he waved the piece of paper at the waiting reporters. He was bringing back, so he hoped, "peace in our time." He was wrong, of course. Hitler had no intention of keeping his promise. Nor did he intend, in spite of what he had said, to leave what was left of Czechoslovakia in peace. A year later, Europe was at war.

7. The Yalta Photograph

The last time the three great Allied leaders of the Second World War met was in the Crimean resort town of Yalta. The photograph shows a gaunt Roosevelt (he was dead two months later) between Churchill and Stalin. All three men are smiling, but in reality the conference was a difficult one that foreshadowed the breakup of the Grand Alliance and the beginning of the Cold War. While Roosevelt talked hopefully of the new United Nations, Churchill did his best to plead for independence for the countries in the centre of Europe. Stalin gave vague and, in the end, worthless assurances. With his armies occupying the centre of Europe, the Soviet Union started to consolidate its grip on countries such as Poland and Czechoslovakia.

8. Kennedy's Visit to West Berlin

The East Germans took the West by surprise when they threw up the wall between East and West Berlin one night in August 1961. Although the United States and its allies considered a military response, they did nothing. President Kennedy, though, went to West Berlin the following year and told the enthusiastic crowds, *"Ich bin ein Berliner."* The *ein* was a mistake, and his carefully memorized sentence translated as "I am a jelly doughnut."

9. Dulles's Snub

The Geneva conference of 1954, which was supposed to wrap up the Korean War and settle the fate of French Indochina, was one of the first times that representatives of the new People's Republic of China appeared on the international stage. As Chou Enlai, the urbane Chinese foreign minister, advanced towards John Foster Dulles with his hand outstretched, the American secretary of state turned away. The Chinese did not forget the snub; when President Nixon went to Beijing in 1972, he had to assure the Chinese that this time there would be a handshake.

10. The Ambassador's Tears

On August 2, 1914, Count Friedrich von Pourtalès, the German ambassador in St. Petersburg, delivered Germany's declaration of war on Russia. German troops were already moving towards Belgium and France; Austria-Hungary was preparing to invade Serbia; and the British were under intense pressure to support France and Russia. The general European war, which had threatened to explode for so long, was under way. Pourtalès, who had never believed that

Russia and Germany would go to war, wept as he handed over the declaration to the Russian foreign minister.

11. Sadat's Trip

In 1977, the Egyptian president, Anwar Sadat, stunned his fellow Arabs and the world when he declared that he was ready to go to the ends of the earth, even to Israel itself, in the cause of peace. That November, he flew to Ben Gurion Airport, the first Arab statesman to pay an official visit to the Jewish state. At the Knesset, Sadat pleaded for an end to the bloodshed that had destroyed so many Arab and Jewish lives. Israel had a right to exist, he affirmed, at peace with its neighbours, as a state in the Middle East. Two years later Egypt and Israel signed a peace treaty. In 1981 Sadat paid the ultimate price for his courage: an Islamic fundamentalist assassinated him.

12. Clemenceau's Revenge

The great Hall of Mirrors in Louis XIV's palace at Versailles has seen many events in the long struggle between Germans and French for control of Europe. In 1871, in the aftermath of a French defeat, the new German Reich was proclaimed there and the King of Prussia crowned as the German emperor. In 1919, at the end of the First World War, Georges Clemenceau arranged for German delegates to come to the Hall of Mirrors to sign the Treaty of Versailles, which marked, for a time, Germany's defeat by France and its allies.

Places

28 FAILED NAMES FOR CANADA

Canada comes from the Huron-Iroquois word *kanata*, which means "village" or "settlement."

Jacques Cartier first heard it in reference to Quebec City, but it was soon used to refer to the whole region. Looking back, *Canada* seems like an obvious pick for our country, but that was not the case in 1867, when the Fathers of Confederation went looking for a name. Many suggestions were made, but fiery Member of Parliament Thomas D'Arcy McGee made the case for adopting *Canada* on February 9, 1865, when he pointed out that the alternatives were absurd: "Now I would ask any Hon. Member of the House how he would feel if he woke up some fine morning and found himself, instead of a Canadian, a Tuponian or Hochelagander?" His words rang true, evidently, and on July 1, 1867, when the British North America Act was declared, the name Canada was formally adopted. Here is a list of the names for Canada that were suggested and rejected:

1. Acadia
2. Albertland or Albertsland
3. Albionara
4. Albona
5. Alexandrina
6. Aquilonia
7. Borealia
8. British North America
9. Brittania or Britannica
10. Cabotia
11. Canadensia
12. Colonia
13. Efisga
14. Hochelaga
15. Laurentia
16. Mesopelagia
17. New Albion
18. Niagarentia
19. Norland
20. Superior
21. Transatlantia
22. Transatlantica
23. Transylvania
24. Tuponia
25. Ursulia
26. Vesperia
27. Victorialand
28. Victorialia

8 WILD AND WOOLLY OCCURRENCES AT TIM HORTONS

1. Snake Throwing and Unicorn BLTs

In December 2014, two 20-year-old men were captured on video throwing a snake at a Tim Hortons staffer in Saskatoon. The incident unfolded as the pair ordered an elaborate meal including an "extra large triple-triple coffee," a breakfast biscuit with undercooked sausage and a BLT with "extra-fresh lettuce, nice diced tomatoes [and] the best kind of BLT bacon in the house—the kind of BLTs unicorns are made of." When the clerk explained they could neither fill this order nor add the requested teriyaki sauce and double bacon, mayhem ensued. Clearly agitated, one man reached into the other man's coat pocket and yelled, "I'm going to release my snake." He threw the garter snake over the counter. Staff screamed and ran out of the store. Christopher Jordon Cook received six months' probation for causing mischief and a public disturbance. His co-accused did not show up for his court date.

2. Deer Crashing through Store Windows

On June 11, 2015, a deer in Chatham, Ontario, broke through a front window and ran out an exit door, apparently unharmed. In July 2010 in Glace Bay, Nova Scotia, a deer smashed through the glass and was trapped in the store until Cape Breton police helped it escape by holding open a door. On September 19, 2016, in Kitchener, Ontario, another deer broke through a Timmy's window but cut its neck so severely it had to be euthanized. According to wildlife experts, deer sometimes wander into settled areas looking for food or avoiding coyotes and get disoriented. When startled, their defence is to flee, and they can mistake glass windows for a darkened passageway or escape route.

3. Drive-Thru Rage

People craving a caffeine fix can become extremely cranky. In April 2016 in Winnipeg, one driver thought the driver in front was taking too long at the window and let him know it. The now irritated 65-year-old exited his vehicle and punched the 21-year-old in the car behind him, who then stabbed the senior. The injuries were not life threatening, and both were charged with assault. On Vancouver Island in December 2015 another raging drive-thru customer chased a Timmy's patron down the highway, forced him to pull over and promptly smashed his windows, headlights and hood with a sledgehammer. In Yarmouth, Nova Scotia, Robert Chetwynd was charged with threatening to kill a police constable in September 2003 after he "tried to ram" the officer's car with his horse while attempting to order coffee from the saddle. The rider had been banned from the drive-thru for previous attempts to order coffee while mounted on his gelding, Dillon. He eventually got six months' house arrest, three years' probation and was ordered to pay fines and restitution for the cost of looking after his horse, who was not injured during the incident.

4. Stubborn Goat

On September 27, 2015, a small brown goat entered a Tim Hortons in Warman, Saskatchewan, and refused to leave. He sat down just inside the sliding doors and could not be coaxed to exit. Mounties on the scene led the goat outside, but he kept turning around and entering through the automated doors. Police concluded the goat was cold, so they put him in their cruiser and drove around to local farms trying to find his owner. When they were not successful, the goat was boarded overnight at a vet's and was reunited with its owners the next day.

5. Bus Hijacking

On March 17, 2016, a man boarded a Toronto transit bus, wielded a switchblade and demanded to be taken to a Tim Hortons a few kilometres east along Steeles Avenue. He waited while the driver got the other passengers off the bus, then forced him to speed along the busy arterial, running red lights, to get to a Timmy's near York University. He exited the bus and explained to staff he wanted to call 911 to report being high on drugs. Police showed up, saw him seated and drinking coffee, determined he was acting erratically but not violently and took him to the hospital for assistance. Daniel Ferreira was charged with assault, mischief, endangering life, forcible confinement, uttering threats and taking a motor vehicle without consent.

6. No Pants, No Service

Risking limb not life, a naked male driver ordered a piping hot beverage at the Timmy's drive-thru in Bracebridge, Ontario, in the spring of 2010. He also visited the drive-thru at a nearby A&W and was spotted strolling through a local park. All of this landed him in court, charged with being nude in public. His defence lawyer, Clayton Ruby, challenged the constitutionality of Canada's nudity laws, claiming that his client, Brian Coldin, was wearing sandals, and thus not naked at the time. Justice Jon-Jo Douglas was having none of it, however, declaring that it was not too much to ask that a person put on pants before appearing in public, and "not only must those who live in glass homes not throw stones, they must buy curtains." Far from being a rare occurrence, flashers routinely hit the Tim Horton's drive-thru across Canada.

7. A 15-pack of Timbits

An enterprising female employee at a Tim Hortons in Halifax devised a way to sell marijuana to discerning drive-thru customers. The manager sensed

something was up when he heard some drivers order a 15-pack of Timbits—
he knew they only came in packs of 20 and 45. He waited until the next order
came through, watched the 22-year-old staffer retrieve something from the
back and return with a coffee cup in hand. The manager intercepted the order
and found a plastic bag of dope inside. Kari Royea was charged and fined with
trafficking marijuana.

8. Man Punches Cougar to Save Dog

Electrical contractor William Gibb was on his way to work one morning when
he pulled into the Timmy's in Whitecourt, Alberta. He let his two huskies out
for a whiz by a wooded patch at the back of the parking lot. Before long he heard
five-year-old Sacha yelp in pain. He ran into the woods and saw the dog being
mauled by a furry beast. Without thinking, he jumped on top and punched it in
the head repeatedly, only to realize it was a full-sized cougar. The cat backed off,
pawed at Gibb for a bit, then turned tail and ran. Seriously injured, Sacha was
rushed to a nearby vet clinic where her lacerations and puncture wounds were
stitched up. She survived and Gibb was unscathed from the attack.

With research files from Stephanie Chambers.

NICK PURDON'S 5 EXPEDITIONS IN THE CANADIAN NORTH THAT ENDED BADLY

Nick Purdon is a reporter for The National *on CBC TV, and an avid paddler.*

1. Eating Shoe Leather and Each Other, Part 1

Sir John Franklin could be on this list twice. In 1819 he led an expedition to
map part of what is now the Canadian Arctic coastline. On a desperate return
journey overland, several of Franklin's men ran out of food. They attempted
to subsist on *tripe de roche* (a black and nearly nutritionless lichen) and boiled
shoe leather. In the end, nine of them died of starvation and exposure. Another
man was killed because he was thought to have resorted to cannibalism. But
the biggest disaster was yet to come. In 1845 the famous explorer set sail from
England in search of the Northwest Passage. With well over 100 men on board
his two ships, and enough food to last several years (including 8,000 cans of
meat, vegetables and soup), Franklin's was the best-equipped expedition ever.
Unfortunately, they were never heard from again. Both ships became trapped

in the Arctic ice in 1848. By then, Franklin and 23 others had died. The commonly held belief has always been that the 10 trudged south across the mainland, some apparently resorting to cannibalism along the way. None was ever found alive. One popular theory was that either scurvy or lead poisoning from badly soldered tins killed the majority of the men.

But when Franklin's ships, the HMS *Erebus* and *Terror*, were located in 2014 and 2016, respectively, all the old narratives were thrown into question. The *Terror* was found in pristine condition (even its windows were still intact), as if it had been secured for winter before it ultimately sank. One researcher wondered: if you brought the *Terror* to the surface and pumped out the water, would it still float? The other surprise was that both ships were found much farther south than anyone ever expected. Some experts suggest all of this could mean that at least some of the desperate Franklin survivors may have secured the HMS *Terror*, and then fled in the expedition's flagship vessel, the HMS *Erebus*, only to meet their grisly fate trying to sail south to safety.

2. Eating Shoe Leather and Each Other, Part 2

In the summer of 1881, American lieutenant Adolphus Greely's supply ship sailed from Newfoundland to Lady Franklin Bay (there's that name again). Greely and his 25 men were dropped in the remote Canadian High Arctic with a whopping 350 tons of gear and food. It wouldn't be enough. The men built a base camp on Ellesmere Island. From there the plan was to gather scientific data and to trek farther north than the record-setting English had gone decades before. Greely's men achieved both goals, toughed out the harsh winter and waited to be picked up, but no ship arrived the following summer as was the plan. Nor did a ship come the summer after that. Both times the rescue vessels were stopped by ice. After waiting for three years, the men gave up hope, and on August 9, 1883, they abandoned their camp and made a desperate attempt to reach a known rendezvous point to the south. Along the way, there was mutiny, starvation, suicide, more consumption of shoe leather and cannibalism. By the time a ship finally did reach the expedition in June 1884, only seven of Greely's 25 men were still alive, and one of them died shortly thereafter. A subsequent investigation cleared Greely of any wrongdoing. He went on to write a book about his adventures.

3. Hubbard Goes Hungry

Leonidas Hubbard was an American writer who wanted to make a name for himself as an explorer. So, in 1903, along with two companions, he embarked on a canoe trip to explore the interior of Labrador. However, almost immediately after leaving civilization, the three men made a critical blunder: they read their map incorrectly and turned up the wrong river. For months the explorers paddled and portaged deeper and deeper into the wilderness, becoming more and more lost. Finally, with their food supplies dwindling and winter upon them, they turned back. Nearing the end of their strength, and with Hubbard deathly ill, his companions left him behind and made a dash for help. Hubbard wrote in his diary, "acute pangs of hunger have given way to indifference. I am sleepy. But let no one suppose that I expect it. I am prepared, that is all. I think the boys will be able with the Lord's help to save me." In fact, they couldn't. Hubbard died of starvation, alone in his tent. Two years later, his wife, Mina, embarked on the same journey and route, completing it without a problem.

4. Troubles on the Thelon

There is a point along the Thelon River in northern Canada where the barren tundra gives way to an oasis of spruce trees. It was there in 1926 that legendary trapper John Hornby planned to spend the winter with his 17-year-old nephew Edgar Christian and another young man named Harold Adlard. Hornby's theory was that, because of the trees, some of the migrating caribou would stick around for the winter. Hornby was wrong. By mid-winter the group's meagre food supply was almost gone. By early spring Hornby and Adlard had both starved to death. Christian, too weak to hunt, subsisted on the fur and bones the group had thrown out earlier in the year. He lay in his bed and wrote a diary as he slowly wasted away. When spring arrived and the animals returned to the area, Christian was too weak to pick up the loaded gun he kept by the door. His final journal entry was on June 1, 1927: "Got out too weak and all in now. Left Things Late." The three bodies weren't recovered until more than two years after Christian's death. The story of the three men starving in the Canadian wilderness became an international media sensation.

5. Moffatt Goes Mad

It was supposed to be the expedition of a lifetime, but instead it's often used as an example of how not to plan a canoe trip. In 1955 American Arthur Moffatt, an experienced canoeist and filmmaker, led a group of five young men across the Canadian tundra and down the remote Dubawnt River. By late summer, delayed by high winds and Moffatt's filming, the group was running out of food. Then it began to snow. According to one of the participants, George Grinnell, whose book *Death on the Barrens* was published in 1996, a kind of insanity brought on by hunger and fatigue overcame the group. Instead of quickening their pace at this point, the paddlers slowed down. They took rest days and went hiking. Then, on September 14, 75 days into their expedition, two of the three canoes dumped in a set of rapids. The water was almost freezing. The young men managed to drag their leader to shore, but Moffatt died of exposure. The rest of the group barely survived. In 1984 disaster struck Grinnell again when two of his sons went missing on James Bay after a canoe trip down the Albany River. They were never found. In 2014 another member of the group, Fred "Skip" Pessl, who long believed people were too hard on Moffatt, wrote his own account of the Dubawnt disaster using Moffatt's personal journals.

THE 15 LEAST POPULOUS INDEPENDENT NATIONS

		Population
1.	Nauru	9,591
2.	Tuvalu	10,959
3.	Palau	21,347
4.	Monaco	30,581
5.	San Marino	33,285
6.	Liechtenstein	37,937
7.	Saint Kitts and Nevis	52,329
8.	Marshall Islands	73,376
9.	Dominica	73,757
10.	Andorra	85,660
11.	Seychelles	93,186
12.	Antigua and Barbuda	93,581
13.	Federated States of Micronesia	104,719
14.	Tonga	106,513
15.	Kiribati	106,925

Source: U.S. Census Bureau, International Database, 2016.

JOHN LORINC'S 8 CANADIAN URBAN PLANNING BLUNDERS

The relatively brief history of urban planning—as a discipline, it's scarcely a century old—encompasses an impressively long list of planning blunders, which could be defined, loosely, as mistakes inflicted on the face of the city that go beyond mere cosmetics. The most infamous can permanently alter commerce and traffic, foster crime and produce social isolation. Herewith, a sample of Canada's most notorious planning errors.

John Lorinc is a Toronto journalist who frequently writes about urban and municipal affairs for publications such as the Globe and Mail, Toronto Star, Spacing *and* Canadian Business. *He has written two urban affairs books and is the co-editor of* Coach House *anthologies, including* The Ward: The Life and Loss of Toronto's First Immigrant Neighbourhood *and* Any Other Way: How Toronto Got Queer.

1. Allen Road, Toronto

This stub expressway, extending south from the 401 and terminating mid-town, is one of a few examples of what happens when a controlled-access highway slams into a residential neighbourhood. The reformist narrative of Toronto in the late '60s and early '70s pivots around a David-and-Goliath story of how Annex activists, among them author and urbanist Jane Jacobs, blocked a proposed highway linking the 401 to the core by slashing through residential areas and the University of Toronto. When then premier Bill Davis cancelled the project in 1971, the northern portion of the Spadina Expressway had been half excavated. The municipal government finished that stretch, thereby producing a traffic snarl that keeps on giving to this day.

2. Turcot Interchange, Montreal

The concrete spaghetti tangle at the spot where the trenched Autoroute Décarie merges with Highway 720, which forces cars into Montreal's business core, is a textbook example of how expressways can sterilize and divide urban neighbourhoods. The Décarie is Montreal's equivalent of Toronto's Spadina Expressway, except it was actually built. The 720 carves a slash across the city's escarpment, throws destructive off-ramp tendrils into the downtown and then burrows under old Montreal. The tunnelling, meant to blunt the visual impact of a downtown highway, produced a kind of DMZ through the core and spawned several heavy-handed renewal schemes. Montreal has several other downtown highway snarls—one at the north end of the Décarie, and another at the base of the Mercier Bridge.

3. Cogswell Interchange, Halifax

This road to nowhere cuts Halifax's downtown in half, separating a north-end community from the rest of the city with significant social consequences. It also served to limit the growth of the city core. The project dates to a late-1960s scheme to build an elevated highway along the waterfront, but the city, in a classic example of putting the cart before the horse, built the interchange and then cancelled the highway just a year later, thus transforming it into a space-hogging monument to bad traffic planning. The Halifax Regional Municipality has embarked on plans to remove the Cogswell, although calls for its demolition date to the late 1990s.

4. De-pedestrianizing Portage and Main, Winnipeg

In the mid-1970s, as part of a downtown revitalization scheme, City of Winnipeg officials cut a 50-year deal with several developers that owned land on the four corners of the city's storied but windswept hub: if they would construct underground retail concourses linking the proposed office towers, the city would take steps to ensure that pedestrians used those new tunnels. The solution: the installation of chest-high barriers on the corners that physically prevent pedestrians from crossing at grade. Former mayor Glen Murray came closest to negotiating an end to the deal, but didn't manage to get all the owners on side. With the deal set to expire, the city is looking at re-opening the intersection and building a roundabout.

5. NIMBY-ism Writ Regional, Vancouver

Legendary planning chief Larry Beasley brought city-defining zoning changes to the West End that created a widely praised form of intensification featuring high-rise point towers but with extensive investment in the neighbourhood's public spaces, resulting in density but also lively street life. Vast tracts of Vancouver and Burnaby, however, remain protected by zoning rules that make it exceedingly difficult for developers to add mid-rise density to main streets serving exceedingly expensive single-family residential neighbourhoods. Vancouver's beauty and constrained geography have driven up house prices to outrageous levels, but municipal officials and residents steadfastly oppose zoning changes that would make housing more affordable.

6. Transit and Pedestrian Malls, Ottawa

Ottawa's planning has traditionally been greatly complicated by the role of the

National Capital Commission, which owns and plans all federal lands and exerts a strong gravitational force on the city. Two optimistic examples of 1970s/80s-vintage planning serve as an object lesson in how to eliminate pedestrian activity. The Sparks Street pedestrian mall succeeded in killing much of the retail along one of Ottawa's main streets. Meanwhile, the Rideau Street transit mall—a buses-only stretch just east of Parliament Hill that abuts the ByWard Market—succeeded in sterilizing the street life on those blocks (the redevelopment of the area with large enclosed malls on either side didn't help).

7. Putting Subways in the Wrong Place, Toronto

When Bill Davis iced the Spadina Expressway, the provincial government pledged new rapid-transit investment, specifically an extension of the University subway line north of Bloor Street. But while transit advocates were pushing for the line to go under Bathurst Street, Metro Toronto politicians opted to route the new Spadina subway, which opened in 1978, beneath a ravine and then along the middle of Allen Road, thereby relegating the route to chronic under-utilization. The legacy of that mistake persists as the city continues to build increasingly expensive subways into low-density suburban areas that don't have the population to support rapid transit.

8. Block-busting, various cities

Seized by a desire to clear so-called slums, municipal officials in cities across Canada approved the expropriation and demolition of older working-class or immigrant/racialized-minority enclaves—Vancouver's Hogan's Alley, Montreal's Chinatown, Halifax's Africville, Toronto's Cabbagetown—to make way for large-scale urban renewal schemes, many of which involved monolithic 1960s-vintage public-housing projects. Self-righteous postwar planners and municipal politicians could only see rundown houses and social ills when they pulled the plug on these neighbourhoods, but the cure—a debased public realm, the eradication of small-scale commercial spaces, and the lack of services—was almost always worse than the disease.

6 DREAMERS AND DESIGNERS UNDONE BY THEIR BUILDINGS

1. Antoni Gaudí and Sagrada Família

Barcelona's audacious architect Antoni Gaudí was inspired by bold colours, shapes and curves from nature, giving his work a surreal, almost psychedelic effect. He had many lucrative commissions for homes and commercial buildings, but starting in 1883, he devoted the last half of his life to designing the massive Catholic church Sagrada Família that is still being built today. By 1914 he had moved into his studio inside the building's shell. He worked obsessively on every design detail, became reclusive, gave up meat and alcohol, fasted and let his hygiene habits slip. On his way to daily mass and confession on June 7, 1926, Gaudí was hit by a tram, but nobody recognized the gaunt, unkempt old master who clung to life for two more days. Barcelona mourned his death and buried him in the Sagrada Família crypt. Work on his building continues around him, and is now expected to be finished in 2026, the 100th anniversary of his death.

2. Henry Pellatt and Casa Loma

Henry Pellatt made a fortune in electrical utilities, arc-lighting streets and powering the streetcars first in Toronto and then in cities around the world. At age 45 he embarked on building a fairy tale–inspired castle that would become his undoing. Pellatt was not one to scrimp on details: the main building had 98 rooms, including 30 bathrooms, three bowling alleys, secret passageways, solid mahogany floors, bronze doors and a shooting range. The price tag was a cool $3.5 million, or about $80 million in today's terms. The Pellatts moved in around 1914, but the epic society parties and champagne fountains started in earnest after the war. The source of Pellatt's wealth, private electrification, dried up as more municipalities made their electricity utilities public. By 1923, the Pellatts were up to their eyeballs in debt and staring down imminent foreclosure. Lady Pellatt keeled over and died of a heart attack in the spring of 1924, and Henry signed over the property to the City of Toronto for back taxes. Casa Loma sat vacant for years and ultimately became a tourist attraction and event facility. Pellatt lived another 15 years, in relative obscurity, never regaining his affluence or status.

3. Robert Dunsmuir and the Craigdarroch Castle

Victoria's Scottish Baronial 39-room mansion, Craigdarroch Castle, was built in the late 1800s for coal baron Robert Dunsmuir. The eye-popping design by architect Warren Heywood Williams featured intricate brick, stone, glass and woodwork. The building was intended to cement the family's social standing and wealth, but both architect and client died before the building was completed. Dunsmuir's sons eventually finished the castle at a cost of over $500,000, but when Joan Dunsmuir, the widow, died, it was sold to real estate speculator Griffith Hughes for a mere $38,000. Hughes hit on hard times, raffled off the building and the winner, Solomon Cameron, went bankrupt trying to leverage the white elephant to finance other deals. By 1919 Craigdarroch Castle had slipped into the hands of a creditor, the Bank of Montreal, though it survives today as a tourist attraction run by a non-profit historical society.

4. Rod Robbie and SkyDome

The downtown Toronto home of the MLB Blue Jays has never been a hit with architectural critics, but when it opened in 1989 with the world's first retractable roof and huge seating capacity, SkyDome could boast some impressive design and engineering feats. Architect Rod Robbie was driven to the brink with the pressures of the job and huge budget overruns that saw the project go from initial estimates of $125 million to final costs of $650 million. Financially hanging by a thread, Robbie submitted a claim for $36 million in fees, but after much wrangling, agreed to be paid only $24 million. His company was finished and his reputation in tatters. Rogers Communications picked up SkyDome for a song in 2005, with taxpayers covering the bulk of the capital losses.

5. The Reichmann Brothers and Canary Wharf

The Reichmann brothers of Montreal made a fortune in the 1980s and '90s with their internationally successful development company Olympia & York. Paul and Edward were practically wiped out, however, when they overextended themselves on what was the biggest development project in the world at that time, London's Canary Wharf. With troubles exacerbated by the recession of the early '90s, Olympia & York collapsed under the pressure of $20 billion dollars of debt, and the Reichmanns lost most of their family fortune. Paul eventually clawed his way out of the basement, even becoming the chair of Canary Wharf for a stint. The project itself has proven very profitable to a range of investors including George Soros, Brascan and Morgan Stanley.

6. Brigitta Hennig and Wolfgang Spiegelhauer and Aspotogan Sea Spa

Big dreams can sometimes lead to big nightmares. Just ask (if you can find them) German siblings Brigitta Hennig and Wolfgang Spiegelhauer, who saw their audacious dream to build a year-round luxury resort and spa on Nova Scotia's pristine South Shore turn into a major financial nightmare. The Aspotogan Sea Spa was to have 131 rooms, each boasting a sweeping view of the Atlantic Ocean. The estimated price tag was $37.5 million. Construction began in 1992, but Hennig and Spiegelhauer quickly ran into trouble raising the cash they needed to keep building. Within a year, they had run out of money, and construction ground to a halt, leaving in its wake unhappy tradespeople and creditors and an unfinished five-storey white stone shell of a building. The siblings quietly slipped away, never to be seen in Nova Scotia again. The building was eventually sold by its creditors for about half a million dollars, but the new owners couldn't figure out what to do with it. In 2015, more than 20 years after construction began, what was left of the Aspotogan Sea Spa was finally demolished.

With Annabel Vaughan.

THE 7 WONDERS OF THE ANCIENT WORLD

Who created one of the earliest and most enduring of all lists, a list that arbitrarily named the seven most spectacular sights existing in the world 150 years before the birth of Jesus Christ? The list was created by a most respected Byzantine mathematician and traveller named Philon. In a series of arduous trips, Philon saw all of the Western civilized world there was to see in his time, and then he sat down and wrote a short but widely circulated paper entitled "*De Septem Orbis Spectaculis*" ("The Seven Wonders of the World").

1. The Great Pyramid of Cheops (Egypt)

Begun as a royal tomb around 2600 BCE, and standing in splendour for 2,000 years before any of the other six wonders were built, this largest of Egypt's 80-odd pyramids is the only wonder to have survived to this day. Located outside Cairo, near Giza, the burial tomb of King Cheops was made up of 2.3 million blocks of stone, some of them weighing 2 1/2 tons. With a height of 147 metres and a base width of 230 metres on each side, it's large enough to enclose London's Westminster Abbey, Rome's St. Peter's, and Milan's and Florence's main cathedrals.

2. The Hanging Gardens of Babylon (Iraq)

When Nebuchadnezzar brought home his new wife, a princess from Media, she pined for the mountains and lush growth of her native land. To please her, in 600 BCE the king started to build a man-made mountain with exotic growths. Actually, it was a square climbing upward, each balcony or terrace densely planted with grass, flowers and fruit trees, irrigated from below by pumps manned by slaves or oxen. Inside and beneath the gardens, the queen held court amid the vegetation and artificial rain. Due to the erosion of time and the influx of conquerors, the Hanging Gardens had been levelled and reduced to wilderness when Pliny the Elder visited them before his death in AD 79.

3. The Statue of Zeus at Olympia (Greece)

The multicoloured Temple of Zeus, in the area where the Greek Olympic Games were held every fourth year, contained the magnificent statue of Zeus, king of the gods. Sculpted by Phidias (who had done Athena for the Parthenon) sometime after 432 BCE, the statue was 12 metres high, made of ivory and gold plates set on wood. Zeus, with jewels for eyes, sat on a golden throne, feet resting on a footstool of gold. Ancients came from afar to worship at the god's feet. A Greek writer, Pausanias, saw the statue intact as late as the second century AD. After that, it disappeared from history, probably the victim of looting armies and fire.

4. The Temple of Diana at Ephesus (Turkey)

Summing up his seven wonders, Philon chose his favourite: "But when I saw the temple at Ephesus rising to the clouds, all these other wonders were put in the shade." The temple, a religious shrine built after 350 BCE, housed a statue of Diana, goddess of hunting, symbol of fertility. The kings of many Asian states contributed to the construction. The temple, 69 metres wide and 160 metres long, was supported by 127 marble columns 18 metres high. As quoted in the New Testament, St. Paul railed against it, saying, "the temple of the great goddess Diana should be despised, and her magnificence should be destroyed, whom all Asia and the world worshippeth." The craftsmen of the temple disagreed: "And when they heard these sayings, they were full of wrath, and cried out, saying, 'Great is Diana of the Ephesians.'" Ravaged and brought down by invaders, the temple was rebuilt three times before the Goths permanently destroyed it in AD 262. In 1874, after 11 years of digging, the English archaeologist J.T. Wood unearthed fragments of the original columns.

5. The Tomb of King Mausolus at Halicarnassus (Turkey)

King Mausolus, conqueror of Rhodes, ruled over the Persian province of Caria. His queen, Artemisia, was also his sister. When he died in 353 BCE, he was cremated and his grieving widow drank his ashes in wine. As a memorial to him, she determined to build the most beautiful tomb in the world at Halicarnassus, now called Bodrum. She sent to Greece for the greatest architects and sculptors, and by 350 BCE the memorial was complete. There was a rectangular sculpted marble tomb on a platform, then 36 golden-white Ionic columns upon which sat an architrave, which in turn held a pyramid topped by a bronzed chariot with statues of Mausolus and Artemisia. The monument survived for 1,900 years, only to tumble down in an earthquake. What remains of it today is the word "mausoleum."

6. The Colossus of Rhodes on the Isle of Rhodes (Aegean Sea)

To celebrate being saved from a Macedonian siege by Ptolemy I, the Rhodians, between 292 and 280 BCE, erected a mammoth statue to their heavenly protector, the sun god Apollo. Chares, who had studied under a favourite of Alexander the Great, fashioned the statue. The nude colossus was 37 metres tall, with its chest and back 18 metres around, built of stone blocks and iron and plated with thin bronze. It did not stand astride the harbour, with room for ships to pass between the legs, but stood with feet together on a promontory at the entrance to the harbour. In 224 BCE it was felled by an earthquake. It lay in ruins for almost 900 years. In AD 667 the Arabs, who controlled Rhodes, sold the 327,000 kilograms of broken statue for scrap metal to a Jewish merchant. When the merchant hauled his purchase to Alexandria, he found that it required 900 camel loads.

7. The Lighthouse on the Isle of Pharos (off Alexandria, Egypt)

On the orders of Ptolemy Philadelphus, in 200 BCE the architect Sostratus of Cnidus constructed a pharos, or lighthouse, such as the world had not seen before. Built on a small island off Alexandria, the tiers of the marble tower— first square, then round, each with a balcony—rose to a height of 122 metres. At the summit, a huge brazier with an eternal flame was amplified by a great glass mirror so that the fire could be seen 483 kilometres out at sea. Half of the lighthouse was torn down by occupying Arabs, who hoped to find gold inside. The rest of the structure crashed to the ground when an earthquake struck in 1375.

10 BIG CANADIAN PLACES

1. Big Dam, Quebec
2. Big Woody, Manitoba

3. Big Ovens, New Brunswick
4. Big Wheel Flats, British Columbia
5. Big Hole, New Brunswick
6. Big Oven Cave, Newfoundland & Labrador
7. Big Kettle Fumarole, British Columbia
8. Big Beaver, Saskatchewan
9. Big Head, Newfoundland & Labrador
10. Big Bon Mature Lake, Nova Scotia

"ROSIE" ROWBOTHAM'S 8 FAVOURITE SOURCES FOR HASHISH

In the 1960s and early '70s, Robert "Rosie" Rowbotham was one of Canada's leading importers of marijuana and hashish. He supplied a substantial portion of the soft drugs that fuelled the infamous drug scene at Toronto's Rochdale College. But federal authorities did not appreciate Rosie's entrepreneurial spirit. He spent most of the years between 1977 and 1997 locked up in various federal institutions. After his release, Rosie worked as a journalist for CBC Radio. During his years of incarceration, Rosie never lost his appreciation for fine-quality hashish. Here are the sources of eight of his road-tested favourites. (See also Rosie's list about the legalization of marijuana in chapter 8.)

1. Mazar-e Sharif, Afghanistan
In the northwest frontier region is the timeless hub of hashish production steeped in centuries of tradition and pride. The bulk of Afghan commercial hash production is derived by beating cannabis plants over a series of screens and collecting the consequent pollen. This crude pollen is then pounded into kilo blocks—with animal fat or milk added for adhesion and as a preservative—by ancient presses, usually made of stone. But with primo Afghan hashish, the pollen is hand-pressed with only water. Buddha Bob, from Timothy Leary's brotherhood, introduced me to Afghan "surfboards," which the hippies brought into California through Mexico. Each plate was 10 by 25 centimetres long and 0.5 centimetre thick, and weighed about 200 grams. Black outside and a smooth, creamy brown inside. Kneads up easily and burns with a clear white ash. Strong, smooth, sweet taste and pungent smoke. Kick-ass buzz!

2. Chitral, Pakistan

This frontier area between Pakistan and Afghanistan is adjacent to the ancient Silk Road, and although claimed by Pakistan, is controlled by a loose association of over 20 tribes. Marijuana cultivation and hashish production dates back centuries in this area. It's the world's oldest and ultimate free trade zone, since before Marco Polo. Commercial "Chitrali" hashish is shaken and pounded by ancient presses and is known for average or below-average quality. However, if you look far enough, you'll find a farmer who hand-presses for his own personal stash. If you can get your hands on a couple of kilos of this, you'll find that the texture, smell and quality is of a primo variety. Black on the outside, more greenish than brown on the inside. Superb high.

3. Kashmir

You're wondering what rubbed hashish is? On massive plantations of marijuana fields, women run naked through the fields, and mature cannabis plant resin sticks to their bodies. Men wear wetsuits, because of body hair. Resins and pollen are collected and rubbed with goat's milk or ghee. Hashish has a coarse, crude, grainy texture, with the odd seed, stalk or stem. Excellent high.

4. Minali, Kulu Valley, India

Unlike Kashmir hashish, Minali is smooth outside, but with a grainy blackish brown inside. Don't be surprised if you find sticks, stems, and a yak hair or two. Fine cross between taste and texture—between Nepalese and Kashmir. White willowy smoke definitely knocks your socks off.

5. Nepal

Soft, distinct smell, grainy texture, kneads up easily. Like Minali, Nepal hashish needs to be wrapped airtight or it will turn brittle and mouldy. Long slabs called Nepalese fingers or hand patties usually give a kilo weight. Don't be fooled by temple balls—they're not rolled by Buddhist monks. Nepalese are the true connoisseurs. Kick-ass.

6. Bekáa Valley, Lebanon

Could I be the Rose of Lebanon?—sorry, I wander. This is one of the least expensive yet most consistent when it comes to quality and packaging. You always know what you're getting. Blond, brown Lebanese hashish is commercial and low quality. Moist, red Lebanese is as good as any hashish in the world. Shaken and heated before being pressed into one-kilo cheesecloth sacks. Smokes beautifully, primo taste and nice buzz.

7. Atlas Mountains, Morocco

If you follow the mountains from Lebanon westward towards Morocco, you reach the Atlas Mountains and the last decent hash of the Middle East. "oo" Moroccan is the prize. Special aged pollen, shaken and carefully screened. Brownish green colouring and distinct flavour. Not top shelf, but often a nice surprise. Don't be a tourist and get fooled by the green, powdery, low-rider "keef." It's garbage, like Turkish, Israeli and less mentionable hashish.

8. Western Hemisphere

North American hash is a relatively new phenomenon. Resins from the more potent *Cannabis sativa* strain—not Middle Eastern *Cannabis indica* plants—are collected and rubbed. The most popular is the Jamaican "rub." More recently, North American bubble and ice hashish have rewritten potency levels. Fine crystalline particles are flash-frozen and collected with ice hashish, or shaken screened with water, for hashish looking like keef. But don't let the colour fool you. Extremely potent—nice buzz, but irritates the throat.

9 CANADIAN PLACE NAMES RECLAIMED BY FIRST NATIONS

What's in a name? A lot, as it turns out, when it comes to Canadian place names and First Nations.

There are hundreds of Canadian places whose names are derived from various Indigenous languages, like Canada ("village" or "settlement" in the Saint-Lawrence Iroquoian language), and Quebec ("strait" or "narrows" in the Mi'kmaq language). But in recent years, as First Nations peoples demand greater self-determination and recognition under the law, they have also lobbied to reclaim place names that do not reflect their presence.

When the Truth and Reconciliation Commission released its final report in 2015, it called for the Canadian government to fully implement the UN Declaration on the Rights of Indigenous Peoples. Article 13 of that declaration enshrines the right of Indigenous peoples "to designate and retain their own names for communities [and] places." That process is now underway in Canada, but it has not always gone smoothly. Here are nine places where changes have already happened, or are still to come.

1. Frobisher Bay/Iqaluit (Nunavut)

This area of the eastern Arctic had been a traditional Inuit hunting and fishing grounds for thousands of years. The Inuit called it Iqaluit, which means "place of many fish" in Inuktitut. In 1942, the U.S. Air Force established a base on the shores of Frobisher Bay, named for the English navigator Sir Martin Frobisher, who, during his search for the Northwest Passage in 1576, became the first European to visit the area. The community took the name of Frobisher Bay in 1955, and kept it until January 1, 1987, when it officially reverted back to its traditional Inuit name.

2. Ellesmere Island National Park/ Quttinirpaaq National Park (Nunavut)

Canada's northernmost national park was known as Ellesmere Island National Park Reserve until Nunavut was created in 1999. The name was then changed to Quttinirpaaq, and it became a national park the following year. The word *quttinirpaaq* means "top of the world" in Inuktitut.

3. Queen Charlotte Islands/ Haida Gwaii (British Columbia)

The Queen Charlotte Islands were changed to Haida Gwaii under the terms of the Haida Gwaii Reconciliation Act of 2010. The name means "the islands of the Haida people." Queen Charlotte was the wife of King George III, famous for losing the American colonies.

4. Port Simpson/Lax-Kw'alaams (British Columbia)

The name of the small northern B.C. community of Port Simpson was changed to Lax-Kw'alaams, which means "place of the wild roses" in the language of the Tsimshian Nation.

5. Mackenzie River/Dehcho (Yukon, Northwest Territories)

Canada's longest river system, named after explorer Alexander Mackenzie, has not officially been renamed yet, but increasingly the Dene refer to it as Dehcho, which means "big river." Similarly, Great Slave Lake is now more commonly referred to as Tucho, which means "big water," or Tu Nedhe, which means "big lake" in Dene Soline.

6. Mount Douglas/Pkols (British Columbia)

Mount Douglas, on the Saanich Peninsula on Vancouver Island, was named after Sir James Douglas, the second governor of the Vancouver Island colony. The mountain is located on the lands of the Saanich Nations and the Songhees and Esquimalt First Nations, who have traditionally referred to it as Pkols, which means "white head" in the Songhees language. In 2013, a group of First Nations activists erected a sign on the summit of the mountain declaring it would now be known as Pkols. The B.C. government has not yet officially agreed to the name change, and the mountain is likely to continue to have two names for some time to come.

7. Fort Good Hope/ Radilih Koe (Northwest Territories)

Situated on the east bank of the Mackenzie River (Dehcho), the community of Fort Good Hope was established by the North West Company in 1805. It boasts the oldest building in the Northwest Territories, Our Lady of Good Hope Church, built in 1865. Most of the people who live there are Dene, and they are currently negotiating a land claims settlement with the Government of Canada. For them, Fort Good Hope is Radilih Koe, which means "place of the rapids."

8. Holman/Ulukhaktok (Northwest Territories)

The Hudson's Bay Company established this outpost on the west coast of Victoria Island in 1939 and named it Holman, after J.R. Holman, who was a member of an 1853 expedition that set out in search of Arctic explorer John Franklin. In 2006, the community was officially renamed Ulukhaktok, which is Inuktitut for "place where there is material for ulus." Ulus are all-purpose knives usually made of slate or copper, materials that can be found in the bluffs that overlook the town.

9. Trout Lake/ Sambaa K'e (Northwest Territories)

This tiny Dehcho community in the southern NWT, near the Alberta border, officially changed its name in June 2016 from Trout Lake to Sambaa K'e, which means "place of trout" in the Dene language.

15 POSSIBLE EXPLORERS OF AMERICA BEFORE COLUMBUS

1-2. Hsi and Ho (c. 2640 BCE), Chinese

Based on evidence derived from the geography text *Shan Hai Ching T'sang-chu* and the chronicle *Shan Hai Jing*, it is argued that the Chinese imperial astronomers Hsi and Ho were the first explorers of America in the 27th century BCE. Ordered by the emperor Huang Ti to make astronomical observations in the land of Fu Sang—the territories to the east of China—the two men sailed north to the Bering Strait and then south along the North American coastline. They settled for a while with the "Yao people," ancestors of the Pueblo Indians living near the Grand Canyon, but eventually journeyed on to Mexico and Guatemala. Returning to China, they reported their astronomical studies and geographic discoveries to the emperor. However, a short time later, they were both executed for failing to predict a solar eclipse accurately.

3-6. Votan, Wixepecocha, Sume and Bochia (c. 800-400 BCE), Indian

According to Hindu legends and to Central American tribal legends, seafaring Hindu missionaries reached the Americas more than 2,000 years before Columbus. Sailing from India to Southeast Asia, they voyaged to the Melanesian and Polynesian islands and then across the Pacific to South and Central America. Votan was a trader from India who lived among the Mayans as a historian and chieftain, while his contemporary, Wixepecocha, was a Hindu priest who settled with the Zapotecs of Mexico. Two more Hindu emigrants were Sume, who reached Brazil and introduced agriculture to the Cabocle Indians, and Bochia, who lived with the Muycas Indians and became the codifier of their laws.

7. Hui Shun (458), Chinese

Using official Chinese imperial documents and maps from the Liang dynasty, scholars have reconstructed the travels of Chinese explorer and Buddhist priest Hui Shun, and have proposed that he arrived in North America in the fifth century. Sailing from China to Alaska in 458, Hui—accompanied by four Afghan disciples—continued his journey on foot down the North American Pacific coast. Reaching Mexico, he taught and preached Buddhism to the Indians of central Mexico and to the Mayans of the Yucatan. He allegedly named Guatemala in honour of Gautama Buddha. After more than 40 years in America, he returned to China, where he reported his adventures to Lord Yu Kie and Emperor Wu in 502.

8. St. Brendan (c. 550), Irish

Two medieval manuscripts, *The Voyage of Saint Brendan the Abbot* and the *Book of Lismore*, tell of an Irish priest who, with 17 other monks, sailed west from Ireland and reached the "Land Promised to the Saints." Employing a curragh—a leather-hulled boat still in use in Ireland—Brendan and his companions made a sea pilgrimage that lasted seven years during the sixth century AD. They travelled to Iceland, Greenland and Newfoundland, and one authority asserts that Brendan reached the Caribbean island of Grand Cayman, which he called the Island of Strong Men. Brendan returned safely to his Irish monastery and reported on his travels, but died soon after. In 1977 Timothy Severin, sailing a modern curragh, retraced Brendan's voyage to America.

9. Bjarni Herjulfsson (986), Norse

According to two medieval Icelandic narratives, *Flateyjarbok* and *Hauksbok*, a young Norse merchant named Bjarni Herjulfsson sailed from Iceland towards Greenland to visit his father, who lived there, but was blown off course by a gale. When the storm ended, Bjarni sighted a hilly, forested land, which is now thought to have been Cape Cod. Wanting to reach the Norse settlements on Greenland before winter, he did not drop anchor and send men ashore to explore. Instead, he sailed north to Greenland. He was criticized by the Greenlanders for not investigating the new land, and his discoveries stimulated further exploration of North America.

10. Leif Ericson (1003), Norse

In 1003 Ericson bought Bjarni Herjulfsson's ship and, with a 35-man crew, sailed for North America. While most scholars agree that Ericson did land in North America, there is disagreement about where. The only Viking site ever found in the New World is L'Anse aux Meadows in Newfoundland, which was discovered in 1960 and excavated for the next eight years by Helge Ingstad, a Norwegian explorer. According to Ingstad, Ericson's first landing was on Baffin Island, which he named Helluland; his second was in Labrador, which he called Markland; and his third was in Newfoundland, which he christened Vinland. To Leif and his companions, Vinland was an abundant country, rich in game, wild wheat and timber, and its climate was mild compared with that of Iceland and Greenland. The explorers spent the winter in Vinland, where they constructed a village of "big houses." In 1004 Leif returned to Greenland, where he was given the honorary name "Leif the Lucky."

11. Thorvald Ericson (1004), Norse

The Icelandic sagas record that, soon after Leif Ericson returned to Greenland, he gave his ship to his brother Thorvald. In the autumn of 1004, Thorvald sailed to Leif's Vinland settlement and wintered there. The next summer, while exploring the St. Lawrence region, Thorvald and his crew attacked a band of Indians, killing eight of them. In retaliation, the Indians ambushed the Norsemen, and

Thorvald was killed in the ensuing battle. In 1007 the expedition's survivors returned to Greenland and took with them Thorvald's body, which was delivered to Leif for burial.

12. King Abubakari II (1311), Malian

According to medieval Arab historical and geographical documents and Malian oral epics, King Abubakari II of Mali, a Black Muslim, sailed from West Africa to northeastern South America. After learning from Arab scholars that there was land on the west side of the Atlantic, King Abubakari became obsessed with the idea of extending his kingdom into these as yet unclaimed lands. He mobilized the resources of his empire to hire Arab shipbuilders from Lake Chad to build a fleet. (Their descendants were employed by Thor Heyerdahl to construct his reed boat, *Ra I*.) In 1311 the king and his crew sailed down the Senegal River and across the Atlantic. It is believed that, while he sighted the north coast of South America, he made his first landfall in Panama. From there, King Abubakari and his entourage supposedly travelled south and settled in the Inca Empire.

13. Henry St. Clair (1398), Scottish

The voyage of St. Clair, the Prince of Orkney and Earl of Rosslyn, is described in the 15th-century *Zeno Narrative*, allegedly written by the grandnephew of St. Clair's Venetian navigator, Antonio Zeno. During a trip to Iceland and Greenland in 1393, St. Clair reportedly learned of a land to the west. Five years later, he led an expedition consisting of 13 ships and 200 to 300 men that landed in Nova Scotia. He left behind a group of settlers, who may have travelled as far south as New England. St. Clair died in a battle at Kirkwall in August 1400, just after his return from America. His sudden death severed all links with the colony in the New World.

14-15. Johannes Scolp and João Vaz Corte-Real (1476), Danish and Portuguese

King Alfonso of Portugal and King Christian I of Denmark arranged a joint expedition to North America to find a sea route to China. Danish sea captain Johannes Scolp and a Portuguese nobleman named João Vaz Corte-Real were appointed as commanders of the combined fleet. Sailing from Denmark across the North Atlantic to the Labrador coast, they explored Hudson Bay, the Gulf of St. Lawrence and the St. Lawrence River. Failing to find a sea passage to Asia, they returned to Denmark, where their discoveries were largely ignored.

SOBRIQUETS OF 10 CANADIAN CITIES

1. Peterborough, Ontario—"The Electric City"

Peterborough was the first city in Canada to use electric streetlights.

2. Medicine Hat, Alberta—"The Gas City"

Medicine Hat sits on large natural gas fields.

3. Moose Jaw, Saskatchewan—"The Mill City"

The Robin Hood flour mill was the city's oldest and biggest building until it closed in 1966.

4. Fredericton, New Brunswick—"The Celestial City"

This name was first attached to Fredericton in the 1840s because of the number of churches being built there.

5. Trail, British Columbia—"Home of Champions"

The Trail Smoke Eaters won the world hockey championship in 1961, but the "Home of Champions" label dates from 1988 when a monument was erected downtown to honour "individuals and groups from the Greater Trail area who have excelled in their chosen field of endeavour."

6. Dawson City, Yukon—"Paris of the North"

This name dates back to the Gold Rush days of the 1890s, when millions of dollars' worth of gold were pulled from the ground, and Dawson City was suddenly filled with newly wealthy men anxious to spend their money on the finest food, drink, clothes and women.

7. Kingston, Ontario—"The Limestone City"

Many of Kingston's famous heritage buildings were constructed from local limestone.

8. Saskatoon, Saskatchewan—"The City of Bridges"

Seven bridges span the South Saskatchewan River.

9. Guelph, Ontario—"The Royal City"

In 1714, Queen Anne, a Stuart, died without a direct Protestant heir to the British throne. The crown passed to her second cousin, George Guelph (also known as Guelf or Welf), from the German House of Hanover, who became George I. The current British royal family traces its lineage back to him.

10. Steinbach, Manitoba—"The Automobile City"

The first Ford dealership in western Canada opened in Steinbach in June 1914. From that point on, Steinbach became a mecca for car buyers from across the Prairies who made pilgrimages there to check out the newest models. By the 1950s Steinbach's car salesmen were the tops in the country on a per capita basis, selling about 250 automobiles a year, and the town adopted the slogan "The Automobile City."

13 POSSIBLE SITES FOR THE GARDEN OF EDEN

"And the Lord God planted a garden eastward in Eden. . . . And a river went out of Eden to water the garden; and from thence it was parted and became into four heads. The name of the first is Pison: that is it which compasseth the whole land of Havilah, where there is gold; And the gold of that land is good: there is bdellium and the onyx stone. And the name of the second river is Gihon: the same is it that compasseth the whole land of Ethiopia. And the name of the third river is Hiddekel: that is it which goeth toward the east of Assyria. And the fourth river is Euphrates" (Gen. 2:8–14).

1. Southern Iraq

Many biblical scholars believe that the Garden of Eden, the original home of Adam and Eve, was located in Sumer, at the confluence of the Euphrates and Tigris (or Hiddekel) rivers in present-day Iraq. They presume that the geographical references in Genesis relate to the situation from the ninth to the fifth centuries BCE, and that the Pison and Gihon were tributaries of the Euphrates and Tigris that have since disappeared. In fact, they may have been ancient canals.

2. Eastern Turkey

Other students of the Bible reason that if the four major rivers flowed *out* of the garden, then the garden itself must have been located far north of the

Tigris–Euphrates civilization. They place the site in the mysterious northland of Armenia, in present-day Turkey. This theory presumes that Gihon and Pison may not have been precise geographical designations, but rather vague descriptions of faraway places.

3. Northern Iran

British archaeologist David Rohl claims that Eden is a lush valley in Iran, located about 16 kilometres from the modern city of Tabriz. Rohl suggests that Gihon and Pison are the Iranian rivers Araxes and Uizhun. He also identifies nearby Mount Sahand, a snow-capped extinct volcano, as the prophet Ezekiel's Mountain of God.

4. Israel

There are those who say that the garden of God must have been in the Holy Land, and that the original river that flowed into the garden *before* it split into four separate rivers must have been the Jordan, which was longer in the days of Genesis. The Gihon would be the Nile, and Havilah would be the Arabian Peninsula. Some supporters of this theory go further, stating that Mount Moriah in Jerusalem was the heart of the Garden of Eden, and that the entire garden included all of Jerusalem, Bethlehem and Mount Olivet.

5. Egypt

Supporters of Egypt as the site of the Garden of Eden claim that only the Nile region meets the Genesis description of a land watered not by rain but by a mist rising from the ground, in that the Nile ran partially underground before surfacing in spring holes below the first cataract. The four rivers, including the Tigris and Euphrates, are explained away as beginning far, far beyond the actual site of Paradise.

6-7. East Africa and Java

Since Adam and Eve were the first humans, and since the oldest human remains have been found in East Africa, many people conclude that the Garden of Eden must have been in Africa. Likewise, when archaeologists discovered the remains of *Pithecanthropus* in Java in 1891, they guessed that Java was the location of the Garden of Eden.

8. Sinkiang, China

Tse Tsan Tai, in his work *The Creation, the Real Situation of Eden, and the Origin of the Chinese* (1914), presents a case for the garden being in Chinese Turkestan, in the plateau of eastern Asia. He claims that the river that flowed through the garden was the Tarim, which has four tributaries flowing eastward.

9. Lemuria

In the mid-19th century a theory developed that a vast continent once occupied much of what is now the Indian Ocean. The name Lemuria was created by British zoologist P.L. Sclater in honour of the lemur family of animals, which has a somewhat unusual range of distribution in Africa, southern India and Malaysia. Other scientists suggested that Lemuria was the cradle of the human race; thus, it must have been the site of the Garden of Eden.

10. Praslin Island, Seychelles

General Charles "Chinese" Gordon supported the theory that Africa and India used to be part of one massive continent. While on a survey expedition for the British government in the Indian Ocean, he came upon Praslin Island in the Seychelles group. So enchanted was he by this island, and by its Vallée de Mai in particular, that he became convinced that this was the location of the original Garden of Eden. The clincher for Gordon was the existence on Praslin of the cocodemer, a rare and exotic tree that is native to only one other island of the Seychelles, and which Gordon concluded was the tree of the knowledge of good and evil.

11. Mars

In his book *The Sky People*, Brinsley Le Poer Trench argues that not only Adam and Eve but Noah lived on Mars. He states that the biblical description of a river watering the garden and then parting into four heads is inconsistent with nature. Only canals can be made to flow that way, and Mars, supposedly, had canals. So the Garden of Eden was created on Mars as an experiment by Space People. Eventually, the north polar ice cap on Mars melted, and the descendants of Adam and Eve were forced to take refuge on Earth.

12. Galesville, Wisconsin

In 1886 the Reverend D.O. Van Slyke published a small pamphlet that expounded his belief that Eden was the area stretching from the Allegheny Mountains to the

Rocky Mountains, and that the Garden of Eden was located on the east bank of the Mississippi River between La Crosse, Wisconsin, and Winona, Minnesota. When the deluge began, Noah was living in present-day Wisconsin, and the flood carried his ark eastward until it landed on Mount Ararat.

13. Jackson County, Missouri

While travelling through Davies County, Missouri, Mormon Church founder Joseph Smith found a stone slab that he declared was an altar that Adam built shortly after being driven from the Garden of Eden. Declaring, "This is the valley of God in which Adam blessed his children," Smith made plans to build a city called Adam-ondi-Ahram at the site. The Garden of Eden itself, Smith determined, was located 64 kilometres south, near the modern-day city of Independence.

BECKY MASON'S 12 FAVOURITE RIVERS TO CANOE

Becky Mason is a canoeist, artist and environmentalist who acquired her paddling skills and her fondness for canoes from her father, the author, artist and National Film Board filmmaker Bill Mason. Becky runs her own canoe school and has produced two award-winning DVDs, Classic Solo Canoeing *and* Advanced Classic Solo Canoeing *that profile her canoeing skills and her love of paddling.*

1. South Nahanni River (Northwest Territories)

From top to bottom, perhaps the greatest combination of wild whitewater, eye-popping scenery, wildlife and a fascinating history of murder, mystery and hidden gold—all this and the fact that it is protected within the confines of a 30,000-square-kilometre national park and includes the incomparable Virginia Falls, a UNESCO World Heritage Site. Even if I never return to the Nahanni, I am pleased to know it is protected—not for me, or even for future generations, but for the sake of the land and river itself.

2. French River (Georgian Bay, Ontario)

This is the river where I learned all about swimming in rapids. I had many formative moments here as a kid, canoeing with my family. To this day I can still feel the sun-warmed rocks, taste the mists of Blue Chute and hear the lazy humming of cicadas as I revisit in my mind the seemingly endless lazy days of childhood summers gone.

3. Rivière Saguenay (Quebec)

Perhaps not the safest place for a canoe (here I must concede that sea kayaks do have their advantages!), but where else can you paddle in such spectacular fjords and, where the river joins the St. Lawrence, share the water with seals, belugas and even mighty blue whales?

4-6. Rivers of the North Shore (Lake Superior, Ontario)

The best part of all of the North Shore rivers is . . . Lake Superior itself. This is such a unique, awe-inspiring and powerful place that at times it leaves me speechless. I have had more spiritual, strange and downright unsettling experiences here than anywhere else in my travels, and that's one of the reasons I continue to return. A few of my favourite North Shore rivers are:

a. Dog River. It doesn't get much more rugged than this. You have to be tough as nails to run the Dog (now part of Nimoosh Provincial Park), but it's wilderness canoe-tripping at its best. The portage around Denison Falls was once listed by *Paddler Magazine* as one of the top 10 worst portages on the planet. If that doesn't deter, you'll discover that nothing beats the thrill of descending this rarely canoed river down to the coast.

b. Pukaskwa River. I think the black flies carried us down most of the Puk, but the section of Superior coastline we paddled is unparalleled. Firing up a trapper's old sod sauna we found one cold evening at Oiseau Bay is a memory and a luxurious feeling I'll not soon forget.

c. Sand River. Just like the Group of Seven did way back in the 1920s, you catch a ride on the Algoma Central Railway to start this trip. And getting dropped off in the middle of nowhere with your canoe and packs to start a trip has to be the most romantic and hopelessly clichéd Canadian experience one can have. And it feels fantastic!

7. Rivière du Lièvre (Quebec)

It seems like way too much fun to fit into one weekend. A challenging stretch of turbulent river that includes chutes, ledges, a "can't scout" white-knuckle canyon run and a kilometre-long continuous roller-coaster ride that, trust me, you don't want your friends to swim through . . .

8. Petawawa River (Ontario)

Although it's famous for its thrilling whitewater, what really draws me to the Petawawa is its natural beauty and how it fuels my creative side. Tom Thomson popularized Algonquin Park and the Petawawa River through his paintings, and you can't help but feel his presence in the early morning mist and cool river currents. My dad and I paddled here many times, but the most memorable was a painting trip we took together after I graduated from art college. Although we did some paintings, he showed me that it was just as important to take the time to stop and experience the land with *all* of your senses.

9. Red Deer River (Alberta)

I've only paddled on the Red Deer River once, for a day, where it winds through Dinosaur Provincial Park, but it blew my mind. This is about as far from stereotypical Canadian canoe country as I can imagine. Fossils, rattlesnakes, cacti, hoodoos . . . wow! I'll be back.

10. Missinaibi River (Ontario)

One of the great things about canoeing in Canada is the immediacy of our history. Much of this country was explored and mapped by canoe, a watercraft whose design has remained virtually unchanged for millennia. Even today, with a few skills and a lot of determination, one can go into the bush with nothing but a crooked knife, flint and a pot and build a craft that could cross the continent. Like many of our rivers, the Missinaibi was a highway first for Indigenous people and then voyageurs, and evidence of their presence can be found everywhere. When on rivers like this one, it is well worth it to read the old explorers' trip journals and marvel at their exploits while revelling in the history of the land.

11. Bloodvein River (Ontario, Manitoba)

Canada's boreal forest is an awe-inspiring place to be. Stretching from coast to coast across the north, it is like a vast green halo of virtually pristine forests, lakes, rivers and swamps. The Bloodvein, a Canadian Heritage River, is a long blue ribbon that winds and tumbles through the heart of the boreal forest. As I travel, I marvel at the jet-black spruces and jack pine sculpting the skyline. I wonder and give thanks at the numerous ancient pictograph sites we pass. I smile as I feel the gentle caress of wild rice brushing my hands. And I tremble at the roar of the falls and rapids we approach. The boreal forest and its vast mossy bogs and wetlands act as critical filters for the entire planet, and there is no better way to journey through this wild and rugged land than by canoe.

12. Miramichi River (New Brunswick)

And finally, if after canoeing all of these rivers you are tired of sitting and paddling, stand up, pick up a pole and head down east. The Mirimachi watershed is huge, and much of it is shallow, wide and fast-moving. It's a beautiful, diverse river environment that's perfect for poling your canoe. That's right, out in these parts standing up in your canoe is encouraged! On the calm placid stretches or in the rapids and pools, when you are standing up and poling you get a brand new perspective and a spectacular view. You can see every river feature, including the salmon, so don't forget your fishing pole too!

CHAPTER 12

Literature and Words

16 BEGINNINGS TO CANADIAN NOVELS

1. "Our house was taken away on the back of a truck one afternoon late in the summer of 1979."
   —*All My Puny Sorrows*, Miriam Toews

2. "When I hear the sea wind blowing through the streets of the city in the morning, I can still feel my father and the Old One—together—lifting me up to perch on the railing of a swaying deck; still feel the steady weight of Father's palm braced against my chest and Poh-Poh's thickly jacketed arm locked safely around my legs."
   —*All That Matters*, Wayson Choy

3. "He had been walking around Halifax all day, as though by moving through familiar streets he would test whether he belonged here and had at last reached home."
   —*Barometer Rising*, Hugh MacLennan

4. "Catherine Tekakwitha, who are you?"
   —*Beautiful Losers*, Leonard Cohen

5. "Sadie turned seventeen years old on top of her boyfriend, Jimmy, in the Woodbury family boathouse."
   —*The Best Kind of People*, Zoe Whittall

6. "I am a Newfoundlander."
   —*The Colony of Unrequited Dreams*, Wayne Johnston

7. "She stands up in the garden where she has been working and looks into the distance."
   —*The English Patient*, Michael Ondaatje

8. "My lifelong involvement with Mrs. Dempster began at 5:58 p.m. on 27 December 1908, at which time I was ten years and seven months old."
   —*Fifth Business*, Robertson Davies

9. "I was driving you up to Prince George to the home of your grandfather, the golf wino."
   —*Life After God*, Douglas Coupland

10. "Snowman wakes before dawn."
    —*Oryx and Crake*, Margaret Atwood

11. "One morning—during the record cold spell of 1851—a big menacing black bird, the likes of which had never been seen before, soared over the crude mill town of Magog, swooping low again and again."
    —*Solomon Gursky Was Here*, Mordecai Richler

12. "Above the town, on the hill brow, the stone angel used to stand."
    —*The Stone Angel*, Margaret Laurence

13. "It happens that I am going through a period of great unhappiness and loss right now."
    —*Unless*, Carol Shields

14. "All day there are glaring omens that go undetected."
    —*The White Bone*, Barbara Gowdy

15. "Here was the least common denominator of nature, the skeleton requirements simply, of land and sky—Saskatchewan prairie."
    —*Who Has Seen the Wind*, W.O. Mitchell

16. "Hello. Howaya? Feh. You think those are the only words I know? Boychik, you don't know from knowing. You ain't seen knowing. I may be *meshugeh* crazy, but I know from words. You think I'm a fool shmegegge? I'm *all* words."
    —*Yiddish for Pirates*, Gary Barwin

KYO MACLEAR'S 7 GLORIOUSLY GLOOMY BOOKS FOR THE VERY YOUNG

Adults love to project simplicity and happiness on children, ignoring the fact that childhood is a pretty complicated time for most. Life can be operatic for the kinder-set. There is brooding and bewilderment, anxiety and injustice. Hearts are shattered on a regular basis. Is it any wonder young children cry lavishly several times a day? As a children's writer, I believe there is a time to be pleasant and optimistic but there is also a time to affirm the emotional wilderness and Sartrean mindset of the young. In the spirit of the latter, here is my list of books for and about the wondrously woeful and wilful.

Kyo Maclear is a celebrated children's author. Her books include Spork (2010), Virginia Wolf (2012), Julia, Child (2014) *and* The Liszts (2016), *among others. She is also the author of the memoir* Birds Art Life (2017).

1. Outside Over There by Maurice Sendak (1989)

The story is seriously bizarro: a baby is snatched away by faceless cloaked goblins. A grotesque ice replica is left in her place. The baby's sister, Ida, fights to bring her back by playing tunes on her wonder horn. Told in incantatory and puzzling prose, Sendak's story is accompanied by lysergic images of twisting capes and swirling seas. A deeply psychedelic and unforgettable odyssey.

2. Three Robbers by Tomi Ungerer (1961)

Another story of abduction—this one by Ungerer, enfant terrible of children's literature (and subversive maker of raucously erotic art for adults). The villains here are three fierce, black-hatted, cape-wearing thieves. Their weapons: a blunderbuss, a pepper sprayer and huge red axe. Their prey: a little orphan girl. Murky shadows and nocturnal blues hint at possible violence to come. But this dark tale for youngsters ends with a nice, subversive twist.

3. The Doubtful Guest by Edward Gorey (1957)

A Converse-wearing creature arrives at a family's home one day. Inexplicably, the flummoxed occupants never ask their uninvited guest to leave, enduring his mischievous and mournful moods for *17 years.* True to Gorey, the characters are all exquisitely gloomy, with draping robes, heavy furs and dreary, doleful faces.

4. Duck, Death and The Tulip by Wolf Erlbruch (2007)

In this brave story, first published in German by the venerated Erlbruch, Duck strikes up a wary friendship with Death. "You've come to fetch me?" asks Duck. Death, sporting a fashionable plaid coat that could have come from Comme des

14. Don't judge a book by its cover.
    Clothes make the man.

15. The squeaky wheel gets the grease.
    Silence is golden.

16. Birds of a feather flock together.
    Opposites attract.

17. The pen is mightier than the sword.
    Actions speak louder than words.

8 CANADIAN POETS AND HOW THEY EARNED A LIVING

You don't go into poetry expecting to get rich, though some poets manage to cobble together a living in the related fields of teaching, editing and wordsmithing. Undaunted, Canada's poets put pen to paper with gusto, and in some cases, find ways of making ends meet that double as both a grind and grist for the mill.

1. Milton Acorn (1923-86)

For a man whose friends called him "the people's poet" and who was accustomed to hearing himself described as a working-class hero, Milton Acorn's employment history was decidedly un-proletarian. Although later in his life he liked to speak about his days working as a union carpenter in Prince Edward Island, it appears that those days were actually few and far between. Acorn's family was decidedly middle class and white collar, and young Milton followed firmly in that path. He started working as a clerk with the New Brunswick Unemployment Insurance Commission in Moncton in July 1944, and he stayed there for three years. Indeed, he spent more of his time working as a civil servant than doing anything else, apart from writing.

2. Leonard Cohen (1934-2016)

In the winter of 1958, Leonard Cohen was 23 years old, a published poet (*Let Us Compare Mythologies*), and had already had a taste of the bohemian beat culture of New York's Greenwich Village. But now he was back in Montreal and facing a dilemma: should he continue to live the precarious life of the poet, or follow the path his family expected of him, joining the successful clothing business Freedman Company, owned by his uncles. He chose the latter. Among his many tasks, he was a "bundle boy," carrying bundles of material from one stage of production to another. For his efforts, he was mocked by friend and fellow poet Irving Layton: "Now Leonard Cohen has decided to bemuse all our wits by entering the family business, the making of suits for unpoetic characters across the land to buy and wear. Our great lyricist is now a shipping clerk, penning odes to wrapping paper and string." Fortunately for all of us, in April 1959 the Canada Council awarded Cohen a grant of $2,000 to write a novel, eventually published as *The Favourite Game*, that would be drawn from visits to Rome, Athens and Jerusalem. It marked the end of Cohen's dalliance in the *schmatte* trade.

3. Irving Layton (1912-2006)

Layton was a devout Communist as a young man, and his main ambition was to further the revolution by working for the Co-operative Commonwealth Federation (CCF). He even went to work on his brother's farm in New York, hoping the party would be impressed by his agrarian roots. Alas, Layton proved to be a bit too far to the left for the CCF, and in 1939, while trying to figure out what to do with his life, he became a Fuller Brush man in Halifax. He proved to be spectacularly unsuccessful at peddling brushes door to door. But then, by all accounts, he never really tried very hard, preferring to spend most of his day stretched out under a tree on the Dalhousie University campus, smoking a pipe and reading. After six months of doing that, he embarked on an equally unsuccessful attempt at selling insurance for Confederation Life. Recalling that period in a letter written later in life, Layton admitted, "I broke no Olympic records in either enterprise."

4. Gwendolyn MacEwen (1941-87)

Gwendolyn MacEwen was a purist. She left school in Toronto at age 18 to live the life of a poet and writer. There was no factory or retail work on her resumé, no door-to-door sales, no secretarial work. In the early 1960s, as she was beginning to establish her reputation as one of Canada's best young poets, she was able to make some money doing poetry readings and reviewing manuscripts for her publisher, Macmillan. She also survived, as did most Canadian writers of the time, by being awarded Canada Council grants, and by selling scripts to *Anthology*, the CBC Radio program produced by the legendary Robert Weaver.

The CBC paid only $150 for each program, but MacEwen assured Weaver years later that "that would have kept me in Kraft Dinners for three or four months." But MacEwen took greatest pride in the money she earned through publishing her writing. "I don't think the poet should be subsidized," she once wrote. "The world doesn't owe him a living. I like to work for what I get. In a recent *Atlantic* there's a Canadian section and they published one of my poems. That's how I like to get paid all the time."

5. Jay Macpherson (1931-2012)

Jay Macpherson, author of the prize-winning lyric poetry opus *The Boatman*, sought to live a life surrounded by poetry and scholarship from an early age. Growing up in Ottawa she published poems as a teenager. After graduating from Carleton with a BA in English she headed to Europe for inspiration and adventure. Through introductions from her father, she wound up working as a nanny for poet and classicist Robert Graves in Majorca. In search of a more "practical" way of supporting herself, she returned to Canada to study library sciences, eventually earning two more degrees, a master's and a PhD at the University of Toronto. She eventually earned a tenured teaching spot, but before then, augmented her meagre wages by living in campus residences as the don of women students. Hardworking, modest and so shy she sent the jacket designer to pick up her Governor General's Award for Poetry in 1957, Macpherson went out of her way to help emerging writers and poets, including publishing poetry chapbooks by the likes of Dorothy Livesay and Al Purdy on the side and taking in Margaret Atwood as a roommate when Atwood was just out of high school.

6. Al Purdy (1918-2000)

Al Purdy has been called the most distinctively Canadian poet of his generation. He had an innate sense of the country and a close connection to its people, derived, in part, from living and working in more of Canada than most Canadians will ever experience. At age 17, bored and restless, he left his home in Trenton, Ontario, and rode the rails west to Vancouver. When the Second World War broke out, he joined the RCAF, and also managed to publish his first book of poetry, *The Enchanted Echo* (1944). After the war, he moved to Belleville, Ontario, where he joined up with his father-in-law to run a taxi company, and tried, with limited success, to write poetry. In his 1993 autobiography, *Reaching for the Beaufort Sea*, Purdy wrote about drinking bouts, and driving 12-hour shifts, 7 days a week and "writing some pretty awful poems. None survive now, scribbled frenziedly when the ideas came, sitting in rented rooms, or idling taxis outside the taxi office." When the taxi business went broke in 1948, he moved back to Vancouver, and went to work as a machine operator at the Vancouver Bedding Co. Purdy was still writing poems, many of which were based on his experiences at the mattress factory. He continued to work at various blue-collar jobs, and published his next book of poems in 1955. The author of 39 books of poetry, he is considered by many to be the unofficial poet laureate of Canada. In 1992 he declared his income as $11,000 to the Canada Revenue Agency and asked that they delete his name from their listings, saying, "at my age [73] it isn't likely that my income will increase. A gross income from writing of the above amount seems to place me below the poverty line, whatever that is."

7. Duncan Campbell Scott (1862–1947)

Scott had a full-time job as a deputy supervisor and then head of the Department of Indian Affairs. He was first hired on by Sir John A. Macdonald, who assigned him the job of temporary copying clerk at the rate of $1.50 a week. In between negotiating treaties and advocating forcefully for assimilation of Canada's Indigenous people, Scott penned eight books of poetry, earning him a place as one of Canada's Confederation Poets alongside Bliss Carman and Archibald Lampman.

8. Raymond Souster (1921–2012)

The words *banker* and *poet* rarely go together, but Raymond Souster spent a lifetime as both. He published more than 50 volumes of his own poetry and edited a dozen more. He won the Governor General's Award for Poetry in 1964, and was considered the unofficial poet laureate of Toronto, the city where he lived his entire life. Along with Irving Layton and Louis Dudek, he founded Contact Press, which was a first home to many young Canadian writers, including Margaret Atwood. But he led a double life. In 1939 he was hired as a teller at the Canadian Bank of Commerce at 25 King Street West, and there he stayed, with the exception of a few years in the RCAF during WWII, until he retired in 1984. His job, by the end, was keeper of the vault. After leaving the bank at 5 p.m., still in his grey banker suit, he would often stroll the streets of the city, taking notes that would eventually find their way into his poems. His two worlds rarely collided, but in 1969 Souster organized the Metro Poetry Festival, and invited a group of poets to read for the bank's personal loan department. He wrote his last poem, about cancer, two weeks before dying of the disease in 2012.

20 WORDS WE NEED IN ENGLISH

1. Waldeinsamkeit (German)
A philosophical, peaceful state of mind generated by being in the woods alone and feeling connected to nature.

2. Komorebi (Japanese)
Sunlight filtered by trees in the forest.

3. Sprezzatura (Italian)
A studied carelessness or elegant nonchalance, suggestive of the beauty of imperfection, like a tie knot with a perfectly placed crease.

4. Hygge (Danish)
A Danish mantra connoting coziness, warmth and pleasure in making ordinary things more special or soothing, like lighting candles for every meal.

5. Vacilando (Spanish)
The act of enjoying travelling more than arriving.

6. Nachas (Yiddish)
A mixture of pride and joy, particularly the kind that a parent gets from a child. It is something one relishes, as in "May you only get *nachas* from your son!"

7. Schadenfreude (German)
Taking pleasure in someone else's misfortune, literally translated as "joy in damage."

8. Fremdschämen (German); Myötähäpeä (Finnish)
At least two languages have words for this more empathetic variation on *schadenfreude*, the feeling of being embarrassed for someone else.

9. Mudita (Sanskrit and Pali)
Taking joy in other people's happiness and good fortune.

10. Ubuntu (Bantu)
An ethical concept from Southern Africa positing that human-ness is embodied in the act of showing kindness and compassion to others.

11. Voorpret (Dutch)
Feeling happy and content about an enjoyable event or party planned for the future.

12. Cafuné (Brazilian Portuguese)
The act of affectionately running your fingers through your lover's hair.

13. Koi No Yokan (Japanese)
A sense that you will fall in love with this person on first meeting them.

14. La douleur exquise (French)
The exquisite agony of wanting someone you can't have.

15. Buksvåger (Swedish)
A word for a person with whom you and your friend have had sex—on different occasions.

16. Kummerspeck (German)
Literally means "grief bacon," the extra pounds put on as a result of emotional overeating.

17. Seigneur-terraces (French)
Customers who stay at coffee shops for a long time but barely spend any money.

18. Tartle (Scottish)
The polite cure for namenesia when stumbling and forgetting someone's name when being introduced—"I'm sorry about my tartle."

19. Esprit de l'escalier (French)
The clever retort you think about after the fact, the "spirit of the staircase" is what comes to you as you ascend to your bedroom or head for the door after the party.

20. Prozvonit (Czech)
A cost-saving phone tactic where you call someone and let it ring once so they will call you back on their dime.

MARGARET ATWOOD'S 10 ANNOYING THINGS TO SAY TO WRITERS

Margaret Atwood was born in Ottawa in 1939 and grew up in northern Quebec and Ontario, and later in Toronto. She is the author of more than 40 books, including novels, collections of short stories, poetry, literary criticism, social histories and children's books. Her acclaimed novels include The Handmaid's Tale, The Robber Bride, Cat's Eye, *the Booker Prize–winning* The Blind Assassin *and the Giller Prize–winning* Alias Grace.

    a) What to say
    b) *What the writer hears*

1. a) "I always wait for your books to come in at the library."
    b) *I wouldn't pay money for that trash.*

2. a) "I had to take your stuff in school."
    b) *Against my will.*

Or: *And I certainly haven't read any of it since!*
Or: *So why aren't you dead?*

3. a) "You don't look at all like your pictures!"
    b) *Much worse.*

4. a) "You're so prolific!"
    b) *You write too much, and are repetitive and sloppy.*

5. a) "I'm going to write a book too, when I can find the time."
    b) *What you do is trivial, and can be done by any idiot.*

6. a) "I only read the classics."
    b) *And you aren't one of them.*

7. a) "Why don't you write about _____?"
    b) *Unlike the boring stuff you do write about.*

8. a) "That book by _____ (add name of other writer) is selling like hotcakes!"
   b) *Unlike yours.*

9. a) "So, do you teach?"
   b) *Because writing isn't real work, and you can't possibly be supporting yourself at it.*

10. a) "The story of *my* life—now *that* would make a good novel!"
    b) *Unlike yours.*

DAVID YOUNG'S 5 ESSENTIAL COLD-LIT CLASSICS

Cold-lit classics, the great stories about cold as a crucible of suffering, are found in the literature of exploration—particularly in books written by and about the English. Rotting gums, blackened toes, dog brains for breakfast, the literature of the Heroic Age is without question in the "stinky cheese" category, an acquired taste that offers many shadings and nuances to the true connoisseur. Here are some of my favourites in this frostbitten genre.

David Young is a Canadian playwright, novelist and screenwriter best known for Glenn *(1992), his theatrical portrait of Glenn Gould, and* Inexpressible Island *(1998), a history-based play about six Royal Navy officers and men who overwintered in an Antarctic snow cave in 1912.*

1. The Worst Journey in the World by Apsley Cherry-Garrard (1922)

This is thought by many to be the greatest cold-lit book of all time. Cherry-Garrard, an English gentleman explorer, accompanied Robert Falcon Scott on his fateful voyage south in 1910. Cherry, as he was called, was not only a hero, he was also a writer of great clarity and feeling who was particularly attuned to the metaphysical pings and pangs of the Antarctic landscape. His book—brimming equally with elegiac melancholy and lyric understatement—conjures those days of epic, crucifying hardship at the bottom of the world better than any other. The cheerful threesome pulled their sledges over the hump of Ross Island, enduring temperatures (-62°C) that literally shattered their teeth. All the while, "we did not forget the please and the thank you and we kept our tempers, even with God." The epic peaks when their tent blows away in a hurricane, leaving them in "darkness and cold such as had never been experienced by human beings." After an unimaginable night in the open, they found their tent snagged on the rocky shore and survived. "Our lives had been taken away and given back to us. We were so thankful we said nothing."

2. The Endurance: Shackleton's Incredible Voyage by Caroline Alexander (1998)

Sir Ernest Shackleton obviously belongs in Cherry's company. There are many accounts of his legendary Antarctic expedition in 1914; my favourite version is Alexander's, which is also the most recent. Alexander weaves her finely written tale in and around 135 duotone reproductions of Frank Hurley's expedition-ary photographs. In 1914 Shackleton sailed from England with a crew of 27 and a plan to cross Antarctica on foot. Why? Because nobody else had done it and, from a sentimental point of view, it was the last great polar journey. The *Endurance* sailed into the Weddell Sea and was promptly frozen into the pack ice. Shackleton and his crew overwintered there. Then things went seriously pear-shaped: their ship was smashed to kindling by ice pressure. Shackleton and his men retrieved what they could from the wreck and lived rough on a vast ice floe for four months, drifting far to the north. Inevitably, their ice floe started to break up, forcing them into lifeboats for six days. They went sleepless for 100 horrific hours, weathering a full gale; the open boats almost sank. "At least half the party were insane," according to Frank Wild, Shackleton's second-in-command. The worst was still to come. Shacks parked his crew on Elephant Island and set off with five men in a crudely rigged lifeboat to sail 1,297 kilo-metres of open ocean to South Georgia Island. This is where the survival saga soars into myth and miracle. Alexander's rendering of the sea voyage is flawless, her voice calm and transparent as she takes us inside the precise human detail of an unimaginably extreme experience.

3. The Home of the Blizzard: A True Story of Antarctic Survival by Sir Douglas Mawson (1915)

This is my last nominee for the cold-lit pantheon of the Heroic Age. In 1912 Mawson set off from Cape Denison with his colleagues Xavier Mertz and Belgrave Ninnis to do a bit of summer sledging. They travelled east, mapping the coastline and collecting geological samples. Five hundred kilometres from base camp, Ninnis disappeared down a deep crevasse with a sledge, a team of six dogs, the tent and most of the food and spare clothing. Mawson and Mertz turned around and headed back over dangerous ground in very bad conditions on a five-week return journey. They had nothing to eat but their dogs. Soon Mertz became ill (poisoned by toxic levels of vitamin A from the dog livers). Mawson dragged Mertz under the tent fly and stood by in utter helplessness for a period of days while his friend came unstuck, spun out of control, bit off his own finger and died a raving lunatic. And the nightmare was only beginning. Mawson was alone and without supplies in the middle of a vast crevasse field. One hundred and sixty kilometres of dangerous ground separated him from the safety of the hut at base camp. Mawson arrived at Aladdin's Cave, a depot on the ice cap above Cape Denison, a month after Mertz's death and was trapped there for a week by a raging blizzard. He finally staggered back to the hut on the same day his expedition supply ship sailed for home.

4. The Shining Mountain: Two Men on Changabang's West Wall by Peter Boardman (1984)

After books about the Heroic Age, the next best source for armchair travel to hell frozen over is books by mountaineers. Peter Boardman and Joe Tasker were best friends and, in the late 1970s, two of the boldest young climbers in the world. They died roped together while attempting the unclimbed northeast ridge of Everest in 1982. *The Shining Mountain* is Boardman's classic account of their 1976 two-man winter assault on the unclimbed west face of Changabang (7,000 m). It was the most difficult climb ever attempted in the Himalayas. The horrifyingly exposed route required sleeping in "bat bags" suspended from pegs hammered into the sheer granite face. Boardman and Tasker designed their own gear and tested it by sleeping in a meat locker in Manchester for three nights. *The Shining Mountain* provides a sustained blast of adrenalin that will leave your ears ringing. Here's Boardman contemplating life as he hangs by his fingernails 1,800 metres off the deck: "My mind was working quickly, absorbing all the tiny details around me, bringing movements into slow motion. In the white granite in front of my eyes were particles of clear quartz, silver muscovite and jet black tourmaline. My attention floated to them, they emphasized my insignificance—the fact that I was fragile, warm blooded and living, clinging to the side of this inhospitable world."

5. I May Be Some Time: Ice and the English Imagination by Francis Spufford (1996)

The last required read in the pantheon of cold-lit classics is Spufford's magisterial and deeply felt work. Named in honour of Captain Oates's famous last laconicism, spoken over his shoulder as he staggered away from Scott's tent to perish in the drift, this wonderful book is a learned and elegant historical overview of the way British society built fantasies about the polar regions into the cozy domestic interior of 19th-century life—an ice-cold wing appended to the great house of empire, a place for the long-term storage of romance, heroism and the boyish pleasures of death by frost in a tent. And what an astonishing reliquary it is! There are chapters devoted to the notion of the sublime, to Lady Franklin's hold on the English imagination, to the naming of the features in the Canadian Arctic, and the managed vision of "Eskimos" in the literature of various Victorian nitwits. In the final chapter, Spufford "channels the tent" and gives us an intimate portrait of Scott's final hours, when, knowing his life was lost, he composed those famous letters to the English people: "It is forty below in the tent. The cold comes into him . . . a spearing and dreadful presence turning the cavities of him to blue glass . . . at its tip the cold moves inside him like a key searching for a lock."

THE ORIGINAL TITLES OF 23 FAMOUS BOOKS

1. Final title: *Barney's Version* (1997)
   Original title: *Barney Like a Player Piano*
   Author: Mordecai Richler

2. Final title: *Brick Lane* (2003)
   Original title: *Seven Seas and the Thirteen Rivers*
   Author: Monica Ali

3. Final title: *Catch-22* (1961)
   Original title: *Catch-18*
   Author: Joseph Heller

4. Final title: *The Colony of Unrequited Dreams* (1998)
   Original title: *Landfall*
   Author: Wayne Johnston

5. Final title: *A Complicated Kindness* (2004)
   Original title: *Swivelhead*
   Author: Miriam Toews

6. Final title: *The Cure for Death by Lightning* (1996)
   Original title: *Blood Road*
   Author: Gail Anderson-Dargatz

7. Final title: *Do Not Say We Have Nothing* (2016)
   Original title: *Awake Now and Cross Towards Her*
   Author: Madeleine Thien

8. Final title: *The Favourite Game* (1963)
   Original title: *Beauty at Close Quarters*
   Author: Leonard Cohen

9. Final title: *The Golden Mean* (2009)
   Original title: *The Master of Stageira*
   Author: Annabel Lyon

10. Final title: *Happiness*™ (2001)
    Original title: *Generica*
    Author: Will Ferguson

11. Final title: *Harry Potter and the Goblet of Fire* (2000)
    Original title: *Harry Potter and the Doomspell Tournament*
    Author: J.K. Rowling

12. Final title: *Lady Chatterley's Lover* (1928)
    Original title: *Tenderness*
    Author: D.H. Lawrence

13. Final title: *Naked Lunch* (1959)
    Original title: *Interzone*
    Author: William S. Burroughs

14. Final title: *Portnoy's Complaint* (1969)
    Original title: *A Jewish Patient Begins His Analysis*
    Author: Philip Roth

15. Final title: *The Postman Always Rings Twice* (1934)
    Original title: *Bar-B-Q*
    Author: James M. Cain

16. Final title: *Pride and Prejudice* (1813)
    Original title: *First Impressions*
    Author: Jane Austen

17. Final title: *Roots: The Saga of an American Family* (1976)
    Original title: *Before This Anger*
    Author: Alex Haley

18. Final title: *The Shining* (1977). Altered when King learned that "shine" was a derogatory term for African-Americans, as they were often employed shining shoes; a black man is a central character in the novel.
    Original title: *The Shine*
    Author: Stephen King

19. Final title: *The Sound and the Fury* (1929)
    Original title: *Twilight*
    Author: William Faulkner

20. Final title: *The Stone Angel* (1964)
    Original title: *Hagar*; also *Old Lady Shipley*
    Author: Margaret Laurence

21. Final title: *The Time Machine* (1895)
    Original title: *The Chronic Argonauts*
    Author: H.G. Wells

22. Final title: *Treasure Island* (1883)
    Original title: *The Sea-Cook*
    Author: Robert Louis Stevenson

23. Final title: *War and Peace* (1866)
    Original title: *All's Well That Ends Well*
    Author: Leo Tolstoy

14 MEMORABLE SEX SCENES IN CANADIAN LITERATURE

At first glance, sex and Canadian literature hardly seem to go hand in hand, but on closer consideration, there is indeed a wealth of sex scenes in our books. At times titillating and at others a tad disturbing, the sex scenes below indicate that Canadian writers deal frankly with a broad range of subjects (although, interestingly, there seems to be a trend towards depicting masturbation).

1. Bear by Marian Engel (1976)

A woman on vacation in the woods gets intimate with a bear. Margaret Laurence describes this powerful, iconoclastic novel as follows: "Fascinating and profound, this novel speaks of a woman's strange (some would say bizarre) and moving journey toward inner freedom and strength, and ultimately toward a sense of communion with all living creatures."

2. The Change Room by Karen Connelly (2017)

Eliza is an accomplished modern woman with all the trappings of happiness: a couple of nice kids, a deliciously rumpled math professor husband, a thriving small business selling flowers—what more could she possibly want? A six-orgasm session with a chiselled beauty she's been sizing up at the local public pool, that's what. "With women the sex could go on and on, and on . . . Orgasm could subside and more touching could begin, not the old highway of penetration but another road, barely defined, meandering off into the forest, dipping into the riverbed, remerging into another geography." The Amazon, as Eliza dubs her, is one scorching-hot lover who knows just what to do with a middle-aged woman on the edge of a midlife change-up. Vroom vroom.

3. A Complicated Kindness by Miriam Toews (2004)

Near the end of this novel, Nomi Nickel loses her virginity to her boyfriend, Travis, after she discovers that he has started dating another girl who works with him at the replica pioneer Mennonite village. Nomi's description captures it all: "In a way I think it might have gone better if I hadn't been bald, drunk, depressed and jealous . . . and I hadn't started crying in the truck on the way home and slammed it into reverse for no good reason going fifty miles per hour."

4. The Diviners by Margaret Laurence (1974)

The zealots who wanted this book banned from high schools and community libraries often point to Morag's dalliance with Harold as a sign of the book's immorality. Morag is a single woman and Harold is recently separated—how dare they have a casual sexual encounter? In a letter to Laurence that appears in *Intimate Strangers: The Letters of Margaret Laurence and Gabrielle Roy*, Roy discusses the attempts to ban *The Diviners*, as well as her own book *The Tin Flute*:

"Perhaps we offer books of too vast an experience to young people as yet too young. I know that I always feel a little embarrassed when I hear of adolescents of fifteen or sixteen reading and studying *The Tin Flute* at school. I don't think we had them in mind—do you?—when we wrote our books."

5. Fall on Your Knees by Ann-Marie MacDonald (1996)

"Under a smoky streetlamp I stood face to face with my beloved and pricked my fingers against the diamond studs of her immaculate shirt front." So begins one of the most sensuous lesbian sex scenes in contemporary literature, Canadian or otherwise.

6. Galveston by Paul Quarrington (2004)

For 16 pages (possibly the longest sex scene in a Canadian novel), Caldwell and Beverly have sex while a force-five hurricane rips the roof, walls and doors off their vacation house. Sex (and weather) becomes a metaphor for release and redemption.

7. The Handmaid's Tale by Margaret Atwood (1985)

One of the most chilling moments in this powerful novel is Offred's narration of being pinned between the Commander and his wife, Serena Joy, in order to impregnate her against her will. Not quite a "sex scene" in the consensual sense, but a prescient use of sex in Atwood's novel about a dystopia that no longer feels so futuristic given the state of sexual politics, women's reproductive rights and religious zealotry in North America.

8. Happiness™ by Will Ferguson (2001)

When Edwin de Valu's wife, Jenni, gets hold of *What I Learned on the Mountain*, the all-encompassing self-help book whose publication he tries to prevent, their conjugal bed heats up. Unrelentingly so. Jenni goes as far as to indicate with Post-it notes the spots she wants her husband to explore. This is arguably one of the funniest sex scenes in a Canadian novel.

9. How Should a Person Be? by Sheila Heti (2010)

A self-obsessed confessional about a recently divorced novelist experiencing writer's block who's having lots of harsh, heartless sex with an emotionally unavailable boyfriend. The sex scenes are calculated to drive the reader to question narcissistic urges to be accomplished, self-expressed, an artist—or simply wanted. Here's a sample: "It is your unconcern that makes me want you to do whatever you want to my body, which can be for you while yours cannot be for me. I can see that your body must be for many women, and though I once thought the same of mine—that mine must be for all the men who wanted me—I can just tease you with it if you will keep on fucking me."

10. In the Skin of a Lion by Michael Ondaatje (1987)

Though Ondaatje's *The English Patient* is a masterpiece infused with erotic desire, the most memorable sex scene in his novels is in this one, about Toronto in the 1920s and '30s. A particularly charged passage details the aftermath of a sexual encounter between Clara and Patrick in which his ejaculate becomes a symbol for their interconnectedness: ". . . they passed it back and forth between them till it no longer existed, till they didn't know who had him like a lost planet somewhere in the body."

11. Lives of Girls and Women by Alice Munro (1971)

In the title story of this collection, Del Jordan develops a flirtation with a war veteran that ends with him masturbating in front of her in a field. In one of Canadian literature's most succinct passages, Del describes his penis: "Not at all like marble David's, it was sticking straight out in front of him, which I knew from reading is what they did. It had a sort of head on it, like a mushroom, and its colour was reddish purple."

12. The Pornographer's Poem by Michael Turner (1999)

This isn't the first Canadian novel to feature bestiality, but it is the first one to offer bestiality, S/M play, voyeurism, porn and sex toys in the same scene.

13. We So Seldom Look on Love by Barbara Gowdy (1992)

A young woman who likes sleeping with dead men gets into a relationship with a live one. He becomes obsessed with her obsession and realizes there is only one way to become truly intimate with her. In a review in the *Boston Globe*, Carol Shields describes the book: "Barbara Gowdy invites herself, and us, into taboo territory where love and disgust mingle freely. Nothing seems to hold back the narrative flow, not propriety, not politics, not even that ambiguity we once called good taste."

14. Wish Book: A Catalogue of Stories by Derek McCormack (1999)

In "Backward," a young man has sex with another man in the back of a hayloft and inadvertently burns down a barn and, with it, the CanLit pastoral tradition. In "The Ghost," the narrator is caught masturbating while watching Bing Crosby in the change room of a Peterborough department store.

GREGORY SCOFIELD'S 5 FAVOURITE CREE WORDS

Gregory Scofield is one of Canada's leading Aboriginal writers whose eight collections of poetry and memoir have earned him both a national and an international audience. He is known for his unique and dynamic reading style that blends oral storytelling, song, spoken word and the Cree language.

1. Pêyâhtik (careful, carefully)

In the English-to-Cree dictionary this word is translated as "to be careful" or "to do something carefully." However, I was taught it means "to give something— i.e., a thought or action—a great amount of consideration before acting upon said thought or action." Because everything is considered an act of medicine, one needs to be conscious of the consequence behind each thought or action. One is required "to walk very softly" before speaking or acting.

2. Maci-manitow or maci-manichôs (devil or little devil)

The literal translation of this word is "evil or bad spirit." I love this word because my late aunty often called me a little devil, even long after I grew up. I took her endearment to mean I was full of mischief and trouble, which, of course, I was and still am. Interestingly, *manicôs* is also the word for a bug, as in bedbug. I suppose, in this context, one could see oneself as an evil little bug.

3. Âpihtawikosisân (Métis, half-breed, mixed blood)

The literal translation of this word is "half son." This was one of the first Cree words I learned as a boy. Not only did it tell the *nêhiyawak* (the Crees) that I was a language speaker but that I also "half" belonged to them. Much later on, in reference to being Métis, I learned the word *otipêyimisowak* (the People Who

Own Themselves). This word, I was taught, is a direct reference to the fact that Western Canadian Métis were not seen as "Indians" under the 1876 Indian Act, but rather as a "free" people, who held no trading alliance to either the Northwest Company or the Hudson's Bay Company. This particular word has always made me extremely proud.

4. Wêpanâsowin (offerings [to the spirits])

For many Cree/Métis ceremonial people this is an important word. The act of making food or material offerings such as cloth or tobacco to the spirits is highly important, and is viewed as an act of humility and reverence. It is believed that we are in a constant relationship with those who've passed on; therefore, we are responsible for respecting and honouring them.

5. Sâkihitowin (love)

Again, one of the first words I learned as a boy. And it has become a word that I live by. I learned that one should say *kisâkihtin* (I love you) each and every time you left another person, either remotely or physically. I was also taught the suffix that could be added to the word *kisâkihitin*, which is *mistahi* (a lot, much, a great deal)—*kisâkihitin mistahi* (I love you very much).

7 ADJECTIVES IN WHICH ALL THE VOWELS APPEAR IN ALPHABETICAL ORDER

1. *Abstemious:* practising temperance in living
2. *Abstentious:* characterized by abstinence
3. *Annelidous:* of the nature of an annelid
4. *Arsenious:* of, relating to, or containing arsenic
5. *Casesious:* having a blue colour
6. *Facetious:* straining to be funny or flippant, especially at the wrong time
7. *Fracedinous:* productive of heat through putrefaction

17 WELL-KNOWN SAYINGS ATTRIBUTED TO THE WRONG PEOPLE

1. Anybody who hates children and dogs can't be all bad.
   ATTRIBUTED TO: W.C. Fields
   ACTUALLY SAID BY: Leo Rosten (at a dinner, introducing Fields: "Any man who hates dogs and babies can't be all bad.")

2. Go west, young man!
   ATTRIBUTED TO: Horace Greeley
   ACTUALLY SAID BY: John Soule (article, Terre Haute *Express*, 1851)

3. Everybody talks about the weather, but nobody does anything about it!
   ATTRIBUTED TO: Mark Twain
   ACTUALLY SAID BY: Charles Dudley Warner (editorial, Hartford *Courant*, August 24, 1897)

4. Survival of the fittest.
   ATTRIBUTED TO: Charles Darwin
   ACTUALLY SAID BY: Herbert Spencer (*Principles of Biology* and earlier works)

5. That government is best which governs least.
   ATTRIBUTED TO: Thomas Jefferson
   ACTUALLY SAID BY: Henry David Thoreau (who put it in quotation marks in "Civil Disobedience" and called it a motto)

6. Cleanliness is next to godliness.
   ATTRIBUTED TO: The Bible
   ACTUALLY SAID BY: John Wesley (Sermons, no. 93, "On Dress")

7. A journey of a thousand miles must begin with a single step.
   ATTRIBUTED TO: Confucius
   ACTUALLY SAID BY: Lao-Tzu (*Tao Tê Ching*)

8. God helps those who help themselves.
   ATTRIBUTED TO: The Bible
   ACTUALLY SAID BY: Aesop ("The gods help them that help themselves.")

9. God is in the details.
   ATTRIBUTED TO: Ludwig Mies van der Rohe
   ACTUALLY SAID BY: François Rabelais ("The good God is in the details.")

10. If you can't stand the heat, get out of the kitchen.
    ATTRIBUTED TO: Harry S. Truman

ACTUALLY SAID BY: Harry Vaughan (Truman's friend, whom Truman was quoting)

11. Promises are like pie crust, made to be broken.
    ATTRIBUTED TO: V.I. Lenin
    ACTUALLY SAID BY: Jonathan Swift (*Polite Conversation*: "Promises are like pie crust, leaven to be broken.")

12. Wagner's music is better than it sounds.
    ATTRIBUTED TO: Mark Twain
    ACTUALLY SAID BY: Edgar Wilson ("Bill") Nye (American humorist, 1850–1896)

13. When I hear the word "culture," I reach for my gun.
    ATTRIBUTED TO: Hermann Göring
    ACTUALLY SAID BY: Hanns Johst (1933 play *Schlageter*: "Whenever I hear the word 'culture,' I reach for my Browning.")

14. Winning isn't everything, it's the only thing.
    ATTRIBUTED TO: Vince Lombardi
    ACTUALLY SAID BY: Red Sanders (UCLA football coach; quoted in *Sports Illustrated*, 1955)

15. Spare the rod and spoil the child.
    ATTRIBUTED TO: The Bible
    ACTUALLY SAID BY: Samuel Butler (*Hudibras*, 1664)

16. Float like a butterfly,
    Sting like a bee,
    Your hands can't hit
    What your eyes can't see.
    ATTRIBUTED TO: Muhammad Ali
    ACTUALLY SAID BY: Drew "Bundini" Brown (Ali's good friend)

17. There's a sucker born every minute.
    ATTRIBUTED TO: P.T. Barnum
    ACTUALLY SAID BY: David Hannum (referring to people who had been duped by Barnum)

19 HISTORICAL AND SOMETIMES HYSTERICAL CANADIAN HEADLINES ABOUT QUEER FOLKS

LGBTQ people have always been around, of course, but weren't always openly acknowledged in public. By the early 20th century, however, the love that dare not speak its name began popping up in the pages of periodicals and newspapers with increasing frequency in Canada. Nowhere was this truer than in purple-prose-soaked pages of the muckraking tabloid press. With names such as *Hush*, *Tab*, *Flash*, and *The Tattler*, the tabloids ran stories about queer life with lurid titles designed to titillate and sell papers. Sometimes bemused and often bigoted, the tabloids, with their references to cops and the courts, are a reminder that same-sex relations, whether male or female, in public or private, remained illegal in Canada until Pierre Trudeau famously got the state out of the nation's bedrooms in 1969. But it wasn't all bad news. One unintended consequence of the tabloids' coverage—naming the bars, restaurants and other places in the city where queer people met—is that it provided interested readers with a detailed map to the city's queer spaces. The many not-so-chance encounters found in and facilitated by the tabloids chart the remarkable growth and increasing visibility of queer communities in Canada over the 20th century.

Steven Maynard is a long-time queer activist and historian. His research and writing appears in many academic journals and publications, including Any Other Way: How Toronto Got Queer. *He lives in Kingston, Ontario, where he teaches Canadian history and the history of sexuality at Queen's University.*

1. "Votaries at the Shrine of Lesbia" (*Hush*, December 19, 1928)

2. "Pale Pansies of the Oscar Wilde garden" (*The Tattler*, April 23, 1938)

3. "Sodomy Specialist" (*Hush*, January 3, 1929)

4. "Hell Witches and Shameless Females Beyond the Law" (*Hush*, April 18, 1929)

5. "Masculine Woman: One of those strangest of all distorted, warped beings—a female addicted to delusions that she belonged to the stronger sex" (*Hush*, March 2, 1940)

6. "Love-Sick Pansy Boys" (*Hush*, June 5, 1930)

7. "Two sexual deviates—negro and white man—are given jail terms" (*Justice Weekly*, June 11, 1955)

8. "Lesbian Vermin Plagues Toronto!" (*Tab*, 1963)

9. "Hanky-whirling Henrys" and "Straw-hatted, lavender-tied, white-panted sweethearts" (*Hush*, June 5, 1930)

10. "Fags in Drag" (*Tab*, 1962)

11. "Third Sex at the Ex! 2,000 'Queers' Invade Toronto" (*Tab*, 1959)

12. "Unparalleled Orgies of Perversion Exposed by Intrepid Flash Reporter" (*Flash*, May 2, 1950)

13. "Blonde pistol packin' mamma jailed" (*Hush*, November 30, 1946)

14. "Sky-High Negro Makes Court Appearance in Mini-Skirt!" (*Tab*, 1969)

15. "Butch Broads Battle in Chinatown Area" (*Tab*, 1961)

16. "Cops burst in on mass carnival of homo lust! Simpering creatures dress like girls; lipstick too!" (*Flash*, December 11, 1950)

17. "Lesbians Crowd Local Chinatown—Mostly from Maritimes!" (*Tab*, 1968)

18. "Union Station washroom 'swish boys' love nest" (*Hush*, August 1949)

19. "Beach Belles Turned Out to Be Men in Women's Clothing!" (*Tab*, 1961)

SO TO SPEAK—THE TRUTH ABOUT 14 COMMON SAYINGS

1. All the tea in China

The United Nations Food and Agriculture Organization estimates that, in 2003, all the tea in China amounted to 800,345 metric tons.

2. At a snail's pace

The fastest land snail on record is a garden snail named Archie, who won the 1995 World Snail Racing Championship in Longhan, England, by covering 33 centimetres in 2 minutes. Archie's pace was 0.001 kilometres per hour.

3. Blood is thicker than water

In chemistry, water is given a specific gravity, or relative density, of 1.00 because it is used as the standard against which all other densities are measured. By comparison, blood has a specific gravity of 1.06—only slightly thicker than water.

4. By a hair's breadth

Although the breadth of a hair varies from head to head, the dictionary definition of hair's breadth is 1/19 centimetre.

5. Eats like a horse

A 544-kilogram horse eats about 7 kilograms of hay and 9.4 kilograms of grain each day. This amounts to 1/50 of its weight each day, or seven times its weight each year. The real gluttons in the animal kingdom are birds, who consume more than 90 times their own weight in food each year.

6. Faster than a speeding bullet

The fastest bullet is a calibre .50 Saboted Light Armor Penetrator-Tracer M962. Used in M2 machine guns, it travels 1,219 metres per second. The fastest non-military bullet is the .257 Weatherby Spire Point, which travels 1,166 metres per second.

7. High as a kite

The record for the greatest height attained by a single kite on a single line is 4,422 metres. The kite was flown by a group headed by Richard Synergy at Kincardine, Ontario, on August 12, 2000.

8. Just a moment

According to an old English time unit, a moment takes 1 1/2 minutes. In medieval times, a moment was either 1/40 or 1/50 of an hour, but by rabbinical reckoning a moment is precisely 1/1,080 of an hour.

9. A king's ransom
The largest king's ransom in history was raised by Richard the Lionheart to obtain his release from the Holy Roman Emperor Henry VI in 1194. The English people were forced to contribute almost 150,000 marks to free their sovereign. Nearly as large a ransom was raised by Atahualpa, king of the Incas, when he offered Pizarro a roomful of gold and two roomfuls of silver for his release in 1532. At today's prices, the ransom would be worth more than $7 million. Unfortunately, it was not sufficient to buy Atahualpa his freedom; he was given a mock trial and executed.

10. Knee-high to a grasshopper
According to Charles L. Hogue of the Los Angeles County Museum of Natural History, this figure necessarily depends upon the size of the grasshopper. For the average grasshopper, the knee-high measurement would be about one centimetre.

11. Only skin deep
The depth of human skin ranges from 0.2 millimetres on the eyelid to 5 millimetres on the back.

12. Quick as a wink
The average wink, or corneal reflex blink, lasts 1/10 second.

13. Selling like hotcakes
Sales figures for the International House of Pancakes show that their 1,164 U.S. restaurants sold a total of 700 million pancakes in 2003.

14. Since time immemorial
Time immemorial is commonly defined as beyond the memory of any living person, or a time extending so far back as to be indefinite. However, for the purposes of English law, a statute passed in 1275 decreed that time immemorial was any point in time prior to 1189—the year when Richard I began his reign.

28 WORDS RARELY USED IN THEIR POSITIVE FORM

Negative form	Positive form
1. Inadvertent	Advertent (giving attention; heedful)

2.	*Analgesia*	*Algesia* (sensitivity to pain)
3.	*Antibiotic*	*Biotic* (of or relating to life)
4.	*Unconscionable*	*Conscionable* (conscientious)
5.	*Disconsolate*	*Consolate* (consoled, comforted)
6.	*Incorrigible*	*Corrigible* (correctable)
7.	*Uncouth*	*Couth* (marked by finesse, polish, etc.; smooth)
8.	*Indelible*	*Delible* (capable of being deleted)
9.	*Nondescript*	*Descript* (described; inscribed)
10.	*Indomitable*	*Domitable* (tameable)
11.	*Ineffable*	*Effable* (capable of being uttered or expressed)
12.	*Inevitable*	*Evitable* (avoidable)
13.	*Feckless*	*Feckful* (effective; sturdy; powerful)
14.	*Unfurl*	*Furl* (to draw in and secure to a staff)
15.	*Disgruntle*	*Gruntle* (to put in good humour)
16.	*Disgust*	*Gust* (inclination; liking)
17.	*Disinfectant*	*Infectant* (an agent of infection)
18.	*Illicit*	*Licit* (not forbidden by law; allowable)
19.	*Immaculate*	*Maculate* (marked with spots; besmirched)
20.	*Innocuous*	*Nocuous* (likely to cause injury; harmful)
21.	*Deodorant*	*Odorant* (an odorous substance)
22.	*Impeccable*	*Peccable* (liable or prone to sin)
23.	*Impervious*	*Pervious* (being of a substance that can be penetrated or permeated)
24.	*Implacable*	*Placable* (of a tolerant nature; tractable)
25.	*Ruthless*	*Ruthful* (full of compassion or pity)
26.	*Insipid*	*Sipid* (affecting the organs of taste; savoury)
27.	*Unspeakable*	*Speakable* (able to be spoken of)
28.	*Unwieldy*	*Wieldy* (strong; manageable)

7 REMARKABLE MESSAGES IN BOTTLES

1. Better Late than Never

In 1784, Japanese seaman Chunosuke Matsuyama embarked on a treasure hunt in the Pacific. His ship was caught in a gale and sank, but he and 43 shipmates managed to swim to a deserted coral reef. Matsuyama and his companions eventually died of starvation and exposure, but before they did, Matsuyama attempted to send word home. He wrote the story on chips of coconut shell, sealed them in a bottle and tossed it into the sea. The bottle washed ashore in 1935 on the beach where Matsuyama grew up.

2. Deliver Us This Day

In 1825 one Major MacGregor bottled a message and dropped it into the Bay of Biscay: "Ship on fire. Elizabeth, Joanna, and myself commit our spirits into the hands of our Redeemer whose grace enables us to be quite composed in the awful prospect of entering eternity." The note was found a year and a half later, but the major and his party had already been rescued.

3. Record Holder

Drift bottles have been employed as a means of measuring and mapping ocean currents for centuries. The oldest *Guinness Book of World Records*–certified message in a bottle was retrieved by Scottish fisherman Andrew Leaper near the Shetland Islands in 2011. The bottle he hauled in contained a note from the Glasgow School of Navigation, which had released 1,889 other messages in bottles in 1914. To date, 315 of these bottled mapping missives have been retrieved and catalogued.

4. The Last Message from the Lusitania

In 1916 a British seaman saw a bottle bobbing in the North Atlantic. He fished it from the water, opened it . . . and read the final message sent from the *Lusitania* before it sank a year prior, taking with it some 1,198 passengers: "Still on deck with a few people. The last boats have left. We are sinking fast. The orchestra is still playing bravely. Some men near me are praying with a priest. The end is near. Maybe this note will . . ." And there it ended.

5. A Message from the North Pole

In 1948 a Russian fisherman found a bottle in the sand bordering Vilkitsky Strait in the Arctic. A message was inside, written in both Norwegian and English. It was incomprehensible even when translated: "Five ponies and 150 dogs remaining. Desire hay, fish and 30 sledges. Must return early in August. Baldwin." The bizarre message became clear when it was learned that polar explorer Evelyn Baldwin had sealed the note and sent it in 1902. He managed to survive the Arctic without ever receiving the hay, fish or sledges. Whether or not he made it back in August is unknown.

6. Eighty-Five Years at Sea

On his way to the front in 1914, British soldier Private Thomas Hughes launched a ginger ale bottle into the English Channel containing a letter to his wife. He died days later in France, but the message was recovered by a fisherman in the River Thames in 1999. His wife had died in 1979, but the message was successfully delivered to his surviving daughter, then 86 years old, in New Zealand.

7. From Nova Scotia to Croatia with Love

Members of a kite-surfing club cleaning a beach in Croatia in 2013 came across a bottle with a message inside. It read, "Mary, you really are a great person. I hope we can keep in correspondence. I said I would write. Your friend always, Jonathon. Nova Scotia '85." In 28 years, the bottle had crossed the Atlantic, threaded the Strait of Gibraltar and bobbed around the Mediterranean and Adriatic Seas, likely travelling in excess of 7,000 kilometres.

9 WORDS FOR BODY PARTS YOU DIDN'T KNOW HAD NAMES

1. Canthus

The corners of the eye where the upper and lower eyelids meet.

2. Eponychium

Another term for the cuticle of the fingernail, a narrow band of epidermal tissue that extends down over the margin of the nail wall.

3. Frenum Glandis

Found in the male reproductive system, this delicate fold of skin attaches the foreskin to the undersurface of the glans.

4. Glabella

A flattened area of the frontal bone (forehead area) between the frontal eminences and the superciliary arches (eyebrows), just above the nose.

5. Lunule

The white crescent-shaped mark at the base of a fingernail.

6. Otoliths
Particles of calcium carbonate in the utricles and saccules of the inner ears. The otoliths respond to gravity by sliding in the direction of the ground and causing sensitive hairs to bend, thus generating nervous impulses important in maintaining equilibrium.

7. Phalanx
One of the bones of the fingers or toes. There are two phalanges in each thumb and big toe, while there are three phalanges in all other fingers and toes, making a total of 14 in each hand or foot.

8. Philtrum
The vertical groove in the middle portion of the upper lip.

9. Pudendum
A collective name for the external genitalia of the female; also known as the vulva. It includes the mons pubis, the labia majora and the labia minora.

14 LAST LINES OF CANADIAN NOVELS

1. "'This is also now a housewarming,' Karen said, holding up a new bottle of wine, 'for Red.'" —*After the Fire*, Jane Rule

2. "He felt the boy's concerned hand on his. This sweet touch from the world." —*Anil's Ghost*, Michael Ondaatje

3. "'God's in his heaven, all's right with the world,' whispered Anne softly." —*Anne of Green Gables*, Lucy Maud Montgomery

4. "Oh my God, I thought, breaking into a sweat. I'd better call Saul. I owe Kate an apology. But, oh God, it's too late for Barney. He's beyond understanding now. Damn, damn, damn." —*Barney's Version*, Mordecai Richler

5. "Morag returned to the house, to write the remaining private and fictional words, and to set down her title." —*The Diviners*, Margaret Laurence

6. "Tomorrow begins from another dawn, when we will be fast asleep. Remember what I say: not everything will pass."
   —*Do Not Say We Have Nothing*, Madeleine Thien

7. "'Here, dear,' says Lily, 'sit down and have a cuppa tea till I tell you about your mother.'"
   —*Fall on Your Knees*, Ann-Marie MacDonald

8. "She washed the two plates, returning them to the sideboard for Nusswan and Ruby to dine off at night. Then she dried her hands and decided to take a nap before starting the evening meal."
   —*A Fine Balance*, Rohinton Mistry

9. "I see that I must give what I most need."
   —*Fugitive Pieces*, Anne Michaels

10. "Then he turns and runs off in the direction of the Iberian rhinoceros."
    —*The High Mountains of Portugal*, Yann Martel

11. "Rising from his body, Gabriel Okimasis and the Fur Queen floated off into the swirling mist, as the little fox on the collar of the cape turned to Jeremiah. And winked."
    —*Kiss of the Fur Queen*, Tomson Highway

12. "She kisses his sleeping back and falls asleep."
    —*Pattern Recognition*, William Gibson

13. "Going down, he counts thirteen soft, carpeted safe steps, watches the way her body descends, and he smells the fragrance of her perfume that lingers."
    —*The Polished Hoe*, Austin Clarke

14. "Someone threw a dead dog after him down the ravine."
    —*Under the Volcano*, Malcolm Lowry

Sports

12 OLYMPIC CONTROVERSIES

1. With Too Much Help from His Friends (1908, marathon)

Italian Dorando Pietri was the first marathon runner to enter the stadium in London, England, in 1908. However, Pietri was dazed and headed in the wrong direction. Track officials pointed him the right way. But then he collapsed on the track. He rose, but collapsed again . . . and again, and again. Finally, the officials, fearful that "he might die in the very presence of the Queen," carried him across the finish line. This aid led to his disqualification, and the gold medal went to John Hayes of the United States.

2. Champion with a Dark Secret (1932 and 1936, women's 100 metres)

Competing for Poland, Stella Walsh won the 100 metres in 1932, equalling the world record three times in the process. Four years later, at the Berlin Olympics, Walsh was beaten into second place by American Helen Stephens. A Polish journalist accused Stephens of being a man in disguise. German officials examined her and issued a statement that Stephens was definitely a woman. Forty-four years later, in 1980, Walsh, by then an American citizen living in Cleveland, was shot to death when she stumbled into the middle of a robbery attempt at a discount store. An autopsy concluded that although Helen Stephens may not have had male sexual organs, Stella Walsh did. While Walsh was winning medals and setting records in women's events, she was, by today's rules, a man.

3. Clock vs. Eyes (1960, 100-metre freestyle)

Swimmer Lance Larson of the United States appeared to edge John Devitt of Australia for first place in the 1960 100-metre freestyle. Devitt congratulated Larson and left the pool in disappointment. Larson's official time was 55.1 seconds and Devitt's was 55.2 seconds. Of the three judges assigned the task of determining who finished first, two voted for Larson. However, the three second-place judges also voted 2–1 for Larson. In other words, of the six judges, three thought Larson had won and three thought Devitt had won. The chief judge gave the victory to Devitt, and four years of protests failed to change the results.

4. The Fog of War (1968, slalom)

French skier Jean-Claude Killy, competing at home in Grenoble, had already won two gold medals and only needed to win the slalom to complete a sweep of the men's alpine events. Killy's main challenge was expected to come from Karl

Schranz of Austria. But something curious happened as Schranz sped through the fog. According to Schranz, a mysterious figure in black crossed the course in front of him. Schranz skidded to a halt and demanded a rerun. His request was granted and Schranz beat Killy's time and was declared the winner. But two hours later, it was announced that Schranz had been disqualified because he had missed two gates before his encounter with the mysterious interloper. At a four-hour meeting of the Jury of Appeal, the Austrians said that if Schranz had missed a gate or two it was because a French soldier or policeman had purposely interfered with him. The French claimed that Schranz had made up the whole story to cover up the fact that he had missed a gate. The jury voted 3–1 for Killy, with one abstention.

5. Extra Shot (1972, basketball)

Since basketball was first included in the Olympic program in 1936, teams from the United States had gone undefeated, winning 62 straight games over a 36-year period . . . until the 1972 final against the U.S.S.R. In an era before professionals were allowed in the Olympics, and with most of the best American college players taking a pass, the U.S. team was hard pressed to prevail against the seasoned veterans of the Soviet squad. The Americans trailed throughout and did not take their first lead, 50–49, until there were three seconds left in the game. Two seconds later, the head referee, noting a disturbance at the scorer's table, called an administrative time out. The officials in charge had failed to notice that the Soviet coach, Vladimir Kondrashkin, had called a time out. With one second on the clock, the U.S.S.R. was awarded its time out. When play resumed, they inbounded the ball and time ran out. The U.S. players began a joyous celebration, but then R. William Jones, the British secretary-general of the International Amateur Basketball Federation, ordered the clock set back to three seconds, the amount of time remaining when Kondrashkin originally tried to call the time out. Ivan Edeshko threw a long pass to Sasha Belov, who scored the winning basket. The United States filed a protest, which was heard by a five-man Jury of Appeal. Three members of the jury were from Communist countries, and all three voted to give the victory to the U.S.S.R. With the final vote 3–2, the United States lost an Olympic basketball game for the first time.

6. Wired for Victory (1976, team modern pentathlon)

The favoured team from the U.S.S.R. was fencing against the team from Great Britain when the British pentathletes noticed something odd about Soviet army major Borys Onyshchenko. Twice the automatic light registered a hit for Onyshchenko even though he had not touched his opponent. Onyshchenko's sword was taken away to be examined by the Jury of Appeal. An hour later Onyshchenko was disqualified. Evidently, he had wired his sword with a well-hidden push-button circuit breaker that enabled him to register a hit whenever he wanted. He was forever after known as Borys Dis-Onyshchenko.

7. The Unbeatable Park Si-Hun (1988, light middleweight boxing)

The 1988 Summer Olympics were held in Seoul, South Korea, and the Koreans were determined to win gold medals in boxing, one of their strongest sports. Light middleweight Park Si-Hun made it to the final with a string of four controversial victories, including one in which he disabled his opponent with a low blow to the kidney. In the final, Park faced a slick 19-year-old American named Roy Jones Jr., who dominated all three rounds, landing 86 punches to Park's 32. Yet three of the five judges awarded the decision to Park, who won the gold medal. Park himself apologized to Jones. Accusations of bribery lingered for years, and it was not until 1997 that an inquiry by the International Olympic Committee concluded that no bribery had occurred.

8. Say It Ain't So, Ben (1988, 100 metres)

It was the best of times that quickly became the worst of times. On Saturday, September 24, 1988, Canadian sprinter Ben Johnson won a gold medal in the 100 metres in Seoul, South Korea, in a world record time of 9.79 seconds. Three days later, Johnson was stripped of that medal after testing positive for anabolic steroids. Ben Johnson was the highest-profile athlete ever caught cheating at the Olympic Games, but in the end, something positive did emerge out of the ashes of Canada's worst Olympic nightmare. In February 1989 the Dubin Commission began hearing evidence that stripped bare the widespread use of illegal performance-enhancing drugs among Canadian track stars and weightlifters. The resulting public outcry led to new policies that put Canada at the forefront of drug-free sport. It would take more than a decade before some other countries, most notably the United States, undertook a similar purge of their doped-up Olympic athletes. As for the man who started it all, Ben Johnson continues to insist that he did not take steroids in the days before his race in Seoul, and professes to still be mystified as to how his urine sample came back positive.

9. Scoring Scandal Synchs Swimmer (1992, solo synchronized swimming)

The two leading synchronized swimmers in Barcelona were Sylvie Fréchette of Canada and Kristen Babb-Sprague of the United States. The competition included a round of figures that counted for 50% of the final score. Fréchette, who was strong in figures, hoped to pick up points to offset the gains that Babb-Sprague was expected to make with her free routine. But one of the five judges, Ana Maria da Silveira of Brazil, gave Fréchette's move, the "albatross spin up 180°," the unusually low score of 8.7. She immediately tried to change the score, claiming she had pushed the wrong button. But before the referee could be notified, the judges' scores were displayed and, according to the rules, that meant they could not be changed. When the free routine was completed the next day, it turned out that da Silveira's low score provided the margin of victory that gave the gold medal to Babb-Sprague. Fourteen months later, the International Swimming Federation awarded Fréchette a belated gold medal, while allowing Babb-Sprague to retain hers.

10. Impaired Judgment (2002, pairs figure skating)

The sport of figure skating has a long history of judging controversies; however, the problem reached a head at the Salt Lake City Olympics. Russian skaters had won 10 straight Olympic championships in the pairs event. In 2002 Russians Elena Berezhnaya and Anton Sikharulidze were in first place after the short program, with Jamie Salé and David Pelletier of Canada in second. In the free skate, the Russians made a series of technical errors, while the Canadians skated a clean program. Nonetheless, the judges voted 5–4 to award the gold medals to Berezhnaya and Sikharulidze. The ensuing outrage expressed by the North American media was so great and so prolonged that the International Olympic Committee pressured the International Skating Union into giving a second set of gold medals to Salé and Pelletier. Subsequent investigations revealed behind-the-scenes deals among judges and even the possible involvement of organized crime figures. Lost in the uproar was the possibility that the five judges who voted for the Russian pair simply preferred their traditional balletic style, while considering the exuberance of Salé and Pelletier's performance too glitzy and "Hollywood."

11. A Track Too Fast (2010, luge)

Most Olympic controversies involve disputes over winner and losers. The biggest controversy at the Vancouver/Whistler 2010 games involved life and death.

On February 12, 2010, the day the Games officially began, Georgian luger Nodar Kumaritashvili was fatally injured in a crash during his final training run at the Whistler Sliding Centre, when he lost control in the penultimate turn of the course and was thrown off his luge and over the sidewall of the track, striking an unprotected steel support pole at the end of the run. He was travelling at 143.6 kilometres per hour at the moment of impact. It was probably the fastest he had ever gone down a track, and above the top speed of 135 kilometres per hour recommended by the International Luge Federation (FIL).

After the accident, John Furlong, CEO of the Vancouver Olympic Organizing Committee (VANOC) told the press, "It's not something I prepared for, or ever thought I would have to be prepared for." But it turned out that wasn't exactly true. Documents obtained by the CBC in February 2011 revealed that as early as March 2009 the FIL had expressed concerns about the speed of the Whistler track to the track's designer, and to VANOC. Furlong acknowledged those concerns in a 2009 email: "An athlete gets badly injured or worse and I think the case could be made we were warned and did nothing." Following Kumaritashvili's death, the Whistler course was modified so Olympic lugers never reached the speeds that led to the Georgian's fatal accident.

12. State-Sponsored Doping (2012, 2014)

Doping scandals in the Olympics are nothing new, but there's never been anything quite like the scandal that was finally exposed in 2016 involving Russian sports and government authorities. After an extensive investigation commissioned by the World Anti-Doping Agency, Canadian lawyer Richard McLaren concluded that between 2011 and 2015 the Russian state orchestrated a doping program that enabled 1,000 athletes in 30 sports to take banned performance-enhancing drugs. The sports ministry, the Secret Service and the national anti-doping agency collaborated in the systematic corruption of the 2012 London Olympics and Paralympics, and the 2014 Sochi Winter Olympics and Paralympics. "The desire to win medals superseded their collective moral and ethical compass and their Olympic values of fair play," McLaren declared. What impact the revelations will have on future Olympics is still unclear. Despite the damning evidence presented in McLaren's report, the International Olympic Committee refused to issue an outright ban on Russian athletes for the 2016 Games in Rio, leaving many to wonder what exactly you would have to do to get kicked out of the Olympics.

COLETTE MCAULEY'S 7 THINGS CANADIAN WOMEN ATHLETES HAVE TO DEAL WITH THAT MALE ATHLETES DON'T

Things are definitely better for Canadian women athletes than they used to be. There's more exposure, more recognition, even a bit more money. But it's still a struggle for women athletes in many sports, particularly those not usually associated with women. Take rugby, for example. You don't get much more macho than rugby, but women have been playing rugby at the university level in Canada for about 20 years (the men have been playing for about 80 years), and internationally, there's been a Women's Rugby World Cup since 1991.

While the Canadian men have usually had to take a backseat to rugby powerhouses like Australia and New Zealand, the Canadian women have shone on the international stage, winning a silver medal in the Women's 15s Rugby World Cup in 2013, a bronze medal in the 2016 Rio Olympics, and winning the Sydney Sevens World Series in Australia in 2017.

Despite our success, Canadian women rugby players are still too often treated as second-class citizens. How so? This list is specifically about our rugby team, but women athletes in many other sports will have no trouble identifying with our struggle.

Colette McAuley has represented Canada 21 times for the National Women's 15s team, including World Cups in 2002 and Canada Cups in 2001, 2003 and 2005. After retiring from the national team in 2007, she took over as head women's rugby coach at the University of Guelph after years of assistant coaching and playing for the university. She also coaches the National Women's 15s team, where she sees the athletes still fighting the same fight she did years ago.

1. Posing Naked for a Calendar

Guess what? You can raise more money selling naked pictures than you can selling T-shirts or chocolate bars. Four times since 2004, our women's rugby team has bared it all for fundraising calendars. We received both praise and contempt from the public. Praise for our confidence and creativity, contempt for being exhibitionists and sinking so low to gain exposure for our sport. For me, it was the most practical return on investment of time. Sad but true. While we were proud of how hard we worked for our athletic bodies, it didn't mean it wasn't embarrassing to sign my name across my exposed behind.

2. Not Getting Invited to the Party

While the women's and men's national teams were on their 2016 fall tour in Dublin, Ireland, the men's team was invited to the amazing, 250-year-old Guinness Brewery and Storehouse. The women were about half an hour away at Johnstown Estate, watching it unfold on social media. Not invited. They then proceeded to head to the field for their second practice of the day. The women's team beat Ireland four days later with a whopping score of 48–7. The men lost to Ireland 52–21.

3. No Stars vs. Five Stars

In 2005, the national team was touring France to prepare for the 2006 World Cup. Our accommodations were something less than first class. At one point, we were staying at a kid's camp lodge, sleeping on bunk beds only a metre and a half long, with the farm animals waking us up at dawn. Meanwhile, the men's team was staying at a five-star hotel and sleeping normal hours, their heads probably resting on extra-fluffy pillows.

4. Wearing Clothes That Don't Fit

It's hard to get women's rugby uniforms that fit properly, probably because they're made for men and by men. Women pay for game shorts that need to be rolled up three times at the waist, T-shirts that fall below the elbow, and golf shirts that when belted could be worn as a dress. We sometimes look ridiculous, but we wear it all proudly because it has the maple leaf on it.

5. Explaining That We're Not All Hookers

Yes, we pose naked for calendars, and we're constantly on the prowl for money, but there's only one hooker on a rugby team, and she's on the field, between the two props in the front row, hooking the ball in the scrum, not on a street corner. Men have hookers on their team too, but nobody confuses them with sex workers.

6. Finding a Job That Allows Us to Play for Our Country

When your sport is chronically short of funds, players often struggle to make ends meet. We need to strike a balance between work, family and playing the sport we love. The work part of that equation requires a job that is flexible enough, and a boss who is compassionate enough, to allow for lunch-time training and lots of time off for tours. It's not easy, but thankfully those jobs and bosses are out there.

7. Positioning Canada As One of the Top Three Rugby Countries in the World

You're welcome.

20 OLD-TIME HOCKEY NICKNAMES

Today's hockey players might be bigger, stronger, faster and richer than the men who played in the NHL 60 or 70 years ago, but there's a least one important area where the old-timers have a clear advantage: nicknames. Hockey players used to take great pride in their nicknames. They were often descriptive, sometimes amusing, sometimes nasty and, as you can see from the list below, frequently baffling to the outsider.

By comparison, today's nicknames are seriously lacking in imagination. A hockey player named Burns will invariably be called Burnsy; a Campbell will be Soupy. Wayne Gretzky was "the Great One," so Mario Lemieux had to be "the Magnificent One," Eric Lindros was "the Next One," and Sidney Crosby was just "the Kid." Blame the players, their teammates and the reporters covering the players, who were often the source of the best nicknames. They all need to up their games. To inspire them, here's a salute to some classics from the golden age of hockey nicknames.

1. Murph "Old Hardrock" Chamberlain, Montreal Canadiens, 1939–49
2. Carson "Shovel Shot" Cooper, Boston Bruins, 1924–27
3. Bert "Pig Iron" Corbeau, Montreal Canadiens, 1917–22
4. Hank "Lou Costello" Damore, New York Rangers, 1943–44
5. Eddie "the Great Gabbo" Dorohoy, Montreal Canadiens, 1948–49
6. Frank "the Shawville Express" Finnigan, Ottawa Senators, 1924–34
7. Jimmy "the Blonde Bouncer" Fowler, Toronto Maple Leafs, 1936–39
8. Bill "the Honest Brakeman" Juzda, Toronto Maple Leafs, 1948–52
9. Alex "Sea Biscuit" Kaleta, Chicago Black Hawks, 1945–48
10. Joe "the Duke of Paducah" Klukay, Toronto Maple Leafs, 1946–52
11. Alex "Mine Boy" Levinsky, Toronto Maple Leafs, 1930–34
12. Herbie "the Duke of Duluth" Lewis, Detroit Red Wings, 1932–39
13. Howie "the Stratford Streak" Morenz, Montreal Canadiens, 1923–37
14. Frank "the Pembroke Peach" Nighbor, Ottawa Senators, 1917–30
15. Alf "the Embalmer" Pike, New York Rangers, 1939–43
16. Fred "Chief Running Deer" Sasakamoose, Chicago Black Hawks, 1953–54

17. Wally "the Whirling Dervish" Stanowski, Toronto Maple Leafs, 1945–48
18. Nels "Old Poison" Stewart, Montreal Maroons, 1925–32
19. Lorrain "Larry Half-n-Half " Thibeault, Montreal Canadiens, 1945–46
20. Georges "the Chicoutimi Cucumber" Vézina, Montreal Canadiens, 1917–26

Source: *Total Hockey: The Official Encyclopedia of the National Hockey League.*

LANNI MARCHANT'S 7 GRITTY AND GROUNDBREAKING ATHLETIC PERFORMANCES BY WOMEN

A list generally implies a ranking, yet there is no way to rank what these women have accomplished in their respective sports. As a marathoner and endurance-sport aficionado, I can tell you that it takes all of who you are to find more fuel when the tank feels empty. These women have what it takes, not just in their sport but as people determined to overcome challenge and adversity.

Lanni Marchant is the current Canadian record holder in both the marathon (2:28:00) and half marathon (1:10:47). In 2016 in Rio, Marchant became the first Canadian woman to compete in the 10,000 metre and the marathon at the same Olympic Games.

1. Kathrine Virginia Switzer (first woman to run the Boston Marathon, 1967)

What makes Kathy's run so gritty is that she didn't necessarily set out to make history or to prove a point. She set out to run Boston because, like the hundreds of men who registered each year, she had done the training and wanted to participate in the biggest marathon. It was during the race that her mindset shifted. Within the first few miles Kathy was physically attacked by the race manager, Jock Semple, who shouted, "Get the hell out of my race and give me those numbers!" Kathy would later describe the event as terrifying: "I was dazed and confused. I'd never been up close to physical violence; the power was terrifying and I was shocked at how helpless I, a strong woman, felt against it." Over the next few miles the temptation to drop out shifted to a realization that she was running for more than herself. "I knew if I quit, nobody would ever believe that women had the capability to run 26 plus miles. My fear and humiliation turned to anger."

2. Sylvia Ruegger (first Canadian woman to run the Olympic Marathon, 1984)

Sylvia was the first Canadian woman to run the Olympic Marathon, in Los Angeles, where she finished eighth. She held the Canadian marathon record for 28 years, between 1985 and 2014. I am forever grateful to Sylvia for paving the way for athletes like me. But what makes her even more iconic and fierce is how, tempted to leave the sport after a serious car accident that cut short her elite running career, she used running and reading to connect and empower children from disadvantaged communities. The volunteer-led after-school program Running and Reading operates coast to coast in Canada. It combines training for a 5K and reading to each other to build young people's self-confidence, literacy and strength through sport and education.

3. Brianne Theisen-Eaton (heptathlon bronze medal winner, 2016)

It's impossible to overstate the physical demands of competing in seven gruelling events spread out over two days. I roomed with Bri at the Rio Olympics and got to witness first-hand the determination required to compete, particularly when things are not 100% going to plan. Watching her come back between event sessions, go to her room and come out a few hours later with her game face back on amazed me. The mental and emotional strength it took to reset and go back into the sporting arena is something I try to draw upon when a marathon starts to go off road. The iconic pic of Bri standing at the finish line of the 800 metre in Rio and all the other women lying on the ground around her says it all—go look it up. In that instant you see all of the work she put in to get there and all of the endurance and emotion it took to finish.

4. Abigail "Abby" Hoffman (four-time Olympian, total badass, 1964, 1968, 1972, 1976)

When Abby was nine she wanted to play in a boys' hockey league, so she cut her hair short and registered as "Ab Hoffman." She was known for her speed, skills and determination that matched or bettered those of the boys with whom she played. She went on to compete in four Olympics between 1964 and 1976, medalled at the Pan American Games in the 800 metre, and is still one of our most decorated middle-distance runners. Abby's efforts helped open the University of Toronto's Hart House to women after initially being an all-male facility. She was the first woman to carry the Canadian flag in the Olympic opening ceremonies, at the 1976 Summer Olympic Games in Montreal. After her career as an athlete Abby went on to be the first woman elected to the executive committee on the Canadian Olympic Association as director general of Sport Canada, where she served for 10 years.

5. Karolina Kowalkiewicz (Ultimate Fighting Championship martial-arts fighter, 2016)

Karolina was up against her more skilled and experienced idol, reigning champion Joanna Jedrzejczyk, in the final fight of the 2016 season. Joanna had zero respect for Karolina, and during the bout landed more strikes. But Karolina was tough as nails, getting in a few shots that shocked the reigning champ. You could see the panic on Joanna's face. It went the full five rounds, and though Joanna prevailed, Karolina earned the respect of her hero. They actually hugged before the start of the final round. Watching the reigning champion's attitude shift and seeing the young challenger battle with all that she had made this one of the grittiest athletic feats I have seen in a long while by anyone.

6. Christine Sinclair (three-time soccer Olympian, 2008, 2012, 2016)

Two-time soccer bronze medallist Christine is known for her ability to get the job done, even if that means wearing a face mask to complete a tournament after breaking her nose. Her finest moment came in the 2012 Olympic semi-final when she scored all three goals against the Americans, only to lose the match when controversial calls by the ref enabled the United States to score on penalty kicks, tying up the game and then winning in overtime. The Canadians went on to win the bronze, but Captain Sinclair's six goals in the 2012 Games broke the record for most goals scored in women's soccer. Sinclair remains Canada's all-time leading scorer, second worldwide in international goals after American Abby Wambach. Off the field, Sinclair is a fairly private person, which I believe shows a different type of strength. She's the type of athlete who lets her skill and sportsmanship do the talking.

7. Hayley Wickenheiser (five-time Olympic medallist, 1998, 2002, 2006, 2010, 2014)

Hayley is the longest-serving member of Canada's National Women's Hockey Team. She competed in all five Olympic Games in which women's hockey has been included, winning five medals—four gold and one silver. Of her many career highlights, her accomplishments in the 2002 Olympics stand out, when she scored seven goals and was named tournament MVP. I could list play after play, accolade after accolade to demonstrate how this woman is one of the finest athletes ever. I could lay out the points in her career where she crossed over gender, age and physical barriers, breaking ground for the rest of us. Instead, I'll leave you with a quote from her Sportsnet interview: "I loved to play for Canada and represent the country, and I hope that my impact makes it easier for little girls now to play the game. And that they'll have a chance to love it the way I did."

10 FEATS OF STRENGTH BY LOUIS CYR

Quebec's world-famous strongman Louis Cyr was born on October 10, 1863, in Napierville. Both of his parents were large, robust people, and their first child, Louis, seemed to combine their strengths. He was encouraged to eat large quantities of food and developed bulging muscles working on the family farm. By the age of 11 he could carry calves around on his shoulders and at 12 he worked as a lumberjack. He first appeared as a "strongman" at age 15, carrying a horse around on his shoulders near Boston. He soon became an international sensation as a sideshow attraction in the Barnum & Bailey and Ringling Bros. circuses. His storied career took place before professional weightlifting and standardized measures existed, so his feats of strength were often showy and unusual.

1. He lifted a 220-kilogram boulder.
2. Using just one finger, he lifted a 280-kilogram weight attached to a hook.
3. He lifted a barrel of cement weighing 142 kilograms over his shoulder with one hand.
4. He lifted a 124-kilogram barbell over his head with one hand.
5. He backlifted a platform of 18 men weighing 1,972 kilograms.
6. He backlifted a record 1,604 kilograms of pig iron.
7. He did a one-handed dead lift of a dumbbell that weighed 238 kilograms.
8. He resisted the pull of four horses, which he held back with ropes, two in each hand, while trainers whipped the horses to get them to pull harder.
9. He often balanced a stack of four 23-kilogram weights in one hand while casually walking around.
10. At his Montreal bar on Notre-Dame Street, he tossed huge beer kegs into the air and caught them with one hand.

14 GREAT NAMES IN CANADIAN FOOTBALL

1. Junior Ah You, defensive end, Montreal Alouettes
2. Jack Bighead, tight end, Hamilton Tiger-Cats
3. Trod Buggs, running back, Hamilton Tiger-Cats
4. Lance Funderburk, quarterback, Hamilton Tiger-Cats
5. Admiral Dewey Larry, cornerback, Ottawa Rough Riders
6. Prince McJunkin III, quarterback, Ottawa Rough Riders
7. Wonderful Terrific Monds Jr., cornerback, Ottawa Rough Riders
8. Yo Murphy, receiver, Ottawa Renegades
9. Goodluck Owi, defensive end, Toronto Argonauts
10. Joe Paopao, quarterback, B.C. Lions
11. Loucheiz Purifoy, defensive back, B.C. Lions
12. SirVincent Rogers, offensive lineman, Ottawa Redblacks
13. Terrell Sinkfield Jr., wide receiver, B.C. Lions
14. Annis Stukus, quarterback, Toronto Argonauts

KURT BROWNING'S 9 TURNING POINTS IN FIGURE SKATING HISTORY (+1 THAT HASN'T HAPPENED YET)

Kurt Browning was born in 1966 in Rocky Mountain House, Alberta, and grew up in nearby Caroline. He is a four-time world champion and Canadian champion, a three-time world and Canadian professional champion and the only skater to win the world title with and without compulsory figures. He landed the first quadruple jump in a sanctioned event, putting him in the Guinness Book of Records.

1. Sonja Henie (Olympic gold medal winner, 1928, 1932, 1936)

Simply put, she was such a huge star on and off the ice and screen that her name alone was a turning point in the sport. One of the biggest stars in Hollywood at the time, she put figure skating in the public eye. And, boy, could she run on her toe picks. Wow.

2. Barbara Ann Scott (Olympic gold medal winner, 1948)

Canada's queen and my adopted Gramma, she was the one who made other skaters afraid of Canadians. Of course, they feared her on the ice only; off the ice she was the sweetest person ever, but she could kick butt when it came time to lace up.

3. Prague World Championships (1962)

Only a miracle could have made Donald Jackson the world champion that year, and a miracle he created. Needing to gain back impossible ground lost during the compulsory figure portion of the competition, Donald pulled out all the stops in the free skate to become Canada's first men's world champion. But the historic turning point was his first jump of the program. Donald went for and landed a huge triple Lutz, which had never been done before. Even after he had made history, he kept his cool, adding many more jumps and spins to win the event. The triple Lutz was not duplicated by any other skater for more than a decade. What a leap!

4. Strawberry Ice (1982)

Toller Cranston's outlandish skating style turned the whole sport around and just a little bit upside down. His extension, his music choices, his elegance and his chest hair all made him stand out from his peers. Easily the best skater of his time, he was a hard pill for the judges to swallow. His 1982 TV special, *Strawberry Ice*, gives an excellent illustration of his extraordinary ability.

5. Budapest (1988)

A skinny kid from Caroline, Alberta, with nothing to lose and everything to gain, tried and landed the first four-revolution jump within a competition. Suddenly, three turns was not enough, and soon the "quad" was an expected jump if you were to be champion. This jump changed the boundaries of skating and—possibly more importantly—got the jumper a six-month loan of a slick Audi Quattro car. That made Kurt Browning one cool 22-year-old that summer.

6. Calgary Olympic Games (1988)

Stepping out on the ice in lingerie—I mean, her short-program dress—Katarina Witt shocked the world and broke a few camera lenses. Some liked it, others did not, but it's safe to say the world of skating was never the same. The outfit, or lack thereof, helped make her a superstar, and she has transcended the sport to become a legend.

7. Halifax World Championships (1990)

This was the last event that featured compulsory figures. Figures used to take up most of a skater's training time. They were slow, difficult and expensive, and nobody who watched skating really cared about them. When fans turned on the television, they could not understand why a German or French skater was ahead of, say, me, without being able to jump or spin. It was because of figures, and it was confusing for the audience. TV won out, and figures were gone for good. After the Halifax World Championships, skaters took to the streets dancing and singing, all the while wearing their now-unneeded compulsory figure skates. Sparks flew in celebration of the death of figures.

8. Midori Ito (1988)

Japan's Midori Ito could fly with the best of them. Her jumps easily stacked up against any of the men of her time. Actually, make that of any time. Midori was doing triple-triple combos better than the men, and in 1988, when she became the first woman in the world to land the triple Axel, she cemented her place in history. In case you don't remember her, she is the skater who jumped out of the rink and into a TV camera at the Worlds in 1991. She got up, jumped back onto the ice, bowed a quick apology to the cameraman and continued with her program. An amazingly gifted, and polite, athlete.

9. Salt Lake City (2002)

The French judge did it. Okay . . . everybody did it, but she's the one who got caught. The pairs event at the 2002 Olympics was basically fixed, and the media jumped on the story hard. The frenzy was the start of a chain of events that would change the sport with the establishment of a new and improved judging system in 2004.

+1 That Hasn't Happened Yet. Only 3 Quads in the Long Program?

Evolution is a slow, slow process . . . usually! Since the first quad jump in 1988, the sport has grown in leaps and four-revolution bounds. Now, in 2017, every version of the six classic jumps has been landed in quad form except for one: the Axel. This quad holdout is the only jump that has a forward takeoff. For a jump to be counted in competition it must be landed on a left or right back outside edge. Because of the forward takeoff the skater must complete an extra half revolution to land backward, and this is arguably why it is the hardest of the jumps. The Axel jump was named after Axel Paulsen from Norway who was the World Speed Skating Champion from 1882 to 1890. So, when a skater finally lands a quad Axel, the last jump to resist the onslaught of all the amazing jumpers in this decade, it will truly be a historic moment in figure skating.

9 REALLY BAD CANADIAN SPORTS TEAMS

1. The 1919-20 Quebec Bulldogs

In 24 games in the 1919–20 season, the Quebec Bulldogs of the NHL won just four times, and all of those victories were on home ice. The Bulldogs had serious problems keeping the puck out of their net. In a game on March 3, 1920, the Montreal Canadiens managed to score 16 goals against the Bulldogs' goaltender, an NHL record that still stands. Over the course of the season, opposing teams scored an average of 7.38 goals per game against the Dogs, another record that remains intact more than 80 years later.

2. The 1949 Hamilton Wildcats

Canadian football has had its share of really awful teams, but only a handful can lay claim to the dubious distinction of going an entire season without winning or tying a single game. The last team to do so was the Hamilton Wildcats (who merged with the Hamilton Tigers to become the Tiger-Cats in 1950). They managed to lose all 12 games during the 1949 season. In fact, this group of players holds the record for the longest winless streak ever in Canadian football. Between September 1948 and September 1950, the boys from Steeltown won no games, tied one and lost 19.

3. The 1969 Montreal Expos

The Expos were truly awful in their first year. Although they beat the New York Mets 11–10 at Shea Stadium in their first game and then went on to win their first home opener against the St. Louis Cardinals, they won just 50 more games in the entire season, finishing with a record of 52 wins and 110 losses. That left them a full 48 games behind the division-leading Mets in the National League East.

4. The 1979 Toronto Blue Jays

It took the Blue Jays until their third season to hit rock bottom. Although their record was marginally better than that of the '69 Expos, at 53 wins to 109 losses, they finished a staggering 50.5 games behind the Baltimore Orioles in the American League East.

5. The 1992-93 Ottawa Senators

The worst Canadian professional hockey team of the modern era was undoubtedly the 1992–93 Ottawa Senators. There had been no NHL team in Ottawa since 1934, and the rust was clearly showing on this first edition of the revitalized franchise. Although they managed to beat the Montreal Canadiens 5–3 in their first game in Ottawa, the Senators won just nine of their remaining 81 games, and all but one of those victories was at home. Their 41 road losses tied an NHL record. The Senators were outscored by their opponents 395–202, and finished 85 points behind the Boston Bruins in the Adams Division.

6. The 1996-97 Vancouver Grizzlies
The NBA returned to Canada in 1995 after an absence of 50 years. In the NBA's first season (1945–46), the Toronto franchise, known as the Huskies, won 22 of their 60 games, finished in sixth place and promptly folded. But the Huskies' performance was positively stellar compared with that of the Toronto Raptors and the Vancouver Grizzlies in the 1990s. Both teams were bad, but the Grizzlies were terrible. After winning only 15 games in their first season, the Grizzlies did what no one thought possible: they actually got worse in their second season. They experienced one of the worst seasons in NBA history, winning just 14 games and losing 68. Their opponents outscored the Grizzlies by an average of 10 points a game. In the short, inglorious history of pro basketball in Canada, they were the worst.

7. The 2000-2001 Mississauga Ice Dogs
You can't get much worse than the 2000–2001 Mississauga Ice Dogs of the Ontario Hockey League, a team partly owned by Don Cherry. The team, in its third year of existence, won just three games out of 68. They managed to accumulate 15 points, leaving them 66 points behind the division-leading Sudbury Wolves. The Ice Dogs scored 157 goals in 2000–2001; their opponents scored 380. The Dogs finished their dismal season, appropriately enough, with a 24-game losing streak. Owners of Canadian hockey teams might want to think twice before including the word "dog" in their team's name.

8. The 2003 University of Toronto Blues
How bad a football team was the 2003 edition of the U of T Blues? Well, they lost all of the eight games they played; they scored only 42 points in those eight games, while their opponents scored 438 points; they lost by scores such as 80–0 and 72–0; and they didn't score a point until their fourth game. U of T is Canada's largest university, with 60,000 full-time students. How could there not be at least a couple of dozen guys who know how to play football? After all,

schools such as Acadia and Mount Allison, with only a tiny fraction of the students to draw on, are able to field competitive teams every year. What's wrong with those U of T men, anyway?

9. The 2012 Toronto FC

The Toronto FC had not gotten to the playoffs in their first five seasons in Major League Soccer (MLS), but hope for a post-season appearance ran high as the 2012 season began. The team actually scored a 4–3 aggregate upset against the L.A. Galaxy in a pre-season tournament in March, but it was all downhill from there. They lost their season opener 3–1 in Seattle, and also lost their midfielder and captain Torsten Frings to injury. It was the first game of a nine-game losing streak, the longest run of futility to open a season in league history. A weak starting lineup got even weaker as injuries piled up. The coach, Aron Winter, was fired in June. The team president told fans that "a new message, a new voice, and a slight tweak in direction" should help turn things around. No such luck. With only a few games to go in the season, fullback Richard Eckersley came closer to the truth when he declared, "It's been the worst season imaginable, to be honest. At the moment we're not good enough and we need to get to the end of the season." Toronto FC finished with a record of five wins, 21 losses and eight ties, for a paltry 23 points. They were outscored 62–36. Needless to say, they finished at the bottom of the MLS standings.

14 CANADIAN SPORTS HEROES WHO BECAME POLITICIANS

1. Syl Apps

Syl Apps played 10 seasons in the NHL, all with the Toronto Maple Leafs. He was Rookie of the Year in 1937 and was twice a first-team all-star. In 1963 he was elected to the Ontario legislature as the Conservative member from Kingston, and he served there until 1975. Between 1971 and 1974, he was the minister of correctional services.

2. Lionel Conacher

Lionel "Big Train" Conacher was voted Canada's greatest athlete of the first half of the 20th century, and it is safe to say that no athlete will ever again have a career quite like his. Consider this: he played for 12 years in the NHL, won two Stanley Cups, one Grey Cup in football and one Triple-A baseball championship, and was a Canadian light-heavyweight boxing champ, a star lacrosse player and a member of the Canadian Wrestling Hall of Fame. Conacher finally retired from professional sports in 1937 and was elected as the Liberal member of the Ontario legislature in the riding of Bracondale. He served provincially until 1943. In 1949 he won a federal Liberal seat in Toronto, which he held until his death in 1954.

3. Jacques Demers
He never played the game, but he sure could coach. Jacques Demers was behind the bench for more than a thousand NHL games for five teams. He won the Jack Adams trophy as coach of the year in Detroit in 1987 and 1988, the only man to ever win that award in two consecutive years. In 1993, he coached the Montreal Canadiens to a Stanley Cup championship. When his coaching career ended in 1999, he became a TV analyst for the Habs on the French language RDS network, and that's where he was in August 2009 when Stephen Harper appointed him to the Senate. The appointment raised some eyebrows because in 2005, Demers had revealed that he was functionally illiterate. In 2015 he quit the Conservative Senate caucus to sit as an independent.

4. Ken Dryden
Goaltender Ken Dryden helped lead the Montreal Canadiens to six Stanley Cups in eight years in the 1970s. He won the Vezina Trophy for best goaltender five times and has the highest winning percentage of any goalie in NHL history. In 2004 he won the Toronto seat of York Centre for the Liberals and was named minister of social development by Prime Minister Paul Martin. He lost his seat in the federal election of 2011.

5. Don Getty
Don Getty joined the Edmonton Eskimos in 1955 as their starting quarterback and led them to Grey Cup wins in 1955 and 1956. He retired from football in 1965. Two years later, he became a Conservative member of the Alberta legislative assembly. He left politics in 1979 and returned to the private sector. In 1985 he was elected leader of the Alberta Progressive Conservatives; that same year, he led his party to victory in the provincial election. Getty served as Alberta's 11th premier from 1985 to 1992.

6. Nancy Greene Raine
She was the best woman's alpine skier that this country has ever produced, and

the most decorated skier of either gender. Nancy Greene was known as "Tiger" because she attacked the hills fearlessly and ferociously. During her nine-year racing career she won three U.S. championship titles and nine Canadian titles. Her greatest year was 1968. She easily won her second consecutive World Cup championship, and at the Winter Olympics in Grenoble, she won a silver medal in the slalom and gold in the giant slalom. In 1999, she was voted Canada's Female Athlete of the 20th Century in a poll of editors and broadcasters conducted by the Canadian Press and Broadcast News. Politically, Greene Raine veered to the right. In 1993 she declared her support for the Reform Party of Canada, and in 2009, she accepted an appointment by Stephen Harper to join the Conservative caucus in the Senate.

7. Otto Jelinek

Otto Jelinek and his sister, Maria, formed one of Canada's most successful skating duos, winning the world pairs championship in their native Prague in 1962. In 1972 Jelinek was elected as the Conservative member in the Toronto riding of High Park–Humber Valley. He served in several cabinet portfolios under Prime Minister Brian Mulroney, including minister of state for fitness and amateur sport from 1984 to 1988. He retired from politics in 1993.

8. Red Kelly

Red Kelly played 20 seasons in the NHL (1947–67) with Detroit and Toronto. He accumulated a total of 823 points and won eight Stanley Cups and numerous individual awards. Between 1962 and 1965, while still playing for the Maple Leafs, he served as the Liberal MP for York West.

9. Normie Kwong

Normie Kwong was born in Calgary in 1929 to Chinese immigrants. In 1948 he became the first Chinese-Canadian to play in the CFL and was dubbed the "China Clipper" for his ferocity as a running back. In 13 seasons in the CFL, he won four Grey Cups—one with the Calgary Stampeders when he was only 18, and three consecutive championships from 1954 to 1956 with the Edmonton Eskimos. He is a member of the CFL Hall of Fame and the Order of Canada. In the 1960s Kwong tried his hand at politics but was unable to get elected as a Conservative. In January 2005 he was chosen by Prime Minister Paul Martin to be Alberta's lieutenant-governor.

10. Peter Lougheed

Peter Lougheed was not a great professional football player. He was with the Edmonton Eskimos for only two seasons, 1949 and 1950, and the records show that big number 30 rushed for a total of only eight yards. So it was probably a smart move when he left football to seek an MBA from Harvard. And although it didn't seem like a good idea at the time, it was also wise of him to accept the leadership of the Alberta Conservative Party in 1965. The party had been out of office for decades, but the ruling Social Credit Party was showing signs of age. In 1971 the Conservatives were elected to office. Lougheed moved into the premier's office, where he remained until he retired from politics in 1985.

11. Frank Mahovlich

Frank Mahovlich played 18 seasons in the NHL (1956–74). He scored 626 goals, was selected to nine all-star teams and won a total of six Stanley Cups, four with Toronto and two with Montreal. In 1998 he was appointed to the Senate by Prime Minister Jean Chrétien.

12. Howie Meeker

Howie Meeker played eight seasons with the Toronto Maple Leafs, winning the Rookie of the Year trophy in 1946–47. Like Red Kelly, Meeker served as an MP while he was still playing for the Leafs. He won a federal by-election for the Conservatives in Waterloo South in 1951, and remained an MP until the election of 1953, when he decided not to run again. He then went on to a successful career as a hockey analyst on television.

13. Cindy Nicholas

Cindy Nicholas is one of Canada's greatest long-distance swimmers. In 1974, at the age of 16, she became the fastest swimmer to cross Lake Ontario, with a time of 15 hours, 10 minutes. But that was just the beginning. In 1976 she won the women's world marathon swimming championship. The following year she became the first woman, and the youngest person ever, to swim the English Channel both ways. By 1982 she had crossed the channel 19 times. Ten of those crossings involved two-way swims. In 1987 she was elected as a Liberal member of the Ontario legislature for the Toronto riding of Scarborough Centre. She served until 1990.

14. Steve Paproski

Steve Paproski was another in the remarkable line of former Edmonton Eskimos who went on to political prominence. He played for four seasons, between 1949 and 1953, which meant he was the teammate of a future premier (Lougheed) and a future lieutenant-governor (Kwong). Paproski's political career began in 1968, when he was elected for the Conservatives in Edmonton Centre. He was responsible for fitness, amateur sport and multiculturalism in the short-lived government of Joe Clark (1979–80). Paproski retired from politics in 1993 and died a few months later.

CATHAL KELLY'S 9 MOST COMPELLING PLAYERS IN SOCCER HISTORY

Cathal Kelly is a sports columnist for the Globe and Mail.

1. Socrates

Pelé once said of his Brazilian teammate Socrates that he was better going backward than anyone else going forward. In more than one sense. Socrates was the midfield fulcrum of the great, thwarted Brazil teams of the 1980s. He was also a qualified physician, a leftist agitator, a newspaper columnist, an alcoholic libertine and a football player who refused to practise football. He once arranged his team, Sao Paolo's Corinthians, into a socialist collective. The players voted on everything, including which tactics to deploy in games. As part of his anarchic outreach, Socrates opposed Brazil's ruling junta in a series of public protests. Using sports stardom as his shield, he gave an entire country permission to become activists. He remains a seminal figure in Brazil's chaotic democracy. In the autumn years of his career, Socrates briefly moved to Italy to play professionally. It didn't suit him. "Sometimes I didn't want to train, but to hang out with friends, party or have a smoke," he explained upon returning. "There's more to life than football." No player in history better exemplified the idea.

2. George Best

Though he stands tall in any tallying of the greatest players ever, George Best is better known for what he could have been than what he was.

He was discovered in a Belfast slum, dribbling tennis balls to hone his close control. He became a global star with Manchester United in the late '60s, as big a deal in England as any of the Beatles. After pulling the keeper out of goal to score the winning tally in the 1968 European Cup final, Best said he wished he'd taken the ball up to the line, got down on his hands and knees and headed it across.

Then his extracurriculars began chipping away at his talent. Best would show up for practice drunk. Eventually, it was games. His career was functionally over at age 27. The final image most people have of him is a story told about one wild night at a ritzy London hotel. Early in the morning, Best rang down for a curative bottle. When an attendant brought it up, he found the room in disarray, thousands in pound notes strewn about and the reigning Miss World lying in bed beside the bedraggled star. Best sat there disconsolately, pulling on a cigarette. The distraught waiter approached and said, "George, where did it all go wrong?"

3. Duncan Edwards

No tragedy has more shaped the contours of modern football than the 1958 Munich Air disaster. A plane carrying the Manchester United team home from a European match slid from the runway during takeoff and careened across a road. Twenty passengers, including eight United players, were killed. The most fetishized of them was 21-year-old Duncan Edwards. Edwards was a global phenomenon in utero. Scotland manager Tommy Docherty would later say, "There is no doubt in my mind that Duncan would have become the greatest player ever." Though he played only 18 games for his country, Edwards was the first man inducted into the English Football Hall of Fame. In the wake of Munich, United became the world's sentimental favourite. That's how a decent club from one of England's second cities has become arguably the biggest sports franchise on Earth. That legacy is the only lasting football testament to Edwards, the player who might have been, but didn't get the chance.

4. Diego Maradona

I once made the mistake of speaking during a Diego Maradona press conference. An elderly Argentinian gentleman seated behind me reached out and slapped me hard across the back of the head. When I turned to punch him in the face, he widened his eyes in the universal gesture for "Really?" We agreed to disagree. Many people (including zero Brazilians) will tell you that Maradona is the best ever. Quite possibly. But he is without doubt the most brilliantly polarizing. Maradona was louche in a way no great player had been before or has been since. He cheated; he drank; he did drugs; he stole; he once shot at a group of journalists with an air pistol. He bragged; he insulted; he filibustered; he got fat; he got thin again; he had heart attacks. He was, in short, more than a bit of a mess. He also won the 1986 World Cup essentially by himself. In the quarterfinal game against England, Maradona scored the most infamous goal in football history, the "Hand of God" goal. Four minutes later, he scored what might be the best, slaloming through the entirety of the opposition. He could surprise you like that. Buttressing all the delicious naughtiness was the knee-weakening skill. I'd sooner pay to watch Maradona's pre-match warm-up than attend any final. When the great French star Zinedine Zidane was widely acknowledged as the finest player at work, his countryman Michel Platini used him as a (perhaps too blunt) point of comparison: "What Zidane could do with a ball, Maradona could do with an orange."

5. Hope Solo

The world first caught notice of Solo in the media mixed-zone after her U.S. national team lost in the semis of the 2007 World Cup. Solo watched from the bench. She had a few thoughts on the matter. "[Not starting me] was the wrong decision, and I think anybody who knows anything about the game knows that," she said. "There's no doubt in my mind I would have made those saves."

Until Solo arrived, women's soccer—and women's team sport generally—was the province of genteel, "Good effort!" types. Depending on your perspective, Solo was either the infection or the cure for that. Over the course of her decade on top, she whined, badgered and goaded her many enemies (which always included her friends). She showed shockingly poor impulse control, resulting in a series of high-profile legal bust-ups. When she lost in her final big game at the 2016 Rio Olympics, she called the winning side "a bunch of cowards." She was promptly fired by both country and club. It was the right sort of ending—an *auto-da-fé*, and fittingly, Solo lit the match. She was also indisputably the greatest women's goalkeeper ever, and a winner of every major trophy in the women's game. Her legacy is more cultural than sporting. Solo pioneered the role of villain in women's sport. Many disliked her, but no one could ignore her.

6. Johan Cruyff

Other great players have been more problematic, but none was quite so difficult as Cruyff. He was forever making enemies, usually amongst his friends. As a player, he was the premier exponent of Total Football—the Dutch tactical system in which all 11 players became interchangeable. The defenders were expected to score and the attackers expected to defend. When the Netherlands lost in the final of the 1974 World Cup, Cruyff judged it a species of victory: "I think the world remembers our team more." That he was right didn't make anyone more accepting. As a coach, Cruyff shaped FC Barcelona into the most romantic professional side that has ever been. "Cruyff painted the chapel," his greatest philosophic heir, Pep Guardiola, once said. "Barcelona coaches since either restore or improve it."

In person, Cruyff was defiantly misanthropic. He would eventually fall out with just about everyone he ever worked with. He was a hewer of gnomic aphorisms: "Every disadvantage has its advantage"; "Before I make a mistake, I don't make that mistake." Most importantly, Cruyff was an aesthete. Winning didn't rate much in his books (which explains why he was so often fired). What mattered was how much style was brought to bear. He constructed teams designed to play with flair, and hated when football was reduced to pragmatism. In that sense, while every top athlete is a sort of genius, Cruyff was sport's most complete artist.

7. Lev Yashin

Lev Yashin is not only the greatest goalkeeper in football history, he may be the sport's most complete athlete. While waiting to break into the Dynamo Moscow first team in the early 1950s, he moonlighted as a hockey goalie, winning a Soviet championship. He also excelled at basketball. His class is captured in one statistic: 150 penalty saves. It may be the safest record in all of sport.

Yashin's most notable achievement was putting a human face on the Soviet sports machine. He was a jovial everyman, roundly beloved while the nation he represented was widely despised. He embraced the villain's role so delightedly—never appearing in anything but an all-black ensemble—that he neutered the cliché. He once explained his approach thusly: "The trick is to smoke a cigarette to calm your nerves and then take a big swig of strong liquor to tone your muscles." As a rule, goalkeeping is the most hazardous position on the field. One mistake can tar you forever. Brazil's Moacir Barbosa was blamed for allowing Uruguay to win the 1950 World Cup final. He played professionally for two decades. Upon retirement, Barbosa was gifted the goalposts from Rio's Maracana as a souvenir. He took them home and burned them in his backyard. His bitterness never faded. Yashin was a unique rejoinder to that peril. He made mistakes, but none attached themselves to him. His joy in the game was so evident, he redeemed a whole country. He remains the only goalkeeper to receive the award as world's best player.

8. Zlatan Ibrahimovic

Forget football players. Few people have ever had such towering self-regard as the irresistible Swede. His best quotes read like an Artificial Intelligence algorithm programmed to achieve a singularity of smarminess:

"I can't help but laugh at how perfect I am."

"A World Cup without me is nothing to watch."

"Zlatan doesn't do auditions."

His fondness for speaking in the third person is so renowned that Nike once constructed an ad campaign around it.

In one instance, a reporter asked him who would win an upcoming match. "Only God knows," Ibrahimovic replied. The reporter pointed out that it was rather hard to ask him. "Why?" Ibrahimovic said. "You're looking at him now."

Ibrahimovic has spent a career telling people how great he is. Annoyingly, he then goes out and proves it. Football players are generally small people, built low to the ground for balance. Ibrahimovic is a giant—six foot five—but plays with a compactness few have ever possessed. If you do manage to get in his way, he just runs you over. It's a difficult combination to plan around. In his early 30s, he wrote a book about his life. The *Guardian* called it "the most compelling autobiography ever to appear under a footballer's name." Ibrahimovic's ghostwriter later admitted that all of the subject's quotes had been invented.

The writer, David Lagercrantz, said he'd tried to find "the literary Ibrahimovic" and recounted the moment he'd sent the player his manuscript. "The first thing he said was, 'What the fuck is this? I never said this.' But after a while I think he understood what I was trying to do. Nowadays he thinks it's really his story."

9. Matthias Sindelar

They called Matthias Sindelar "the paper man," owing to the slightness of his frame. He is the only giant Austrian football has ever produced, and outside his own country is largely forgotten now. For a mid-war moment, he may have been the best player alive. With Sindelar leading the attack, the national team became a European powerhouse in the mid-'30s. Then the Nazis annexed the country. The Austrian senior men's side was to be disbanded, and its best players subsumed under the German banner. A final "reunification" game between the two countries was proposed, to be played in Vienna. Sindelar insisted that the Austrians would only participate if they could wear their national strip. The Nazis reluctantly agreed. Government officials decreed that the game must end in a draw or an Austrian loss. Sindelar scored the first goal late in game. His exuberance spread to his teammates. Another goal was scored, prompting Sindelar to dance in front of the VIP section. The game ended in an embarrassing 2–0 Austrian win. Now under suspicion, Sindelar refused both to join the Nazi propaganda machine or to leave the country, though clubs in England would gladly have had him. He quit the game, bought a former teammate's bar and opted for a publican's life. Many of his customers were Jewish—a fact that was noted in Gestapo reports. In 1939, a friend found Sindelar, 36, and his girlfriend dead in their bed. Police called it an accident—carbon monoxide poisoning. The truth of Sindelar's death continues to roil Austrians. Was he killed by the Nazi regime? Did he kill himself? Was he murdered by gangsters or was his lover to blame? The records are gone. All that remains of Sindelar are a few moments of choppy newsreel, but in them a hint of the elegance that typifies truly great players.

12 THESES ABOUT HOCKEY

1. Kimberley Amirault. "Examining Self-Talk of the Canadian Men's Hockey Team." University of Calgary, 2000.

2. Brian Walter Benson. "The Risk of Neck Injuries Among Canadian Intercollegiate Ice Hockey Players Wearing Full Face Shields Compared to Half Shields." University of Calgary, 1998.

3. Chris J. Gee. "Predicting the Use of Aggressive Behaviour among Canadian Amateur Hockey Players: A Psychosocial Examination." University of Toronto, 2010.

4. Zack Goodman. "The Cardiovascular Effects of Recreation Hockey in Middle-Aged Men." University of Toronto, 2013.

5. Tracy L. Heller. "Sources of Stress in NCAA Division 1 Women Ice Hockey Players." McGill University, 2003.

6. Karen V. Lomond. "Three-Dimensional Blade Position and Orientation during a Stationary Ice Hockey Slap Shot." McGill University, 2005.

7. Martin R. Raymond. "The Relationship Between Team Success and Within-Group Differences in Group Cohesion." McGill University, 1995.

8. Norman Rothsching. "The Effect of Shaft Stiffness on the Performance of the Ice Hockey Slap Shot." McGill University, 1997.

9. Alex Trumper. "Comparison of Skate Boot Pressure of Elite and Recreational Hockey Players During the Performance of Forward Crossovers." McGill University, 2006.

10. Alejandro Villasenor-Herrera. "Recoil Effect of the Ice Hockey Stick during a Slap Shot." McGill University, 2004.

11. Gilbert D. Wade. "An Inductive Analysis of Intramural Ice Hockey Officiating: A Case Study." University of Ottawa, 1995.

12. Crysta Ann-Marie Westoby. "Toe Picks and Hockey Sticks: Children and the Gendering of Figure Skating and Hockey." University of British Columbia, 2008.

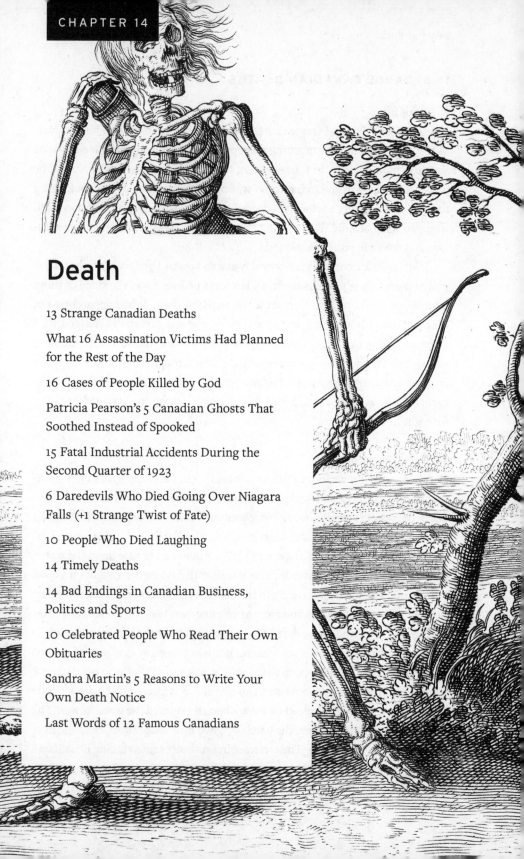

Death

13 STRANGE CANADIAN DEATHS

1. Snake Bit

It was a horrifying and tragic death. Noah Barthe, age four, and his six-year-old brother Connor were enjoying a sleepover at the apartment of Jean-Claude Savoie, a family friend, in Campbellton, New Brunswick, in August 2013. The boys were asleep in the living room when an African rock python belonging to Savoie escaped its enclosure, entered the room through a ventilation duct, wrapped itself around the boys and started biting. The boys died of asphyxiation and multiple puncture wounds.

Noah and Connor had spent the day at a zoo owned by Savoie's father. They petted many of the animals there, and experts believe it was the smell of those animals on the boys' skin that drew the snake to them. It had apparently not been fed for 24 hours prior to the attack. Savoie was eventually charged with criminal negligence causing death. The Crown argued that Savoie should have known that the python was capable of travelling through the ventilation system into the apartment, because it had attempted to escape that way a few weeks earlier. In November 2016, a jury found Savoie not guilty, after deliberating for eight hours.

2. Water Tower Mystery

Here's what we know about Elisa Lam's death. On February 19, 2013, a maintenance worker at Cecil Hotel in Los Angeles climbed up onto the hotel roof to check the water tower following complaints about low water pressure. When he got there, he noticed the hatch was open, and when he looked inside, he saw the naked, lifeless body of the 21-year-old UBC student lying face up in the water. And that is all we really know. She was last seen 18 days earlier, caught on a hotel video camera behaving strangely in the elevator: cowering in a corner, flipping her head frantically as if someone was chasing her. Was someone really after her? Was she having some sort of breakdown? Medical examiners found no signs of drugs or alcohol in her system, nor was there any evidence of trauma on her body. How did she get up to the roof, which was off-limits to hotel guests? The door to the roof was locked and an alarm was triggered if the proper code was not entered. Was she dead or alive when she entered the water tower? The tower was three metres high, the hatch weighed nine kilograms. Could she have gotten in there on her own? The strange circumstances surrounding Elisa Lam's death have sparked years of rumours and conspiracy theories, but the fact is, no one knows how she died, and the sad reality for her family and friends is that we might never know.

3. Coyote Ugly

In the summer of 2009, Taylor Mitchell was a promising 19-year-old Toronto-based country folk singer-songwriter. Her first album, *For Your Consideration*, had received good reviews, as had her appearance at the Winnipeg Folk Festival. In the fall, she embarked on a tour of eastern Canada, and with a few days to spare between concerts, she decided to hike the popular Skyline Trail in Cape Breton Highlands National Park. At 3:25 in the afternoon of October 27, a group of hikers came across Mitchell's body in a clearing, lying in a pool of blood. A coyote was standing over her. It took a shotgun blast from an RCMP officer before the coyote finally fled the scene and allowed rescuers to reach Mitchell. She was bitten over most of her body, and had suffered extreme blood loss. She died in a Halifax hospital the following day.

If an attack like this had been carried out by a bear or a pack of wolves, it would have been considered one of the hazards of hiking in the wild. But this was a coyote, and coyotes don't normally attack people. They try to avoid human contact if possible. Until Mitchell, there had never been a fatal attack by a coyote on an adult in Canada or the United States. Park officials eventually concluded that three coyotes were involved in the attack, but they were never able to determine what caused them to behave so uncharacteristically. Mitchell's death has led to a reassessment of the risk to humans from the predatory behaviour of coyotes.

4. Tree Hugger

Daryl Hatten, 49, was one of British Columbia's most renowned mountain climbers. He had blazed trails in the Canadian Rockies, in California's Yosemite National Park and on the challenging Stawamus Chief, north of Vancouver. But on August 21, 2004, Hatten died from severe internal injuries sustained when he fell 20 metres out of a rain-soaked arbutus tree while trying to rescue a neighbour's cat. The cat remained stranded in the tree.

5. Hat Trick

Forty-four-year-old Derek Keenan of Lethbridge, Alberta, was killed on November 19, 2003, when he crawled underneath a semi-trailer loaded with precast concrete drainage pipe in pursuit of a baseball hat that had blown off his head. The truck began to move just as Keenan dove under it. He tried to grab the hat and make a quick exit, but the truck's rear wheels rolled over his upper body and killed him.

6. A Death Unnoticed

Though his death was not strange in and of itself, the fact that Jim Sulkers's death went unnoticed for 21 months was very strange indeed. Sulkers died of natural causes in the bedroom of his Winnipeg condo sometime during November 2002, but nobody noticed his absence until August 25, 2004. His condo fees and bills were still being paid, his phone was still listed, and his pension was still being deposited into his account. The payments had all been set up for automatic withdrawals and deposits. Sulkers had multiple sclerosis and had withdrawn from neighbours and family over the previous decade. Still, when some relatives were in town in the summer of 2003, a few came knocking at his door. "He didn't answer," said Kim Dyck, a cousin. "You assume he isn't home. You certainly don't assume he's dead." His neighbours didn't recall smelling anything, and while they did wonder where Sulkers had gone, they didn't know him well. His mummified corpse was finally discovered after his father called police to ask them to check in on his son.

7. Bad Bounce

In March 2000, 21-year-old Chad Hildebrand was attending a senior men's hockey league game in Winnipeg. A puck flew into the crowd and glanced off a friend's head before hitting Hildebrand in the temple. Hildebrand went home, collapsed, fell into a coma and died a week later.

8. Last One In...

A hog farm near Lucky Lake, Saskatchewan, proved unlucky for three young Prince Albert farmers, who died after they dived into a giant tank of hog manure on September 25, 1998. Investigators believe one of the men went into the tank without a breathing apparatus, apparently trying to clear a clogged line, and was overcome by hydrogen sulphide fumes. The second man went in when the first didn't reappear, and the third man went in to see about the first two. A fourth man followed, but managed to escape before the gas could overcome him. The tank held more than 32,000 litres of manure. One investigator commented that being overcome by hydrogen sulphide is "like being hit on the head with a two-by-four."

9. Hard to Swallow

Twenty-two-year-old Franco Brun of Toronto died when he choked on a bible he shoved down his throat while in custody at the Metro East Detention Centre on June 9, 1987. Dr. Peter Charlebois, an anaesthetist and respiratory specialist, testified at the inquest into Brun's death that the average person "does not have the will to persistently shove something of such a size, such a solidity" down his throat.

10. One Bad Swing

On June 5, 1963, clothing executive Harold Kalles was hitting out of the rough at a Toronto golf course when disaster struck. The shaft of his five iron hit a tree and snapped in two. The jagged end flew up, hit him in the throat and slashed his jugular vein. Bleeding profusely, Kalles managed to straggle out of the woods. His two playing partners got him to the hospital, where doctors were initially optimistic about his recovery. "He's fine and dandy now," one of them told the *Toronto Daily Star.* But the 41-year-old Kalles died of his injuries five days later.

11. Death by Dynamite

On July 11, 1932, a freak lightning bolt struck a gold mine near Rouyn-Noranda, Quebec, detonating dynamite 60 metres underground and killing two miners instantly. The lightning either struck near two locked safety switches on the surface, jumped across and detonated the dynamite, or struck just inside the mine shaft below the safety switch. The men on the surface were not injured.

12. Death by Phone Call

A storm burst upon Lumsden and Bonavista, Newfoundland, on June 26, 1930. When the telephone rang at the O'Neil residence, Mrs. O'Neil took the receiver but fell to the floor after getting a shock. Her husband and his brother-in-law, James Clarke, revived her. When the phone rang again, Mrs. O'Neil told Clarke it was for him. It was his wife, so he warned her to hang up. Just then, lightning struck and Clarke dropped dead on the floor.

13. Killed by Jazz

Seventy-nine-year-old cornetist and music professor Nicolas Coviello had had an illustrious career, having performed before Queen Victoria, Edward VII and other dignitaries. Realizing that his life was nearing its end, Coviello decided to travel from London, England, to Saskatchewan to pay a final visit to his son. On the way, he stopped in New York City to bid farewell to his nephews, Peter, Dominic and Daniel Coviello. On June 13, 1926, the young men took their famous uncle to Coney Island to give him a taste of America. The elder Coviello enjoyed himself, but seemed irritated by the blare of jazz bands. Finally, he could take it no longer. "That isn't music," he complained, and he fell to the boardwalk. He was pronounced dead a few minutes later. Cause of death was "a strain on the heart."

WHAT 16 ASSASSINATION VICTIMS HAD PLANNED FOR THE REST OF THE DAY

1. Benazir Bhutto (1953-2007)

Former Pakistani prime minister Benazir Bhutto was shot to death on December 27, 2007, shortly after giving a speech to her supporters in the city of Rawalpindi. Two months earlier, Bhutto had narrowly escaped an attempted assassination in Karachi as she returned from eight years of political exile to try to win a third term as prime minister. On the morning of December 27, Bhutto had met with Afghan president Hamid Karzai in Islamabad, and she had reviewed secret documents that she had obtained that pointed to a plot by her rival, President Pervez Musharraf, to rig the results of the upcoming election. Bhutto was scheduled to meet with two leading American politicians for dinner later that evening. She was planning to show them the evidence she had amassed about the vote rigging. But first, there was the rally in Rawalpindi. "I put my life in danger and came here because I feel this country is in danger," she told the crowd. When her speech ended, she left the podium and got into her armoured white Toyota Land Cruiser. As her driver prepared to leave the park, she stood up in the car's sunroof so she could wave to her supporters one last time. She was hit by at least two bullets fired by a gunman at close range. Then a suicide bomber standing near the car detonated his bomb. Twenty other people died in the explosion. Bhutto was rushed to hospital and was declared dead an hour later.

2. Gaius Julius Caesar (100-44 BCE)

Roman statesman and soldier Julius Caesar was assassinated in a hall of the Theatre of Pompey in Rome by a group of 60 conspirators led by Marcus Junius Brutus and Gaius Cassius Longinus on March 15, 44 BCE. In the street a few minutes earlier, a Greek logic teacher named Artemidorus had handed Caesar a note, warning him that it should be read immediately. But Caesar had put it aside. The unread note cautioned him that assassins planned to attack him as he entered the hall. At the theatre, Caesar had expected to attend a meeting of the Roman senate, where he and his followers were to speak in favour of his being crowned king of Rome.

3. Mohandas K. Gandhi (1869-1948)

Indian independence leader Mahatma Gandhi was assassinated in New Delhi, India, by Hindu fanatic Nathuram Godse at 5:13 p.m. on January 30, 1948. Gandhi was killed upon arriving in the Birla House gardens, where he was supposed to lead a prayer meeting attended by several hundred of his followers. After the religious ceremonies, he was to return to the home of Ghanshyam Das Birla, his host in New Delhi. That evening, Gandhi had intended to follow his usual evening routine, which consisted of talking to his relatives and followers for a short time before a session of reading and writing. At about 9 p.m., he would have had his nightly enema before going to bed.

4. James Garfield (1831-81)

President Garfield was shot at the Baltimore and Potomac train depot in Washington, D.C., by Charles J. Guiteau at 9:30 a.m. on July 2, 1881; he died on September 19. Shot while preparing to leave the capital for the Fourth of July holidays, President Garfield had arranged to take the 9:30 train to Elberon, New Jersey, where his wife, Lucretia, and their sons Harry and James were to join him before he proceeded to Williams College in Williamstown, Massachusetts. Garfield was to observe the 25th anniversary of his graduation and enrol his sons in the college's freshman class, after which he expected to spend the evening as an overnight guest at the home of Cyrus Field, the entrepreneur who developed the first transatlantic cable.

5. Indira Gandhi (1917-84)

Indian Prime Minister Indira Gandhi was assassinated at 9 a.m. on October 31, 1984, as she was walking from her residence in New Delhi to her office, about 20 metres away. She was on her way to do a TV interview with the British actor Peter Ustinov. That evening, she was scheduled to host a dinner in honour of the queen's daughter, Princess Anne, who was visiting India. As she walked along the path to her office, Mrs. Gandhi encountered one of her bodyguards, Sardar Beant Singh, who greeted her by saying, "Namaste." Before the prime minister had a chance to reply, Beant Singh reached for his government revolver and began shooting. Then a second bodyguard, Sardar Satwant Singh, appeared from behind a wall, opened fire and emptied the magazine of his Sten gun. Then Beant Singh shot her with another two bullets. In all, 30 bullets were fired in an encounter that lasted only a few seconds. As the prime minister lay dying, Beant Singh put his revolver on the ground and declared, "We have done what we wanted to, now you can do what you want."

6. John F. Kennedy (1917-63)

President Kennedy was assassinated in Dealey Plaza in Dallas, Texas, at 12:30 p.m. on November 22, 1963. After the motorcade—during which he was shot—Kennedy was scheduled to speak at the new Trade Mart building and then to fly to Bergstrom Air Force Base near Austin, Texas, where the coach of the University of Texas Longhorns was to present him with a team-autographed football. In Austin, a second motorcade was planned, to be followed by a Democratic fundraising banquet for which 8,000 steaks had been prepared. Presidential advance man Bill Moyers had found out too late that the menu featured steaks—a highly inappropriate selection for a Catholic president's Friday night dinner. Kennedy had agreed to take a helicopter from Austin to the LBJ Ranch, near Johnson City, Texas, where he was to spend the night. To entertain Kennedy that evening, Vice President Lyndon Johnson had organized a whip-cracking and sheepherding demonstration.

7. Robert F. Kennedy (1925-68)

The Democratic presidential candidate was shot at the Ambassador Hotel in Los Angeles, California, by Sirhan Sirhan and possibly a second gunman at 12:15 a.m. on June 5, 1968; he died the following day. Kennedy was shot while walking through a corridor off the kitchen on his way to the hotel's Colonial Room for a press conference following his victory in the California Democratic primary election. After that, he had planned to return to his room, suite 511, where several dozen celebrities were awaiting him. Once freshened up, he would have gone with his friends and supporters—including Roosevelt "Rosie" Grier, Rafer Johnson and Pierre Salinger—to the Factory, an exclusive and very chic Los Angeles discotheque.

8. Martin Luther King Jr. (1929-68)

Dr. King was assassinated at the Lorraine Motel in Memphis, Tennessee, by James Earl Ray just after 6 p.m. on April 4, 1968. When he was shot, King was leaving his room on his way to a soul-food dinner at the home of the Reverend Samuel (Billy) Kyles. Accompanying King were his friends and supporters, including Dr. Ralph Abernathy, the Reverend Jesse Jackson, the Reverend Andrew Young and lawyer Chauncey Eskridge. King had also promised to attend an evening rally in support of the striking garbage collectors of Local 1733. He had requested that Ben Branch, the lead singer of the Breadbasket Band, which was providing the evening's entertainment, sing "Precious Lord" at the rally.

9. Abraham Lincoln (1809-65)

President Lincoln was shot at Ford's Theater in Washington, D.C., by John Wilkes Booth at 10:15 p.m. on Good Friday—April 14, 1865; he died the next day. Lincoln had intended to watch the play *Our American Cousin* and then be introduced to the cast. From the theatre, he and Mrs. Lincoln, accompanied by two young friends—Major Henry Rathbone and the major's fiancée, Clara Harris—were to return to the White House for a small party, at which refreshments would be served, as the president had missed supper that evening.

10. Thomas D'Arcy McGee (1825-68)

Thomas D'Arcy McGee was shot and killed in the early hours of Tuesday, April 7, 1868, in front of his rooming house on Sparks Street in downtown Ottawa. Earlier that evening, McGee had delivered a rousing speech in the House of Commons in defence of Confederation. It had been well received by his colleagues in the chamber and the roughly 500 spectators who had witnessed it in the gallery. McGee left Parliament that evening feeling tired but exhilarated. He was looking forward to a good night's sleep. In a few days it would be his 43rd birthday, and he was planning to travel to Montreal to celebrate with family and friends.

11. William McKinley (1843-1901)

President McKinley was shot at the Temple of Music at the Pan-American Exposition in Buffalo, New York, by Leon Czolgosz at 4:07 p.m. on September 6, 1901; he died on September 14. Shot during a public handshaking reception, President McKinley had intended to leave three minutes later and take his private carriage to the John Milburn mansion, where he was staying while in Buffalo. That night, McKinley was looking forward to one of those rarities in a president's life, an unscheduled evening of privacy with his wife and a few friends. Before retiring that evening, he would have done some packing, since he was returning to his family home in Canton, Ohio, the next morning.

12. Faisal ibn Abd al-Aziz ibn Saud (1905-75)

King Faisal was assassinated before noon on March 25, 1975, in the Ri'Assa Palace in Riyadh, Saudi Arabia. The assassin was his nephew, ibn Musad Abd al-Aziz. At the time, the king was preparing to meet with a Kuwaiti delegation, which included that nation's oil minister. Matters concerning both nations—such as a territorial dispute over a tract of oil-rich desert—were to be discussed. Also, since it was the birthday of the Prophet Mohammed, Faisal had planned to hold the traditional *majlis*, an open court in which any Saudi Arabian, aristocrat or peasant, could have an audience with the king and ask a personal favour of him.

13. Leon Trotsky (1877-1940)

The exiled Russian revolutionary leader was attacked at his home in Mexico City by Jaime Ramon Mercader just before 6 p.m. on August 20, 1940. Trotsky was reading an article that Mercader had written. Trotsky died the next day. He had expected to have dinner with his wife, Natalia, and possibly would have invited Mercader to join them. After dinner, Trotsky would have studied some recently published French economic statistics and written a few pages of an article on Stalin that was to be published in *Harper's Magazine*.

14. Rafael Leonidas Trujillo Molina (1891-1961)

The dictator of the Dominican Republic was assassinated on the highway between Ciudad Trujillo and San Cristobal by seven men in two automobiles at approximately 10:15 p.m. on May 30, 1961. When hit by machine-gun bullets, Trujillo was on his way to one of his immense ranches, Estancia Fundacion, where he was to spend the night. Awaiting his arrival was at least one of his mistresses. In fact, he may well have been looking forward to an orgy that night. These frequently involved as many as 40 women, who were supplied by a government official whose fee was 10% of all funds allocated for public works.

15. Malcolm X (1925-65)

Malcolm X was shot to death while giving a speech to members of his Organization of Afro-American Unity at the Audubon Ballroom in Harlem on February 21, 1965. A year earlier, Malcolm had broken with the powerful Nation of Islam, led by Elijah Muhammad, and tensions between the two groups were running high. Malcolm worried that Nation of Islam supporters would punish him for his disloyalty. He suspected them of fire-bombing his house the previous week. Malcolm had invited his wife and four children to come hear him speak at the Audubon Ballroom. He was looking forward to spending time with them afterward. But in the dressing room, he was anxious. "I just don't feel right," he told a supporter. "Salaam Aleikum," he said as he stepped onto the stage. Then a shot rang out, then more. Malcolm was hit seven times. He died in hospital later that evening. He was 39 years old. Three members of the Nation of Islam were convicted of killing Malcolm X. They served 20 years in prison.

16. Emiliano Zapata (1877-1919)

The Mexican revolutionary leader was assassinated at Chinameca hacienda near Cuautla, Mexico, by soldiers commanded by Colonel Jesus Guajardo, at 2:10 p.m. on April 10, 1919. Zapata, who was ambushed while riding into the hacienda, had planned to share a dinner of tacos and beer with the treacherous Colonel Guajardo, who, with his 50th Regiment, had tricked Zapata into believing he was defecting from the Mexican federal government. (Actually, Guajardo's sole purpose was to lure Zapata into a trap.) After dinner, Zapata had intended to negotiate the final details of the new alliance and to obtain 12,000 rounds of ammunition for his men. After officially announcing the new partnership, Zapata would have returned to his guerrilla camp at Sauces, 3 kilometres to the south.

16 CASES OF PEOPLE KILLED BY GOD

1. Entire World Population Except Noah and Seven Relatives (Gen. 6, 7)
TRANSGRESSION: Violence, corruption and generalized wickedness
METHOD OF EXECUTION: Flood

2. Entire Populations of Sodom and Gomorrah except Lot, His Wife and Their Two Daughters (Gen. 19)
TRANSGRESSION: Widespread wickedness and lack of respect for the deity
METHOD OF EXECUTION: Rain of fire and brimstone

3. Lot's Wife (Gen. 19)
TRANSGRESSION: Looked back
METHOD OF EXECUTION: Turned into a pillar of salt

4. Er (Gen. 38)

TRANSGRESSION: Wickedness

METHOD OF EXECUTION: Unknown

5. Onan (Gen. 38)

TRANSGRESSION: Refused to make love to his brother Er's widow

METHOD OF EXECUTION: Unknown

6. All the First-Born of Egypt (Exod. 12)

TRANSGRESSION: Cruel to the Jews

METHOD OF EXECUTION: Unknown

7. Pharaoh and the Egyptian Army (Exod. 14)

TRANSGRESSION: Pursued the Jews

METHOD OF EXECUTION: Drowned

8. Nadab and Abihu (Lev. 10)

TRANSGRESSION: Offered strange fire

METHOD OF EXECUTION: Fire

9. Korah, Dathan, Abiram and Their Families (Num. 16)

TRANSGRESSION: Rejected authority of Moses and started own congregation

METHOD OF EXECUTION: Swallowed by earth

10. 250 Followers of Korah (Num. 16)

TRANSGRESSION: Supported Korah

METHOD OF EXECUTION: Fire

11. 14,700 Israelites (Num. 16)

TRANSGRESSION: Murmured against Moses and his brother, Aaron, following execution of Korah and his supporters

METHOD OF EXECUTION: Plague

12. Retreating Amorite Soldiers (Josh. 10)

TRANSGRESSION: Fought the Israelites

METHOD OF EXECUTION: Hailstones

13. Uzzah (2 Sam. 6)
TRANSGRESSION: Touched the ark of God after oxen shook it while pulling it on a cart
METHOD OF EXECUTION: Unknown

14. 70,000 People (2 Sam. 24)
TRANSGRESSION: King David ordered a census of the population
METHOD OF EXECUTION: Plague

15. 102 Soldiers of King Ahaziah (2 Kings 1)
TRANSGRESSION: Tried to capture Elijah the Tishbite
METHOD OF EXECUTION: Fire

16. Ananias and Sapphira (Acts 5)
TRANSGRESSION: Land fraud
METHOD OF EXECUTION: Unknown

PATRICIA PEARSON'S 5 CANADIAN GHOSTS THAT SOOTHED INSTEAD OF SPOOKED

Patricia Pearson is an award-winning journalist whose books have earned her a reputation internationally for upending conventional wisdom. Her most recent books are Opening Heaven's Door: What the Dying May Be Trying to Tell Us About Where They're Going, *and* A Brief History of Anxiety . . . Yours and Mine.

1. Ghost in a Trench
In his memoir about the First World War, Nova Scotian journalist William Bird described what was, for him, the most extraordinary episode in the war. He was in France, in April 1917, sleeping beneath a groundsheet in the maze-like trenches after the Battle of Vimy Ridge, when he was awoken by the grip of hands, urgently shaking him. Opening his eyes, he saw, to his confused surprise, his brother Steve Bird, who had gone missing in action two years earlier.

"Steve grinned as he released my hands, then put his warm hand over my mouth as I started to shout my happiness. He pointed to the sleepers in the bivvy and to my rifle and equipment. 'Get your gear,' he said softly." Bird obediently followed him out into the night and along down the trench until his brother rounded a corner and vanished. He searched anxiously, but then decided that he must have been sleepwalking. Exhausted, he crawled into a funk hole.

The next day, Bird's battalion mates were desperately excited to have found him alive. They took him over to show that the bivvy his brother had led him away from had been hit by a high-explosive shell, the men eviscerated beyond recognition.

2. Following Ghostly Orders

Mountain climber James Sevigny, a 20-year-old graduate student, was so severely injured by an avalanche in Banff National Park in 1983 that he could barely move. The snow smashed his back, his arms, his nose and some ribs. He was bleeding internally. When he tried to stand, he crumpled. He was yielding to shock and hypothermia when a sensed presence materialized, according to the interview he gave journalist John Geiger. "It was something I couldn't see, but it was a physical presence," he said.

The presence berated Sevigny to get up and move, instructing him every raw inch of the way, a 1.5-kilometre elbow crawl through deep-crusted snow to his camp. "All decisions made," he said, "were made by the presence. I was merely taking instructions." As soon as he reached his tent, his bossy and ethereal companion disappeared. Moments later, some cross-country skiers came across him and arranged for a rescue.

3. A Ghostly Hand on the Tiller

In the late 19th century, Nova Scotia–born sailor Joshua Slocum, on a solo voyage in the midst of a battering storm, fell ill with food poisoning and couldn't keep to the helm of his boat. To his astonishment, a tall man somehow appeared, standing solid on the swaying vessel, and told Slocum that he would handle the tiller so that the sailor could recover. Slocum had the impression that this man was "a friend and a sea man of vast experience," as he later wrote in his account, *Sailing Alone Around the World*. The unknown seaman kept Slocum's vessel on course for 145 kilometres, and then—just as inexplicably—dematerialized.

4. Back Seat Ghost Driver

Joe Losinski was driving through the Rocky Mountains en route to Alaska in the spring of 2004 when a snowstorm billowed up, reducing nighttime visibility on the hairpin turns of the Trans-Canada Highway. Hypnotized by the snow and exhausted, the young soldier was on the verge of losing control when he became aware of a calm female voice instructing him.

"'Slow down around this turn,' she would say, or 'Now back the other way, don't overcorrect.' I didn't see her in front of me so much as I was aware of her hovering above my line of vision," he later said. "I was unable to see the lay of the road and adjust accordingly. I was responding only to her commands."

The voice steered Losinski through the darkness for hours, until he drove clear of the blizzard. Although he couldn't imagine why, his impression was that she was an Hispanic woman of middle age with her hair swept up in a bun. He felt sure he would know her instantly if they were ever to meet on the street.

5. A Ghostly Presence

After her father died of a heart attack in 1994, Toronto businesswoman Karen Simons took to driving his big, old Ford Taurus. "It was comforting," she explained, "the way you hang on to people's shirts." On a very cold night about six weeks after his death, Simons was driving on the highway when she suddenly sensed her father settle into the passenger seat. He had a very distinctive lean to the left, due to his chronic back pain, and the seat pressed down accordingly. He rode with his daughter in companionable silence for 20 kilometres. "It was incredibly real, and it was completely transforming. I was almost giddy. I was hoping he would stay." Although she didn't know it at the time, she was amongst the estimated 50% of our bereaved population who are soothed by the spirits of the dead.

15 FATAL INDUSTRIAL ACCIDENTS DURING THE SECOND QUARTER OF 1923

In 2015, there were 852 workplace deaths recorded in Canada. That's a lot of tragic, and often unnecessary deaths, but the workplace used to be a lot more dangerous than it is today. That's partly a result of greater attention being paid to safety, but it's mostly because fewer people are working in agriculture, logging, mining and other resource-based industries, which tend to be much more dangerous than office or retail work. Spending your day sitting in an office cube or working in a mall will not usually kill you, at least not directly.

There are about 18 million Canadians in the workforce today. That means there is approximately one death for every 21,000 workers. Back in 1923, there were about three million Canadian workers, including farm workers, and according to the *Canada Labour Gazette*, in the second quarter of that year, there were

343 workplace fatalities, a pretty standard number for that period. On an annual basis, that works out to about 1,200 deaths a year, or one death for every 2,500 workers. Here's how 15 of those workers died.

Agriculture

1. Picton, Ontario: farmer; fell when horses bolted and was pierced by plough
2. New Finland, Saskatchewan: farmer; fell over dashboard and was dragged through slough by runaway horse
3. Brantford, Ontario: farmhand, age 60; thrown from manure spreader

Logging

4. Granite Falls, British Columbia: logger, age 45; crushed between log and stump when log slid downhill
5. Monteith, Ontario: labourer, age 20; caught in conveyor
6. Dewdney, British Columbia: logger, age 53; falling tree bent back another, which rebounded and struck man on head

Mining

7. Sydney Mines, Nova Scotia: fireman; ankle caught in coal conveyor, shock
8. Cobalt, Ontario: miner; struck by rock due to bad ground while sinking shaft
9. Stonehaven, New Brunswick: employee at cement plant, age 32; scalded by steam escaping from broken pipe

Manufacturing

10. Toronto, Ontario: shipper with chocolate company, age 23; struck by a tub of cream
11. Galt, Ontario: woodworker, age 47; nose scratched by splinter of wood from saw and meningitis developed
12. Winnipeg, Manitoba: engineer at packing plant, age 41; electrocuted while repairing electric motor, the frame of which was not grounded

Transportation and Public Utilities

13. Edmonton, Alberta: brakeman, age 27; crushed; foot caught while uncoupling cars
14. Guelph, Ontario: lineman, age 29; fell off pole when support belt's stitching gave way

15. Montreal, Quebec: powerhouse employee, age 61; electrocuted; backed against high-tension wire while sweeping in transformer room

6 DAREDEVILS WHO DIED GOING OVER NIAGARA FALLS (+1 STRANGE TWIST OF FATE)

People have been stunting in the Niagara gorge since the 1820s. In September 1827 the Eagle Hotel in Niagara Falls, New York, decided to attract tourists to the area by publicizing a bizarre and cruel spectacle: they bought an old schooner, loaded it with two bears, two raccoons, a buffalo, a dog and some birds and sent it over the falls. Apparently, only a goose survived. Since then, the curious call of the falls has been answered by a couple of dozen human daredevils, including two pairs, in contraptions that range from oak barrels to water tanks wrapped in truck inner tubes. In 2003 Kirk Jones of Canton, Michigan, went over wearing nothing but the clothes on his back and suffered only bruised ribs. A friend failed to capture his wild ride on videotape because he was impaired and didn't know how to work the recorder.

Here are the five daredevils who died trying.

1. Charles Stephens

A renowned stunt man from Bristol, England, Stephens was in a rush to make history at the falls and refused all advice to first try sending his barrel over unmanned. He installed heavy straps inside the barrel for his arms and, in order to keep himself floating upright, tied an anvil to his feet as ballast. He wore padded clothing and reluctantly took a small supply of oxygen with him, in the event that his barrel got stuck in a whirlpool. On July 11, 1920, he was launched into the river. When the barrel hit the base of the falls, the anvil crashed through the barrel, taking Stephens down with it. When the barrel was recovered, only Stephens's right arm remained, still strapped into the harness, with a tattoo that read "Forget Me Not Annie."

2. George L. Stathakis

An eccentric Greek chef from Buffalo, New York, Stathakis declared himself a religious mystic, and in an effort to raise funds for the publication of his books, he devised a plan to conquer Niagara. He went over the falls in a huge barrel on July 5, 1930, presumably surviving the fall. However, he suffocated after getting trapped behind the falls for more than 14 hours. His pet turtle "Sonny

Boy," whom he had brought along for the ride, survived. No one ever claimed his body from the morgue.

3. William "Red" Hill Jr.

Hill Jr. was the son of a famous riverman who had shot the rapids in a barrel three times and had pulled 177 corpses from the rapids below. Hill Jr. had helped his father on many of these rescues and had tried several times to revive the family legend and fortune with his own derring-do. Down on his luck, Hill Jr. built a flimsy contraption called "The Thing" from fishnets, canvas straps and 13 truck inner tubes. On August 5, 1951, thousands of people, including his family, gathered to watch The Thing go over Horseshoe Falls and get ripped to shreds in the pounding water. Hill Jr.'s mangled body was recovered the next day.

4. Jesse W. Sharp

On June 5, 1990, Sharp rode the fine line between stunting and suicide when he plunged over Horseshoe Falls in a 3.7-metre plastic kayak. The unemployed 28-year-old bachelor from Ocoee, Tennessee, had planned the stunt for three years. A veteran whitewater kayaker, Sharp was attempting to give his career a boost with his high-profile stunt. Accompanied by three friends who were there to videotape him, Sharp refused to wear a helmet because he wanted his face to be visible on the video. He also shunned a life jacket, maintaining it would hinder his ability to swim underneath the falls and whirlpools. His body was never recovered.

5. Robert Overacker

On October 1, 1995, Overacker became the latest daredevil to die going over the falls. The 39-year-old man from California was hoping to publicize the plight of the homeless by shooting off Horseshoe Falls on a Jet Ski while igniting a rocket-propelled parachute strapped to his back. Witnesses say the rocket lit, but there is some confusion as to whether the parachute deployed or simply fell away from his body because he had forgotten to attach it. In any event, Robert plunged to his death, and the *Maid of the Mist* picked up his body later that day.

6. Kirk R. Jones

In 2003, Kirk R. Jones of Canton, Michigan, became the first of four people known to have survived an unprotected plunge over the falls. The 40-year-old Jones, wearing nothing but the clothes on his back, suffered only broken ribs and bruising. A friend reportedly failed to capture his wild ride on videotape because he was impaired and couldn't work the recorder. On April 19, 2017, Jones died trying to repeat his stunt, this time riding inside an inflatable rubber ball. The *Maid of the Mist* picked up his empty inflatable that day and his body was recovered 20 kilometres downriver two weeks later.

+1. Strange Twist of Fate

On July 3, 1984, riding inside a cylindrical barrel with two eyeholes and a snorkel, Karel Soucek became the first Canadian to survive the falls. Later that year, the Hamilton, Ontario, native was killed recreating his feat at the Houston Astrodome by being dropped from a platform into a water tank. His barrel hit the edge of the tank.

10 PEOPLE WHO DIED LAUGHING

1. Calchas (c. 12th century BCE), Greek soothsayer

Calchas, the wisest soothsayer of Greece during the Trojan War, advised the construction of the notorious wooden horse. One day he was planting grapevines when a fellow soothsayer wandered by and foretold that Calchas would never drink the wine produced from the grapes. After the grapes ripened, wine was made from them and Calchas invited the soothsayer to share it with him. As Calchas held a cup of the wine in his hand, the soothsayer repeated the prophecy. This incited such a fit of laughter in Calchas that he choked and died. (Another version of his death states that he died of grief after losing a soothsaying match in which he failed to predict correctly the number of piglets a pig was about to give birth to.)

2. Zeuxis (5th century BCE), Greek painter

It is said that Zeuxis was laughing at a painting of an old woman he had just completed when his breathing failed and he choked to death.

3. Chrysippus (3rd century BCE), Greek philosopher

Chrysippus is said to have died from a fit of laughter on seeing a donkey eat some figs.

4. Philemon (c. 236–263), Greek poet

This writer of comedies became so engulfed in laughter over a jest he had made that he died laughing.

5. Pietro Aretino (d. 1556), Italian author

Aretino was laughing at a bawdy story being told to him by his sister when he fell backwards in his chair and died of apoplexy.

6. Thomas Urquhart (d. 1660), Scottish writer and translator

Best known for his translation into English of Rabelais's *Gargantua*, the eccentric Sir Thomas Urquhart is said to have died laughing upon hearing of the restoration to the throne of Charles II.

7. Mrs. Fitzherbert (d. 1782), English widow

On a Wednesday evening in April 1782, Mrs. Fitzherbert of Northamptonshire, England, went to Drury Lane Theatre with friends to see *The Beggar's Opera*. When the popular actor Mr. Bannister made his first appearance, dressed outlandishly in the role of "Polly," the entire audience was thrown into uproarious laughter. Unfortunately, Mrs. Fitzherbert was unable to suppress the laugh that seized her, and she was forced to leave the theatre before the end of the second act. As the *Gentleman's Magazine* reported the following week: "Not being able to banish the figure from her memory, she was thrown into hysterics, which continued without intermission until she expired on Friday morning."

8. Alex Mitchell (d. 1975), English bricklayer

Mr. and Mrs. Mitchell were watching their favourite TV comedy, *The Goodies*. During a scene about a new type of self-defence called "Ecky Thump," Mr. Mitchell was seized by uncontrollable laughter. After half an hour of unrestrained mirth, he suffered a heart attack and died. His wife, Nessie, wrote to the Goodies thanking them for making her husband's last moments so happy.

But the story doesn't end there. In 2012, 37 years after Alex Mitchell's death, doctors announced that they believed they'd figured out what likely killed him. It was a rare heart condition called Long QT syndrome. People with Long QT can suddenly faint or pass out during exercise, or when experiencing intense emotions, including laughter. In May 2012, Mitchell's 23-year-old granddaughter experienced a near-fatal cardiac arrest at her home. Doctors diagnosed her with Long QT syndrome, leading them to conclude that her grandfather likely suffered from the same condition.

9. Ole Bentzen (d. 1989), Danish physician

An audiologist who specialized in developing hearing aids for underdeveloped countries, Bentzen went to see the film *A Fish Called Wanda*. During a scene featuring John Cleese, Bentzen began laughing so hard that his heartbeat accelerated to a rate of between 250 and 500 beats a minute. He suffered a heart attack and died.

10. Damnoen Saen-um (d. 2003), Thai ice cream truck driver

It's odd enough to die laughing, even odder to die laughing in your sleep. But that appears to be what happened to Thai ice cream truck driver Damnoen Saen-um in August 2003. According to his wife, Damnoen started laughing in his sleep. She tried to wake him up but couldn't, and about two minutes later, he stopped breathing and died. An autopsy revealed the likely cause of death was a heart attack. "I have never seen a case like this," commented Dr. Somchai Chakrabhand, deputy director-general of Thailand's Mental Health Department, "but it is possible that a person could have heart seizure while laughing or crying too hard in their sleep."

14 TIMELY DEATHS

We read so often in the newspapers about "untimely deaths" that it makes one wonder if anyone ever died a "timely death." Well, people have. Here are some examples.

1. Domitian (AD 51-96), Roman emperor

Early astrological predictions had warned that he would be murdered on the fifth hour of September 18, AD 96. As the date approached, Domitian had many of his closest attendants executed to be on the safe side. Just before midnight marked the beginning of the critical day, he became so terrified that he jumped out of bed. A few hours later he asked the time and was told by his servants (who were conspiring against him) that it was the sixth hour. Convinced that the danger had passed, Domitian went off to take a bath. On the way, he was informed that his niece's steward, Stephanus, was waiting for him in the bedroom with important news. When the emperor arrived, Stephanus handed him a list of conspirators and then suddenly stabbed him in the groin. Domitian put up a good fight, but he was overcome when four more conspirators appeared. He died as predicted, on the fifth hour of September 18, AD 96.

2. Thomas Jefferson (1743–1826), American president

The 83-year-old former president was suffering from a bad case of diarrhea, but he had hopes of lasting until July 4, 1826, the 50th anniversary of the signing of the Declaration of Independence. From his sickbed, he asked, "This is the fourth?" When he was informed that it was, he died peacefully.

3. John Adams (1735–1826), American president

Adams, like Jefferson, held on until July 4, 1826, before dying at the age of 90. He is reported to have said, "Thomas Jefferson survives. . . . Independence forever," unaware that his old friend had died a few hours earlier.

4. Dr. Joseph Green (1791–1863), English surgeon

While lying on his deathbed, Dr. Green looked up at his own doctor and said, "Congestion." Then he took his own pulse, reported a single word, "Stopped," and died.

5. Henrik Ibsen (1828–1906), Norwegian poet and dramatist

On May 16, 1906, Ibsen was in a coma in his bedroom, surrounded by friends and relatives. A nurse told the others in the room that the famed playwright seemed to be a little better. Without opening his eyes, Ibsen uttered one word: "*Tvertimod*" ("On the contrary"). He died that afternoon without speaking again.

6. Mark Twain (1835–1910), American humorist

Born in 1835, the year of Halley's Comet, Twain often stated that he had come into the world with the comet and would go out of the world with it as well. Halley's Comet next returned in 1910, and on April 21 of that year Twain died.

7. Arnold Schönberg (1874–1951), Austrian composer

Schönberg's lifelong fascination with numerology led to his morbid obsession with the number 13. Born in 1874 on September 13, he believed that 13 would also play a role in his death. Because the numerals seven and six add up to 13, Schonberg was convinced that his 76th year would be the decisive one. Checking the calendar for 1951, he saw to his horror that July 13 fell on a Friday. When that day came, he kept to his bed in an effort to reduce the chance of an accident. Shortly before midnight, his wife entered the bedroom to say good night and to reassure him that his fears had been foolish, whereupon Schönberg muttered the word "harmony" and died. The time of his death was 11:47 p.m., 13 minutes before midnight on Friday, July 13, in his 76th year.

8. Leonard Warren (1911–60), American opera singer

Warren was performing in Verdi's *La Forza del Destino* on the stage of the Metropolitan Opera in 1960. He had just begun the aria "O Fatal Urn of My Destiny." When he reached the word "fatal," he suddenly pitched forward, dead of a heart attack.

9. Elizabeth Ryan (1892–1979), American tennis player

Ryan won 19 Wimbledon tennis championships between 1914 and 1934—a record that stood for 45 years. On July 6, 1979, the day before Billie Jean King broke Ryan's record by winning a 20th Wimbledon title, the 87-year-old Ryan became ill while in the stands at Wimbledon. She collapsed in the clubhouse and died that night.

10. Charles Davies (1927–95), British singer

Davies, age 67, was giving a solo rendition of the old soldiers' song "Goodbye" at the annual dinner of the Cotswold Male Voice Choir in Eckington, England, on January 3, 1995. He finished with the words, "I wish you all a last goodbye." As the crowd applauded, Davies collapsed and died.

11. Charles Schulz (1922–2000), American cartoonist

In 1999 Schulz, the creator of the popular comic strip *Peanuts*, announced his decision to retire because of poor health. He died on February 12, 2000, the night before the last original *Peanuts* ran in the Sunday newspapers. The timing was "prophetic and magical," said close friend and fellow cartoonist Lynn Johnston (*For Better or for Worse*). "He made one last deadline. There's romance in that."

12. George Story (1936–2000), American journalist

In 1936 the premier issue of *Life* featured a picture of newborn baby George Story under the headline "Life Begins." Over the years, the magazine periodically updated readers about the "*Life* baby," as Story married twice, had children and retired. On April 4, 2000, just days after *Life* had announced that it would cease publication, Story died of heart failure. The final issue of *Life* featured one last article about Story. The headline: "A Life Ends."

13. Pierre Berton (1920-2004), Canadian writer, columnist, nationalist

Berton's politics shaded towards the left. His views on organized religion bordered on the hostile. So it is not surprising that his opinion of the right-wing fundamentalist Christian president of the United States, George W. Bush, was far from positive. On November 30, 2004, President Bush was in the middle of his first state visit to Canada when Berton died at the age of 84. Faced with the choice of covering the visit of a much-disliked American president or the death of a much-loved author, most Canadian media chose to emphasize the latter. The Berton story led the CBC national news that evening. In fact, the network's Berton coverage ran for more than 10 minutes. The next day, Berton all but shoved Bush off the front page of the nation's newspapers. Somewhere, Pierre Berton was smiling.

14. Stafford Smythe (1921-1971), hockey executive

Stafford Smythe was a hockey blue blood. His father, Conn Smythe, had bought the Toronto St. Pats' hockey team in 1927 and changed their name to the Toronto Maple Leafs. Four years later, he built Maple Leaf Gardens. In 1957, the elder Smythe chose Stafford to chair a seven-man committee to run the foundering hockey club. In 1961, Stafford, along with fellow committee members Harold Ballard and John Bassett, bought control of the Leafs and the Gardens from Conn Smythe for $2.3 million. The team went on to win four Stanley Cups in the 1960s, but in 1971, the RCMP charged Smythe and Ballard with income tax evasion, and accused them of using Gardens' money to pay for renovations of their homes and other personal expenses. Their lawyer urged them to accept a plea bargain that would see them spend a year or two in jail. Ballard supported the idea, but Smythe refused. "I will never go to jail," he vowed. He didn't. On October 13, 1971, just 12 days before the trial was scheduled to start, Stafford Smythe died as the result of complications arising from a perforated ulcer. He was just 50 years old. In 1972, a jury found Ballard guilty of 48 out of 50 charges of theft and fraud. He wound up serving a year in prison.

14 BAD ENDINGS IN CANADIAN BUSINESS, POLITICS AND SPORTS

In Canadian Business

1. Micheline Charest

After years of legal and financial problems, the controversial co-founder of Cinar, the well-known Montreal animation house, finally looked as if she was ready to move on with her life. She had sold her shares in her company and had paid a $1 million fine to the Quebec Securities Commission. On April 14, 2004, she checked herself into a private clinic to undergo a facelift and a nip and tuck to her breasts. But the operation took longer than expected, and Charest was under general anaesthesia for about seven hours. After surgery, she was moved to the recovery room, and the breathing tube in her windpipe was removed. But the muscles in her larynx went into spasm, blocking her ability to breathe. She went into cardiac arrest and died a few moments later. She was 51 years old.

2. Michael de Guzman

On March 19, 1997, de Guzman jumped out of the back of an Alouette III helicopter over the jungles of Indonesia and plunged 240 metres to his death. De Guzman was the chief geologist in Indonesia for Bre-X Minerals Ltd. It was his surveys that had convinced investors that Bre-X had discovered one of the world's largest gold reserves. But by March 1997, there was growing evidence that there was no gold there and that de Guzman had fabricated his surveys. Rather than live with the consequences of his actions, de Guzman decided to end his life. Rescuers searched for four days through the dense forest before finally locating the body. The injuries caused by the fall, combined with the ravages of the insects and animals in the jungle, left de Guzman's body so grotesque that authorities decided not to allow his family to see it.

3. Guy Lamarche

Guy Lamarche was born in Timmins, Ontario, and made his living promoting dubious stocks and other shady investment deals. The man who shot him to death in the lobby of Toronto's Royal York Hotel on March 9, 1987, was Lamarche's boyhood friend, Timmins Bissonnette, who had made millions running carnival shows and gambling for big stakes in Las Vegas. But business is business, and when Lamarche refused to repay $80,000 that Bissonnette had loaned him two years earlier, something had to be done. Bissonnette confronted Lamarche in the hotel lobby, demanding his money. Lamarche refused to pay. "He called me a bum and a lot worse," Bissonnette later recalled. "That was the end of it. The light went out. I went and got my gun." Bissonnette shot his old friend twice in the heart, then spat on his body. He fled the scene but was captured by police a few moments later. He was convicted in February 1988 and sentenced to life in prison.

4. Ambrose Small

Ambrose Small's disappearance remains one of the most intriguing unsolved whodunits in Canadian history. Small was a wealthy Toronto businessman and socialite. He lived in a Rosedale mansion and owned several theatres that specialized in racy shows about the misadventures of young, single, working-class women alone in the big city. He was also a renowned gambler and womanizer. On December 2, 1919, at the age of 53, Small completed the sale of some of his theatres and deposited a cheque for $1 million in his bank account. Later that day, he walked out of his office and was never seen or heard from again. Much speculation focused on his long-suffering wife as a possible suspect in her philandering husband's disappearance, but no proof of her involvement was ever established.

In Canadian Politics

5. George Brown

George Brown played a prominent role in the Quebec and Charlottetown conferences that led to Confederation, but he was probably best known as the crusading editor of the Toronto *Globe*. On March 25, 1880, a disgruntled former *Globe* employee came to Brown's office and, after a brief scuffle, shot the editor in the leg. The wound was considered to be minor, and Brown returned home to recuperate. But over the next few weeks, as Brown continued to work from home, the wound became infected. He became feverish, then delirious, and eventually slipped into a coma. He died on May 9 at the age of 61.

6. John Buchan, 1st Baron Tweedsmuir

On February 6, 1940, Governor General Lord Tweedsmuir suffered a stroke while shaving at Rideau Hall. He fell and severely injured his head. Dr. Wilder Penfield, the renowned Montreal neurosurgeon, was called in and, over the next several days, performed two operations. But it was to no avail. Lord Tweedsmuir died on February 11, becoming the first governor general to die while in office.

7. Jim Flaherty

Jim Flaherty had every reason to look forward to a slower, less stressful life outside the political fishbowl. On March 18, 2014, he announced his resignation as minister of finance in the government of Stephen Harper. He planned to move to a job in the private sector. Flaherty had been finance minister for eight years, a long time to be the nation's top money man. In addition, in 2013, Flaherty announced he was suffering from a painful skin condition that he was treating with powerful steroids, but he insisted health was not a factor in his decision to resign. On April 10, 2014, just three weeks after leaving cabinet, Flaherty suffered a heart attack and died in his Ottawa condo. He was 64.

8. Shaughnessy Cohen

Shaughnessy Cohen was first elected to the House of Commons from Windsor in 1993, and quickly established herself as one of the hardest-working and most popular MPs in the House. On the afternoon of December 9, 1998, Cohen was seated at her desk in the Commons, chatting with one of her fellow Liberal MPs, when she started bleeding from the mouth and collapsed on the floor beside her desk. She had suffered a massive brain hemorrhage. Efforts to revive her failed, and she died in hospital later that evening. She was 50 years old.

9. Donald Summerville

Donald Summerville was just two years into his term as mayor of Toronto on the night of November 19, 1963, when he donned his goalie pads to take part in a charity hockey game in aid of Italian flood victims. The game was only five minutes old, and the 48-year-old mayor, a former practice goalie for the Maple Leafs, had already made several solid saves, when he skated shakily off the ice. He made it to the dressing room but then collapsed from congestive heart failure. He was pronounced dead on arrival in hospital, the only Toronto mayor to die while in office.

10. Sir John Thompson

On December 12, 1894, Prime Minister Thompson was summoned to Windsor Castle to be sworn in as the Right Honourable Sir John Thompson. After the ceremony, he was invited to stay for lunch with the Queen. Shortly after taking his seat in the dining room, he fainted. He was taken to a nearby room and, after a few moments, felt well enough to return to the table. But before he could eat his first bite of food, he suddenly collapsed, falling into the arms of Sir John Watt Reid, the Queen's doctor, who had been seated beside him. The prime minister had suffered a massive heart attack, and he died moments later.

11. Sir Samuel Leonard Tilley
Sir Samuel Leonard Tilley was premier (twice) and lieutenant-governor of New Brunswick, a minister in Sir John A. Macdonald's first cabinet and a Father of Confederation. Early in June 1896 he cut his foot while vacationing at his summer home in Rothesay, New Brunswick. Within a few days, blood poisoning had spread through his entire system. He died on June 25 at the age of 78.

In Canadian Sports

12. Lionel Conacher
Lionel "Big Train" Conacher was the best all-around athlete Canada has ever produced, a star of hockey, football, baseball, boxing and several other sports. On May 26, 1954, as a Liberal MP, Conacher was playing in a softball game between MPs and members of the parliamentary press gallery. In the sixth inning, Conacher hit a long fly ball into left field and started running the bases. Just as he was pulling into third base, he collapsed of a heart attack. Within 20 minutes, the man voted Canada's greatest athlete of the first half of the 20th century was dead at 53 years of age.

13. Owen Hart
On May 23, 1999, Owen Hart, a member of Calgary's famed Hart family of professional wrestlers, was killed when a stunt he was performing at a World Wrestling Federation event in Kansas City misfired. Hart was planning to descend 30 metres into the ring from the top of the arena. He was supposed to be guided down by wires attached to his costume, but the release cord mechanism malfunctioned, and Hart plunged into the ring, smashing into the padded turnbuckle. Many of the 16,200 fans in the arena thought the wrestler's crash landing was part of his act. Paramedics quickly rushed in to try to resuscitate Hart, but they were unsuccessful. He was pronounced dead at the hospital.

14. Owen "Bud" McCourt

On March 8, 1907, Owen "Bud" McCourt became the only player in Canadian hockey history to die as a direct result of an on-ice attack. McCourt, who played for the Cornwall Wanderers of the Federal Amateur Hockey League, was clubbed over the head with the hockey stick of a player for the Ottawa Victorias during a fight-filled game in Cornwall. McCourt died several hours later in hospital. Charles Masson of the Victorias was arrested the day after the game and charged with murder. The charge was later reduced to manslaughter, but when the case went to trial, Masson was acquitted because, in those days before video replays, the Crown was unable to prove conclusively which Ottawa player had struck the fatal blow.

10 CELEBRATED PEOPLE WHO READ THEIR OWN OBITUARIES

1. Hannah Snell (1723-1792)

When Hannah Snell's husband walked out on her and joined the British army, she borrowed an outfit from her brother-in-law and enlisted as well, hoping to track down her wayward husband. She first served in the army, and later joined the Royal Marines, sailing to India to fight in the battle of Pondicherry. During the battle, she sustained a groin injury, but she managed to keep her sex a secret by treating the injury herself. Upon her return to England, she revealed her sex to her shipmates and sold her story to a London publisher. She became a celebrity, and once out of the army she performed in public houses as the Female Warrior. On December 10, 1779, when she was 56, she opened a copy of the *Gentlemen's Magazine* and read her own obituary, which informed her that she had died on a Warwickshire heath. Perhaps she was superstitious, because reading her death notice snapped something in her mind. Her mental health slowly deteriorated, and in 1789 she was placed in London's Bethlehem Hospital, where she remained until her death in 1792.

2. Daniel Boone (1734-1820)

The great American frontiersman had retired and settled down in Missouri. In 1818 a newspaper in the eastern United States trumpeted the news that the renowned hunter had been found dead near a deer lick, kneeling behind a tree stump, his rifle resting on the stump, a fallen deer 90 metres away. The obituary was picked up across the nation. Daniel read it and laughed. Although he could still trap, he was too old and weak to hunt and could no longer hit a deer, even close up. Two years later, at the age of 86, Boone finally did die. His best-known obituary was seven stanzas devoted to him in Lord Byron's *Don Juan*.

3. Lady Jane Ellenborough (1807-1881)

She was one of the most beautiful and sexual women in all history. Her name was Jane Digby. At 17 she married Lord Ellenborough, Great Britain's lord of the privy seal, then left him to run off with an Austrian prince. During her colourful career she was the mistress of novelist Honoré de Balzac, King Ludwig of Bavaria and Ludwig's son, King Otto of Greece. Her last marriage, of 26 years, was to Sheik Medjuel, an erudite Bedouin, head of the Mezrab tribe in the Syrian desert. Returning from a desert trip with Medjuel, the 66-year-old Lady Ellenborough learned that she was dead. Her obituary appeared prominently in *La Revue Britannique*, published in Paris in March 1873. It began: "A noble lady who had made a great use—or abuse—of marriage has died recently. Lady Ellenborough, some 30 years ago, left her first husband to run off with Count von Schwarzenberg. She retired to Italy, where she married six consecutive times." The obituary, reprinted throughout Europe, called her last husband "a camel driver." The next issue of the publication carried a eulogy of Lady Ellenborough written by her friend Isabel Burton, the pompous and snobbish wife of Burton of Arabia. Mrs. Burton claimed she had been authorized to publish the story of Lady Ellenborough's life, based on dictated notes. Appalled, Lady Ellenborough vehemently wrote to the press, denying her death—and having dictated an "authorized" book to Mrs. Burton. Lady Ellenborough outlived her obituary by eight full years, dying of dysentery in August 1881.

4. James Butler Hickok (1837-1876)

In March 1873 "Wild Bill" Hickok, legendary sheriff and city marshal in the Midwest and a constant reader of Missouri's leading newspaper, the *Democrat*, picked up a copy and learned that he was a corpse. Hickok read: "The Texan who corralled the untamed William did so because he lost his brother by Bill's quickness on the trigger." Unsettled by his supposed demise, Wild Bill took pen in hand and wrote a letter to the editor: "Wishing to correct an error in your paper of the 12th, I will state that no Texan has, nor ever will, 'corral William.' I wish to correct your statement on account of my people. Yours as ever, J.B. Hickok." Delighted, the editor of the *Democrat* printed Hickok's letter and added an editorial: "We take much pleasure in laying Mr. Hickok's statement before the readers of the *Democrat*, most of whom will be glad to read from his pen that he is 'still on the deck.' But in case you should go off suddenly, William, by writing us the particulars we will give you just as fine an obituary notice as we can get up, though we trust that sad pleasure may be deferred for years." Three years later Hickok was murdered while playing poker.

5. Alfred Nobel (1833-1896)

As the inventor of dynamite, Alfred Nobel, a moody yet idealistic Swede, had become a millionaire. When Nobel's older brother, Ludwig, died of heart trouble on April 12, 1888, a leading French newspaper misread the report and ran an obituary of Alfred Nobel, calling him "a merchant of death." Upon seeing the obituary, Nobel was stunned, not by the premature announcement of his passing but by the realization that in the end he would be considered nothing more than a merchant of death. The printed summary of his life reflected none of his hopes for humanity, his love of his fellow beings, his generosity. The need to repair this false picture was one of several factors that led him to establish, in his will, the Nobel Prizes, to be given to those who did the most to advance the causes of peace, literature and the sciences.

6. P.T. Barnum (1810-1891)

At 80, the great American was ailing and knew that death was near. From his sickbed, he told a friend that he would be happier if he had "the chance to see what sort of lines" would be written about him after he was dead. The friend relayed this wish to the editor of the *Evening Sun* of New York City. On March 24, 1891, Barnum opened his copy of the *Evening Sun* and read: "Great and Only Barnum. He Wanted to Read His Obituary; Here It Is." According to the preface, "Mr. Barnum has had almost everything in this life, including the woolly horse and Jenny Lind, and there is no reason why he should not have the last pleasure which he asks for. So here is the great showman's life, briefly and simply told, as it would have appeared in the *Evening Sun* had fate taken our Great and Only from us." There followed four columns of Barnum's obituary, illustrated by woodcuts of him at his present age, of him at 41, of his mother, of his deceased first wife, Charity, and of the Swedish singer Jenny Lind. Two weeks later, Barnum was dead.

7. Leopold von Sacher-Masoch (1836-1895)

This police commissioner's son, born in Galicia and raised in Austria, was fascinated by cruelty and loved pain and degradation. His first mistress, Anna von

Kottowitz, birched him regularly and enjoyed lovers whom Sacher-Masoch found for her. His second mistress, Fanny Pistor, signed a contract with him, agreeing to wear furs when she beat him daily. She fulfilled the contract and treated him as a servant. He had become a famous writer when he met and married a woman named Wanda. She thrashed him with a nail-studded whip every day of their 15-year marriage and made him perform as her slave. After she ran off, Sacher-Masoch married a simple German woman named Hulda Meister. By this time, he was slipping into insanity, and he tried to strangle her. In 1895 she had him secretly committed to an asylum in Mannheim and announced to the world that he had died. The press published obituaries praising his talent. Undoubtedly, in lucid moments, he read some of his death notices. He finally did die 10 years later. Because of Sacher-Masoch's life, psychiatrist Richard von Krafft-Ebing coined the word "masochism."

8. Mark Twain (1835-1910)

In 1897 the noted American author and humourist was in seclusion, grieving over a death in his family, when he learned that he too had been declared dead. A sensational American newspaper had headlined his end, stating that he had died impoverished in London, England. A national syndicate sent a reporter to Mark Twain's home to confirm the news. Twain himself appeared before the bug-eyed reporter and issued an official statement: "James Ross Clemens, a cousin of mine, was seriously ill two or three weeks ago in London, but is well now. The reports of my illness grew out of his illness. The reports of my death are greatly exaggerated." Twain finally lived up to his premature obituaries in 1910.

9. Bertrand Russell (1872-1970)

Once, in the 1930s, while the English philosopher was visiting Beijing, he became very ill. Japanese reporters in the city constantly tried to see Russell, but were always denied access to him. The journalists decided he must be dead and notified their newspapers of his demise. Word of his death went around the world. Wrote Russell, "It provided me with the pleasure of reading my obituary notices, which I had always desired without expecting my wishes to be fulfilled." One missionary paper had an obituary notice of one sentence: "Missionaries may be pardoned for heaving a sigh of relief at the news of Mr. Bertrand Russell's death." All of this inspired Russell to compose his own obituary in 1937 for *The Times* of London. He wrote of himself: "His life, for all its waywardness, had a certain anachronistic consistency, reminiscent of the aristocratic rebels of the early nineteenth century . . . He was the last survivor of a dead epoch." He told *The Times* to run it in 1962, the year in which he expected to die. *The Times* did not need it until 1970.

10. Edward V. Rickenbacker (1890-1973)

The former auto racer turned fighter pilot emerged from the First World War as America's leading ace, with 26 confirmed kills. In peacetime he was an executive in the automobile and aviation industries. With the onset of the Second World War, Rickenbacker volunteered to carry out missions for the U.S. War Department. In October 1942, on an inspection tour, Rickenbacker's B-17 went down somewhere in the Pacific Ocean. An intensive air search of the area was made. There was no sign of survivors. Newspapers across the United States declared Rickenbacker dead. The following month, on Friday, November 13, there were new headlines: Rickenbacker and seven others had been spotted alive in the Pacific, having survived on a raft for 23 days. Waiting for Rickenbacker when he returned home was a pile of his obituaries. One, in the *New York Daily News*, was a cartoon showing a black wreath floating on water, with the caption "So Long, Eddie." Another, in the *New York Journal*, bore the headline "End of the Roaring Road?" Grinning, Rickenbacker scrawled across it, "Hell, no!"

SANDRA MARTIN'S 5 REASONS TO WRITE YOUR OWN DEATH NOTICE

Sandra Martin is the author of several books including Great Canadian Lives: A Cultural History of Modern Canada Through the Art of the Obit. *As a feature writer, she has written obituaries of dozens of prominent Canadians, including Jane Jacobs, Bertha Wilson, Pierre Trudeau, Maurice Rocket Richard, Mordecai Richler, Arthur Erickson and Kenojuak Ashevak.*

1. Accuracy

You will ensure the facts of your life are reported accurately and save your loved ones from a genealogical scramble (and possibly an argument) at an already stressful time if you provide the information about the year you graduated from college, enlisted in the armed forces, or divorced your second and third spouses.

2. Control the Narrative

You can control the narrative, leaving out pesky details like career reversals and love affairs gone sour, and inserting loving testimonials from your children.

Otherwise, you may be at your survivors' mercy. Siblings Katherine and Patrick Reddick lashed out at their mother, Marianne Theresa Johnson-Reddick in the *Reno Gazette-Journal* after the former nun and alleged madam died alone and friendless in 2013. Her children accused her of neglecting and abusing them when they were small and stalking and torturing "anyone they dared to love" as adults. Finally, they celebrated "her passing from this earth" in the hope that "she lives in the after-life reliving each gesture of violence, cruelty and shame that she delivered on her children." Clearly, the Reddicks were unfamiliar with the adage "never speak ill of the dead."

3. Comfort the Living
You can include comforting messages for your survivors. After the American actor James Rebhorn died of melanoma in March 2014, his church posted a posthumous letter from him on its website. The hawk-nosed character actor, best known for supporting roles on *Seinfeld* and *Homeland*, sent a poignant deathbed message saying that without his family "at the centre of his being," his life "would have been little more than a vapour." And he entreated his daughters to "grieve his passing only as long as necessary," because they have "much good work to do and they should get busy doing it." The message went viral, and even now I tear up when I reread it.

4. Get the Last Word In
You can get a final lick in at those who wronged you in life. Best to outlive your enemies because the dead can't sue your estate, or make the references subtle but devastating.

5. Make Them Smile
There's no such thing as an uninteresting life. If you write the announcement with flair and humour, you may attract the attention of a journalist like me. As an obituary writer, I found some of my favourite subjects in the classified death notices: a spy, a survivor of a Japanese prisoner-of-war camp, a theatrical promoter and all sorts of other unknowns—all of whom caught my interest because their death notices intrigued me.

LAST WORDS OF 12 FAMOUS CANADIANS

1. "Now, God be praised, I will die in peace."
   —General James Wolfe, September 13, 1759. He was mortally wounded in the Battle of the Plains of Abraham, but lived long enough to learn that Quebec had been taken.

2. "Push on, brave York volunteers."
   —Sir Isaac Brock, October 13, 1812, spoken just before he was shot and killed by American soldiers

3. "Good morning. It is morning now."
   —Thomas D'Arcy McGee, April 7, 1868. A friend had just wished McGee "good night," but since it was already 2 a.m., McGee corrected him. Moments later, he was gunned down in front of his Ottawa rooming house.

4. "I am dying."
   —George-Étienne Cartier, May 20, 1873, spoken to his wife and doctors

5. "In our opinion, his powers of life are steadily waning."
   —last bulletin issued to the public by Sir John A. Macdonald's doctors, hours before the prime minister died, June 6, 1891

6. "Oh, take me home."
   —former prime minister Alexander Mackenzie, April 17, 1892, spoken to his wife and daughter

7. "I am feeling very sick."
   —former premier of Ontario and federal Liberal leader Edward Blake, March 1, 1912, spoken to his family

8. "*C'est fini.*"
   —Sir Wilfrid Laurier, February 17, 1919, spoken to his wife, Zoë

9. "Hold up my head."
   —Dr. William Osler, December 29, 1919, spoken to a friend at his bedside

10. "Did I behave pretty well? Was I a good boy?"
    —Stephen Leacock, March 28, 1944, spoken to the radiologist treating him for throat cancer

11. "I'm afraid to die, but it pains too much to live."
    —Samuel Bronfman, July 10, 1971, spoken to his doctor

12. "Please, my near and dear ones, forgive me and understand. I hope this potion works. My spirit is already in another country, and my body has become a damn nuisance. I have been so fortunate."
    —last words of the suicide note written by Margaret Laurence, January 5, 1987

Miscellaneous

10 SENSATIONAL SAVANTS

Savant syndrome is a rare condition in which people who have been diagnosed with mental disabilities, autism or schizophrenia nonetheless possess an unusual ability in a single field, most often relating to music, art or numbers.

1. Clarence Asham (1954-)

Asham is blind and unable to speak, and has an IQ of 32. For 28 years, he lived in an institution in Portage la Prairie, Manitoba. One day, his nurse gave him an accordion, and Clarence immediately proceeded to play hundreds of songs that he had heard on the radio over the years. It turns out that Asham has an extraordinarily highly developed musical memory. He can play any piece of music on the piano, even a complex classical score, after hearing it only once.

2. Thomas "Blind Tom" Bethune (1849-1908)

Although his vocabulary was limited to fewer than 100 words, Blind Tom could play more than 5,000 pieces on the piano, an instrument he had mastered as a four-year-old slave on a Georgia plantation. At the age of 11, he performed at the White House for President James Buchanan. He learned each piece after hearing it only once; his repertoire included Mozart, Beethoven, Bach and Verdi.

3. Ellen Boudreaux (1957-)

Ellen Boudreau is a blind, autistic musical savant, able to remember, perform, improvise and transpose a broad array of music on piano and guitar. But she also uses echolocation to move around in indoor and outdoor spaces without bumping into objects. She makes chirping noises as she moves that bounce back to her, reflecting the placement of obstacles, walls and openings. It's a human sonar system functioning much like those used by bats, whales or submarines.

4. Alonzo Clemons (1959-)

Clemons, who has an IQ of 40, lives in a home for the developmentally disabled in Boulder, Colorado. An exceptionally talented sculptor, he has sold hundreds of pieces, including one for $45,000. Many buyers have purchased his work unaware that it was created by a mentally handicapped artist.

5. Thomas Fuller (1710-90)

Born in Africa, Fuller was taken to Virginia as a slave in 1724. He was a calculating wonder who could easily multiply nine-digit numbers. At the age of 78, Fuller, who was never able to learn to read or write, was asked, "How many seconds has a man lived who is 70 years, 17 days and 12 hours old?" Ninety seconds later he gave the answer—2,210,500,800. Informed that he was wrong, Fuller corrected his interrogator by pointing out that the man had forgotten to include leap years.

6. Leslie Lemke (1952-)

Leslie was born prematurely and suffered brain damage, cerebral palsy and retinal damage that led to the removal of his eyes shortly after birth. When he was given up for adoption, a caretaker devoted herself to keeping him alive, teaching him to eat food, walk and play instruments. He learned piano rapidly, his erratic hand movements subsiding completely, and eventually mastered complex classical and jazz pieces by age 12. A resident of Milwaukee, Wisconsin, Leslie continues to perform publicly, do media appearances and has been the subject of two films, *An Island of Genius* and the Emmy-winning *The Woman Who Willed a Miracle*.

7. Jonathan Lerman (1987-)

Lerman, who was diagnosed as autistic at the age of three, has a tested IQ of 53. His verbal abilities are quite limited, but he began drawing at 10, shortly after the death of his maternal grandfather, Burt Markowitz, who had always insisted that Jonathan had promise. His charcoal drawings have been compared to Matisse and Picasso, and sell for $500 to $1,200. A book of his artwork, *Jonathan Lerman: The Drawings of a Boy with Autism*, was published in 2002.

8. Kim Peek (1951-2009)

"Megasavant" Peek could perform complex mathematical calculations and accurately recall the contents of thousands of books he'd speed-read on topics as diverse as sports, history, literature and geography. He lived in Utah and was the inspiration for the character played by Dustin Hoffman in the 1988 Academy Award–winning film *Rain Man*. Despite his gifts, he was socially awkward, tested at a general IQ of 87 and struggled with basic tasks like buttoning his shirt. Peek seemed to enjoy his celebrity, appearing publicly often with an Oscar statuette given to him by screenwriter Barry Morrow. Peek's story is told in the book *The Real Rain Man* (1997).

9. Grant Reimer (dates unknown)

Grant Reimer of Steinbach, Manitoba, is unable to live on his own, but he possesses one narrow streak of brilliance. Give Grant a date from any year as far back as the 19th century, and he will instantly be able to tell you what day of the week that date fell on. He is also able to tell you, with extraordinary accuracy and precision, what the weather was on any day of his life. When asked to explain his amazing talent, Reimer replied, "I have a computer in my mind."

10. Stephen Wiltshire (1974–)

Wiltshire, who lives in London, England, is able to glance briefly at a building and then draw it in exquisite detail. Wiltshire has produced several books of drawings and has travelled the globe drawing 10-metre-long panoramas of cities including Tokyo, Dubai, New York and Jerusalem. In 1993 he was discovered to also be a musical savant, with perfect pitch. In 2006 Queen Elizabeth named Stephen a member of the Order of the British Empire in recognition of his gifts to the world of art and design.

8 NOTABLE CANADIAN CANOES

by Jeremy Ward

The Canadian Canoe Museum in Peterborough, Ontario, is dedicated to exploring and preserving the history, art and culture of paddled watercraft. Founded in 1997, the museum's collection of more than 600 historic and contemporary vessels spans the canoe and kayak traditions of Canada, including the great dugouts of the First Nations of the Pacific Northwest to the skin-on-frame kayaks of northern peoples from Baffin Island in the east to the Mackenzie River Delta in the northwest.

Jeremy Ward is the curator of the Canadian Canoe Museum and led a team of volunteers building an authentic, functional canot du maître, *the workhorse vehicle of the Canadian fur trade.*

1. Dugout Canoe, Smoke Lake, Ontario (19th century)

This canoe, recovered from a lakebed near Algonquin Park in Ontario, was hewn from a single large pine log. Although eroded and damaged, tool markings left by steel axe and adze may still be seen across its surfaces. A robust canoe like this would have been best suited for local fishing, hauling short distances and used by both Indigenous people and pioneers. Hundreds of these dugouts have been discovered in muddy rivers or lake bottoms, and some speculate they may have been submerged deliberately to protect them from harsh winter conditions.

2. Birch Bark Canoe, St. Lawrence basin (18th century)

Exquisitely crafted over 240 years ago, this canoe features a magnificent 7-metre sheet of birch bark laid its full length and stretched tight by the assembled internal framework of hand-carved cedar ribs and sheathing. The canoe's gunwales, still bearing scratched measurement markings, are assembled with wooden pegs and the entire hull sewn and lashed together using coniferous tree roots that have been deftly peeled and split to a uniform thickness. All of the hull's seams have been made watertight with a resinous pitch made from spruce gum blended with animal fat.

This canoe was likely made along the shores of the St. Lawrence River in the late 18th century and is one of the oldest documented birch bark canoes in the world. It was donated to the Canadian Canoe Museum in 2012 by descendants of one of its earliest owners. Although significantly damaged in storage at some point, it is one of only a handful of birch bark canoes that have survived this long. Despite the damage, however, the dramatic profile of its long cutwaters and overall grace in form may still be appreciated.

3. Beothuk Canoe Model

This exquisite canoe model was made circa 1826 by Nancy Shanawdithit, the last known member of Newfoundland's indigenous Beothuk people. These were a highly skilled canoeing people who plied Newfoundland's inland waterways and shoreline, even making open water crossings in bark canoes to islands 60 kilometres away. Before her death, Shanawdithit made a precise 54-centimetre model of a Beothuk canoe that featured the characteristic "half moon" profile and the high, peaked sections at the bow, stern and midsection. Shanawdithit's wonderful canoe model can be seen at the National Maritime Museum, Greenwich. A replica may be seen at the Canadian Canoe Museum.

4. Voyageur Canoe

The largest of the birchbark canoes, the 11-metre *canot du maître* (Montreal canoe) was a workhorse for the Canadian fur trade. Given their size and draft, they were restricted to larger waterways and followed the major freight routes from Montreal and posts in the Great Lakes region, or *pays d'en haut*. Across each of the 36 or so portages between Montreal and Lake Superior, these canoes could be lifted and carried empty by as few as four voyageurs while the rest began shuttling the payload across. However, once back on the water with its crew of eight to 12, the canoe would transport over 3,500 kilograms of cargo when loaded.

The bark canoe itself is truly an engineering marvel that met perfectly the challenges of centuries of travellers across much of the Canadian landscape. On terrain interrupted by countless river systems and lakes, it was an essential key for unlocking an otherwise challenging geography, and its construction allowed for it to be easily repaired. Most birchbark canoes of this size today are replicas, given the difficulty of providing long-term storage and that, due to their extreme uses, they tended to last only a season or two.

5. Tom Thomson's Chestnut Cruiser

The discovery of celebrated Canadian artist Tom Thomson's distinctive canoe on Algonquin Park's Canoe Lake on July 8, 1917, led to the recovery of his body. Thomson was likely paddling a Chestnut Canoe Company 16-foot Cruiser, made in Fredericton, New Brunswick. A wood-and-canvas canoe, it was rugged and sleek, ideal for woodsmen and veteran paddlers. Thomson created and applied the distinctive dove-grey colour to the canoe's canvas covering, making the colour by blending a tube of cobalt paint into conventional grey enamel. The whereabouts of Thomson's iconic canoe is unknown.

6. Paddle-to-the-Sea

Near Lake Nipigon in northern Ontario, an Anishinaabe boy carves a wooden model of a birchbark canoe and paddler. Along its weighted bottom, he carves the words "I am Paddle-to-the-Sea. Please put me back in the water." One spring he sets his carving free in the icy waters of Lake Superior to find its way to the Atlantic Ocean. So begins Holling C. Holling's enchanting tale, and the short film adaptation directed by naturalist, artist and foremost canoeing authority Bill Mason. As anyone who was in school during 1967 and after can tell you, the model canoe wends its way across the Great Lakes basin, over Niagara Falls and out to the ocean via the St. Lawrence, imparting the majesty and power of Canada's geography and watersheds. To make the film, Mason carved several copies of the toy-sized sculpture, setting them afloat as others were lost or damaged during shooting. The Canadian Canoe Museum has a painted resin casting of this iconic miniature canoe, also used in filming, in its collection.

7. West Coast Dugout Canoe: Victor Adams's Eagle Canoe

In 1969, Victor Adams of Masset, Haida Gwaii, was commissioned to carve a traditional northern-style dugout canoe for the Kanawa Museum (forerunner of the Canadian Canoe Museum). At that time, construction details dwelled only in the memories of community elders. Adams's work marks the earliest indication of the revival of Haida sea-going canoe-making traditions that flourishes today and is carried on by his family two generations later. The Haida created great centres for canoe-building and exported their craft to the remotest parts of the Northwest Coast. This dugout represents the significance of the canoe in Haida culture both past and present.

8. Odeyak Hybrid Canoe-Kayak

The *Odeyak* is a symbolic hybrid of canoe and kayak that served both as a seaworthy vessel and a potent symbol of Cree and Inuit resistance to external exploitation. Like the boat's design, its name is a combination of the Cree word *ode*, for "canoe", and the Inuktitut word *kayak*. Made by Billie Weetaltuk in 1990, the *Odeyak* is eight metres long, made in the method of a canvas-covered freighter canoe typical of the region, and features colourful vignettes along its hull depicting traditional northern life threatened by a hydroelectric project. It was paddled by a group of Inuit and Cree from Whapmagoostui, in northern Quebec, to New York City to protest the proposed Great Whale Hydroelectric Project in the same year. After the successful protest held on Earth Day in 1990, the *Odeyak* was displayed for many years at the Canadian Canoe Museum. It is an important expression of Indigenous self-determination and statesmanship and has recently been returned to northern Quebec for display at the Aanischaaukamikw Cree Cultural Institute in Oujé-Bougoumou.

14 MOST-CANADIAN HEADLINES OF 2016

by Stephanie Chambers

I've always been tickled by our not-so-mythic national character traits: a self-effacing nation of bear-punching census-filler-outers in hot pursuit of the bronze medal, for example. As a news researcher and librarian, I run headlong into these stereotypes with alarming frequency. So I started making a list, and here, offer up some of the fine examples of these iconic headlines drawn from 2016. You can debate the merits of these national characterizations, but you can't deny that these incidents happened. No fake news here, though it often seems like the headline writers and the folks LOL-sharing them widely on social media are in on the joke. We're good sports, eh.

Stephanie Chambers is a news researcher for the Globe and Mail.

1. Ontario budget: Restraint is fine, but is it enough? (*Globe and Mail*, February 26)

2. Canadian showdown: Mountie halts highway traffic for stubborn beaver (ctvnews.ca, March 25)

3. Canada's enthusiasm for census brings down StatsCan website (CBC.ca, May 3, 2016)

4. Sorry, says knife-wielding robber who stole smokes, beer in Corner Brook holdup (CBC.ca, May 5)

5. Sudbury man punches black bear in the face (CBC.ca, July 5)

6. When polite signage isn't enough: "the polite signage wasn't working," says councillor (Metro Canada, July 12)

7. $1.5 million in antlers stolen from Caledon taxidermy shop (*Toronto Star*, August 12)

8. Thieves make off with 20,000 litres of maple syrup from Montreal storage depot (CBC.ca, August 12)

9. Canadian wrestler Dori Yeats just misses winning bronze (*Toronto Star*, August 17)

10. B.C. man strips nude at gas station after getting bear spray down pants (*Toronto Star*, August 31)

11. Newfoundland driver hits moose while looking at other driver who hit moose—and three other moose crashes (*National Post*, October 13)

12. Thief rappels into Canadian sports store to steal $120,000 worth of hockey sticks (UPI.com, October 19)

13. "I am sorry to Chad": P.E.I. officer apologizes for threatening to punish drunk drivers with Nickelback (*National Post*, Dec 5)

14. Peak Canadiana: Alberta man takes Zamboni through Tim Hortons drive-thru (CBC.ca, December 21)

14 FREE THINGS ON CRAIGSLIST

by Mark Laba

Ever since humans were told there's no such thing as a free lunch, the obsessive desire to find free stuff seems like the only reason some folks get out of bed. What is it about a Craigslist free offering that impels a person to waste gas money driving for miles to a total stranger's house in order to pick up their trash? Likewise, what is it that inspires an individual to post, say, a mouldy and partially chewed rubber bathtub plug instead of just throwing it in the garbage? Is it a desire for company? Or maybe a strange need to pass on worn, torn and shredded household crap? These are the mysteries of human nature that I like to probe via the Craigslist free listings. Enjoy, exactly as written.

Mark Laba is the author of several books and chapbooks of poetry, including Dummy Spit *and* Movies in the Insect Temple. *His chapbook* The Mack Bolan Poems *won the bpNichol Chapbook Award.*

1. Scratch and Sniff Memory Game

Memory game with a Canadian theme. Some of the pieces are scratch-and-sniff pieces.

2. Free Cukoo Marans

Five Roosters and fifteen cukoo maran hens. Please bring your own container to pick them up. No slaughtering on our property. Thank you.

3. Large Amount of Bacon Fat

Large amount of bacon fat available for cooking or whatever other purpose you might have for it. We know that it might be a long shot to find somebody who wants it, but if you might have a use for it it's here.

4. Cans of Shaving Gel and Shaving Cream

2 cans. One is of a gel with a broken dispenser. It will still dispense but the nozzle is a little wobbly since the surrounding plastic got shattered when it fell in the shower. And a can of shaving cream that works okay. Both are around half full.

5. Kryolan Mustache

Hand made, human hair Light blonde mustache, never used

6. Basket Ball Sized Rocks

I've recently dug up 4 big basket ball sized rocks. Not sure what you could use it for. Basket ballish sized. Pretty heavy.

7. Student Magicians Only: Free Copies of Linking Ring Mag +

To make room, I am giving away copies of the magicians magazine The Linking Ring (70 copies), plus other assorted magic magazines. However, I will only give these away to serious, preferably student of magic who can answer a few questions that any student of magic would know.

8. Free Wingchun/Martial Art Wooden Dummy

Home made Wooden Dummy for Wing Chun or other Martial Artists to practice. This dummy is made out of wooden pallets as the back board and solid wood as the three hands, no leg, not an art or anything.

9. Brand New Enema Board for Colon Cleansing

Brand new, never used, enema board. Table like platform for colon cleansing enemas.

10. Free TV Supper Condition with Manuel

37 samsung TV in a very clean home. Remote control and manual. Very good working condition. We did not watch it often. YOU NEED to MOVE it by YOURSELF, It is very heavy!! two people with a trolly should be able to do it.

11. Free Trophies

I don't know, use them for crafting? I got them way back for reciting bible verses but they have no value now soooo some of them are pretty big and others are basic. Think sports trophies. There is one standard(ish) size moving box full first to come by gets them all. Not available piecemeal. I am around all day today and want them gone.

12. Collection: Inedible Food Items

I would not try eating any of these, outside of the apocalypse. I can't even recall how many years I have had the Dried Meat in a jar. Perhaps you need a hobby? Or like odd collections? If so, this is it. Also Holiday Luncheon Meat in a can, dehydrated French Fried onions and some old spaghetti noodles.

13. Partially Damaged Suitcase—Pick Up ASAP

OK, so here are the issues with it - The handle bar mechanism doesn't work properly (i.e you can't use it anymore unless you find a way to repair it). However, I have an old brown dog leash that you can use to strap it together.

14. Plastic Cup

Free plastic cup with straw. Must pick up.

10 AMAZING ATTIC EVENTS (+1 THAT WASN'T)

1. Thomas Chatterton Commits Suicide (1770)

As a boy, Thomas Chatterton was a prodigious poet and scholar. An early Romantic, at the age of 10 he wrote on a par with his adult contemporaries. His family was poor, his mother a widowed seamstress, and privacy was difficult to come by in their small Bristol, England, home. So young Thomas set up a writing room in the attic, which he jealously guarded as his secret domain. In the attic room, among his books and papers, stood Ellinor, a life-sized doll made of woven rushes, which his mother used for dress fittings. Thomas loved Ellinor and always took care to powder her face and do her hair. However, when he moved to London to pursue his literary career, he left his beloved Ellinor behind. He rented a garret reminiscent of his attic study at home. Thereafter suffering repeated personal and professional disappointments, including failure to sell a series of forgeries he claimed had been written by a 15th-century monk, Chatterton took arsenic and died at the age of 17.

2. Marconi Invents the Wireless Telegraph (1894-96)

Guglielmo Marconi was 20 years old when he began experimenting in earnest with radio waves. Because his father took a dim view of such "childish" pursuits as physics, and even went so far as to destroy his son's electronic equipment, young Marconi had to set up a secret laboratory in the attic of their villa in Bologna. There, among his mother's trays of silkworms, Marconi determined that radio waves could carry a message in Morse code across the room. In time, he proved that the effectiveness of his invention was not bound by the four attic walls; radio waves could transmit messages over great distances.

3. Baird Constructs and Demonstrates the First Television (1922-26)

In 1922 British scientist John Logie Baird rented an attic room above an artificial-flower shop at 8 Queen's Arcade in Hastings, England, to continue research on his primitive television sets. He used a tea chest as the base for his motor and a biscuit tin to house the projection lamp. He held the whole contraption together with darning needles, scraps of wood, string and sealing wax. In 1924 he took his "working" apparatus to London. There he rented two attic rooms at 22 Frith Street in Soho. He struggled for another two years before he gave the first demonstration of true television on January 26, 1926, for an audience of 50 scientists. The British Broadcasting Corporation inaugurated

Baird's system in 1929 and used it until 1935, when a more sophisticated system was adopted.

4. Hitler Attempts Suicide (1923)

After the failure of his Beer Hall Putsch in Munich, Germany, Hitler hid in an attic bedroom at Uffing, the country estate of his follower Ernst "Putzi" Hanfstangl. Hitler tried to commit suicide by shooting himself when the police came to arrest him. A police agent managed to disarm him before he could pull the trigger.

5. The Kühns Commit Espionage at Pearl Harbor (1939-41)

Ruth Kühn was only 17 years old when she became the mistress of Nazi leader Joseph Goebbels. But like all of his mistresses, Ruth was soon discarded. When the affair ended in 1939, Goebbels decided to send Ruth out of Germany. He arranged for her and her parents, Bernard and Friedel, to move to Hawaii and act as espionage agents for the Japanese. Ruth set up a beauty parlour in Honolulu, which became her chief source of information, since it was frequented by the wives of American military men. The next step was to figure out a way to transmit this information to the Japanese. The Kühns devised a simple code system and sent signals from the attic window of their small house overlooking Pearl Harbor. On December 7, 1941, towards the end of the Japanese surprise attack, their signals were noticed by two American naval officers. The U.S. Navy Shore Patrol arrested the family, and all were imprisoned for espionage.

6. Anne Frank Writes Her Diary (1942-44)

Forced into hiding when the Nazis overran the Netherlands, Anne Frank, her parents and sister, and four other Jews shared a musty Amsterdam attic above a warehouse and office building. They hid there for two years, obtaining food and other necessities from Gentiles on the floor below. Anne, a precocious girl in her early teens, kept a diary in which she chronicled not only the details of their imprisonment, but also her personal feelings about life, love, the future and her budding sexual awareness. Finally, in August 1944, the Gestapo, acting on a tip from Dutch informers, raided the hiding place. All of the Franks died in concentration camps (Anne of typhus) except Otto Frank, Anne's father. He returned to the attic after the war and found his daughter's diary, which was first published under the title *The Diary of a Young Girl*.

7. Franz Schubert's Lost Piano Score Is Discovered (1969)

The score for a fantasy for piano by Franz Schubert was discovered in an attic in Knittlefield, Austria, in 1969. The piece is believed to have been written by the Viennese composer in 1817.

8. Frédéric Chopin's Lost Waltzes Are Discovered (1978)

Several waltzes dedicated to Clementine de la Panouse were discovered by Vicomte Paul de la Panouse in the attic of the family chateau near Paris in 1978. The waltzes were stored in a heavy trunk belonging to the French aristocratic family. They had been hidden—along with many other documents—in various locations prior to the German invasion of France during the Second World War.

9. Schindler's List Is Discovered (1998)

When a German couple found an old grey suitcase in a loft belonging to the husband's late parents in Hildesheim, they didn't think much about it, until they saw the name on the handle: O. Schindler. Inside were hundreds of documents, including a list of the names of Jewish labourers that factory owner Oskar Schindler gave the Nazis during the Second World War. By giving Jewish workers fake jobs and otherwise manipulating the system, Schindler saved 1,200 Jews from extermination. His story inspired Thomas Keneally's novel *Schindler's Ark* (1982) and the movie *Schindler's List* (1993). The documents had apparently been stored in the loft by friends of Schindler and then forgotten. In 1999 the suitcase and its contents were donated to the Yad Vashem Holocaust Museum in Jerusalem.

10. Van Gogh Painting Discovered in Attic Is Authenticated (2013)

The authenticity of the painting *Sunset at Montmajour* had long been in question. It appeared to have been painted by the great Dutch master Vincent van Gogh, but there remained lingering doubts about whether it was genuine, largely because the canvas was unsigned. In 1908, a Norwegian industrialist named Christian Nicolai Mustad bought the painting and hung it in his home. But a houseguest, the French ambassador to Sweden, advised Mustad that the painting was probably not by van Gogh, so Mustad took it down and put it in his attic, where it remained until his death in 1970. In the 1990s, members of Mustad's family approached the Van Gogh Museum with the painting, but the museum refused to authenticate it. In 2011, it agreed to have another look, using some newly developed techniques to determine its authenticity. After a two-year investigation, on September 9, 2013, the museum announced, at a public unveiling of the painting, that *Sunset at Montmajour* had indeed been painted by van Gogh in 1888. It was the first full-sized painting by van Gogh to be confirmed since 1928.

+1 That Wasn't: Picasso Painting Not Found in Attic (2015)

It seemed too good to be true, and it was. Dominic Currie, a 58-year-old Scottish artist, caused quite a stir in June 2015 when he announced that he had opened a suitcase that had long been stored in his attic, and inside had discovered a rolled-up canvas that, according to Mr. Currie, had been painted by Pablo Picasso and given to Currie's mother by a Russian soldier with whom she'd had an affair. Art historians and dealers expressed scepticism about Currie's story, but he insisted it was true, at least for a few weeks. In July, just before the painting was to be examined by auctioneers at Christie's, Currie admitted that the whole story was a hoax, or, to be more precise, a piece of performance art. "I don't do hoaxes but it was an experiment," he told *The Scotsman*. "It was a piece of performance art in order to raise awareness of the struggling artists in Scotland. It's got a lot of media attention because any kind of celebrity gets a lot of attention. What doesn't get the attention is the struggling artist in Scotland."

15 "REMARKABLE OCCURRENCES" OF 1885

Every year between 1878 and 1887, the federal government of Canada published *The Dominion Annual Register and Review*, an eclectic compendium of stories and information that managed to capture a broad slice of Canadian life. One of the most informative chapters was called "A Journal of Remarkable Occurrences." Here is a sample of some of those "remarkable occurrences" from October to December 1885, as described in the 1885 edition.

1. October 2
The Hudson's Bay Company ship *Princess Royal* is driven ashore at Sandhead beach, near the mouth of Moose River, during a heavy gale. She is laden with furs.

2. October 4
A dispatch to Victoria B.C. announces an accident on the C.P.R. near Kamloops, by which 1 white man and 5 Chinese are killed.

3. October 7

At Halifax, it transpires that H.Y. Clarke, cashier of the Union Bank of Halifax, is a defaulter to the extent of $33,000, and has been dismissed from his position.

4. October 12

In Toronto, Jas. Wilson, 26, is run over by a wagon, and dies in a few minutes.

5. October 20

Kyle & Mustard's roller, flouring and sawmills at Egmondville, Ont., are destroyed by fire. Loss $35,000; insurance $5000.

6. October 28

A meeting in Quebec to express disapproval of the execution of Riel, breaks up in a general row.

At Peterboro Ont., Mr. Wm. Hopkins is killed by being thrown out of his buggy while driving.

7. October 29

At Halifax, a somewhat novel case is tried before the Supreme Court. Dr. Rigby sues Dr. Slayter for $1000 for assault. Slayter, it appears, refused to go to the North-West with his battalion when called on for active service. Rigby taunted him upon the fact, and called him a coward, for which Slayter knocked him down. Rigby obtains a verdict for $20.

8. October 30

Mr. C.S. Chapman, a clerk in the Department of the Interior, Ottawa, formerly an officer in H.M.'s 54th Reg., is found in bed suffocated to death, with his wife lying insensible beside him. It is supposed they were overcome by the fumes of gas, generated by a coal stove.

The Montreal Harbour Commissioners tug *St. John*, while proceeding to Pointe-aux-Trembles, takes fire and is run on a sand-bank where she is completely consumed. Some sporting gentlemen on board have a narrow escape from being burned to death.

9. November 12

Three men are dashed to death by falling from the roof of the Montreal drill hall which they were engaged in painting.

Adolphe Sharpe, sailor on board the steamboat *Speedwell* falls from the mast whilst the vessel is at the Niagara dock and is instantly killed.

10. November 18
The existence of 18 cases of smallpox causes much alarm at Charlottetown P.E.I. No services are held at the churches, and all public meetings are forbidden.

11. November 28
The first car of oatmeal exported from Manitoba is shipped to Montreal.

12. December 9
Samuel Perry is killed in the Union Phosphate Mine, Portland West, P.Q., by the falling of a piece of ice, about a ton in weight, into the pit where he is working.

13. December 16
Chief of Police McMillan of Brandon, Man., accidentally shoots himself with a rifle, and dies from the effects of the wound.

14. December 24
The annual Christmas distribution of the Toronto St. George's Society includes 7,000 lbs. of beef and 2,500 4-lb. loaves, besides tea and sugar. 750 families and 200 casuals are relieved.

15. December 31
John Napier, a farmer at Coveyhill P.Q., while lying intoxicated in his farm yard, has his nose and fingers eaten off by hogs.

9 UNUSUAL DISASTERS

1. The St. Pierre Snake Invasion
Volcanic activity on the "bald mountain" towering over St. Pierre, Martinique, was usually so inconsequential that no one took seriously the fresh, steaming vent holes and earth tremors during April 1902. By early May, however, ash began to rain down continuously, and the nauseating stench of sulphur filled the air. Their homes on the mountainside made uninhabitable, more than 100 fer-de-lance snakes slithered down and invaded the town. The 1.8-metre serpents killed 50 people and innumerable animals before they were finally

destroyed by St. Pierre's giant street cats. But the annihilation had only begun. On May 5 a landslide of boiling mud spilled into the sea, followed by a tsunami that killed hundreds. Three days later, on May 8, Mount Pelée finally erupted, sending a murderous avalanche of white-hot lava straight towards the town. Within three minutes St. Pierre was completely obliterated. Of its 30,000 population, there were only two survivors.

2. The Shiloh Baptist Church Panic

Two thousand people jammed into Shiloh Baptist Church in Birmingham, Alabama, on September 19, 1902, to hear an address by Booker T. Washington. The brick church was new. A steep flight of stairs, enclosed in brick, led from the entrance doors to the church proper. After Washington's speech, there was an altercation over an unoccupied seat, and the word "fight" was misunderstood as "fire." The congregation rose as if on cue and stampeded for the stairs. Those who reached them first were pushed from behind and fell. Others fell on top of them until the entrance was completely blocked by a pile of screaming humanity 3 metres high. Efforts by Washington and the churchmen down in front to induce calm were fruitless, and they stood by helplessly while their brothers and sisters, mostly the latter, were trampled or suffocated to death. There was neither fire nor even a real fight, but 115 people died.

3. The Great Boston Molasses Flood

On January 15, 1919, the workers and residents of Boston's North End, mostly Irish and Italian, were out enjoying the noontime sun of an unseasonably warm day. Suddenly, with only a low rumble of warning, the huge cast-iron tank of the Purity Distilling Company burst open, and a great wave of raw black molasses, two storeys high, poured down Commercial Street and oozed into the adjacent waterfront area. Neither pedestrians nor horse-drawn wagons could outrun it. Seven and a half million litres of molasses originally destined for rum engulfed scores of people—21 men, women and children drowned or suffocated, while another 150 were injured. Buildings crumbled, and an elevated train track collapsed. Those horses not completely swallowed up were so trapped in the goo that they had to be shot by police. Sightseers who came to see the chaos couldn't help but walk in the molasses. On their way home, they spread the sticky substance throughout the city. Boston smelled of molasses for a week, and the harbour ran brown until summer.

4. The Pittsburgh Gasometer Explosion

A huge cylindrical gasometer—the largest in the world at the time—located in the heart of the industrial centre of Pittsburgh, Pennsylvania, developed a leak. On the morning of November 14, 1927, repairmen with an open-flame blow-torch set out to look for the leak. At about 10 o'clock they apparently found it. The tank, containing 1.5 million cubic metres of natural gas, rose in the air like a balloon and exploded. Chunks of metal, some weighing more than 45 kilo-grams, were scattered great distances, and the combined effects of air pressure and fire left 1.6 square kilometres of devastation. Twenty-eight people were killed, and hundreds were injured.

5. The Gillingham Fire "Demonstration"

Every year the firemen of Gillingham, England, would construct a makeshift "house" out of wood and canvas for the popular firefighting demonstration at the annual Gillingham Park fete. A few local boys were selected from many aspi-rants to take part in the charade. On July 11, 1929, nine boys—aged 10 to 14— and six firemen costumed as if for a wedding party climbed to the third floor of the "house." The plan was to light a smoke fire on the first floor, rescue the "wedding party" with ropes and ladders and then set the empty house ablaze to demonstrate the use of the fire hoses. By some error, the real fire was lit first. The spectators, assuming the bodies they saw burning were dummies, cheered and clapped, while the firemen outside directed streams of water on what they knew to be a real catastrophe. All 15 people inside the house died.

6. The Empire State Building Crash

On Saturday morning, July 28, 1945, a veteran army pilot took off in a B-25 light bomber from Bedford, Massachusetts, headed for Newark, New Jersey. The co-pilot and a young sailor hitching a ride were also aboard. Fog made visibility poor. About an hour later, people on the streets of midtown Manhattan became aware of the rapidly increasing roar of a plane, and watched with horror as a bomber suddenly appeared out of the clouds, dodged between skyscrapers and plunged into the side of the Empire State Building. Pieces of plane and build-ing fell like hail. A gaping hole was gouged in the 78th floor, one of the plane's two engines hurtled through seven walls and came out the opposite side of the building, and the other engine shot through an elevator shaft, severing the cables and sending the car plummeting to the basement. When the plane's fuel tank exploded, six floors were engulfed in flame, and burning gasoline streamed down the sides of the building. Fortunately, few offices were open on a Saturday, and only 11 people—plus the three occupants of the plane—died.

7. The Texas City Chain Reaction Explosions

On April 15, 1947, the French freighter *Grandcamp* docked at Texas City, Texas, and took on some 1,400 tons of ammonium nitrate fertilizer. That night a fire broke out in the hold of the ship. By dawn, thick black smoke had port authorities worried because the Monsanto chemical plant was only 213 metres away. As men stood on the dock watching, tugboats prepared to tow the freighter out to sea. Suddenly, a ball of fire enveloped the ship. For many, it was the last thing they ever saw. A great wall of flame radiated outward from the wreckage, and within minutes the Monsanto plant exploded, killing and maiming hundreds of workers and any spectators who had survived the initial blast. Most of the business district was devastated, and fires raged along the waterfront, where huge tanks of butane gas stood imperilled. Shortly after midnight, a second freighter—also carrying nitrates—exploded, and the whole sequence began again. More than 500 people died, and another 1,000 were badly injured.

8. The Basra Mass Poisoning

In September 1971, a shipment of 90,000 metric tons of seed grain arrived in the Iraqi port of Basra. The American barley and Mexican wheat, which had been chemically treated with methylmercury to prevent rot, were sprayed a bright pink to indicate their lethal coating, and clear warnings were printed on the bags—but only in English and Spanish. Before they could be distributed to the farmers, the bags were stolen from the docks, and the grain was sold as food to the starving populace. The Iraqi government, embarrassed at its criminal negligence or for other reasons, hushed up the story, and it was not until two years later that an American newsman came up with evidence that 6,530 hospital cases of mercury poisoning were attributable to the unsavoury affair. Officials would admit to only 459 deaths, but total fatalities were probably more like 6,000, with another 100,000 suffering such permanent effects as blindness, deafness and brain damage.

9. The Chandka Forest Elephant Stampede

In the spring of 1972, the Chandka Forest area in India—already suffering from drought—was hit by a searing heat wave as well. The local elephants, who normally were no problem, became so crazed by the high temperatures and lack of water that the villagers told authorities they were afraid to venture out and to farm their land. By summer the situation had worsened. On July 10, the elephant herds went berserk and stampeded through five villages, leaving general devastation and 24 deaths in their wake.

18 BAD PREDICTIONS

1. The Telephone
"This 'telephone' has too many shortcomings to be seriously considered as a means of communication."
—*Western Union internal memo, 1876*

2. Canada's Future
"Canadian nationality being a lost cause, the ultimate union of Canada with the United States appears now to be morally certain; so that nothing is left for Canadian patriotism but to provide that it shall be a union indeed, and not an annexation."
—Goldwin Smith, in his book *The Political Destiny of Canada*, 1877

Political gadfly Goldwin Smith did not see much hope for the future of the new nation when he published his book. His prediction about the union of Canada and the United States has not come true—yet.

3. Canada in the World
"The nineteenth century was the century of the United States. I think we can claim that it is Canada that shall fill the twentieth century."
—Wilfrid Laurier, Canadian prime minister, speech to the Canadian Club, Ottawa, January 1904

Laurier never said "the twentieth century belongs to Canada," although most people think he did. But even his more modest claim that Canada will "fill" the 20th century would probably have to be judged as overly optimistic. It wasn't a bad century, but it would be pretty hard to deny the United States the title of Most Important Country for the second century in a row. Any bets on this one?

4. The 1929 Stock Market Crash

"While no doubt a number of people have suffered owing to the sharp decline in stocks, the soundness of Canadian securities generally is not affected. Business was never better, nor faith in Canada's future more justified."
—William Lyon Mackenzie King, Canadian prime minister, October 30, 1929

Mackenzie King made this statement the day after the stock market crashed. His optimism about the soundness of the Canadian economy on the eve of the greatest economic downturn in history proved to be completely unjustified.

5. Hitler

"I still stake my belief in Hitler's word that the people themselves do not want war, and that he, himself, has primarily the interests of the people at heart."
—William Lyon Mackenzie King, Canadian prime minister, 1937

After their meeting, Mackenzie King confided to his diary that Hitler was "a calm, passive man, deeply and thoughtfully in earnest."

6. Computers

"I think there is a world market for maybe five computers."
—Thomas Watson, chairman of IBM, 1943

7. The Atomic Bomb

"That is the biggest fool thing we have ever done.... The bomb will never go off, and I speak as an expert in explosives."
—Admiral William Leahy, U.S. Navy officer, speaking to President Truman in 1945, shortly before the U.S. dropped the bomb on Hiroshima

8. Landing on the Moon

"Landing and moving around the moon offers so many serious problems for human beings that it may take science another 200 years to lick them."
—*Science Digest*, August 1948

It took 21 years.

9. Fashion in the 1970s

"So women will wear pants and men will wear skirts interchangeably. And since there won't be any squeamishness about nudity, see-through clothes will only be see-through for reasons of comfort. Weather permitting, both sexes will go about bare-chested, though women will wear simple protective panties."
—Rudi Gernreich, American fashion designer, 1970

10. The Montreal Olympics

"The Olympics can no more have a deficit than a man can have a baby."
—Jean Drapeau, mayor of Montreal, 1973

The mayor's prediction about the financial legacy of the 1976 Olympic Games proved to be slightly off the mark. The Games ended up more than $1 billion in the red, and Montrealers spent nearly 30 years paying down the debt. The mayor never did have that baby.

11. The Collapse of the Soviet Union

"We must expect the Soviet system to survive in its present brutish form for a very long time. There will be Soviet labour camps and Soviet torture chambers well into our great-grandchildren's lives."
—Newt Gingrich, U.S. Representative (and future Speaker of the House), 1984.

The Soviet Union collapsed in 1989.

12. The Fall of the Berlin Wall

"Liberalization is a ploy . . . the Wall will remain."
—George Will, columnist for the *Washington Post*, November 9, 1989—the day the Berlin Wall fell

13. Invasion of Iraq #1

"There is a minimal risk of conflict."
—Heino Kopietz, senior Middle East analyst, on the possibility of Iraq invading Kuwait, in *The Times* of London, July 26, 1990

Iraq invaded Kuwait five days later.

14. 9/11

"Who cares about a little terrorist in Afghanistan?"
—Paul Wolfowitz, U.S. deputy secretary of defence, dismissing concerns about al Qaeda at an April 2001 meeting on terrorism

15. Invasion of Iraq #2

"I have no doubt we're going to find big stores of weapons of mass destruction."
—Kenneth Adelman, U.S. Defense Policy Board member, in the *Washington Post*, March 23, 2003

"[The war] could last six days, six weeks. I doubt six months."
—Donald Rumsfeld, U.S. secretary of defence, to U.S. troops in Aviano, Italy, February 7, 2003

"[My] belief is we will, in fact, be greeted as liberators. . . . I think it will go relatively quickly, weeks rather than months."
—Dick Cheney, U.S. vice president, March 16, 2003

No weapons of mass destruction were ever found, and the war, which began in 2003, in many ways continues to this day.

16. The 2015 Canadian Federal Election

"Harper is going to win. He's got a very efficient vote, he has a whole bunch of new seats in British Columbia and Ontario and Alberta, and those are in ridings where he's highly competitive. And he's going to have the ability to motivate those voters because the quality of his research is better than the other two parties." —Warren Kinsella, former Liberal election strategist, July 7, 2015

In October 2015 the Liberals won a majority government.

17. The iPhone

"Everyone's always asking me when Apple will come out with a cell phone. My answer is, 'Probably never.'"
—David Pogue, *New York Times* technology columnist, 2006

18. The 2016 U.S. Presidential Election

"Trump has a better chance of cameoing in another *Home Alone* movie with Macaulay Culkin—or playing in the NBA Finals—than winning the Republican nomination." —Harry Enten of the polling website fivethirtyeight.com, June 16, 2015

"If you want absurd specificity, I recently estimated Trump's chance of becoming the GOP nominee at 2 percent." —Nate Silver of fivethirtyeight.com, August 16, 2015

Donald Trump officially became the Republican nominee for president in July 2016.

13 REMARKABLE TREES OF CANADA

1–2. The Carmanah Giant and the Renfrew Red Creek Fir

The Pacific rainforest is home to Canada's most imposing and majestic trees. The Carmanah Giant, a Sitka spruce in Carmanah Walbran Provincial Park, is Canada's tallest known tree, standing at 95.73 metres tall and with a circumference of 13.28 metres. The largest (height combined with circumference) Douglas fir is the Red Creek Tree, near the San Juan River in British Columbia. It is 73.8 metres tall and has a circumference of 22.8 metres.

3. The Cheewhat Lake Cedar

The Cheewhat Lake Cedar in Pacific Rim National Park is Canada's biggest overall tree. It is a western red cedar 18.3 metres in circumference and 55.5 metres tall. It is considered the biggest because it combines its height and circumference with many branches and a massive crown. A partial core sample of the tree taken by conservationist Randy Stoltmann reveals that the tree is at least 1,212 years old, and possibly 2,000. The red cedar is revered by the Indigenous peoples of the northwest coast, who use the wood and bark for clothing, medicine, rituals, totem poles, dugout canoes and housing material. According to the Coast Salish, the Great Spirit created the red cedar to honour a man who was always helping others.

4. Eastern White Cedars

There's an ancient forest of eastern white cedars that grows on the limestone, sandstone and shale cliff faces of the Niagara Escarpment in southwestern Ontario. The trees grow very slowly, and as a result are twisted and stunted. A tree survey was done in 2000, and over 73 trees were found to be more than 500 years old; 17 of them were over 700 years old. The oldest cedar, found in Lion's Head, is 1,053 years old, making it the oldest tree in Canada east of the Rocky Mountains.

5. The Golden Spruce, Kiidk'yaas

The 300-year-old golden spruce, the only living tree of its kind, stood in the old-growth forest of Haida Gwaii, British Columbia, until January 1997, when a disturbed "conservationist," Grant Hadwin, took a chainsaw and hacked at the tree as a political statement against logging. It fell a couple of days later. This Sitka spruce had a genetic mutation and lacked 80% of the regular amount of chlorophyll, rendering its needles golden yellow instead of green. Considered sacred by the local Haida, the tree, 2 metres in diameter, stood perfectly straight and conical. Scientists gave the tree its own scientific name, *Picea sitchensis aurea*. Hadwin was arrested and charged but disappeared before coming to trial, his whereabouts still unknown. Eighty cuttings of the fallen spruce were taken, and many of the grafts have been successful, producing golden needles on a regular Sitka stem.

6. The McIntosh Apple Tree

The McIntosh apple was developed and nurtured from a wild sapling discovered by John McIntosh in 1801 in Dundela, Ontario. For many years, the original tree produced abundant fruit and healthy grafts for the propagation of the species. In 1893 the original tree was damaged by fire, and it died in 1910. Today, five trees still stand in Dundela that grew from grafts of the original McIntosh apple tree.

7. The Newton Apple Tree

On the front lawn of the National Research Council in Ottawa grows the Newton Apple Tree. A small but sturdy tree, it is believed to be a direct descendant of the apple tree under which Sir Isaac Newton lay on that fateful day when an apple fell on him—the "eureka" moment when he formulated the basis of his theory of gravity.

8. The Hanging Garden

Meares Island, off Tofino, British Columbia, is home to a grove of ancient-rainforest hemlock, fir, cedar and spruce trees. Nestled among them is a cedar dubbed the Hanging Garden that is 18.3 metres in circumference and approximately 1,500 years old. Supported in its branches that twist and jut off in all directions is an entire ecosystem of mosses, lichens, fungus, shrubs and ferns; it looks like a massive, mossy candelabra. Tourists come from around the world to stare at and photograph it.

9. The Eik Cedar

The Eik Cedar became the old-growth mascot of Tofino, British Columbia, due to a heated campaign to rescue it from the chainsaws in 2001. The 800- to 1,000-year-old western red cedar was the last example of old-growth forest in the town, but was declared a safety hazard by town councillors because of some rot inside its trunk. When Tofino residents heard about the plan to chop it down, they quickly conspired to save the tree with a publicity and fundraising campaign. Two local men, Brad Lindey, 17, and Dominic Beaulieu, 24, scrambled up the trunk and lived in its canopy for 37 days. The standoff allowed everyone time to think up creative options for saving the tree. Ultimately, engineers and arborists encircled the cedar with a $60,000 girdle of steel rods anchored in the bedrock to prevent it from falling; it should stand for centuries to come.

10. The Swamp Cottonwood

Swamp cottonwood is scattered throughout the eastern seaboard of the United States, but the first known example growing in Canada was discovered in November 2002 by botanists John Ambrose, Lindsay Rodger and Gerry Waldron. Out for a walk at Bickford Oak Woods, south of Sarnia, Ontario, Ambrose was amazed when he came across the tree: "Since the late 1700s or early 1800s people have been documenting what is here and we are still finding new trees. And these aren't obscure little orchids or whatever, but big trees."

11. The Burmis Tree

The Burmis Tree, named after a now-deserted village 250 kilometres southwest of Calgary, is said to be Canada's most photographed tree. The twisted and weathered pine, 5 metres tall and roughly 600 years old, is a much-loved landmark for people living around Crowsnest Pass. A spectacular example of the limber pine species, its flexible branches and twigs can be tied in knots without breaking. Although the Burmis Tree died 25 years ago, its many fans and defenders have twice rescued it from decay and destruction by rebuilding it. In 1998 the tree fell over in high winds, and it was raised and replanted using steel bands and bolts to anchor it to the bedrock. In 2004 vandals hacked off several branches, which were then reattached to the tree with rods and wooden dowels.

12. The Burford Sweet Chestnut Trees

The Burford sweet chestnut trees represent a botanical find akin to the discovery of a living dinosaur. Arborist and conservationist Bruce Graham stumbled upon four mature sweet chestnut trees growing just outside Burford, a southwestern Ontario farm town. Sweet chestnuts were thought to have been wiped out everywhere by a deadly disease that has infected an estimated 3.5 million trees in Canada and the United States since 1904. Graham collected seeds from the large, robust specimens, and in recent years has planted and raised thousands of them. The public is encouraged to buy seedlings and grow them to help the sweet chestnut re-establish itself in Canada.

13. Laing Street Silver Maple

A venerable silver maple that grew in east-end Toronto is said to have inspired Alexander Muir to write the patriotic standard "Maple Leaf Forever" in 1867, the year of Confederation. It blew down in a 2013 windstorm, but the salvaged wood is being used in dozens of commemorative carpentry projects, including a bench for the House of Parliament honouring Jack Layton and a guitar that will be passed around amongst Canadian musicians starting with members of Blue Rodeo, who live nearby.

10 FUNGUSES THAT CHANGED HISTORY

1. The Yellow Plague (Aspergillus flavus)

A. flavus is an innocent-looking but deadly yellowish mould also called aflatoxin. Undoubtedly the cause of countless deaths throughout history, it was not suspected of being poisonous until 1960. That year, a mysterious disease killed 100,000 young turkeys in England, and medical researchers traced the "turkey-X disease" to *A. flavus* growing on the birds' peanut meal feed. Hardy, widespread and lethal, aflatoxin is a powerful liver cancer agent. Even so, people have long cultivated *A. flavus*—in small amounts—as part of the manufacturing process of soy sauce and sake. But *A. flavus* can get out of control easily. It thrives on warm, damp conditions, and as it breeds—sometimes to lethal proportions within 24 hours—the mould produces its own heat, which spurs even faster growth. Some of A. *flavus*'s favourite dishes are stored peanuts, rice, corn, wheat, potatoes, peas, cocoa, cured hams and sausage.

2. The Mould That Toppled an Industry (Aspergillus niger)

This common black mould, most often found on rotting vegetation, played a key role in the collapse of a major industry. Until the early 1920s, Italy produced about 90% of the world's citric acid, using low-grade lemons. Exported mainly to the United States as calcium citrate, citric acid was a costly ingredient—about $1 a pound—used in food, pharmaceutical and industrial processing. When American chemists discovered that A. *niger*, the most ordinary of moulds, secreted citric acid as it grew in a culture medium, they seized the opportunity to perfect citric-acid production using the easily grown mould. Charles Pfizer & Co., of Brooklyn, New York, became known as the "world's largest lemon grove"—without a lemon in sight. Hard-working acres of A. *niger* were soon squirting out such quantities of citric acid that by 1923 the price was down to 25 cents a pound and the Italians were out of business.

3. St. Anthony's Fire (Claviceps purpurea)

A purplish-black spur-shaped mass, C. *purpurea* is a formidable and even frightening fungus that has long plagued humankind. But in addition to its horrible effects, C. *purpurea* also has valuable medical uses if the greatest care is taken to use tiny amounts. The fungus is a powerful muscle contractor and can control bleeding, speed up childbirth and even induce abortion. It is also the source of the hallucinogenic LSD-25. In doses larger than microscopic, C. *purpurea*—commonly called ergot—produces ergotamine poisoning, a grisly condition known in the Middle Ages as St. Anthony's fire. There is still no cure for this hideous, often fatal disease caused by eating fungus-infected rye. The victim suffers convulsions and performs a frenzied "dance." This is often accompanied by a burning sensation in the limbs, which turn black and fall off. Some victims of medieval ergotism went insane and many died. In AD 994 more than 40,000 people in two French provinces died of ergotism, and in 1722 the powerful fungus forced Peter the Great of Russia to abandon his plan to conquer Turkey when, on the eve of the Battle of Astrakhan, his entire cavalry and 20,000 others were stricken with ergotism. The last recorded outbreak of ergot poisoning was in the French village of Pont-Saint-Esprit in 1951.

4. The Nobel Mould (Neurospora crassa)

The humble bread mould *N. crassa* provided the means for scientists to explore the most exciting biological discovery of the 20th century: DNA. As anyone with an old loaf of bread in the bread box knows, *N. crassa* needs only a simple growing medium, and it has a short life cycle. With such co-operative qualities, this reddish mould enabled George Beadle and Edward Tatum to win the Nobel Prize in Medicine/Physiology in 1958 for discovering the role that genes play in passing on hereditary traits from one generation to the next. By X-raying *N. crassa*, the researchers produced mutations of the genes, or components of DNA, and then found which genes corresponded with which traits.

5. The Bluish-Green Lifesaver (Penicillium notatum or Penicillium chrysogenum)

A few dots of a rather pretty bluish-green mould were Dr. Alexander Fleming's first clue to finding one of the most valuable life-saving drugs ever developed. In 1928 he noticed that his petri dish of staphylococcus bacteria had become contaminated with symmetrically growing, circular colonies of *P. notatum*. Around each speck, all the bacteria were dead. Fleming further found that the mould also killed pneumonia, gonorrhea and diphtheria germs—without harming human cells. The unassuming bluish-green mould was beginning to look more interesting, but Fleming could not isolate the active element. Not until 1939 did Howard Florey and Ernst Chain identify penicillin, a secretion of the growing mould, as the bacteria-killer. The first important antibiotic, penicillin revolutionized treatment of many diseases. Fleming, Florey and Chain won the Nobel Prize in Physiology/Medicine in 1945 for their pioneering work with the common fruit mould that yielded the first "miracle drug."

6. The Gourmet's Delight (Penicillium roquefortii)

According to an old legend, a French shepherd forgot his lunch in a cave near the town of Roquefort, and when he found it weeks later, the cheese had become blue-veined and was richly flavoured. No one knew why this had happened until American mycologists discovered the common blue mould *P. roquefortii* in 1918. All blue cheeses—English Stilton, Italian Gorgonzola, Norwegian Gammelost, Greek Kopanisti and Swiss Paglia—derive their tangy flavour from the energetic blue mould that grows rapidly in the cheese, partially digesting it and eventually turning the entire cheese into mould. Of course, it's more appetizing to say that *P. roquefortii* ripens the cheese instead of rotting it, but it's the same process.

7. The Famine-Maker (Phytophthona infestans)

The political history of the world changed as a result of the unsavoury activity of *P. infestans*, a microscopically small fungus that reduced Ireland to desperate famine in 1845. Hot, rainy July weather provided perfect conditions for the white fungus to flourish on the green potato plants—most of Ireland's food crop—and the bushes withered to brown, mouldy, stinking clumps within days. The entire crop was devastated, causing half a million people to starve to death, while nearly two million emigrated, mostly to the United States. *P. infestans* dusted a powdery white death over Ireland for six years. The fungus spread rapidly, and just one bad potato could infect and ruin a barrel of sound ones. British prime minister Robert Peel tried to get Parliament to repeal tariffs on imported grain; while the MPs debated, Ireland starved. Relief came so slowly and inadequately that Peel's government toppled the next year, in 1846.

8. The Temperance Fighter (Plasmopara viticola)

A soft, downy mildew infecting American-grown grapes was responsible for nearly ruining the French wine industry. In 1872 the French unwittingly imported *P. viticola* on grafting stock of wine grapes grown in the United States. Within 10 years, the mild-mannered mildew had quietly decimated many of France's finest old vineyards. But in 1882 botanist Pierre-Marie-Alexis Millardet discovered a miraculous cure for the ravages of *P. viticola*. He noticed that Medoc farmers painted their grape leaves with an ugly paste of copper sulphate, lime and water to prevent theft. Called Bordeaux mixture, this paste was the first modern fungicide. The vineyards of France recovered as the entire world sighed with relief.

9. Merchant of Death (Saccharomyces cerevisiae)

Ordinary brewer's yeast, *S. cerevisiae*, used to leaven bread and make ale, was once employed as a wartime agent of death. During the First World War, the Germans ran short of both nitroglycerin and the fat used in its manufacture. Then they discovered that the usually friendly fungus *S. cerevisiae* could be used to produce glycerine, a necessary ingredient in explosives. Fermenting the fungus together with sucrose, nitrates, phosphates and sodium sulphite, the Germans produced more than 1,000 tons of glycerine per month. According to some military sources, this enabled them to keep their war effort going for an additional year.

10. The TB Killer (Streptomyces griseus)

A lowly mould found in dirt and manure piles, *S. griseus* nevertheless had its moment of glory in 1943, when Dr. Selman Waksman discovered that it yields the antibiotic streptomycin, which can cure tuberculosis. Waksman went to the United States in 1910 as a Russian refugee, and by 1918 he had earned his doctorate in soil microbiology. He had worked with *S. griseus* before, but not until a crash program to develop antibiotics (a word coined by Dr. Waksman himself) was launched did he perceive the humble mould's possibilities for greatness. Streptomycin was first used successfully on human beings in 1945, and in 1952 Dr. Waksman was awarded the Nobel Prize in Physiology/Medicine.

14 FAMOUS EVENTS THAT HAPPENED IN THE BATHTUB

1. The Poisoning of Pelias

According to Greek mythology, Medea murdered Jason's uncle (Pelias, king of Thessaly) by showing his daughters that they could rejuvenate him if they chopped him up and bathed him in her cauldron of herbs. They believed her, and he died.

2. The Murder of Agamemnon

Shortly after his return from the Trojan War, the Greek hero Agamemnon was murdered by his wife, Clytemnestra, who struck him twice with an axe while he was relaxing in the tub.

3. Archimedes's Discovery

While soaking in the bathtub, the Greek scientist Archimedes formulated the law of physics—known as the Archimedean principle—that a body immersed in fluid is buoyed up by a force equal to the weight of the fluid it displaces. He became so excited about his discovery that he rushed out stark naked into the streets of Syracuse, Sicily, shouting "Eureka!" ("I have found it!")

4. Franklin's Pastime

Benjamin Franklin is reputed to have imported the first bathtub into America. He improved its design, and contemporary reports indicate that he carried on much of his reading and correspondence while soaking in the tub.

5. Marat's Assassination

Jean-Paul Marat played an active part in the French Revolution. As editor of the journal *L'Ami du Peuple*, he became known as an advocate of extreme violence. The moderate Girondists were driven out of Paris and took refuge in Normandy. There, some of them met and influenced a young woman called Charlotte Corday. Convinced that Marat must die, she went to Paris and bought a butcher's knife. When she arrived at Marat's house on July 13, 1793, he was taking a bath. (He spent many hours in the tub because of a painful skin condition.) Overhearing Corday, he asked to see her. They discussed politics for a few minutes, then Corday drew her knife and stabbed Marat to death in the bathtub.

6. The Bonapartes' Argument

While Napoleon was taking a bath one morning in 1803, his brothers Joseph and Lucien rushed in, seething with rage because they had just heard of his plan to sell Louisiana to the Americans. They were furious because he refused to consult the legislature about it. Lucien had worked hard to make Spain return the colony to France, and now his work would be for naught. Joseph warned Napoleon that he might end up in exile if he carried out his plan. At this, Napoleon fell back angrily in the tub, splashing water all over Joseph. Napoleon's valet, who was standing by with hot towels over his arm, crashed to the floor in a dead faint.

7. Wagner's Inspiration

Composer Richard Wagner soaked in a tub scented with vast quantities of Milk of Iris perfume for several hours every day while working on his final opera, *Parsifal* (1882). He insisted that the water be kept hot and heavily perfumed so that he could smell it as he sat at his desk, clad in outlandish silk and fur dressing gowns and surrounded by vials and sachets of exotic scents.

8. Rostand's Writing

Edmond Rostand, French poet and playwright, hated to be interrupted while he was working, but he did not like to turn his friends away. Therefore, he took refuge in the bathtub and wrote there all day, creating such successes as *Cyrano de Bergerac* (1898).

9. Smith's Murders

George Joseph Smith of England earned his living by his almost hypnotic power over women. In 1910 he met Bessie Mundy, married her (without mentioning that he already had a wife) and disappeared with her cash and clothes. Two years later they met by chance and began living together again. After Smith persuaded Bessie to write a will in his favour, he took her to a doctor on the pretence that she suffered from fits. (Both she and the doctor took his word for it.) A few days later she was found dead in the bathtub, a cake of soap clutched in her hand. Everyone assumed she had drowned during an epileptic seizure. Smith married two more women (Alice Burnham and Margaret Lofty), took out insurance policies on their lives and described mysterious ailments to their doctors. They too were found dead in their bathtubs. When Alice Burnham's father read of Margaret Lofty's death, he was struck by its similarity to his daughter's untimely end. The police were notified, and Smith was tried for murder and sentenced to be executed. His legal wife, Edith, testified at the trial that she could remember only one occasion when Smith himself took a bath.

10. Bennett's Death

R.B. Bennett, who had the misfortune of being prime minister of Canada during the Great Depression, spent most of the 1940s in self-imposed exile at his English estate, Juniper Hill. At 10:30 on the evening of June 26, 1947, Bennett drew a hot bath and climbed in. Shortly thereafter, the former prime minister suffered a massive heart attack and died. He was found the next morning by his butler. The floor of the bathroom was covered with water. His dog, Bill, was asleep on the bed, no doubt awaiting the master who would never return.

11. King Haakon's Fall

On June 29, 1955, the reign of King Haakon VII, who had ruled Norway from the time of its independence in 1905, effectively came to an end when the beloved monarch fell in the royal bathtub at his palace in Oslo. The elderly king lingered on for over two years before succumbing on September 21, 1957, to complications resulting from his fall.

12. A Hiccup in Glenn's Career

The momentum of what contemporary experts considered to be an unstoppable political career was interrupted in 1964 when astronaut hero John Glenn fell in the bathtub and had to withdraw from his race for senator of Ohio. He was finally elected to the Senate in 1974.

13. Morrison's Death

Rock idol Jim Morrison was living in exile in an apartment in Paris. On the morning of July 3, 1971, he was found dead in his bathtub. The cause of death was ruled "heart failure." He was 27 years old.

14. Whitney Houston's Drowning

Whitney Houston almost had it all. She was beautiful, famous, rich, a movie star and one of the best selling female vocalists of all time. Her voice was perhaps the greatest of her generation. But she was also addicted to booze, drugs and tobacco, and locked in an unhappy, tumultuous marriage to fellow singer and addict, Bobby Brown. On the afternoon of February 11, 2012, Houston was found face-down in a bathtub full of water in her room at the Beverley Hilton Hotel. The cause of death was accidental drowning. According to a report by the L.A. County Coroner, there was "a plethora of prescription medicine bottles" in her room, along with open bottles of champagne and beer. Several drugs were found in her system at the time of her death, including cocaine, which she apparently ingested shortly before entering the bathtub. She was 48 years old.

16 LAST CANADIAN FACTS

1. The Last Beothuk

On June 6, 1829, Nancy Shawnadithit, the last living Beothuk, died of tuberculosis in St. John's, Newfoundland, at the age of 23. She had spent the last five years of her life working as a maid for a white family. She spoke little English, but when encouraged to record details about her ancestors, language and culture, she made many detailed drawings.

2. The Last Duel in Upper Canada

The last fatal duel in Upper Canada was fought in Perth, Ontario, on June 13, 1833. John Wilson squared off with Robert Lyon over the affections of the local schoolteacher, Elizabeth Hughes. Lyon was shot and killed, and Wilson was charged with murder. The place where these events unfolded is now called Last Duel Park.

3. The Last Wish of Robert Baldwin

The last wish of Robert Baldwin, two-time former premier of Upper Canada, was that an incision be made in his corpse below his waistline that would mirror the surgical scar his long-dead wife had from her caesarean section. His wish was granted in 1858.

4. The Last Spike of the Canadian Pacific Railway

The last spike connecting eastern and western Canada was driven into the rail by the Honourable Donald Alexander Smith at Craigellachie, British Columbia, on November 7, 1885.

5. The Last Canadian WWI Casualty

The last Canadian soldier to die in battle during the First World War is believed to be Private George Lawrence Price of Port Williams, Nova Scotia. He was killed on November 11, 1918, at Mons, Belgium, about two minutes before the signing of the Armistice. He was 25 years old.

6. The Last Woman Hanged in Canada

The last woman to be hanged in Canada was Marguerite Pitre, on January 9, 1953, for "abetting" Albert Guay, the man responsible for planting a bomb on a Canadian Pacific airplane that killed 23 people.

7. The Last Men Hanged in Canada

The last men to be hanged in Canada were Ronald Turpin, 29, and Arthur Lucas, 54. Turpin was convicted of murdering a Toronto cop, and Lucas of murdering an FBI informant working in Canada. They were hanged just after midnight on December 11, 1962, at the Don Jail in Toronto, where they had been held.

8. The Last Race of Northern Dancer

The last race run—and won—by the horse Northern Dancer was the 2-kilometre Queen's Plate on June 30, 1964. His time was 2:02, capping a career record of winning 14 of 18 starts.

9. The Last Films of Buster Keaton

The last two films of Buster Keaton—*The Railrodder* and *Buster Keaton Rides Again*—were made in Canada in 1965. The first was silent, a comedy about riding a railway scooter across Canada. The second, which had sound, was a documentary directed by John Spotton on how Keaton worked and lived.

10. The Last RCMP Dogsled
The last RCMP dogsled was driven between Old Crow, Yukon, and Fort McPherson, Northwest Territories, between March 11 and April 5, 1969. After that, the RCMP switched to snowmobiles.

11. The Last Direct Link to the Inventor of Insulin
The last and longest-living link to the inventor of insulin was Theodore Ryder. He was close to death from diabetes at age five when he was given an experimental injection of insulin by Dr. Frederick Banting at the Toronto General Hospital in 1922. He instantly revived and recovered. By using insulin regularly to keep his diabetes in check, he lived a long, healthy life. He died at the age of 76 on March 8, 1993, of heart failure.

12. Last Canadian WWI Veteran
John Babcock didn't get to fight in the First World War, but it wasn't for lack of trying. Born on an Ontario farm in 1900, he lied about his age, joined the Canadian Expeditionary Force in 1916, and was shipped to England. But in August 1917, the truth was uncovered, and Babcock was sent to the "Boys' Battalion," a group of 1,300 too-young soldiers training to join the regular army when they turned 18. But peace intervened before Babcock made it to the front lines, a fact that he regretted for the rest of his life. He died in 2009 at the age of 109, the last Canadian to wear a uniform in "The Great War."

13. Last Montreal Expo in Major League Baseball
The Expos played their final season in Montreal in 2004, before moving south and becoming the Washington Nationals the following year. When the 2017 baseball season started, only one player who wore an Expos uniform was still playing in the major leagues. Pitcher Bartolo Colón was already 29 years old when he was traded to the Expos in the middle of the 2002 season. That's an age when most pitchers' careers have peaked and begun to decline. But in 2017, at the age of 44, Colón is still in baseball, on the major-league roster of the Minnesota Twins, and the last Expo standing.

14. Last of the original Reform Party Members of Parliament

The Reform Party shook up Canadian politics in 1993 when it increased its standing in Parliament from one seat before the election to 52 after the votes were counted. All but one of those seats were won west of Ontario. By the 2015 election, only six of the original 52 remained in the House, all under the banner of the Conservative Party of Canada. Four of them, Diane Ablonczy, Leon Benoit, Dick Harris and Garry Breitkreuz, did not seek re-election in 2015. Of the two who sought re-election, one, John Duncan, was defeated, while the other, Stephen Harper, won his seat in Calgary, but his government fell to the Liberals. Harper subsequently gave up his seat in the House, and with his retirement, all of the original Reformers were gone.

15. The Last Canadian Soldier Killed in Afghanistan

The Canadian combat mission in Afghanistan ended in July 2011, but 950 soldiers stayed behind in the country to train Afghan soldiers. One of them was Master Corporal Byron Greff of the 3rd Battalion Princess Patricia's Canadian Light Infantry, based in his home province of Alberta. On October 29, 2011, Greff was travelling in a bus filled with NATO personnel outside the capital of Kabul when it was rammed by a car loaded with explosives. Seventeen people, including Greff, died in the suicide bombing. The Taliban claimed responsibility for the blast. The last Canadian soldiers left Afghanistan in March 2014. Byron Greff was the last Canadian soldier killed there.

16. The Last Message from the Authors to the Readers

We hope you have enjoyed the 2017 edition of *The Book of Lists*.

Credits

Expert Contributors

"Jann Arden's 5 Most Important Things You Need to Travel with a 5-Pound Dog" © 2017 Jann Arden

"Margaret Atwood's 10 Annoying Things to Say to Writers" © 2017 Margaret Atwood

"Kurt Browning's 9 Turning Points in Figure Skating History (+1 That Hasn't Happened Yet)" © 2017 Kurt Browning

"14 Most-Canadian Headlines of 2016" © 2017 Stephanie Chambers

"Lynn Coady's 8 Canadian '80s Pop Acts Who Were More '80 Than the '80" © 2017 Lynn Coady

"7 Digital Innovations Down on the Farm" © 2017 Courtney Denard

"'Is It Something I Said?' John Duffy's Dirty Dozen: 12 Election-Losing Clunkers" © 2017 John Duffy

"Naomi Duguid's 10 Favourite Cookbooks" © 2017 Naomi Duguid

"Charlotte Gray's 10 Women Who Liven Up Canadian History" © 2017 Charlotte Gray

"Robert Harris's 10 Little-Known Canadians Who Changed the Course of Music History" © 2017 Robert Harris

"Daniel Henry's 10 Memorable Moments in Free Expression and the Media" © 2017 Daniel Henry

"Lorraine Johnson's 7 Gardens Brought Before the Law" © 2017 Lorraine Johnson

"Andrew Kear's 6 Favourite Nudes and Prudes in Canadian Art Before '69" © 2017 Andrew Kear

"Cathal Kelly's 9 Most Compelling Players in Soccer History" © 2017 Cathal Kelly

"21 Free Things on Craigslist" © 2017 Mark Laba

"Chuck Lazer's 13 Canadian TV Shows That Mattered" © 2017 Chuck Lazer

"Mark Leiren-Young's 7 Canadian Whales Who Made Huge Waves" © 2017 Mark Leiren-Young

"8 Canadian Urban Planning Blunders" © 2017 John Lorinc

"Daniel MacIvor and Daniel Brooks's 14 Essential Canadian Plays and the Playwrights Who Wrote Them" © 2017 Daniel MacIvor and Daniel Brooks

"Kyo Maclear's 7 Gloriously Gloomy Books for the Very Young" © 2017 Kyo Maclear

"Margaret MacMillan's 12 Favourite 20th-Century Diplomatic Incidents" © 2017 Margaret MacMillan

"Lanni Marchant's 7 Gritty and Groundbreaking Athletic Performances by Women" © 2017 Lanni Marchant

Index

Ira Basen is a Toronto writer, teacher and broadcaster. At CBC Radio he was responsible for the creation of several network shows, including *The Inside Track*, *This Morning* and *Workology* (with Jane Farrow). He was also senior producer at *Quirks and Quarks* and *Sunday Morning*. He currently produces documentaries for *The Sunday Edition* on CBC Radio One.

Jane Farrow is a writer, former CBC broadcaster and advocate for livable cities. Her books include the bestselling *Wanted Words 1 & 2* and, as co-editor, *Any Other Way: How Toronto Got Queer*. She worked as a CBC Radio One producer (*This Morning, Sunday Edition*) and hosted *And Sometimes Y* and *Workology*. Jane has helped people tell the stories of their neighbourhoods as the first director of Jane's Walk, a global movement of free, citizen-led walking tours celebrating urbanist Jane Jacobs's ideas about livable, walkable cities.